Living & Working in
FRANCE

● A Survival Handbook ●

David Hampshire

First published in 1991
Eleventh edition published 2017

Copyright © Survival Books 1993, 1996, 1999, 2002,
2003, 2004, 2006 (twice), 2008, 2012, 2017
Cover photograph: Rocamadour, Lot © Francisco Oreja (www.dreamstime.com)
Illustrations, cartoons and maps © Jim Watson

Survival Books Limited
Office 169, 3 Edgar Buildings, George St, Bath, BA1 2FJ, United Kingdom
+44 (0)1305-246283, info@survivalbooks.net
www.survivalbooks.net and www.londons-secrets.com

British Library Cataloguing in Publication Data
A CIP record for this book is available
from the British Library.
ISBN: 978-1-909282-88-9

Printed in China by D'Print Pte Ltd.

Acknowledgements

*T*he publisher would like to thank all those who contributed to the successful publication of the 10th edition of *Living and Working in France* and previous editions of this book. In particular, thanks are due to Peter Read for research and updating this edition; Robbi Atilgan for editing; David Woodworth for proofreading and additional research; John Marshall for desktop publishing, photo selection and cover design; and Jim Watson for the cartoons and maps. Also special thanks are due to the many photographers – the unsung heroes – whose beautiful images add colour and bring France to life.

La Ciotat, Bouches-du-Rhône

What Readers and Reviewers Have Said About Survival Books:

"If I were to move to France, I would like David Hampshire to be with me, holding my hand every step of the way. This being impractical, I would have to settle for second best and take his books with me instead!"

Living France

"We would like to congratulate you on this work: it is really super! We hand it out to our expatriates and they read it with great interest and pleasure."

ICI (Switzerland) AG

"I found this a wonderful book crammed with facts and figures, with a straightforward approach to the problems and pitfalls you are likely to encounter. The whole laced with humour and a thorough understanding of what's involved. Gets my vote!"

Reader (Amazon)

"Get hold of David Hampshire's book for its sheer knowledge, straightforwardness and insights to the Spanish character and do yourself a favour!"

Living Spain

"Rarely has a 'survival guide' contained such useful advice – This book dispels doubts for first time travellers, yet is also useful for seasoned globetrotters – In a word, if you're planning to move to the US or go there for a long term stay, then buy this book both for general reading and as a ready reference."

American Citizens Abroad

"It's everything you always wanted to ask but didn't for fear of the contemptuous put down – The best English language guide – Its pages are stuffed with practical information on everyday subjects and are designed to complement the traditional guidebook."
Swiss News

"A must for all future expats. I invested in several books but this is the only one you need. Every issue and concern is covered, every daft question you have but are frightened to ask is answered honestly without pulling any punches. Highly recommended."
Reader (Amazon)

"Let's say it at once. David Hampshire's Living and Working in France is the best handbook ever produced for visitors and foreign residents in this country; indeed, my discussion with locals showed that it has much to teach even those born and bred in l'Hexagone. It is Hampshire's meticulous detail which lifts his work way beyond the range of other books with similar titles. This book is absolutely indispensable."
The Riviera Reporter

"Covers every conceivable question that might be asked concerning everyday life – I know of no other book that could take the place of this one."
France in Print

"It was definitely money well spent."
Reader (Amazon)

"The ultimate reference book – Every conceivable subject imaginable is exhaustively explained in simple terms – An excellent introduction to fully enjoy all that this fine country has to offer and save time and money in the process."
American Club of Zurich

Important Note

*F*rance is a diverse country with many faces, a variety of ethnic groups, religions and customs, as well as continuously changing rules, regulations, exchange rates and prices. A change of government in France can have a far-reaching influence on many important aspects of life, particularly taxes and social security. We cannot recommend too strongly that you check with an official and reliable source (not always the same) before making any major decisions or taking an irreversible course of action. However, don't believe everything you're told or read – even, dare we say it, herein!

The historic vote by the British people in 2016 to leave the European Union (see page 17) will also have consequences for British people planning to live or work in France, although nothing is expected to change until the UK actually leaves the EU in 2019.

To help you obtain further information and verify data with official sources, useful websites and references to other sources of information have been included in all chapters and in Appendix A. Important points have been emphasised throughout the book, some of which it would be expensive or foolish to disregard.

Note

Unless specifically stated, the reference to any company, organisation or product in this book doesn't constitute an endorsement or recommendation. None of the businesses (except advertisers), organisations, products or individuals have paid to be mentioned.

Contents

9. EDUCATION 101

10. PUBLIC TRANSPORT 121

11. MOTORING 135

16. SPORTS 229

17. SHOPPING 241

Author's Notes

♦ Frequent references are made in this book to the European Union (EU), which comprises Austria, Belgium, Bulgaria, Croatia, Cyprus, the Czech Republic, Denmark, Estonia, Finland, France, Germany, Greece, Hungary, Ireland, Italy, Latvia, Lithuania, Luxembourg, Malta, the Netherlands, Poland, Portugal, Romania, Slovakia, Slovenia, Spain, Sweden and the UK. The European Economic Area (EEA) comprises the EU countries plus the European Free Trade Association (EFTA) countries of Iceland, Liechtenstein and Norway, plus Switzerland (which is an EFTA member but not a member of the EEA). In this book, references to the EU countries generally also apply to the EEA countries and Switzerland.

♦ All times are shown using the 12-hour clock; times before noon are indicated by the suffix 'am' and times after noon by 'pm'.

♦ Prices quoted should be taken only as estimates, although they were mostly correct when going to press and fortunately don't usually change overnight. Although prices are sometimes quoted exclusive of value added tax (*hors taxes/HT*) in France, most prices are quoted inclusive of tax (*toutes taxes comprises/TTC*), which is the method used when quoting prices in this book. To convert from other currencies to euros or vice versa, see www.xe.com.

♦ His/he/him also means her/she/her (please forgive me ladies). This is done to make life easier for both the reader and the author, and isn't intended to be sexist.

♦ The French translation of many key words and phrases is shown in *italics* in brackets.

♦ British English and spelling is used throughout the book.

♦ A list of **Useful Websites** is contained in **Appendix A**.

♦ **Maps** – departments, airports and ports, TGV rail lines and motorways – are shown in **Appendix B**. A physical map of France is shown inside the front cover.

Introduction

Whether you're already living or working in France or just thinking about it – this is THE BOOK for you. Forget about all those glossy guidebooks, excellent though they are for tourists; this book was written especially with you in mind and is worth its weight in truffles. Furthermore, this fully updated and re-designed 11th edition is printed in colour. *Living and Working in France* is intended to meet the needs of anyone wishing to know the essentials of French life – however long your planned stay in France, you'll find the information contained in this book invaluable.

General information isn't difficult to find in France (provided you speak French) and a multitude of books are published on every conceivable subject. However, reliable and up-to-date information in English specifically intended for foreigners living and working in France isn't so easy to find, least of all in one volume. This book was written to fill this void and provide the comprehensive practical information necessary for a relatively trouble-free life. You may have visited France as a tourist, but living and working there is a different matter altogether. Adjusting to a different environment and culture and making a home in any foreign country can be a traumatic and stressful experience – and France is no exception.

Living and Working in France is a comprehensive handbook on a wide range of everyday subjects and represents the most up-to-date source of general information available to foreigners in France. However, it isn't simply a monologue of dry facts and figures, but a practical and entertaining look at life.

Adapting to life in a new country is a continuous process, and, although this book will help reduce your beginner's phase and minimise the frustrations, it doesn't contain all the answers. (Most of us don't even know the right questions to ask!) What it will do, however, is help you make informed decisions and calculated judgements, instead of uneducated guesses. **Most importantly, it will save you time, trouble and money, and repay your investment many times over.**

Although you may find some of the information a bit daunting, don't be discouraged. Most problems occur only once and fade into insignificance after a short time (as you face the next half a dozen!). The majority of foreigners in France would agree that, all things considered, they love living there. A period spent in France is a wonderful way to enrich your life and hopefully please your bank manager. We trust this book will help you avoid the pitfalls of life in France and smooth your way to a happy and rewarding future in your new home.

Bon courage!

David Hampshire

January 2017

1.
FINDING A JOB

*F*inding work in France isn't always as difficult as the unemployment figures may suggest, particularly in Paris and other large cities, depending of course on your profession or trade, qualifications and, most importantly, your ability to speak French. Nationals of EU/EEA countries (see Brexit below) have the right to work in France or any other member state without a work permit, provided they have a valid passport or national identity card and comply with the member state's laws and regulations on employment.

EU nationals are entitled to the same treatment as French citizens in matters of pay, working conditions, access to housing, vocational training, social security entitlements and trade union rights, and their families and immediate dependants are entitled to join them and enjoy the same rights.

If you don't qualify to live and work in France by birthright or as an EU national you must obtain a long-stay visa, which is dependent upon obtaining employment. However, France has had a virtual freeze on the employment of non-EU nationals for many years, which has been strengthened in recent years due to the high unemployment rate. The employment of non-EU nationals must be approved by the Pôle Emploi (formerly the Agence Nationale Pour l'Emploi/ANPE), which can propose the employment of a French national instead, although this is rare.

For a permanent position, the prospective employer must have advertised the post with the Pôle Emploi for at least five weeks and must also obtain authorisation to employ a non-EU national from the French Ministry of Labour (Ministère du Travail, des Relations Sociales et de la Solidarité, www.travail-solidarite.gouv.fr) or the Direction Départementale du Travail, de l'Emploi et de la Formation Professionnelle (DDTEFP) where the business is registered.

If you aren't an EU national it's essential to check whether you'll be eligible to work in France, before your arrival (see **Chapter 3**).

BREXIT

The most important consideration for British citizens planning to live or work in France, either in the short or long term, is Britain's historic decision to leave the European Union (EU) – termed Brexit (British Exit) – in a referendum held on 23rd June 2016. The actual mechanism to leave the EU will begin with the invoking of Article 50 – due to happen before the end of March 2017 (after this book had gone to press) – after which the UK will have two years to 'negotiate' its exit from the EU.

Leaving the EU won't only affect the UK's relationship and trade with the EU and the 27 other member countries, but it will also influence the relationship between England and the other countries that make up the United Kingdom (not least Scotland, which voted to remain in the EU, and Northern Ireland, which has a land border with the Republic of Ireland, an EU member). It will also have far-reaching consequences for Britain's future European and world trade relations, exchange rates, cost of living, laws, and – not least – the ability of Britons to live, work and study in France and other EU countries (and French citizens to live and work in Britain).

The consequences of the UK leaving the EU will take many years to become clear, but a certain amount of turmoil is expected in the short to medium term. However, the immediate Armageddon forecast by the remain campaign had yet to materialise six months after the vote (although the pound had predictably fallen in value against the Euro), although the uncertainly regarding future trading arrangements with the EU was causing anxiety among many businesses. However, many experts and analysts believe that the UK could eventually be better off as an independent nation able to make its own trade deals.

ECONOMY

France is one of the world's wealthiest countries and its sixth-largest economy in 2015, with one of the highest per capita gross domestic products (GDP) in the EU of US$44,444.84 in 2014, although this had fallen to $38,653 in 2015 (source: www.statista.com). The country experienced stagnant growth between 2012 and 2014, with the economy expanding by 0% in 2012, 0.8% in 2013 and 0.2% in 2014, though it picked up in 2015 with growth of 1.2% and forecast growth of 1.5% for 2016. Since 2008, the French economy has grown by around 3 per cent, while in the same period the German economy has grown 6 per cent, the UK by 8 per cent and the US by some 10 per cent.

Since the start of the new millennium, inflation has generally been low at around 2 per cent; in the ten years from 2006-2015 the highest annual rate was 2.3 per cent in 2012 (the rate for 2015 was 1.53 per cent).

France is among the world's largest exporters of goods and services and in 2015 was ranked sixth in the world for total exports. The country has experienced an economic transformation in the last few decades, during which its traditional industries have been thoroughly modernised and a wealth of new high-tech industries created. However, increasing competition, particularly from Far Eastern countries (known collectively as *le low-cost!*), has meant that traditional industries such as steel, clothing and textile production have become less competitive. Nevertheless, the manufacture of chemicals, ships, cars, aeroplanes and defence equipment remains significant.

Less labour and capital intensive industries such as electronics, pharmaceuticals and communications have flourished since the '80s,

although the largest growth in recent years has been in service industries, e.g. banking, insurance, advertising and tourism, which together account for over 70 per cent of GDP, compared with around 25 per cent for industry and under 3 per cent for agriculture. Despite the continuing decline in the number of farms, France remains Europe's largest agricultural producer and the world's second-largest after the USA.

WORKFORCE

French workers enjoy an affluent lifestyle in comparison with those in many other western countries, with high salaries (especially for executives and senior managers) and excellent employment conditions (see **Chapter 2**). Much of the French 'working class' (France is supposedly a classless society) consists of skilled (*qualifié*) workers and technicians, with engineers part of the elite (as in Germany) and highly respected. France has a well-educated and trained workforce, and even employees doing what many would consider menial jobs, such as shop assistants and waiters, have trade training (although seldom in politeness!) and aren't looked down on.

> Most French don't dream of becoming entrepreneurs or businessmen but of working in the public sector, which constitutes some 25 per cent of the country's workforce compared with around 15 per cent in most other EU countries, and where benefits are second to none, e.g. up to three months' annual holiday and retirement at 55 or even 50!

WORK ATTITUDES

French companies have traditionally been expected to care for their employees and most have a paternalistic attitude. Experience, maturity and loyalty are highly valued (although

qualifications are even more valuable), and newcomers generally find it difficult to secure a senior position with a French company. The traditional hierarchical structure of French businesses with little contact between management and workers, both of whom are reluctant to take on responsibilities outside their immediate duties, has given way to a more 'modern' reward-for-achievement attitude and relations between management and staff have generally improved. However, the French 'old boy' network is still alive and well and may prevent foreigners achieving the promotion they deserve (see **Industrial Relations** on page 22).

As in the US, French employers tend to expect high standards and are intolerant of mistakes or inefficiency. However, it's difficult and expensive to fire employees. When it comes to hiring new employees (particularly managers and executives) and making important business decisions, the process is slower in France than in many other developed countries. Many foreigners, particularly Americans, find that they need to adjust to a slower pace of working life. Most French managers and executives rarely take work home and they seldom work at weekends, which are sacrosanct.

Don't be misled by the apparent lack of urgency and casual approach to business – the French can be just as hard-headed as any other race. Business relations tend to be formal: colleagues usually address each other as *vous* rather than *tu* and often use surnames instead of first names, while socialising with work colleagues is rare. Attire is generally formal, although in some companies Fridays are declared 'casual dress' days.

WORKING WOMEN

The number of working women in France has increased dramatically in recent years, and some two-thirds of French women (and the vast majority of those under 40), including 70 per cent of women with one child, now work – the highest percentage in Europe outside Scandinavia. However, around 30 per cent of women work part-time, compared with just 5 per cent of men. Most women are employed in distribution and transport, nursing and health care, education, secretarial professions and service industries such as retailing.

Male chauvinism is alive and well in France and most French women are more concerned with equal rights in the workplace and benefits (such as paid maternity leave and state-run nurseries) than the opportunity to reach the top. Women must generally be twice as qualified as a man to compete on equal terms, although the 1983 law on professional equality (*loi Roudy sur l'égalité professionnelle*) made it easier for women to break into male-dominated trades and professions. However, women still find it difficult to attain management positions, particularly in technical and industrial fields, where there has long been a tradition of prejudice against them.

Women have had some success in reaching the top in the professions and in sectors such as finance, insurance, the media, personnel, advertising and retailing. Career women are generally more accepted and taken more seriously in Paris, which has a more progressive outlook than the provinces. Nevertheless, over a quarter of France's 2.5 million businesses are run by women, by far the highest proportion in Europe. Since 1997, women have had the right to earn 90 per cent of a full-time salary if they work a four-day week, e.g. taking Wednesday off to look after their children.

A woman doing the same or broadly similar work to a man and employed by the same employer is legally entitled to the same salary and other terms of employment. However, despite the Equal Pay Act of 1972, women's salaries are an average of around 15 per cent lower than men's. Around 15 per cent of women earn the minimum wage (see page 22), which generally reflects the fact that most women work in lower paid industries and hold lower paid positions than men (including more part-time jobs), rather than discrimination.

However, the situation has improved considerably in recent years, and women are much less exploited in France than in many other western European countries. Women continue to face the additional hazard of sexual harassment, as 'flirting' is an unwritten part of French life. If it's any consolation, refusing a sexual advance from your boss rarely results in your losing your job, as it's difficult to fire employees in France.

SALARY

French executive salaries were lower than the international average in the '70s and early '80s, but rose much faster than the rate of inflation in the '80s and '90s and were augmented by lucrative bonuses and profit-sharing schemes. They've now caught up and even surpassed those in some other Western countries, although in recent years university graduates and school-leavers have been willing to accept almost any wage in order to get a foot on the career ladder. Annual salary increases have been minimal since the recession in 2008.

☑ SURVIVAL TIP

If you've friends or acquaintances working in France or who've worked there, ask them what an average or good salary is for your particular trade or profession. If locality is your prime consideration, you can consult the website (www.salairemoyen.com) to check the average salary in a particular area.

Salaries often vary considerably for the same job in different parts of France. Those working in Paris and its environs are generally the highest paid, primarily due to the high cost of living, particularly regarding accommodation. When comparing salaries, you need to take into account compulsory deductions such as tax and social security (see **Chapters 13** and **14**), and also the cost of living.

For many employees, particularly executives and senior managers, their remuneration is much more than what they receive in their monthly salary. Many companies provide a range of benefits for executives and managers that may include a company car, private health insurance and health screening, expenses-paid holidays, private school fees, inexpensive or interest-free home and other loans, rent-free accommodation, free or subsidised public transport tickets, free or subsidised company restaurant, sports or country club membership, non-contributory company pension, stock options, bonuses and profit-sharing schemes, tickets for sports events and shows, and 'business' conferences in exotic locations (see also **Chapter 2**).

Many employees in France also receive an extra month's salary at Christmas, known as a 13th month's salary, and some companies also pay a 14th month's salary before the summer holiday period.

Salaries in many industries are decided by collective bargaining between employers and unions, either regionally or nationally. When there's a collective agreement, employers must offer at least the minimum wage agreed, although most major companies exceed this. Agreements specify minimum wage levels for each position within main employment categories in a particular industry or company, and often require bonus payments related to the age or qualifications of employees or their length of service with the company (*prime d'ancienneté*). This means that wage levels are effectively fixed. The government doesn't regulate cost of living increases for salaries above the minimum wage (see below), although the collective agreement may provide for annual increases based on cost of living figures.

The introduction of the 35-hour week (see **Working Hours** on page 38) included guarantees that salaries couldn't be reduced from the levels paid on a 39-hour week basis. Government incentives available to employers for hiring additional workers did little to mitigate the cost of reducing the working week, and it's likely that most salaries will remain static with pay rises few and far between for the foreseeable future.

You can obtain a rough guide to salaries from many websites, including World Salaries (www.worldsalaries.org/france.shtml) and Votre Salaire (www.votresalaire.fr/main/salaire – in French).

Minimum Wage

At the lower end of the wage scale, there has been a statutory minimum wage (*salaire minimum de croissance/SMIC*) since 1950. When the cost of living index rises by 2 per cent or more in a year, the minimum wage is increased. In practice, the minimum wage rises each year, usually in July and especially when elections are coming up! In 2016, the minimum wage was €9.67 per hour, equal to gross pay of €1,466.62 per month for 151.67 hours (the standard under the terms of the 35-hour working week). Working hours above 35 per week are considered overtime.

There's a lower *SMIC* for juveniles, those on special job-creation schemes and disabled employees. Unskilled workers (particularly women) are usually employed at or near the minimum wage, semi-skilled workers are usually paid 10 to 20 per cent more, and skilled workers 30 to 40 per cent more (often shown in job advertisements as '*SMIC + 10, 20, 30, 40%*'). Note, however, that many employees, particularly seasonal workers in the farming and tourist industries, are paid below the minimum wage, despite it being illegal. Part time workers can't legally receive a lower wage than the SMIC.

Young people under 17 years of age with less than 6 months experience can be paid 80 per cent of the SMIC between the ages of 16-17 and 90 per cent between the ages of 17-18. Young students on apprenticeship contracts usually receive between 25 and 78 per cent of the SMIC in accordance with their age and the number of years they have served. Young people on work experience don't receive wages but may get an expense allowance, which is compulsory by law for work experience of more than two consecutive months.

INDUSTRIAL RELATIONS

The French are notorious for their strikes (*grèves*, euphemistically known as *mouvements sociaux*), which are a common feature of French 'working' life – particularly in the public sector, where employees have long been known for their propensity to stop work at the drop of a beret. Recent years have seen strikes among public transport employees and among self-employed groups such as farmers, fishermen, truck drivers, doctors and other medical professionals, and strikes become increasingly common in the run-up to elections and in response to announcements of plant closures or sales of businesses to foreign investors.

There was a period when strikes in private companies were almost unheard-of in France, but they've recently started to become a popular means of protesting against threats to job security. In both the public and private sectors strikes are often seen as the only effective means of communicating with the government and elected officials, as it's the government rather than employers who are expected to resolve most work-related issues. Despite negligible union membership (less than 10 per cent and falling) most workers in France are automatically covered by industry-wide and legally recognised collective agreements (*conventions collectives*).

Nevertheless, there has been a huge reduction in strikes in the last decade or so and a less confrontational relationship between employers and employees, which is due both to high unemployment and new legislation requiring both sides to discuss their differences and imposing a cooling-off period before a strike can be called.

UNEMPLOYMENT

The French unemployment rate fell to 9.9 per cent in mid-2016, which was the lowest since Autumn 2012. The rate has averaged 9.25 per cent between 1996 and 2016, reaching an all-time high of 10.7 per cent in early 1997 and a record low of 7.2 per cent in 2008. In comparison, the unemployment rate in autumn 2016 was 4.2 per cent in Germany, 4.8 per cent in the UK, 11.4 per cent in Italy and 19.5 per cent in Spain.

Unemployment remains a major problem in France, particularly for those aged under 25 among whom it's almost three times the national average. France spends more on job creation schemes than any other EU country, yet has the worst job creation record in the OECD, and the government's recent attempt to introduce a 'youth employment contract' was a disaster.

Other groups badly affected by unemployment are older people, women and blue collar workers, the last currently suffering unemployment rates five times as high as executives and managers. Although unemployment has hit manufacturing industries the hardest no sector has survived unscathed, including the flourishing service industries in the Paris region. Some of the worst hit industries have been construction, electronics, communications, the media and banking.

Long-term unemployment is a huge problem, where the average period of unemployment is a year (the longest in Europe) and over a million people have been unemployed for over two years. Anyone aged over 50 who loses his job is unlikely to work again with an indefinite-term contract (*contrat à durée indéterminée/CDI*)

unless they're highly qualified and their skills are in demad.

EMPLOYMENT PROSPECTS

Being attracted to France by its weather, cuisine, wine and lifestyle is understandable but doesn't rate highly as an employment qualification. You should have a positive reason for living and working in France. Simply being fed up with your job or the weather isn't the best motive for moving to France. It's extremely difficult to find work in rural areas and it isn't easy in cities and large towns (even Paris), especially if your French isn't fluent.

You shouldn't plan on finding employment in France unless you've special qualifications or experience for which there's a strong demand. If you want a good job you must usually be extremely well qualified and speak fluent French. If you plan to come to France without a job you should have a plan for finding employment on arrival and try to make some contacts before you arrive.

 Caution

An increasing number of people in France turn to self-employment or starting a business to make a living (see page 32), although this path is strewn with pitfalls for the newcomer.

If you've a job offer you should ensure that it's in writing (preferably in French). France has a reasonably self-sufficient labour market and doesn't require a large number of skilled or unskilled foreign workers. In recent years however French companies have been keen to expand into international markets which has created opportunities for foreign workers, particularly bilingual and tri-lingual employees. In recent years there has been a marked increase in French investment abroad, and France is experiencing a brain drain as executives and entrepreneurs (not to mention football players!) leave the country, creating something of a vacuum – particularly in high-tech industries such as information technology. There are some 2,000 affiliates of US firms in France, employing over half a million people.

QUALIFICATIONS

The most important qualification for working (and living) in France is the ability to speak French fluently (see Language below). Once you've overcome this hurdle you should establish whether your trade or professional qualifications and experience are recognised in France. If you are new to the world of full time employment French employers expect studies to have been in a relevant discipline and to have included work experience (*un stage*).

Professional or trade qualifications are required to work in most fields in France, where qualifications are also often necessary to be self-employed or start a business. It isn't just a matter of hanging up a sign and waiting for the stampede of customers to your door. Many foreigners are required to undergo a 'business' course before they can start work in France (see **Self-employment & Starting a Business** on page 32).

Theoretically, qualifications recognised by professional and trade bodies in one EU country should be recognised in France. However, recognition varies from country to country and in some cases foreign qualifications aren't recognised by French employers or professional and trade associations. All foreign academic qualifications should also be recognised, although they may be given less prominence than equivalent French qualifications.

All EU member states issue occupation information sheets containing a common job description with a table of qualifications.

These cover a large number of trades and are intended to help someone with the relevant qualifications look for a job in another EU country. For information about equivalent qualifications you can contact the Centre d'Études et de Recherche sur les Qualifications (CEREQ, 04 91 13 28 28/01 44 08 69 10, www.cereq.fr) or ENIC-NARIC run by the European Network of Information Centres (www.enic-naric.net). A list of professions and trades in France can be found on the website of the Office National d'Information sur l'Enseignement et les Professions (ONISEP, www.onisep.fr).

Further information can be obtained from the Bureau de l'Information sur les Systèmes Educatifs et de la Reconnaissance de Diplômes of the Ministère de la Jeunesse, de l'Education Nationale et de la Recherche (01 55 55 10 10, www.education.gouv.fr) and the Ministère de l'Enseignement Supérieure et de la Recherche (www.enseignementsup-recherche.gouv.fr).

LANGUAGE

Although English is the *lingua franca* of international commerce and may help you to secure a job in France, the most important qualification for anyone seeking employment is the ability to speak fluent French. Although most French children learn English at school and the majority of educated French people can speak some English, many of them are reluctant to do so, as they have an ingrained fear of making mistakes and 'losing face'.

☑ **SURVIVAL TIP**

The most common reason for negative experiences among foreigners in France, whether they be visitors or residents, is that they can't – or won't – speak French.

(Two-thirds of French people claimed to speak only French and less than 25 per cent admit to speaking English 'well'.) The French are extremely proud of their language (to the point of hubris) and – not surprisingly – expect everyone living or working in France to speak it.

If necessary you should have French lessons before arriving in France. A sound knowledge of French won't just help you find a job or perform your job better, but will also make everyday life much simpler and more enjoyable. If you come to France without being able to speak French you'll be excluded from everyday life and will feel uncomfortable until you can understand what's going on around you. You must usually speak French if you wish to have French friends.

However bad your grammar, limited your vocabulary or terrible your accent, an attempt to speak French will be appreciated more than your fluent English. Don't, however, be surprised when the French wince at your torture of their beloved tongue, pretend not to understand you even though you've said something 'correctly', or correct minor grammatical or pronunciation errors!

If you don't already speak good French don't expect to learn it quickly, even if you already have a basic knowledge and take intensive lessons (see **Learning French** on page 118). It's common for foreigners not to be fluent after a year or more of intensive lessons in France. If your expectations are unrealistic you'll become frustrated, which can affect your confidence. It takes a long time to reach the level of fluency needed to be able to work in French. If you don't speak French fluently you should begin French lessons on arrival and consider taking a menial or even an unpaid voluntary job, which is one of the quickest ways of improving your French.

Your ability in French and other languages must be listed on your curriculum vitae (CV/résumé) and the level of proficiency stated as follows: some knowledge (*notions*); good (*bien*); very good (*très bien* or *parle, lis, écris*); fluent (*courant*); and mother tongue (*langue maternelle*). When stating your French language ability it's important not to exaggerate. If you state that your French is very good or fluent you'll be interviewed in French, which may also happen even if you've only a little knowledge.

When doing business in France or writing letters to French businesses communication should always be in French. Most business letters must be written in a very precise style with proper opening and closing greetings.

France also has over 70 regional languages, the most widely spoken including Alsatian (spoken in Alsace), Basque (Pyrenees), Breton (Brittany), Catalan (Roussillon), Corsican (Corsica), Gascon (southwest) and Occitan (Languedoc). In some areas schools teach in the regional language as well as in French. However fluent your French, you may still have problems understanding these, as well as some accents – particularly those of the south – and local dialects (*patois*).

JOB HUNTING

As many as 60 per cent of job vacancies in France aren't advertised but rather are filled by word of mouth. When looking for a job, it's therefore best not to put all your eggs in one basket – the more job applications you make, the better your chance of finding the right (or any) job. Contact as many prospective employers as possible by writing, telephoning or calling on them in person.

Whatever job you're looking for it's important to market yourself appropriately. For example, the recruitment of executives and senior managers is handled almost exclusively by recruitment consultants. At the other end of the scale, manual jobs requiring no previous experience may be advertised at Pôle Emploi offices (see below), in local newspapers and on notice boards, and the first suitable applicant may be offered the job on the spot. Job hunting resources are listed below.

EMPLOYMENT AGENCIES
Government Employment Service

The French national employment service Pôle Emploi (*www.pole-emploi.fr*) operates offices throughout France with both local and national job listings, although jobs on offer are mainly for non-professional skilled, semi-skilled and unskilled jwork, particularly in industry, retailing and catering. Around 75 per cent are temporary (*intérimaire*) or short-term (*CDD*) opportunities, although higher-level jobs are offered by specialist offices (see below). You can search for your nearest office online under *Administrations du Travail et de l'Emploi* or *Pôle Emploi*.

Pôle Emploi offices provide free telephones for calling prospective employers (not your mum!). The Pôle Emploi website provides access to many of its services, including a searchable database of job vacancies. To apply for most of the jobs listed online you must contact a Pôle Emploi office, but a few of the listings give you the name and address of the company so that you can apply directly. The website also contains general information about job hunting in France (in French).

Pôle Emploi services are available to all EU nationals and foreign residents in France. However, offices have a reputation for being unhelpful to foreign job-seekers unless they've previously been employed in France or are unemployed and receiving unemployment benefit. Being a government department, the Pôle Emploi isn't service-oriented and the quality of service varies with the region, the office and the person handling your case.

Some Pôle Emploi offices specialise in certain fields and industries. For example, in Paris there are offices dealing exclusively with hotel and restaurant services, tourism, journalism, public works, civil aviation, the entertainment industry and jobs for the disabled. Around 20 Pôle Emploi offices are termed *Points Cadres* and handle executive jobs. The Pôle Emploi also operates Jeunes Diplômés, a service for young graduates (www.jd.apec.fr); the Association Pour l'Emploi des Cadres (APEC, www.cadres. apec.fr) for managers and engineers; and the Association Pour l'Emploi des Cadres, Ingénieurs, Techniciens de l'Agriculture (APECITA, www.apecita.com) for professionals in the agriculture industry.

La Cité des Métiers

La Cité des Métiers is a careers resource centre at the Cité de Sciences et de l'Industrie (known as 'La Villette'), where you'll find information on over 2,500 jobs, magazines and periodicals, mini-computers and staff to help with job applications. Its website (www. cite-sciences.fr – follow the links to Cité des Métiers) provides information about the various services and resources available, opening hours, job fairs and exhibitions sponsored by La Villette.

EURES

The European Employment Service (EURES) network covers all EU countries plus Iceland and Norway. Members regularly exchange information about job vacancies and you can have your personal details circulated to the employment service in selected countries, e.g. to the Pôle Emploi in France. Details are available in local employment service offices in each member country, where advice on how to apply for jobs is provided.

In the UK you can contact your local Employment Service, which publishes information about working in France (ask for the Jobcentre Plus service). EURES has a website (https://ec.europa.eu/eures/public/ homepage) where you can find contact information for job counsellors in the UK and other EU countries specialising in public sector jobs in France.

RECRUITMENT CONSULTANTS

International recruitment consultants or executive search companies (*cabinet de recrutement*) and 'head hunters' (*chasseur de têtes*) act for French companies, although they mainly handle executive and management positions. Britons seeking work in France can obtain an *Overseas Placement List* from the Recruitment and Employment Confederation in London (020-7009 2100, www.rec.uk.com), which lists agencies that specialise in finding overseas positions.

Many foreign (i.e. non-French) recruitment consultancies post job vacancies on the main internet job sites with links to their own recruitment websites. See **Internet** below for the most popular online job sites.

NEWSPAPERS & OTHER PUBLICATIONS

Most Parisian and regional newspapers contain job sections (*offres d'emploi*) on certain days and most newspapers also post job advertisements on their websites. The most popular Parisian newspapers for job advertisements are *Le Monde*, *Le Figaro*, *France-Soir*, *Libération*, *Le Parisien* and *Les Echos* (the daily financial and stock exchange journal). The best newspapers depend on the sort of job you're seeking. If you're looking for a management or professional position, you should see *Le Monde*, *Le Figaro*, *Libération* and *Les Echos*. Those seeking employment as technicians, artisans, secretaries, sales clerks,

For links to the websites of the major French newspapers, see www.onlinenewspapers.com/ france.htm and www.world-newspapers.com/ france.html.

factory workers and manual labourers should try *France-Soir* and *Le Parisien*. *Libération* has adverts for all job categories.

In addition to the above, there are many important regional newspapers in France, e.g. *Sud-Ouest* and *Ouest-France*. There are also a number of newspapers and magazines devoted to careers and jobs, such as *Carrières et Emplois* (which publishes regional issues), *Carrières Publiques et Privées*, *Emploi*, *Entreprise et Carrières*, *Job Pratique*, *Le Mardi du Travail* and *Rebondir*. Specialist publications include *Courrier Cadres* for management level jobs (published by Pôle Emploi), the *Journal de l'Hôtellerie* (www.lhotellerie.fr) for hotel and catering jobs, *L'Usine Nouvelle* for factory jobs and *L'Etudiant* for student summer jobs

Most professions and trade associations publish journals containing job offers (see *Benn's Media Directory Europe*). Jobs are also advertised in various English-language publications, including the *International Herald Tribune*, *Wall Street Journal Europe*, and *France-USA Contacts* (fortnightly – see www.fusac.fr).

INTERNET

The internet has hundreds of sites for jobseekers, including business, recruitment company and newspaper sites. Most of the main international job-finding sites have sections devoted to vacancies in France. Some of the best known are listed below (unless otherwise stated, sites cover all types of jobs in all parts of France).

◆ Bale.fr (www.bale.fr) for IT and communications jobs

◆ Cadremploi (www.cadremploi.com) for management jobs

◆ Emailjob.com (www.emailjob.monster.fr)

◆ Emploi.com (www.emploi.com)

◆ Eurojobs (www.eurojobs.com/browse-by-country/france)

◆ Indeed (www.indeed.co.uk/jobs?q=france&l=)

◆ Jobs in Paris (www.jobsinparis.fr) for English-speaking professionals

◆ Keljob (www.keljob.com)

◆ The Local (www.thelocal.fr/jobs) for English-language jobs

◆ Monster (www.monster.fr)

◆ Offre-emploi.com (www.offre-emploi.com)

◆ Regions Job (www.regionsjob.com) for jobs in a particular French region

◆ Talents.fr (www.talents.fr) for media and culture jobs

Many of the above websites include articles about job hunting in France and information about work permits and qualifications. Don't forget to check the websites of large companies and international organisations.

SEASONAL JOBS

Seasonal jobs are available throughout the year, the vast majority in the tourist industry.

> Fluency in French is required for all but the most menial and worst paid jobs and is more important than your experience and qualifications, although fluent French alone won't guarantee you a well paid job.

Many seasonal jobs last for the duration of the summer or winter tourist seasons, May to September and December to April respectively, although some are simply casual or temporary jobs for a number of weeks.

Seasonal jobs include most trades in hotels and restaurants, couriers and representatives, a variety of jobs in ski resorts, sports instructors, jobs in bars and clubs, fruit and grape picking and other agricultural jobs, and various jobs in the construction industry. Seasonal employees in the tourist industry have traditionally been paid below the minimum wage, although the authorities have clamped down on employers in recent years.

If you aren't an EU national you may require a visa. Check with a French embassy or consulate in your home country well in advance of your visit. Foreign students in France can obtain a temporary work permit (*autorisation provisoire de travail*) for part-time work during their summer holiday period.

Note that seasonal workers have few rights and little legal job protection in France, unless they're hired under standard employment contracts (usually *CDD*s), and they can generally be fired without compensation at any time.

Lists of summer jobs can be found via the internet, e.g. *www.pole-emploi.fr*, www.cidj.com and www.jobs-ete-europe.com. There are a number of books for those seeking holiday jobs, including *Work Your Way Around the World* (Crimson).

Hotels & Catering

Hotels and restaurants are the largest employers of seasonal workers, with jobs available all year round for roles from hotel manager to kitchen hand. Experience, qualifications and fluent French are required for all the best and highest paid positions, although a variety of jobs are available for the untrained, inexperienced and those who don't speak fluent French. Bear in mind that if accommodation with cooking facilities or full board isn't provided with a job it can be expensive and difficult to find, therefore you must ensure that your salary is sufficient to pay for accommodation, food and other living expenses.

The weekly trade magazine *L'Hôtellerie* (www.lhotellerie-restauration.fr) is a good source of hotel and catering vacancies, as is *L'Echo Touristique* (www.echotouristique.com).

Language Teachers

Language teaching (particularly English) is a good source of permanent, temporary or part-time work all year round, but particularly in summer. This may entail teaching a foreign language at a language school or privately, or even teaching French to expatriates if your French is up to the task. Language schools don't always require a teaching qualification and a university degree may suffice, although you should take as many educational certificates with you as possible. However, some schools insist that teachers have a Teaching English as a Foreign Language (01349-800 600, www.tefl.org.uk) qualification. Further information about teaching English in France is available from TESOL France (www.tesol-france.org).

You could also try placing an advertisement in a French newspaper or magazine offering private lessons. You can also apply directly to state schools for a position as a language assistant(e), although they're usually paid only a nominal salary – much less than that offered to a qualified French native teacher. Information about teaching in France can be obtained from the Ministry of Education (www. education.gouv.fr).

Grape & Fruit Picking

One of the most popular summer jobs in France – particularly among young people – is grape picking (*vendange*), although it's hard, back-breaking work. Thousands of foreigners are employed on French farms each summer, most of whom are 'professionals' from Morocco, Portugal and Spain who return to the same region each year. Accommodation and cooking facilities can be primitive, and the cost of food and accommodation is usually deducted from your wages.

The grape harvest begins in the south around mid-September and moves up towards Alsace by the middle of October. It's possible to move from area to area, particularly as growers recommend workers to one another. The best (often only) way to find work in a vineyard is to turn up and ask for a job (it's almost impossible to arrange work from outside France). Grape pickers can obtain a *contrat vendange* valid for one month and renewable for a further month, which exempts them from paying social security charges.

Useful websites for finding grape-picking jobs include www.grapepicking.co.uk, www.

vinomedia.fr, www.viti-vini.com and the French government employment site, *www. pole-emploi.fr*. Information about general farm work can be obtained from the Service des Echanges et des Stages Agricoles dans le Monde (SESAME, www.agriplanete.com).

Increasing competition from Eastern European workers has made grape and fruit-picking work harder to find, and it may also be less well paid than previously.

Holiday Camps

There are many children's and youth holiday 'camps' (*colonie de vacances*) in France, where French (and many foreign) parents sensibly off-load their offspring during the long summer break from June to September, which offer various job opportunities. Information about children's holiday centres is available from local Directions Départementales de la Jeunesse et des Sports, the addresses of which can be obtained from French embassies or online.

One of the largest British recruiters of summer seasonal workers is PGL Young Adventure (0844-371 0101, www.pgl.co.uk), which operates around ten activity centres in France and recruits some 1,000 staff from May to September (applications should be made by March for the summer season). PGL offers a variety of jobs, including couriers, group and entertainment organisers, chalet staff, sports instructors (particularly water-sports), teachers, caterers and cooks, and various support staff.

Winter Jobs

Ski resorts require an army of temporary workers to cater for the annual invasion of winter sports enthusiasts. Such jobs can be a lot of fun. You'll get fit, improve your French and make friends, and may even be able to save some money. Note, however, that although a winter job may be a working holiday to you (with lots of skiing and little work), to your employer it means exactly the opposite!

In addition to jobs in the hotel and catering trades already mentioned above, a variety of winter jobs are available, including couriers, resort representatives, chalet staff, ski technicians, and (for the suitably qualified) ski instructors and guides. As a general rule, the better paid the job, the longer the working hours and the less time off there is for skiing and other pleasurable activities. Employment in a winter resort usually entitles employees to a discounted lift pass (but no time to use it!).

AU PAIRS

The au pair system provides an excellent opportunity to travel, improve your French, and generally broaden your education while living and working in France. Single males and females aged between 18 and 27 from most countries are eligible for a position as an au pair. (Although 'au pair' is French, the French commonly refer to a *fille au-pair* and the official term is a *stagiaire aide-familiale*.) Au pairs must usually have had a high school education or the equivalent and have a good knowledge of French, and must attend French classes organised for foreign students.

If you're an EU national, you need only a valid passport and aren't required to arrange a position before arriving in France, although it's usually wise. Applicants from non-EU countries need a long-stay visa and require an 'engagement agreement' (*déclaration d'engagement*) with a French family and a certificate of registration for French classes at a language school. If applicable, these must be presented to your local French embassy or consulate with your passport when applying for a visa.

Au pairs are usually contracted to work for a minimum of six and a maximum of 18 months. Most families require an au pair for at least the

whole school year, from September to June. The best time to look for an au pair position is therefore before the beginning of the school year. You should apply as early as possible and not later than a month prior to your preferred start date or at least two months if you need a visa.

Working hours are officially limited to 5 hours a day (30 per week), six days per week, plus a maximum of three evenings' baby-sitting. You should be given time off to attend French classes and religious services. Au pairs usually holiday with the family, or they may be free to take Christmas or Easter holidays at home.

According to French law, your host family must pay you pocket money, which corresponds to 75-90 per cent of the so-called *minimum garanti*, which is re-evaluated each year. In 2016 this was between €264 and €316.80 per month (it's higher in Paris), as agreed with your host family and detailed in your contract. You're required to pay your own fare from your home to Paris (and back), although if you're employed in the provinces the host family pays the rail fare from Paris.

An au pair position can be arranged privately with a family or through an agency. There are au pair agencies in France and many other countries, e.g. www.aupairworld.com/en/

au_pairs and www.newaupair.com. The better agencies vet families, make periodic checks on your welfare, help you overcome problems, whether personal or with your family.

Many au pairs grow to love their children and families and form lifelong friendships. On the other hand, abuses of the au pair system are common in all countries, and you may be treated as a servant rather than a member of the family and be expected to work long hours and spend most evenings baby-sitting. If you've any complaints about your duties, you should refer them to the agency that found you the position.

It's possible for responsible English-and French-speaking young women to obtain employment as a nanny (*nurse, nanny* or *nounou*, sometimes called *garde d'enfants*). Duties are basically the same as for an au pair job (see above), although a position as a nanny is a proper job with full employee rights and a real salary!

SELF-EMPLOYMENT & STARTING A BUSINESS

France is traditionally a nation of small companies and sole traders, where the economic philosophy encourages and even nurtures the creation of small businesses, although many exist on a shoe string. (Around 11 per cent of the French workforce is self-employed, compared with around 16 per cent in the UK.) Being self-employed in France is no simple matter and requires planning, preparation, determination and a good deal of luck. If you're planning to start a business, you must also do battle with the notoriously obstructive French bureaucracy (*bonne chance!*).

If you're an EU-national, you can work as a self-employed individual (*travailleur independent*) or as a sole trader (*entreprise individuelle* or *micro-entrepreneur*). A non-EU

national with a long-term residence permit (*carte de résident*) can also be self-employed or a sole trader. However, it's difficult for non-EU nationals to obtain a residence permit to become self-employed.

There are three main categories of self-employed people in France: *profession libérale* (e.g. accountants, doctors, lawyers, writers), *commerçant* (traders and shopkeepers) and *artisan* (craftsmen and tradesmen).

> **Caution**
>
> To be self-employed in certain trades and professions, you must have an official status (*statut* or *régime*) and it's illegal simply to hang up a sign and start business.

Registration with the appropriate professional or trade organisation is no longer necessary if you opt for the *micro-entrepreneur* (formerly *auto- entrepreneur*) system for new small businesses, aimed at reducing the taxes and financial costs of being self-employed or running a small business in France. Prior to the *micro-entrepreneur* status, a small business was charged a maximum fixed percentage of their turnover in social charges, while under the new regime (officially *micro-social*) social charges are based on actual earnings, calculated from previous months' turnover.

A *micro-entrepreneur* doesn't need to register for VAT and limits are placed on annual turnover of €82,200 for commercial businesses and €32,900 for service professionals and artisans. The regime has fewer restrictions on those working from home and is particularly helpful to the self-employed and those with a secondary income, including British expats or retirees looking to make a little extra income from home (under the previous system they would have faced high social charges, irrespective of whether any income had actually been earned!). See the French Entrée website for more information (www.frenchentree.com/news/new-autoentrepreneur-system-for-small-businesses).

The regime has been adopted by many service providers, including those engaged in sales, bar/restaurant businesses and letting accommodation. It also applies to independent professionals, including some ancilliary health and well-being professionals, paralegals, surveyors, accountants, consultants and other entrepreneurs.

The majority of businesses established by foreigners in France are linked to the leisure and catering industries, followed by property investment and development. These include holiday accommodation (e.g. bed and breakfast, *chambres d'hôtes* and *gîtes*, chalets, apartments and cottages to let), caravan and camping sites, building and allied trades, farming (e.g. dairy, vineyards, fruit, fish and fowl), catering (e.g. bars, cafés and restaurants), hotels, shops, franchises, estate agencies, translation services, language schools, landscape gardening, and holiday and sports centres (e.g. tennis, golf, squash, shooting and horse-riding schools). Before deciding on a business model, it's essential to research the demand and competition for a particular business in the local area.

> Comprehensive information about setting up and running a holiday accommodation business in France are provided in our sister publication, *Running Gîtes and B&B in France* (Survival Books).

As a self-employed person in France you aren't entitled to unemployment benefits should your business fail and there are no benefits for accidents at work (except for artisans), although you're insured against invalidity. As a self-employed person you risk bankruptcy if your business fails, but no longer necessarily ruin, as since 1st January 2011 creditors have had no claim on your private estate if you operate as a sole trader limited company (entrepreneur individuel à responsibilité limitée). This protection covers micro-entrepreneurs, commerçants (retailers), self-employed sales agents, artisans, farmers and professions libérales.

For more information about self-employment or starting a business in France, see the Expatica website (www.expatica.com/fr/employment/self-employment), French Property (www.french-property.com/guides/france/working-in-france/starting-a-business) and www.startbusinessinfrance.com.

2.
EMPLOYMENT CONDITIONS

*F*rench employees, particularly state employees, enjoy excellent employment conditions, which are variously based on the French Labour Code (*Code du Travail*), collective agreements (*conventions collectives de travail*), individual employment contracts (*contrat de travail*), and an employer's in-house rules and regulations (*règlements intérieurs/règlements de travail*).

Employees have extensive rights under the French Labour Code, which details the minimum conditions of employment, including working hours, overtime payments, holidays, trial and notice periods, dismissal conditions, health and safety regulations, and trade union rights.

The Labour Code is described in a number of books, including the *Code du Travail* (VO Editions). Information about employment conditions is available from the Legifrance website (www.legifrance.gouv.fr), some of which is in English, and from the government website (www.service-public.fr).

Collective agreements (*conventions collectives*) are negotiated between industry associations (*syndicats*) and employers' associations in many industries, and specify the rights and obligations of both employees and employers in a particular industry or occupation. Agreements specify minimum wage levels for each employment category in a particular industry or company and include around 75 per cent of the French workforce.

Employment regulations are supervised by local work inspectors (*inspecteur du travail*)

and the Direction Départmentale du Travail et de l'Emploi. Employment laws can't be altered or nullified by private agreements. In general, French law forbids discrimination by employers on the basis of sex, religion, race, age, sexual preference, physical appearance or name, and there are specific rules regarding equal job opportunities for both men and women (see **Working Women** on 19).

Salaried foreigners are employed under the same working conditions as French citizens, although there are different rules for certain categories of employee, e.g. directors, managers and factory workers. As in many countries, seasonal and temporary workers aren't always protected by employment laws and have fewer legal rights than other workers. However, part-time employees receive the same rights and benefits (on a pro rata basis) as full-time employees.

This chapter covers the content of an employment contract and general employment conditions, and highlights things to check when negotiating the terms for a job, some of which apply to all positions and some to executive and managerial positions only.

EMPLOYMENT CONTRACTS

Legally an offer of employment in France (and, in practice, the receipt of regular salary slips for an indefinite-term contract) constitutes an employment contract (*contrat de travail/d'emploi*), although it's advisable to insist upon a formal written contract. Employees usually have a formal contract stating such details as their job title, position, salary, working hours, benefits, duties and responsibilities, and the place and duration of their employment.

 Caution

Some employers offer their foreign employees a translated version of the official French contract – if yours does then consider it a gift, but also bear in mind that the only document which carries any legal weight is the contract drafted in French.

All employment contracts are subject to French labour law and references may be made to other regulations such as collective agreements. Anything in contracts contrary to statutory provisions and unfavourable to an employee may be deemed invalid. There are two main kinds of employment contract in France: an indefinite-term contract and a term contract. There are also temporary contracts.

An **Indefinite-term Contract** (*contrat à durée indéterminée/CDI*) or open-ended contract is the standard employment contract for permanent employees. Surprisingly, it doesn't have to be in writing (unlike a fixed-term contract), although you should insist on this; a standard contract form (*modèle de contrat de travail à durée indéterminée*) can be obtained from URSSAF offices. A *CDI* often includes a trial period of one to three months (three months is usual), depending on

collective agreements, before it becomes legal and binding on both parties.

A **Fixed-term Contract** (*contrat à durée déterminée/CDD*) is, as the name suggests, a contract for a pre-determined limited period. This is normally a maximum of 18 months, although it's limited to nine months if a position is due to be filled permanently and can be extended to two years if the position is due to be suppressed (there's no minimum term). It can be renewed twice for a term no longer than the original contract, provided it doesn't exceed two years in total. A *CDD* must be in writing and can be issued when a permanent employee is on leave (including maternity or sick leave), when there's a temporary increase in business or at any time in the construction industry or for youth employment schemes.

*CDD*s are strictly regulated, mainly because they're considered a contributing factor to the ever-increasing precariousness of employment (*précarité d'emploi*) in France. For example, the salary of an employee hired on a *CDD* mustn't be less than that paid to a similarly qualified person employed in a permanent job. An employee has the right to an end-of-contract bonus (*indemnité de fin de contrat*) equal to 10 per cent of his salary, in addition to other agreed bonuses, although this doesn't always apply to seasonal and temporary workers which fall under the same rules as a *CDD*.

Temporary Contracts: A temporary contract (*contrat de travail temporaire* or *intérim*) has no minimum or maximum duration and can be issued only in certain circumstances. Any other type of short-term contract is regarded as a fixed-term contract. A worker engaged on a temporary contract is known as a *salarié intérimaire* or simply *intérimaire*.

Trial & Notice Periods

For most jobs in France there's a trial period (*période d'essai*) of one to three months,

depending on the type of job and the employer (three months is usual). A trial period isn't required by law, although there's no law forbidding it, the length of which is usually stated in collective agreements. During the trial period either party may terminate the employment contract without notice or financial penalty, unless otherwise stated in a collective agreement.

If at the end of the trial period an employer hasn't decided whether he wishes to employ you permanently, he may have the right to repeat the trial period, but only once and only to the maximum period permitted by the collective agreement for the industry. After this period, if you haven't been officially dismissed, you're deemed to be hired permanently irrespective of whether an employment contract exists.

Notice (préavis) periods are governed by the law and collective agreements, and usually vary with the length of service. The minimum notice period is usually a month for clerical and manual workers, two months for foremen and supervisors, and three months for managerial and senior technical staff. The minimum notice period for employees with over two years' service is two months.

SALARY & BENEFITS

Your salary (salaire) is stated in your employment contract; salary reviews, planned increases, cost of living rises, etc., may also be included. Salaries may be stated in gross (brut) or net (net) terms and are usually paid monthly, although they may be quoted in contracts as hourly, monthly or annually. If a bonus is paid, such as a 13th or 14th month's salary (see below), it's stated in your contract.

General points such as the payment of your salary into a bank or post office account and the date of salary payments are usually included in employment conditions. Salaries above €1,500 per month must be paid by cheque or direct transfer (not cash), although it isn't wise to receive your salary in cash as it makes you subject to close scrutiny by the tax authorities! You receive a pay slip (bulletin de paie) itemising your salary and deductions, which you must keep indefinitely as they may be required to show proof of your earnings, social security payments and other insurances, even after your death!

Salaries must be reviewed once a year (usually at the end of the year), although employers aren't required by law to increase salaries that are above the minimum wage (see page 22), even when the cost of living has increased. Salary increases usually take effect on 1st January. See also **Salary** on page 20.

13th Month's Salary & Bonuses

Many employers in France pay their employees a bonus in December, known as the 13th month's salary (13ème mois). A 13th month's salary isn't mandatory unless it's part of a collective agreement or when it's granted regularly, in which case this should be stated in your employment contract. In your first and last years of employment, your 13th month's salary (if there is one) and other bonuses should be paid pro rata if you don't work a full calendar year.

Some companies also pay a 14th month's salary, usually in July before the summer holiday period. A few companies, e.g. banks and other financial institutions, may pay as many as 15 or 16 months' salary. Where applicable, extra months' salary are guaranteed bonuses and aren't pegged to the company's performance (as with profit-sharing). In some cases, they're paid monthly rather than in a lump sum at the end or in the middle of the year. Senior and middle managers often receive extra bonuses, perhaps linked to profits, equal to around 10 to 20 per cent of their annual salary, although these are more restricted since the recession in 2008.

Expenses

Expenses (*frais*) paid by your employer are usually listed in his general conditions. These may include travel costs from your home to your place of work, usually consisting of a second-class rail season ticket or the equivalent amount in cash (paid monthly with

your salary). In the Paris area, most employers pay 50 per cent of the cost of an employee's monthly public transport pass (*Carte Orange* – see page 129). Otherwise, travelling expenses to and from your place of work are tax deductible.

Companies without a restaurant or canteen may pay a lunch allowance or provide 'luncheon vouchers' (*chèques* or *tickets restaurant*) that can be purchased for half their face value and may be used in local restaurants and some food shops.

Relocation Expenses

The payment of relocation expenses (*frais de voyage*) depends on your agreement with your employer and should be included in your employment contract or conditions. Most employers pay travel and relocation costs to France up to a specified amount, although you may be required to sign a clause stipulating that if you leave the employer before a certain period (e.g. five years), you must repay a percentage of the costs.

If you change jobs within France, your new employer may pay your relocation expenses when it's necessary for you to move house. Don't forget to ask, as he may not offer to pay.

If you're hired from outside France, your air ticket and other travel to France are usually booked and paid for by your employer or his overseas representative. In addition, you can usually claim any onward travel costs, e.g. the cost of transport to and from airports. If you travel by car, you can usually claim a mileage rate or the equivalent air fare.

WORKING HOURS

Traditionally, the French have had a flexible attitude to working hours and the idea of fixed office hours is particularly alien to executives

and managers. For example, taking a long lunch break, perhaps for a game of tennis or some other kind of 'game', isn't frowned upon, provided you put in the required hours and don't neglect your work. It isn't unusual for a parent to leave work early to collect children from a nursery and some employees work only a half-day on Wednesdays, when children don't attend school.

In 2002 a mandatory 35-hour working week was introduced for all large employers. The objective of the scheme, referred to as the 'working hours reduction' programme (*réduction du temps de travail* or *RTT*), was to dramatically reduce unemployment by spreading the existing amount of work across more workers. Some industries were allowed to recognise seasonal workload variations by granting extra time off during the off-season to compensate employees for longer hours necessary at peak times of the year. Predictions (mostly governmental) that the scheme would create a million new jobs proved wildly optimistic and many employers claim the 35-hour week has escalated labour costs and handicapped French companies struggling to compete in global markets.

Many of the original provisions have been amended and restrictions relaxed, so that the 35-hour week has generally become the 39-hour week and working practices have largely reverted to tradition, although some have changed irrevocably. Companies currently have to pay between 10 and 50 per cent extra per hour if they want employees to work more than 35 hours a week. However, France urgently needs labour reforms to revive its stagnant economy and halt the rise of unemployment, and there are proposals to give employers the right to renegotiate longer hours and lower overtime pay with staff (not surprisingly, bitterly opposed by unions).

Many workers traditionally have a two-hour lunch break, particularly in the provinces, although it's no longer standard practice in most companies. Lunch may be anything from a marathon to a quick bite at a café (eating at your desk is generally frowned upon unless you've urgent work to complete).

The good news is that weekends are sacrosanct and almost no office employees work at weekends. Even most shops are closed on Sundays (and many also on Mondays).

Overtime & Time Off in Lieu

In principle, if you work over 35 hours per week, you must be paid overtime or be given time off in lieu. Employees can be asked to do overtime but can't be compelled to do over 220 hours per year, although this can be altered by collective agreements and/or the government. The total hours worked per week mustn't exceed an average of 44 over 12 consecutive weeks or an absolute maximum of 48 hours per week.

The minimum legal pay for overtime is the normal rate plus 25 per cent for the first eight hours above the standard 35-hour week (i.e. up to 43) and plus 50 per cent for additional hours (i.e. above 43). Employees can be granted time off in lieu at overtime rates (i.e. 1.25 hours for each hour of overtime worked) instead of being paid. Employees can't be obliged to work on

Sundays unless collective agreements state otherwise, although if an employee agrees to work on a Sunday normal overtime rates apply.

Salaried employees, particularly directors (*dirigeants*) and managers/executives (*cadres*), aren't generally paid overtime, although this depends on their contracts. Most managers are subject to both *RTT* and maximum work time regulations, even though their work time may not be tracked on an hourly basis but measured in days per year. Directors, managers and executives generally work long hours, even allowing for their occasionally long lunch breaks, but may be accorded additional holiday time to meet *RTT* requirements.

HOLIDAYS & LEAVE
Annual Holidays

French workers enjoy longer holidays than those in any other country: an average of 39 days per year compared with 24 in the UK, 17 in Australia and just 14 in the US. French 'working' life revolves around holidays (*les vacances*). Under labour laws, an employee is entitled to 2.5 days' paid holiday (*congé*) for each full month he works. After working for a full year you're therefore entitled to 30 days off, which equals five weeks (including Saturdays, which are 'traditionally' counted as work days).

Legally, you earn your holiday entitlement over the course of a year that runs from 1st May to 30th April. Therefore, if you start work in January, by 1st May you'll have earned ten days' holiday, which you can take during the subsequent year, i.e. starting 1st May. By the next 1st May, you should have accrued a full five weeks' holiday, which is available to you over the next 12 months.

Some collective agreements grant extra days off (usually from one to three) for long service and many grant additional days off in lieu of overtime or to meet *RTT* regulations. Employers can't include official French public holidays (see below) in the annual holiday entitlement.

Employees are legally entitled to take up to four weeks' paid holiday in a single block between 1st May and 31st October, unless business needs dictate otherwise (although other agreements are possible). Most employees take a three-or four-week summer holiday between July and August and one or two weeks in winter (often around the Christmas and New Year holiday period).

Traditionally August was the sole month for summer holidays, many businesses closing for the whole month. However, the government has been trying to encourage companies to stagger their employees' holidays throughout the summer and it's becoming more common for employees to take their main summer holiday in July or between the two summer public holidays, 14th July and 15th August.

Almost half of companies, particularly small businesses and local shops, close for the entire month of July or August, which naturally has an adverse effect on the economy.

When a company closes during summer, employees are obliged to take their holiday at that time. Many large manufacturers are forced to close because their component suppliers shut during this period and

Public Holidays	
Date	**Public Holiday**
1st January	New Year's Day (*Nouvel An/Jour de l'An*)
March or April	Easter Monday (*Lundi de Pâques*)
1st May	Labour Day (*Fête du Travail*)
8th May	VE Day (*Fête de la Libération/Victoire 1945/Anniversaire 1945*)
May	Ascension Day (*Ascension*) – the sixth Thursday after Easter
14th July	Bastille Day (*Fête Nationale*)
15th August	Assumption (*Fête de l'Assomption*)
1st November	All Saints' Day (*Toussaint*)
11th November	Armistice Day (*Fête de l'Armistice*)
25th December	Christmas Day (*Noël*)

they don't carry large enough stocks to keep them going. Even in companies that remain open throughout the summer, roughly half of employees are on holiday during July and August.

Public Holidays

The only public holiday (*jour férié*) that an employer in France is legally obliged to grant with pay is 1st May, irrespective of which day of the week it falls on. However, most collective agreements allow paid holidays on some or all of the ten public holidays show in the table (Pentecost isn't an official holiday, but many employers allow it).

When a holiday falls on a Saturday or Sunday, another day (e.g. the previous Friday or following Monday) isn't usually granted as a holiday instead. However, when a public holiday falls on a Tuesday or Thursday, the day before or the day after (i.e. Monday or Friday respectively) may be declared a holiday, depending on the employer. This practice is called 'making a bridge' (*faire le pont*). If a holiday falls on a Wednesday, it's common for employees to take the two preceding or succeeding days off.

In May there are usually three or four public holidays and it's possible to have a two-week break while only using a few days of your annual holiday. In some years, France virtually grinds to a halt due to the *ponts de mai*.

All public offices, banks, post offices, etc., are closed on public holidays, when only essential work is carried out. Note that foreign embassies and consulates usually observe French public holidays, plus their own country's national holidays.

Maternity & Paternity Leave

The family is of fundamental importance in France, and female employees are entitled to extensive employment benefits with regard to pregnancy (*grossesse*) and infant care. Social security benefits are also generous and are designed to encourage large families (see page 177).

Maternity leave (*congé maternité*) is guaranteed for all women irrespective of their length of employment. The permitted leave period is 16 weeks: six weeks prior to birth (*congé prénatal*) and ten weeks afterwards (*congé postnatal*); leave is extended for the third and subsequent children as well as for multiple births, caesareans or other complications. A doctor may authorise additional time off, either before or after a birth, in which case a company must continue to pay the employee's salary.

Women aren't obliged to inform their employers that they're pregnant, although if they don't they won't be entitled to benefits. It's normally to your advantage to do so in any case, as most employers are flexible regarding time off work in connection with childbirth and child care. For example, you're usually allowed to arrive late (especially if your journey to work involves travelling on public transport), have more work breaks and paid time off for routine antenatal examinations. If you're breastfeeding, they must also reduce your daily work time by one hour for your child's first year but aren't obliged to pay you for this hour.

New fathers are entitled to paternity leave (*congé paternité*) in addition to the three days off usually granted on the birth of a child (*congé de naissance* – see **Compassionate & Special Leave** below), provided they've been making health insurance contributions for at least ten months. The permitted paternity leave period is 11 days for a single birth and 18 days for a multiple birth, which must be taken in a continuous period during the four months following a birth. Both employees and the self-employed can claim a daily allowance of

around €70 and fathers are entitled to a further three months' unpaid paternity leave. Parents also have the right to an additional year of unpaid parental leave (*congé parental*), which applies equally to parents of adopted children.

Provided you don't extend your leave beyond the permitted period, your employer must allow you to return to the same job at the same or a higher salary, taking into account general increases in wages and the cost of living. See also **Childbirth** on page 168.

Compassionate & Special Leave

Most companies provide days off for moving house, your own or a family marriage, the birth of a child, the death of a close relative and other such events. Grounds for compassionate leave (*congé pour convenance personnelle*) are usually defined in collective agreements and may include leave to care for a seriously ill or disabled child (*congé de présence parentale*). The regulations allow 12 days a year for each child, although a doctor's certificate (*fiche médicale pour enfant*) must be provided.

The number of days' leave granted varies according to the event, e.g. four days off for your own wedding (but not if you get married during a holiday!) and one day off to attend a child's wedding or the funeral of a parent (including in-laws), brother or sister.

Employees who've worked for a company for at least three years and have worked for a total period of at least six years are entitled to take from between six and 11 months off – naturally without pay!

Sick Leave

Employees in France don't receive a quota of sick days as in some countries (e.g. the US) and there's no limit to the amount of time you may take off work due to sickness or accidents. You must, however, obtain a doctor's certificate (*arrêt de travail*) on the first day of your sickness, otherwise it counts as a day's holiday.

INSURANCE

All employers in France are required to publish a document listing the dangers and risks to the health and safety of their employees, and provide a minimum level of health and safety insurance. All French employees, foreign employees working for French companies and the self-employed must contribute to the French social security (*sécurité sociale*) system. Social security includes healthcare (plus sickness and maternity benefits), salary insurance (during sickness or after an accident), compensation for injuries at work, family allowances, unemployment insurance, old age benefits (i.e. pensions), and invalidity and death benefits.

> Social security contributions are high and total an average of around 60 per cent of gross pay, although some 40 per cent is paid by employers. For details see **Social Security** on page 177.

Contributions are calculated as a percentage of your gross income and are deducted at source by your employer.

Health Insurance

Comprehensive health insurance is provided by the French social security system (see page 177), but many industries and professions have their own supplementary health insurance schemes (*mutuelle*) that pay the portion of medical bills that isn't covered by social security – usually 20 to 30 per cent (see page 160). Membership may be obligatory and contributions may be paid wholly by your employer or split between employee and employer. Some employers, particularly foreign companies, provide free comprehensive private health insurance for executives, senior

managers and their families. For further information about health insurance see page 180.

In addition to undergoing a medical examination before starting employment, you may need to be examined by a company's *médecin du travail* on an annual basis, attesting to your continued fitness for your job, or at any time if there's a doubt about your physical condition. A medical examination may also be necessary as a condition of membership of a company health, pension or life insurance scheme.

Salary Insurance

Salary insurance (*assurance salaire*) pays an employee's salary during periods of sickness (*congé maladie*) or after accidents, and is provided under social security. After a certain number of consecutive sick days (the number varies with your employer) your salary is no longer paid by your employer but by social security, which is one reason contributions are so high. Some employers opt to pay their employees' full salaries for a limited period in cases of extended disability or illness, in which case state benefits are paid to the employer rather than to the employee.

Unemployment Insurance

Unemployment insurance (*allocation d'assurance chômage*) is compulsory for employees and is covered by social security contributions. In the last decade the government has legalised a form of private unemployment insurance for some categories of self-employed people and owner-managers of small companies who aren't eligible for state unemployment insurance. Statutory unemployment benefit is available to those who are eligible.

RETIREMENT & PENSIONS

The official French minimum retirement age (*retraite*) is 60 for both men and women born before 1st July 1951 and 62 for those born before 1st January 1955. For those born after 1st January 1955, the age of automatic entitlement to a full state pension will rise to 67 (by 2023). The rules apply to most trades and professions and civil servants, although some state employees can retire on a full pension at 55 or even 50.

An employee isn't required to retire when he reaches the minimum retirement age and can retire at any time between the ages of 60 and 70, but after the age of 70 an employer has the right to compulsorily retire an employee (as from 2011). Those who continue to work after the legal minimum retirement age and who've paid contributions for longer than the qualifying period for a full pension (which depends on their year of birth) receive an increased pension.

In addition to contributing to social security, which provides a state pension (see page 179), most employees contribute to a supplementary company pension fund (*caisse complémentaire de retraite*). Almost every trade or occupation has its own scheme and in many companies it's obligatory for employees to contribute. The rates and details vary slightly, depending on whether you contribute to the fund for managers (*cadres*) or for non-managerial workers (*non-cadres*).

UNION MEMBERSHIP

There are numerous trade unions in France, many grouped into confederations, although French unions aren't as highly organised as those in many other developed countries, and their power and influence has been reduced considerably since the late '70s, when labour disputes and strikes (*grèves*) were common.

Since then union membership has declined dramatically; membership of the *Confédération française démocratique du travail* (CFDT) – the largest French trade union confederation – is now around 900,000, while membership of the *Confédération Générale du Travail* (CGT) has fallen from a high of over 2.5 million to around 700,000 today.

Union membership includes just 8 per cent of all employees (down from 30 per cent in the '50s) and just 5 per cent of the private sector workforce – the lowest proportion in the EU. Unions are strongest in traditional industries and services such as railways, automobile manufacturing and stevedoring, but have had little success in new high-tech industries. However, they're still capable of causing widespread disruption, as has been demonstrated in recent years.

Under French law, unions are allowed to organise on any company's premises and 'closed shops' are banned. With the exception of some public sector employees, e.g. the police, employees have the right to strike and can't be dismissed for striking. Workers rights are protected by labour laws irrespective of whether they belong to a union.

All businesses with more than 11 employees must have a workers' (or works) council or a labour management committee comprising employee delegates (*délégués du personnel*) elected by and from the employees. The number of delegates increases in proportion to the number of employees, up to a maximum of 50. Delegates represent employees when they have questions or complaints for management concerning, for example, working conditions, job classification, wages, and the application of labour laws and regulations.

In companies with over 50 employees, employee delegates must be elected to the board of directors and a labour management committee (*comité d'entreprise*) must be formed. Companies with separate locations (e.g. factories or offices) employing over 50 employees must have a local labour management committee (*comité d'établissement*), with representatives of this committee sitting on a central labour management committee (*comité central d'entreprise*).

In addition to matters relating to the terms and conditions of employment, any major changes to the operation, organisation and management of a company must be discussed with the committee before they can be implemented. However, a company isn't usually required to act on the opinion of the labour management committee.

Dismissal & Redundancy

The rules governing dismissal (*licenciement*) and severance pay (*indemnité de licenciement*) depend on the size of a company, an employee's length of service, the reason for dismissal (e.g. misconduct or redundancy), and whether an employee has a protected status, such as that enjoyed by union and employee representatives, who can be dismissed only for 'gross misconduct'.

The two main reasons for dismissal are personal (*motif personnel*) and economic (*motif économique*), i.e. when a company is experiencing serious financial problems. An employee can be dismissed at any time during his trial period (usually the first one to three months) without notice or compensation. Thereafter, you can be dismissed for personal reasons only in the case of a 'valid and serious offence' (*cause réelle et sérieuse*), e.g. stealing from an employer. It's difficult for an employer to dismiss an employee unless he has

demonstrated utter incompetence or is guilty of some form of gross misconduct, when he can appeal against the decision to a union or labour court.

A dismissed employee is entitled to severance pay if he has at least two years' service and compensation in lieu of notice when a notice period can't be observed. Payment must also be made in lieu of any outstanding paid holiday (*indemnité compensatrice de congés payés*) up to the end of the notice period, i.e. for earned holiday not yet used in the current year. Severance pay must equal at least 20 per cent of his average monthly salary for each year of service, i.e. 100 per cent if he's been employed for five years. Collective agreements may provide for increased severance pay, although it may not be payable when an employee is dismissed for a serious breach of conduct.

information about working as an au pair in France, see **Au Pairs** on page 31.

Retirees

Non-EU/EEA retirees require a long-stay visa to live in France for longer than 90 days, and should make a visa application to their local French consulate well before their planned departure date. Non-EU retirees are issued with temporary residence permits, which must be renewed annually.

☑ SURVIVAL TIP

All non-employed residents must provide proof that they have an adequate income or financial resources (including health insurance for non-EU nationals) to live in France without working or becoming a burden on the state.

Student Visas

There are three types of visa for non-EU nationals – 'non européens' is the wording used by the French government on their website (www.service-public.fr) – planning to study in France, depending on the intended length of their stay:

Schengen visa: A Schengen visa (see above) allows multiple entries but is valid for a maximum stay of three months only. Applications are made using a Schengen visa form and the fee is the same.

Temporary Long-stay Visa (*visa d'étudiant pour six mois avec plusieurs entrées*): This allows multiple entries and is valid for three to six months. With this visa it's usually unnecessary to obtain a residence permit. The visa must, however, state that a residence permit is unnecessary, i.e. *le titulaire de ce visa est dispensé de solliciter une carte de séjour* or *le présent visa vaut autorisation de*

séjour. Requirements are the same as for an ordinary long-stay visa (see above).

One-year Visa: This visa is valid for between six months and a year but allows only a single entry. Applications are made using a temporary long-stay visa form (see above) and the fee is the same. On arrival in France, you must have a medical examination by a French doctor approved by the Office des Migrations Internationales (OMI) and apply for a residence permit (*carte de séjour d'étudiant*) – see **Residence Permits** on page 53.

Students with a scholarship from the French government or a foreign government, or on an EU study programme or one arranged by a recognised international organisation, require only a valid passport, a completed visa application form, photographs and a letter confirming the value of the grant and the duration of their intended stay. There's no fee for a visa for students on a scholarship.

Fiancé(e)s & Spouses

The status of the fiancé(e) or spouse of a French resident depends on the nationality of the resident, as detailed below.

Fiancé(e)s

Non-EU nationals coming to France to marry a French citizen may need to apply for a long-stay visa. France doesn't issue a 'fiancé visa'. If you plan to arrive in France less than three months before your marriage, it may be possible to enter the country on a short-stay visa and then regularise your situation immediately after your marriage, claiming full benefit of your status as a spouse of a French national. Ensure, however, that you declare your entry into France (by requesting a declaration of entry or having your passport stamped with the date of arrival).

Spouses

Non-EU nationals married to a French resident (whether of French or foreign nationality) for less than a year require a long-stay visa to enter France; they can't obtain an extension (beyond 90 days) if they enter France as a visitor. It's usually fairly simple for someone married to a French national to obtain a long-stay visa, simply by presenting their marriage certificate and proof of the French partner's citizenship to the appropriate consulate.

Non-EU nationals who've been married to a French resident for more than a year may be permitted to enter France as visitors and then apply for a residence permit, although a long-stay visa is recommended (check with a French consulate abroad).

> The foreign spouse of a French citizen is automatically granted a permanent residence permit (*carte de résident* – see below) provided the couple have been married for at least a year. The non-EU spouse of an EU national resident in France is granted a temporary five-year residence permit (*carte de séjour*) permitting him or her to live and work in France.

The spouse and children under 18 of a non-EU national with a visa to work in France (*visa de séjour salarié*) may usually accompany him to France, although a visa is required for each family member. Applications for visas for family members must be made at the same time as the main applicant's visa application. Family members don't have the right to work in France unless they have their own *visa de séjour salarié*.

Applications

Applications for visas must be made to the nearest French embassy or consulate in your country of residence. Applicants for long-stay visas living in a country other than their country of nationality must apply in their country of nationality unless they've been resident abroad for at least a year.

You can usually apply for a visa in person or by post. If you apply in person you should bear in mind that there are long queues at consulates in major cities (take a large book to read and get there early!). Some consulates only deal with visa applications in the morning and/or close their visa section on one day a week, so check the opening hours. The documentation required for a visa application depends on the purpose of your visit to France. Contact a French embassy or consulate for information. Certain documents may need to be translated into French by a translator approved by your local French consulate, a list (*liste de traducteurs*) of whom is provided by consulates.

WORK PERMITS

The following information is of a general nature. For further details, contact your country's embassy in France or the commercial attaché at a French consulate.

EU nationals don't require a work permit; just proof of residence (a *titre de séjour* or a certificate from their town hall following registration there), which gives them the right to work in France. For more information check with a local French consulate or embassy.

Non-EU Nationals: A combined residence and work permit (*carte unique de séjour et de travail* or *carte de séjour salarié*) is issued to non-EU nationals coming to France to take up permanent employment. When you arrive, you've two months in which to apply for a temporary residence permit (*carte de séjour temporaire salarié* – see **Temporary Residence Permits** below) while your application for a *carte unique de séjour et de travail* or *carte de séjour salarié* is being processed (French bureaucracy at its inimitable best).

Students: After completing their first year of study, students can obtain a temporary work permit (*autorisation provisoire de travail*) for part-time (*mi-temps*) work, provided they have a residence permit (see below) and are attending an educational institution that provides students with French social security health cover or a scholarship (*bourse*).

RESIDENCE PERMITS

In general, all foreigners in France for longer than 90 days in succession for any reason require a residence permit (*titre de séjour*) or a certificate showing that they have registered with their town hall. Where applicable, a residence permit holder's dependants are also granted a permit. Children can be listed on a parent's permit until the age of 18, although they require their own residence permit at the age of 16 if they're working.

Different types of residence permit are issued depending on your status, including permits for long-stay visitors (*visiteur*), salaried employees (*salarié*), transferees (*détaché*), family members (*membre de famille*), students (*étudiant*) and traders (*commerçant*). A combined residence and work permit (*carte unique de séjour et de travail* or *carte de séjour salarié*) is issued to non-EU nationals taking up permanent employment in France (see above).

There are two main categories of residence permit in France: a *carte de séjour* and a *carte de résident*. The *carte de séjour* is referred to below as a temporary residence permit and the *carte de résident* as a permanent residence permit.

Temporary Residence Permits

Until November 2003, a temporary residence permit (*carte de séjour*) was required by all foreigners aged 18 and above, both EU and non-EU nationals, who were to remain in France for over 90 days. A new law (called the *loi Sarkozy* after the then-future President) waived the requirement for EU citizens to obtain a *carte de séjour*, although the actual wording of the law is ambiguous. If you aren't sure whether your citizenship waives the requirement for a *carte de séjour,* you should contact the departmental *préfecture* in order to check whether one is required – particularly as you can be fined for failing to apply for one!

Whether or not you require a *carte de séjour* you must meet the criteria for residence, i.e. adequate financial means of support and,

unless you qualify for state health benefits, private health insurance.

The period of validity of a temporary residence permit varies depending on your circumstances. Note, however, that a temporary residence permit automatically cancelled if you spend over six months outside France or you no longer meet the conditions for which it was issued. The maximum permitted period of continuous residence in France for a holder of a temporary residence permit is three years.

EU Nationals: Unless advised otherwise EU nationals – whether or not they will be working in France – no longer require a residence permit (*carte de séjour de ressortissant d'un état membre de l'UE*). EU nationals who are unemployed and have no proof of income are issued with a one-year temporary residence permit, provided they have the means to support themselves during this period.

Non-EU Nationals: Non-EU employees must apply for a temporary residence permit (*carte de séjour temporaire salarié*) within two months of their arrival. This is valid for a maximum of a year and can be renewed two months before its expiry date, upon application and presentation of a new employment contract or verification of your continued employment. If you're taking up long-term employment, you must apply for a *carte unique de séjour et de travail* or a *carte de séjour salarié* (see above). The non-EU spouses of EU nationals or French residents are granted a five-year residence permit (*carte de séjour*) permitting them to live and work in France, although the dependants of non-EU nationals aren't.

Students: Students on a one-year visa (see above) should apply for a student's residence permit (*carte de séjour d'étudiant*), which is valid for a further year and can be renewed annually for the duration of the course. Students who've studied in France for the preceding two years and have a parent who has lived in France for at least four years don't require a permit.

Permanent Residence Permit

A permanent residence permit (*carte de résident*) is available for non-EU nationals and is usually issued to those who've lived in France for three consecutive years and speak fluent French. It's valid for ten years and renewable provided the holder can provide proof that he's practising a profession in France or has sufficient financial resources to maintain himself and his dependants. A permanent residence permit authorises the holder to undertake any professional activity (subject to qualifications and registration) in any French department, even if employment was previously forbidden.

Applications

An application for a residence permit should be made to the *préfecture de police* in towns that have them, to the local town hall (*mairie*) in small towns and to the police (*gendarmerie/ commissariat de police*) in large towns and cities. If permits aren't issued locally, you'll be referred to the Direction de la Réglementation of your department's *préfecture* or the nearest *sous-préfecture*.

In large towns and cities many police stations have a foreigners' office (*bureau des étrangers*), while in smaller towns this may be located in the town hall. In Paris, applications must be made to the appropriate police centre (*centre d'accueil des étrangers*) for the area (*arrondissement*) where you live. Students should apply to their local town hall or *préfecture* (there's a special counter at the *préfecture* in Paris). You'll be notified of the documentation required, which depends on your situation and nationality.

☑ SURVIVAL TIP

Certain documents may need to be translated by a notarised translator (search for *Traducteurs – Traductions Officielles Certifiées* online), which may vary depending on the area or office and your nationality.

If you arrive in France with a long-stay visa, you must apply for a residence permit within a week. EU nationals who visit France with the intention of finding employment or starting a business have 90 days in which to find a job and apply for a residence permit or register their address at the local town hall. Note that it isn't possible to do this while living in temporary accommodation such as a hotel.

If it isn't possible to issue a residence permit immediately, you'll be given a temporary authorisation (*récipissé de demande de carte de séjour* or an *attestation d'application de résidence*) valid for up to three months and renewable. You should keep this as evidence that you've applied for your residence permit.

An application for renewal of a residence permit should be made one or two months before its expiry date. When you renew your residence permit, you must reconfirm your status and provide the same documentary evidence required for the original application. If you're applying to renew your residence permit and don't have all the necessary documents, you can apply for an extension (*prolongation*).

4.

ARRIVAL

O n arrival in France your first task will be to negotiate immigration and customs. Note that you must obtain any necessary visas (see Chapter 3) before arriving in France, otherwise you could be refused entry. In addition to covering immigration and customs this chapter contains information about registration and useful sources of advice and information (Finding Help) to assist families to settle into their new life in France.

IMMIGRATION

France is a signatory to the Schengen agreement, whereby immigration checks and passport controls take place when you first arrive in a Schengen country (see page 49), after which you can travel freely between Schengen countries. This means that, when you arrive in France from another Schengen country, there are usually no immigration checks or passport controls. Note that this doesn't apply if you're arriving from the UK or Ireland.

Non-EU nationals arriving by air or sea from outside the EU must go through immigration (*police des frontières*) for non-EU citizens. If you require a visa to enter France and attempt to enter without one, you'll be refused entry.

If you think you'll need to prove your date of entry into France, you should obtain a declaration of entry (*déclaration d'entrée sur le territoire*), which may be advisable in any case.

Immigration officials may ask non-EU visitors to produce a return ticket and proof of their accommodation arrangements, health insurance and financial resources. If you're a non-EU national coming to France to work, study or live, you may be asked to produce documentary evidence. The onus is on visitors to show that they won't violate French law and immigration officials can refuse anyone entry solely on the grounds of suspicion.

CUSTOMS

Those arriving from outside the EU (including EU citizens) are subject to customs checks and limitations on what may be imported duty-free. The shipment of personal (household) effects to France from another EU country isn't subject to customs formalities, although an inventory should be provided. There are no restrictions on the import or export of euros or foreign cash or securities, although if you enter or leave France with €10,000 or more in cash or negotiable instruments you must make a declaration to French customs.

If you require general information about customs regulations or have specific questions, contact the Centre de Renseignement aux Usagers des Douanes (08 11 20 44 44, www.douane.gouv.fr) or a local customs office.

For information about the importation of pets, see page 273, and for vehicles see page 136.

Visitors

If you're visiting France (i.e. for less than 90 days) your belongings aren't subject to duty or VAT and may be imported without formality, provided their nature and quantity doesn't imply any commercial aim. This applies to the import of private cars, camping vehicles (including trailers and caravans), motorcycles, aircraft, boats (see below) and personal effects. All means of transport and personal effects imported duty-free mustn't be sold, loaned or given away in France, and must be re-exported before the end of the 90-day period.

If you enter France from another Schengen country (see above), you may drive through the border without stopping. However, any goods and pets that you're carrying mustn't be the subject of any prohibition or restriction (see below). Customs officials can stop anyone for a spot check, e.g. for drugs or illegal immigrants. If you arrive at a seaport by private boat, there are no particular customs formalities, although you must produce the boat's registration papers if asked.

If you arrive at a river port or land border with a boat, you may be asked to produce registration papers for the boat and its outboard motor(s). A foreign-registered boat may remain in France for a maximum of six months in a calendar year, after which it must be re-exported or permanently imported (and duty and tax paid on it).

Non-EU Nationals

If you're a non-EU national planning to take up permanent or temporary residence you're permitted to import your furniture and personal effects free of duty. These include vehicles, mobile homes, pleasure boats and aircraft. However, to qualify for duty-free importation, belongings must have been owned and used for at least six months.

To import personal effects an application must be made to the Direction Régionale des Douanes in the area where you'll be resident. Customs clearance may be carried out by a customs office in an interior town in France, rather than at the border, in which

⚠ Caution

Value added tax must be paid on items owned for less than six months which were purchased outside the EU. If goods were purchased within the EU a VAT receipt must be produced.

case you should obtain a certificate (*carte de libre circulation*) to confirm that you declared your belongings on entry into France and are entitled to travel with them.

All items should be imported within a year of the date of your change of residence – in a single or a number of consignments – although it's best to have one consignment only. After a year's residence in France you must pay French VAT (*TVA*) on further imports from outside the EU, except in certain circumstances such as property resulting from an inheritance.

A complete inventory of items to be imported (even if they're imported in a number of consignments) must be provided for customs officials, together with proof of residence in your former country and proof of settlement in France. If there's more than one consignment, subsequent consignments should be cleared through the same customs office.

If you use a removal company to transport your belongings they'll usually provide the necessary forms and take care of the paperwork. Many of the forms are now available online, either through the Customs website (www.douane.gouv.fr) or by following the links on the Service Public site (www.service-public.fr).

Always keep a copy of forms and communications with customs officials – both in France and in your previous country of residence. An official record of the export of valuables from any country will allow you to re-import them duty-free later.

Prohibited & Restricted Goods

Certain goods are subject to special regulations and in some cases their import (and export) is prohibited or restricted. This applies in particular to certain animal products, plants (see below), wild fauna and flora (and products  derived from them), live animals, medicines and medical products (except for prescribed medicines), guns and ammunition, goods and technologies with a dual civil/military purpose, and works of art and collectors' items. If you're unsure whether any goods you're importing fall into the above categories you should check with French customs.

If you make it through customs unscathed with your car loaded to the gunnels with illicit goods, don't be too quick to break out the champagne in celebration. France has 'flying' customs officials (*douane volante*) with the power to stop and search vehicles at random anywhere within its borders.

REGISTRATION

Non-EU nationals planning to remain in France for over 90 days must register with the local authorities, usually within a week of their arrival, and obtain a residence permit. Although EU nationals no longer require a residence permit, they still need to register with their local town hall within three months of their arrival. For further information see **Residence Permits** on page 53.

Nationals of some countries are required to register with their local embassy or consulate after taking up residence. Even if registration isn't mandatory, most embassies like to keep a record of their country's citizens resident in France (it helps to justify their existence) and it can be to your benefit, e.g. in a personal, national or international crisis.

FINDING HELP

One of the main difficulties facing new arrivals in France is how and where to find help with day-to-day problems, particularly as many administrative matters are handled at a regional, departmental or even local level, rather than nationally. The availability of local information varies depending on your employer, the town or area where you live (e.g. residents of Paris are better served than those living in rural areas), your nationality, your French proficiency and to some extent your sex (women are better served than men through numerous women's clubs). Nevertheless, there are many resources for newcomers, including the following:

Employer: some companies, particularly international companies, employ staff to help new arrivals acclimatise or contract this job out to a relocation consultant.

Colleagues & Friends: In France it isn't what you know but who you know that can make all the difference between success and failure. String-pulling (i.e. the use of contacts) is widespread and invaluable when it comes to breaking through the numerous layers of bureaucracy; a telephone call on your behalf from a French neighbour or colleague can work wonders. But take care! Although colleagues and friends can often offer advice and invariably mean well, you're just as likely to receive irrelevant and inaccurate information as correct information.

Local Community: Your town hall (*mairie*), which is often the local registry of births, deaths and marriages, passport office, land registry, council office, citizens' advice bureau and tourist office rolled into one, should be your first port of call for most kinds of local information, although you'll usually need to speak good French to benefit from it.

It pays to introduce yourself to your local mayor and invite your neighbours for an apéritif within a few weeks of your arrival. This is particularly important in villages and rural areas if you want to be accepted and become part of the community.

Embassy or Consulate: Most embassies and consulates provide their nationals with local information including details of lawyers, interpreters, doctors, dentists, schools, and social and expatriate organisations, although some are more helpful than others (the British Embassy in Paris is supremely unapproachable).

The American Embassy has a particularly good website (http://france.usembassy.gov – click on 'U.S. Citizen Services'), which includes a good deal of information (in English) about living and working in France, including lists of English-speaking professionals from doctors to private investigators. Much of the information comes from their popular *Blue Book: Guide for U.S. Citizens Residing in France*, which can be downloaded from the site or obtained from the US Embassy (01 43 12 22 22, https://fr.usembassy.gov).

Hand-holding services: A number of English-speaking companies and individuals offer a 'hand-holding' service to help expatriates settle in and do whatever is necessary in their first few weeks or months in France (this book was written to help fulfil this need). As with all such services, some are worth their weight in gold while others are a waste of time and money, therefore it's to check their references before parting with any cash. Services may range from help with house hunting (renting or buying), registering for utilities, finding local tradesmen, taking out insurance, buying a car, opening a bank account and completing tax returns.

Expatriate Organisations

There's usually at least one English-language expatriate organisation in most major French cities. In Paris foreigners are well served by English-speaking clubs and organisations (see below) and there are several Anglophone organisations in the Bordeaux and Côte d'Azur regions. Contacts can also be found through many expatriate magazines and newspapers (see www.world-newspapers.com/france.html). An English-speaking counsellor in certain parts of France can be found via www.counsellinginfrance.com.

In Paris, newcomers can obtain assistance from the Association of American Wives of Europeans (01 40 70 11 80, www.aaweparis.org), which is a member of the Federation of American Women's Clubs Overseas (FAWCO) and publishes the snappily titled *Vital Issues: How to Survive Officialdom while Living in France*. Other organisations include The

Association France Grande-Bretagne (01 55 78 71 71, www.afgb.free.fr – in French only), whose aim is to foster links between the two nations, The British & Commonwealth Women's Association (01 47 20 50 91, www.bcwa.org), and WICE (01 45 66 75 50, www.wice-paris. org), an anglophone expatriate organisation that operates a 'Living in France' programme for newcomers.

The British Community Committee (www. britishinfrance.com) publishes a free *Digest of British and Franco-British Clubs, Societies and Institutions*, available from British consulates in France.

AVF

An organisation of particular interest to foreigners moving to France is the Union Nationale des Accueils des Villes Françaises (AVF), a national organisation comprising around 350 local volunteer associations that provide a welcome for individuals and families and helps them settle into their new environment. Each association operates a centre where information and advice is available free of charge. The address of local associations can be found on the AVF website (www.avf.asso.fr), where some information is available in English, and there's a list of groups in each department as well as details such as whether information and services are available in English. Groups often contain at least one fluent English-speaker.

CIRA

If you don't know which administrative department to contact for particular information (which is often the case in France), you can ask the local Centre Interministériel de Renseignements Administratifs (CIRA). As its name suggests, CIRA is a 'pan-governmental' organisation, which can answer questions on a range of subjects, including employment,

finance, accommodation, health, consumer affairs, the environment and education. There are nine information centres (in Bordeaux, Lille, Limoges, Lyon, Marseille, Metz, Paris, Rennes and Toulouse) but only one central telephone number (3939).

The Disabled

Disabled persons can obtain advice and help from the Association des Paralysés de France (www.apf.asso.fr), which isn't just for those who are paralysed, the Fédération des Associations pour Adultes et Jeunes Handicapés (APAJH, www.apajh.org) and the Fédération Nationale des Accidentés de Travail et des Handicapés (www.fnath.org).

Disabled people looking for work or work-related information should contact the Association Gestion du Fonds d'Insertion Personnes Handicapées (AGEFIPH, www. agefiph.fr, which provides contact details for the 18 regional associations).

If you're seriously and permanently disabled you can apply to the Commission Technique d'Orientation et de Reclassement Professionel (COTOREP) for an invalidity card (*carte d'invalidité civile*), which entitles you to a number of benefits.

5.
ACCOMMODATION

*I*n most areas of France, accommodation (to buy or rent) isn't difficult to find, although there are a few exceptions. Accommodation accounts for around 20 per cent of the average family's budget (compared with some 25 per cent in the UK), but can be much higher in expensive areas. Property prices vary considerably depending on the region and city, although in most areas they're much the same as they were ten years ago.

You can buy a small detached modern house or a large property in need of restoration in rural areas from around €100,000, but a tiny studio apartment (20-25m² – 1m² is roughly equal to 10ft²) in a good area in central Paris can cost you €250-400,000 (property prices in Paris are similar to London), which would buy you a large rural property and land in most regions. Property in Paris, the French Riviera and some ski resorts is among the most expensive in the world, although prices are reasonable in most regions and a bargain in rural areas.

Many Parisians (and other city dwellers) rent their principal homes but own a holiday home (or a number), e.g. in the country for weekends, on the Mediterranean coast for summer holidays or in the Alps for winter skiing. Property ownership in France is around 65 per cent (about the same as the UK), slightly below the EU average of 70 per cent, although this is distorted by the fact that many homeowners also rent their principal homes. A 50m² two-bedroom apartment in a reasonable area of Paris will cost you between €1,000 and €2,000 per month to rent but around 50 per cent less in a provincial city such as Bordeaux

In cities and large towns, apartments are much more common than detached houses, particularly in Paris, where houses are rare

and prohibitively expensive. In rural areas there's a depopulation crisis due to the mass exodus of people from the land to the cities in the last 30-40 years. Provincial France is losing its population to the cities at an alarming rate and it's estimated that as many as one in ten properties are vacant in many areas.

FRENCH HOMES

For many foreign buyers France provides the opportunity to buy or rent a size or style of home that they could never afford in their home countries. In most areas, properties range from derelict farmhouses and barns to modern townhouses and apartments with all modern conveniences, from crumbling *châteaux* and manor houses requiring complete restoration to new luxury chalets and villas. French homes are relatively spacious, with the average home around 100m², compared with, for example, the UK's 76m² (the smallest in Europe).

French homes are built to high structural standards and whether you buy a new or an old home it's usually extremely sturdy. Older homes usually have thick walls and contain numerous rooms and a wealth of interesting period features, including vast fireplaces, wooden staircases, attics, cellars (*caves*), and a profusion of alcoves and annexes. Many houses have a basement (*sous-sol* or *cave*), used as a garage and cellar. In most old houses, open fireplaces remain a principal feature, even when central heating is installed.

In warmer regions, floors are often tiled and walls are painted rather than papered, while elsewhere floors are carpeted or bare wood and walls are more likely to be papered. When wallpaper is used it's often garish and may cover everything, including walls, doors and ceilings! Properties throughout France tend to be built in a distinct local (often unique) style using local materials. There are stringent regulations in most areas regarding the style and design of new homes and the restoration of old buildings.

In older rural properties the kitchen (*cuisine*) is the most important room in the house. It's usually huge with a large wood-burning stove for cooking, hot water and heating, a huge solid wood dining table and possibly a bread oven. French country kitchens are worlds apart from modern fitted kitchens and are devoid of shiny

formica and plastic laminates. They're often comparatively stark with stone or tiled floors and a predominance of wood, tiles and marble. Kitchens in older apartments in Paris and other cities may be very basic, although modern fitted kitchens (with dishwashers, cookers and refrigerators) are usually found in new properties, and fitted American-style kitchens are increasingly common.

Refrigerators (*frigidaire* or *frigo*) and cookers (*cuisinière*) are generally quite small. Cookers in rural homes are usually run on bottled gas or a combination of bottled gas and electricity. Many homes have a gas water heater (*chaudière*) that heats the water for the bathroom and kitchen. Most houses don't have a separate utility room and the washing machine and drier are stored in the kitchen. A separate toilet (*toilette* or *WC*) is popular, and the bathroom (*salle de bains*) often has a toilet, bidet, bath (*baignoire*) and/or shower (*douche*). Baths are more common than showers in older homes, although showers are found in most modern homes.

Many rural properties have shutters (*volets*), both for security and as a means of insulation. External shutters are often supplemented by internal shutters, which are fixed directly to the window frames. In the south and southwest many rural homes have swimming pools and homes throughout France have a paved patio or terrace that's often covered. Old farmhouses invariably have a number of outbuildings such as barns, which can usually be converted into additional accommodation.

A huge variety of new properties is available in France, including city apartments and individually-designed detached houses. Many new properties are part of purpose-built developments. Note, however, that many developments are planned as holiday homes and may not be attractive as permanent homes (they're also generally expensive). New homes usually contain features such as deluxe bathroom suites, fitted kitchens, smoke and security alarms, and coordinated interior colour schemes. They're usually sold *décorée*, which means not only that they're decorated but also that they have a fitted kitchen.

France's bold and innovative architecture, as portrayed in its many striking public buildings, doesn't often extend to private dwellings, many of which seem to have been designed by the same architect. However, although new properties are often lacking in character, they're usually spacious and well-endowed with mod cons and services. The French generally prefer modern homes to older houses with 'charm and character' – which to the locals mean 'expensive to maintain and in danger of falling down' – although new homes often have pseudo period features such as beams and open fireplaces.

> Central heating, double-glazing and excellent insulation are common in new houses, particularly in northern France, where they're essential. Central heating may be electric, gas or oil-fired. However, on the Côte d'Azur, where winter temperatures are higher, expensive insulation and heating may be considered unnecessary (don't you believe it!).

Note that most French families live in apartments or detached homes and semi-detached and terraced properties built more than four or five decades ago are relatively rare. Some 30 per cent of the population live in apartments (compared with just 15 per cent in the UK), which are common in cities and large towns. Around two-thirds of French families live in urban areas compared with an average of over 70 per cent in the whole of Europe and over 85 per cent in the UK.

In the major cities there are many (hugely expensive) beautiful *bourgeois* apartments

built in the 19th or early 20th century, with large rooms, high ceilings and huge windows. Unless modernised, they have old-fashioned bathrooms and kitchens and are expensive to decorate, furnish, heat and maintain. Many apartments don't have their own source of hot water and heating, which is shared with other apartments in the same building.

RELOCATION COMPANIES

If you're fortunate enough to have your move to France paid for by your employer it's likely that he'll arrange for a relocation company to handle the details. There are fewer relocation consultants in France (most are based in Paris) than in many other European countries, and they usually deal only with corporate clients. Fees depend on the services required, but packages usually run into €thousands.

The main service provided by relocation consultants is finding accommodation (for rent or purchase) and arranging viewings. Other services include conducting negotiations, drawing up contracts, arranging mortgages, organising surveys and insurance, and handling the move. Consultants may also provide reports on local amenities and services, such as schools, health services, public transport, and sports and social facilities. Some companies provide daily advice and help dealing with officials.

Finding rental accommodation for single people or couples without children can usually be done in a matter of weeks, while locating family homes may take a month or more depending on the location and requirements. However, you should usually allow two to three months between your initial visit and moving into a purchased or rented property.

MOVING HOUSE

After you've found a home in France, it usually takes just a few weeks to have your belongings shipped from within continental Europe. From anywhere else the time varies considerably, e.g. four weeks from the east coast of America, six weeks from the west coast and the Far East, and around eight weeks from Australasia.

Customs clearance isn't necessary when shipping your household effects within the EU. However, when shipping your effects from a non-EU country to France, you should enquire about customs formalities in advance; if you fail to follow the correct procedure, you can encounter numerous problems and delays and may be charged duty or even fined. The relevant forms to be completed by non-EU citizens depend on whether your French property will be your main residence or a holiday home. Removal companies usually take care of the paperwork (red tape) and ensure that the right documents are provided and correctly completed (see also **Customs** on page 57).

☑ SURVIVAL TIP

For international removals you should use a company that's a member of the International Federation of Furniture Removers (FIDI, www. fidi.com) or the Overseas Moving Network International (OMNI, www.omnimoving.com), with experience in France.

Some removal companies have subsidiaries or affiliates in France, which can be useful if you encounter problems or need to make an insurance claim. American removal companies with offices in France include Biard International (www.biard.fr), Team Relocations (www.teamrelocations.com) and Grospiron International (www.grospiron.com). It's advisable to obtain a number of written quotations before choosing a company.

Make a list of everything to be moved and give a copy to your removal company. Don't include anything illegal (e.g. guns, bombs, drugs and pornography) with your belongings, as customs checks can be rigorous and penalties severe. Provide the shipping company with detailed instructions how to find your French address from the nearest motorway (or main road) and a telephone number where you can be contacted. Note that if your new home has restricted access or is surrounded by soft ground you may incur additional costs – but make sure you inform the shipping company in advance!

Be sure to fully insure your belongings during removal with a well-established insurance company. Insurance premiums are usually 1 to 2 per cent of the declared value of your goods, depending on the type of cover chosen. It's prudent to make a photographic or video record of valuables for insurance purposes. Note that china, glass and other breakables are usually included in an all-risks policy only when they've been packed by the removal company.

Bear in mind that when moving home everything that can go wrong often does, so allow plenty of time and try not to arrange your move from your old home on the same day as the new owner/tenant is moving in. That's just asking for fate to intervene! See also the checklists in **Chapter 20**.

BUY OR RENT?

Whether you buy or rent a home in France will usually depend on how long you're planning to stay. If you'll be living in France for only a few years renting is usually the best option, and it's also the answer for those who don't want the trouble, expense and restrictions associated with buying a property.

Even if you're planning to buy, it's often prudent to rent for a period in order to reduce your chance of making an expensive error. This allows you to become familiar with a region and its climate, and gives you plenty of time to look around for a permanent home.

Renting is common in France where over 35 per cent of the population live in rented accommodation. Tenants have security of tenure, and rental costs are strictly controlled under French law. It's possible to rent every kind of property, from a tiny studio apartment (bedsitter) to a huge rambling *château*.

If you decide to buy you should be clear about your long-term plans and goals. Buying a house or an apartment is usually a good long-term investment and preferable to renting over a period of three or more years, but you shouldn't expect to make a quick (or any) profit, particularly in rural areas (although in cities – particularly Paris – prices rise much faster). During the boom years from 1997 to 2007 French house prices surged by over 100 per cent, but since 2008 they have been largely stagnant, increasing by just 2 per cent.

Rural property is considerably cheaper than in many other developed countries and many foreign buyers find that they can buy a size or style of home that they couldn't possibly afford in their home countries (French property prices are generally around half of those in the UK).

RENTAL ACCOMMODATION

If you want a long-term rental to move into as soon as you arrive in France, you should start looking a few months before your planned arrival date and may need local help. This could be your employer (if applicable), an estate agent or a property search agent or relocation company. It also helps if you've friends or contacts living in your chosen area(s) who may get wind of a suitable property before it comes onto the open market.

Try to avoid the *rentrée* months of September and October, when the French return from their summer holidays and students in university towns and cities may still be chasing accommodation. It's wise to make your search radius as wide as possible, which will improve your chances of finding somewhere suitable, and not limit yourself to just one town or city neighbourhood.

Rental Terms

Rents vary considerably depending on the size and quality of a property, its age and the facilities provided. In large cities, the district (*quartier*) – there are over 100 in Marseille, for example – and area (*arrondissement*) in which a property is located also have a considerable impact on rental costs. Prices, particularly for apartments, are calculated according to the number of rooms (*pièces*), excluding the obligatory kitchen, bathroom(s) and toilet(s) and any other 'utility' rooms, and the overall habitable floor area (in square metres, m^2) which includes a converted attic room provided the ceiling height is at least 1.8m. Room dimensions are rarely given in property descriptions, although a room's surface area may be mentioned.

A one-room apartment has a combined living and sleeping room, with possibly a separate kitchen, and is called a *studio*. A two-room (*deux-pièces*) apartment has either a bedroom or a room that converts into a bedroom, and a living room. A three-room (*trois-pièces*) apartment has two bedrooms, a four-room (*quatre-pièces*) apartment may have three bedrooms or two bedrooms and separate dining and living rooms – an apartment with two bedrooms and a through lounge-dining room is a *faux quatre-pièces* – and so on. Apartment descriptions often begin with '*F*' or '*T*' followed by the number of rooms other than the 'utility' rooms. Thus '*faux F4*' is an abbreviation of '*faux quatre-pièces*'.

Finding a Rental

There are numerous property websites offering rentals in France. Two of the most prominent – available in English – are www.seloger.co.uk and www.french-property.com. The French National Federation of Estate Agents website (www.fnaim.fr – click on *louer*, then on *location*

and complete the boxes) also contains a wide choice of rentals, as does the property magazine *Logic-immo* (www.logic-immo.fr – click on *louer* and complete the boxes). Other property portals include www.avendrealouer.fr, www.century21.fr, www.explorimmo.com, www.lavieimmo.com, www.lokaviz.fr (for students), www.pap.fr, and www.seloger.com. Many websites offer free subscription to an email update, which informs you about new properties in your chosen areas.

The property rental section of weekly free-sheets such as *Topannonces* (www.topannonces.fr) can also be accessed via the internet. Most French newspapers have websites, many of which can be found via Online Newspapers (www.onlinenewspapers.com/france.htm), while World Newspapers (www.world-newspapers.com/france.html) is a good source for expatriate English-language publications.

There are numerous estate agency chains in France, including Foncia whose specialty is rentals (www.foncia.fr – full search and completion service). Agents can be found online under *Agences immobilières* and *Locations d'appartements*. If you want a furnished rental (which is more difficult to find) search for *Maisons, appartements, chambres meublés* (*location*).

Rents

Rents are based on the prevailing market value of a property (*indice*), but the most significant factor is its location: the region, city and neighbourhood. With a dominant owner-occupied sector and long-term renting trends, it can be tricky finding affordable – and decent – rental accommodation, particularly in major cities and popular neighbourhoods, where demand outstrips supply.

Rental accommodation in Paris is always in short supply and prices are among the highest in Europe, at least double those in other French cities. In central Paris it isn't unusual to pay around €750 per month for a tiny studio apartment of 20m² in a good area, while a one-bedroom apartment of around 50m² costs €1,500 per month and a two- or three-bedroom apartment of 125m² in a top-drawer area such as the 16th *arrondissement* can cost over €5,000 per month, (the sky's the limit for a renovated apartment in a listed Haussmann building). However, as you venture further into the suburbs, rents fall dramatically.

The lowest rents are in small towns and rural areas, although there's less choice. Generally, the further a property is from a large city or town (or town centre), the sea, public transport or other facilities, the cheaper it is. You can rent a two-bedroom apartment or village house/cottage over five years old (*ancien*) in many departments for under €500 a month, while the rent for a large three-bedroom (*quatre pièces*) detached house with a garden in rural areas is around €750 to €1,000 per month.

Rental rates for short-term lets, e.g. less than a year, are higher than for longer lets, particularly in popular holiday areas and properties with a sea, lake or mountain view. If you rent on a weekly basis you may experience up to five different seasonal weekly rates in a six-month period, from low to peak season, with the peak season rate up to three times as high as the low season. The rates depend on the standard, number of beds – including sofa beds – and the facilities provided. A *studio* sleeping four people costs around €600 to €800 per week on the Côte d'Azur in the peak season.

The rent for a one-bedroom *gîte* sleeping two to four is €300 to €500 per week in summer (€500 to €700 for two bedrooms) and slightly less in spring and autumn. However, when renting for several months outside the peak season rents are usually around 50 per cent lower in most regions.

Until recently rents have been freely set and could be revised once a year, but by no more than the INSEE rental index (www.insee.fr). However, in 2014 the French parliament passed a new bill – the *Loi pour l'accès au logement et un urbanisme rénové* (ALUR, improving access to housing and updating town planning) – also known as the 'Loi Duflot' after the housing minister Cécile Duflot. This put a cap on long-term rental costs in the urban areas of 28 major cities (with over 500,000 inhabitants), which should be no more than 20 per cent above the average rent set by the *prefect*.

CHARGES OR EXTRA COSTS

There are usually extra costs (*charges*) in addition to the monthly rent, especially for those renting in apartment blocks, although they're much less common if you rent a house or maisonette. This is because while the landlord pays for major repairs and new equipment, the tenant pays for small repairs, rubbish collection and the general upkeep of the common areas in the building, grounds and outside areas, including lift and lighting costs. Charges average around 10 per cent of the rent, but can be considerably more if you rent an apartment of *grand standing* in a residential block with large grounds or gardens, concierge, electronic surveillance, gardener, swimming pool, tennis court and gym.

In a joint-ownership block of flats the landlord or agent must tell the tenant exactly how the charges are split between the apartments, depending on their size. Check the accounts carefully as landlords and managing agents (*syndics*) often make 'mistakes'. Building repairs, facelifts (*ravalement*) and property tax (*taxe foncière*) aren't a tenant's responsibility, but residential or occupant's tax (*taxe d'habitation*) is if your rental period includes the 1st January (see page 201).

Lift maintenance can form a part of a building's running costs, and the higher an apartment is in a block the more a tenant must pay, while ground floor tenants don't pay lift charges. In apartment blocks with a central heating unit, all accommodation must have its own meter unless this is technically impossible. Apartments heated by a central unit in the block must have heating appliances that can be regulated by the occupant.

GARAGE OR PARKING SPACE

A garage isn't normally included with an apartment and must be purchased or rented separately. Modern apartment blocks generally have single lock-up garages (*box*), outside parking spaces or underground parking with reserved parking spaces. A simple *box* with just a light bulb and no tap costs from around €100 per month and garages of '*grand standing*' with a pit, taps and electrical points run to double this. Centrally located garages in towns with a parking shortage (i.e. most towns) are in huge demand and can cost much more. Some car parks offer special rates for residents (*tarif spécial résident*), such as those run by the VinciPark group (www.vincipark.com).

Most property websites also carry advertisements for garage and parking space rentals, as does the website for *De Particulier A Particulier* magazine (www.pap.fr).

BUYING A HOME

There are many ways of finding homes for sale in France, including via a wealth of real estate agents (most of whom have websites – see below), ads in newspapers and magazines (including many English-language publications) and property exhibitions such as www. thefranceshow.com and www.fpeolympia.com).

Some agents and companies organise discovery tours in various regions of France, allowing you to get a feel for an area and the type of properties for sale. If you prefer to look for homes under your own steam, one way to find them is simply to tour the areas that you're interested in looking for FOR SALE (*A VENDRE* or sometimes simply *AV*) signs. Ensure you avoid public holidays (see page 41) and also the Monday before a holiday if it falls on a Tuesday and the Friday after if it falls on a Thursday.

When house hunting in France it's advisable to take a calculator (to work out how few euros you'll get for your money!), a mobile phone (and a charger and plug adapter), a camera and/or video camera, as well as a notepad, maps and contact numbers, and – if necessary – a French dictionary or phrase book.

REAL ESTATE AGENTS

Only some 50 per cent of property sales in France are handled by real estate agents (*agent immobilier*). However, where foreign buyers are concerned the vast majority of sales are made through agents or handled by *notaires* (see below). It's common for foreigners in many countries, particularly the UK, to use an agent in their own country who works with one or more French agents. A number of French agents also advertise abroad in foreign property magazines (and publications in France targeted at expatriates) and many have English-speaking staff, so don't be discouraged if you don't speak fluent French.

If you want to find an agent in a particular town or area, the easiest way it to use a search engine such as Google (simply enter 'estate agents xxxxx', where 'xxxxx' is the town or department you are interested in). If you're using a local estate agent it's best to visit them and view properties at the earliest opportunity (French agents don't generally send out property details and when they do they're usually sparse).

Most French estate agents are members of a professional body, the main one being the French association of estate agents (Fédération Nationale de l'Immobilier/NAIM, www.fnaim.fr). The Syndicat National des Professionnels Immobiliers (SNPI, www.snpi.com) represents property agents and property managers, while the Union Nationale de la Propriété Immobilière (UNPI, www.unpi.org) is one of the national associations representing property owners' managing agents.

Foreign Agents

Very few foreign agents in France possess the coveted *carte professionnelle* (see above). Previously foreigners were permitted to act as self-employed 'sales representatives' (*agents commerciaux*) of French-registered agents, requiring no particular qualifications. This practice has now been outlawed, however, and you should avoid making any binding agreements with an *agent commercial* and certainly shouldn't pay any money to one or any unregistered 'property agent' or 'search agent'. In fact, you shouldn't even view properties with anyone who can't produce a *carte professionnelle* (or who isn't employed by someone with one); if you've an accident while

visiting a property you won't be able to make a claim unless an agent is legal and registered.

> If you're dealing wth an *agent commercial*, you should check that he's listed on the local *registre du commerce* (he should have a registration number and a *SIRET* number) and that the agent he represents is a member of one of the recognised professional bodies (see above).

Members of the Federation of Overseas Property Developers (www.nfopp.co.uk), which is a member of the National Association of Estate Agents International Division (NAEA, UK 0192-649 6800, www.naea.co.uk), are bound by a code of ethics requiring them to meet local licensing requirements, and must therefore be French-registered if they have offices in France.

There may be advantages in using a foreign agent, particularly an English-speaking one who's experienced in selling to foreign buyers and is familiar with the problems they can encounter. Among the leading UK French property agents are France Property Shop (www.francepropertyshop.com), French Property (www.french-property.com), and French Entrée (www.frenchentree.com).

If a foreign agent refers clients to a French agent or agents, he may share his commission with the French agent(s) or charge extra for his services – in some cases a great deal extra – therefore you should check what's included (and what isn't) in a price quoted by a foreign agent. See also **Fees** below.

Notaires

Around 15 per cent of property sales in France are negotiated by *notaires* (a peculiarly French official, whose functions aren't the same as a notary or notary public), who also have a monopoly on conveyancing for all property sales in France. *Notaires* have a strict code of practice and aren't, for example, permitted to display property details in their offices, which means that most have a working relationship with a number of estate agents.

When a *notaire* is the selling agent, his 'agency' commission isn't included in the asking price and is paid by the buyer, which should be taken into account when calculating the overall cost of the property. However, the 'agency' fees charged by a *notaire* are usually lower than those levied by estate agents and are standard throughout France. Although there may appear to be a conflict of interest when a *notaire* is instructed by the seller but receives his fee from the buyer, in practice there are usually no problems. Value added tax/VAT (*TVA*) at 20 per cent must be added to all fees.

Fees

There are no government controls on estate agents' fees in France, although they're obliged to post a list of charges (*barème*) in their offices. Fees are usually levied on a sliding scale between 5 and 10 per cent: the cheaper the property, the higher the percentage, e.g. 10 per cent on properties priced at €20,000 reducing to 5 per cent on properties costing €150,000 or more. For expensive properties an agent's fee may be negotiable.

An agent's fees may be paid by the vendor, the buyer or be shared, although it's normal for the vendor to pay, i.e. the fee is 'included' in the purchase price. A price quoted as *net vendeur* excludes the selling agent's fees; *commission comprise* (written as C/C) or *frais d'agence inclus* (FAI) indicates that the price includes the agent's commission. Make sure when discussing the price that it's C/C or FAI and not *net vendeur*.

If you're buying a garage separately through an agent, don't be surprised to find that the price includes a hefty agent's fee. Garage prices range from around €10,000 to over €50,000, depending on their location and the services included.

When buying, check in advance whether you need to pay commission or any extras in addition to the sale price (apart from the usual fees and taxes associated with buying a property in France). The agent's fee is usually payable on completion, but may be payable sooner.

PROPERTY PRICES

Apart from the obvious points such as size, quality and land area, the most important factor influencing the price of a house is its location. A restored or modernised two-bedroom house may cost just €100,000 in a remote rural area but may cost two or three times as much in a popular village or town. The closer you are to the coast (or Paris), the more expensive property is.

Note that when people talk about 'inexpensive' homes, they invariably mean something that needs restoring, which usually necessitates spending as much as the purchase price to make it habitable. The French think that the British are particularly insane for buying up their tumbled down farmhouses and crumbling *châteaux*. Few Frenchmen share the British passion for spending their holidays and weekends up to their elbows in bricks and mortar! They do, however, have a grudging

---

☑ SURVIVAL TIP

You can track house price changes on the LPI (Les Prix de l'Immobilier, http://lespriximmobiliers. com) index, which shows weekly house price changes using data from banks and financial institutions including Sogeprom, Gecina, Crédit Foncier, as well as from the Syndicat National des Professionnels Immobiliers (SNPI).

admiration for the British for their painstaking and sensitive restorations.

A slice of *la bonne vie* needn't cost the earth, with habitable cottages and terraced village homes available from around €100,000 and detached homes from as little as €125,000. In some rural areas it's still possible to buy an old property for as little as €50,000, although you usually need to carry out major restoration work which can cost as much as building from scratch. A modern two-bedroom bungalow or renovated cottage in a rural area costs from around €100,000. However, if you're seeking a home with three or more bedrooms, a large plot and a swimming pool, you'll need to spend at least €200,000 to €300,000 (depending on the area), while luxury apartments in Paris and villas in the south of France will set you back €millions.

In addition to the purchase price, you must allow for various costs associated with buying a house in France, which are higher than in most other countries and can amount to around 25 per cent of the purchase price for old properties and as much as 40 per cent of new properties (although most fees are included in the asking price). If you negotiate a reduction, check that the agent or vendor hasn't excluded some fees from the price (to be added later).

Between 2006 and 2015, house prices in France increased by just 2 per cent on average, compared with a 30 per cent increase in the UK and a 21 per cent rise in Germany.

SECURITY

When moving into a new home, it's wise to replace the locks (or lock barrels) as soon as possible and fit high-security locks, as you've no idea how many keys are in circulation for the existing ones. Some apartments and houses may be fitted with door locks that are individually numbered; extra keys for these can't be made by an ordinary locksmith (*serrurerie*) and you must obtain details from the previous owner or the landlord to have additional keys cut or to change the lock barrels. At the same time as changing locks, you may wish to have an alarm system fitted, which is the best way to deter intruders and may also reduce your home contents insurance.

If you're likely to be leaving your home unoccupied for long periods, your insurance company may insist on extra security measures such as two, or even three, locks on external doors (one a mortise lock) and internally-lockable shutters (or grilles) on windows, which must be locked when the property is vacant. In high-risk areas you may be required to fit extra locks and shutters, security blinds or gratings on windows. However, no matter how secure your home, a thief can usually break in if he's determined enough, e.g. through the roof or by knocking a hole in a wall!

If you've a holiday home it isn't wise to leave anything of great value (monetary or sentimental) there. If you vacate a rented house or apartment for an extended period it may be obligatory to notify your caretaker, landlord or insurance company, and to leave a key with the caretaker or landlord in case of emergencies. If you've a break-in you should report it immediately to your local *gendarmerie* and make a statement (*plainte*), which is required by your insurance company if you make a claim.

Another important aspect of home security is ensuring that you have early warning of a fire, which is easily accomplished by installing smoke detectors. Following recent legislation homes must have at least one smoke detector (*détecteur de fumée*), which should be operated by electricity if you leave a property empty for long periods (batteries can go flat while you're away). You can also fit an electric-powered gas detector that activates an alarm when a gas leak is detected.

UTILITIES

As well as electricity and gas, French homes use oil (*fioul* or *fuel*) and wood (*bois*) for heating and hot water. Electricity and gas are supplied by the partially state-owned Electricité de France/Gaz de France (EDF/GDF, www. edf.fr and www.dolcevita.gazdefrance.fr) and although the market was supposedly opened up to competitors a decade ago, EDF still has a virtual monopoly of 90 per cent of households. EDF's rates are regulated by the government, while rivals set their own prices.

Your rental or real estate agent should be able to advise you on registering with EDF or an alternative supplier.

Château d'Azay-le-Rideau, Indre-et-Loire

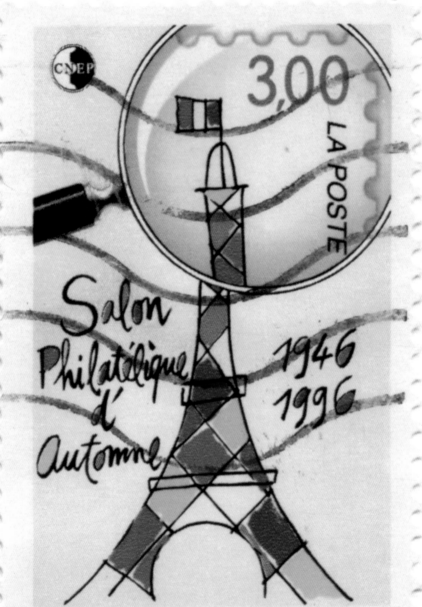

6.
POSTAL SERVICES

*T*he French Post Office (*La Poste*) lost its monopoly on postal delivery in 2005 and became a public-owned company in 2010, although it still handles most letter deliveries. There are over 17,000 post offices (*bureau de poste* or simply *poste*) in France, around a third of which are operated in partnership with other businesses (such as bakeries and general stores) and are known as *Agences Postales* (postal agencies) or *Relais Poste* (postal intermediaries). The identifying colour used by La Poste is yellow, which is the colour of French post office signs, post vans and post boxes, which can be found in most villages, as well as towns and cities. The post office logo looks like a blue paper aeroplane on a yellow background (see image below).

In addition to the usual post-handling services French post offices offer a range of other services, including telephone calls, domestic and international cash transfers, and payment of telephone and utility bills. La Poste also offers email services (free and permanent email addresses as well as e-commerce services for small businesses), banking services (e.g. cheque and savings accounts, mortgage and retirement plans), insurance, currency exchange (*bureau de change*) and cash transfers.

Main post offices usually have separate counters (*guichets*) for different services, e.g. cashing or depositing post office cheques (*CCP*), postal orders (*mandat*), *poste restante* and bulk stamps (*timbres en gros*), although some counters provide all services (*tous services/toutes opérations*). If you need different services you must queue a number

of times if there's no window for all services. Stamps are sold at most windows and most handle letters and packages (*envoi de lettres et paquets*), except perhaps very large parcels. Most main post offices also have a row of automatic postage machines (*guichets automatiques*), with instructions in English, where you can weigh packages, buy stamps, and obtain sticky labels and tape.

> Signs for post offices in towns vary widely and include *PTT* (the old name for the post office), *PT, P et T, Bureau de Poste* or simply *Poste*.

La Poste produces numerous leaflets and brochures and its website (www.laposte.fr) contains information about all services, including a searchable database of post offices.

BUSINESS HOURS

Business hours for main post offices in towns and cities in France are usually from 9am to 7pm Mondays to Fridays and from 9am to noon on Saturdays. In small towns and villages business hours vary considerably and post offices close for lunch, e.g. from noon to 1.30 or even 2.30pm. Main post offices in major towns don't close at midday and also have longer business hours (some even open for a few hours on Sundays), while in Paris the main post office (52 rue du Louvre, 1er) is open 24 hours.

It's best to avoid visiting a post office during lunch hours and late afternoon (when office workers handling business mail create long queues), and Saturday afternoons and Sundays are also best avoided.

LETTERS

La Poste offers three rates for sending domestic mail: first-class (*prioritaire*), second-class (*lettre verte* or green letter) and *Ecopoli*, which is the cheapest (although restricted to a maximum of 250g) and slowest taking three to five days, and is generally used by businesses for mass mailings. *Lettre verte* was introduced in 2011 to provide an ecological alternative (no use of aircraft) to first class, but savings are relatively small. The delivery targets (not always met) are next day for first class and two days for *lettre verte*.

In 2016 it cost 80¢ to send a letter up to 20g first class (up to €6.40 for the maximum of 501g to 3kg), 70¢ by letter verte (€5.60 for 501g to 3kg) and 68¢ by Ecopli (€2.72 for the maximum weight of 101-250g). A full tariff (*tarif*) list is available from post offices. Letter post rates apply only to letters and documents and other items can't be sent using this service, however small, but must be sent as parcels (see below).

If you're sending anything remotely fragile ensure that you pack it well, as it isn't unusual for mail to arrive in tatters.

Stamps

Stamps can be purchased at tobacconist shops (*bureau de tabac*) as well as post

offices, many of which have machines that print postage labels (*vignettes d'affranchisement* or *etiquettes*). Self-adhesive (*auto-collant*) stamps for domestic letters up to 20g are sold in sheets of ten (*carnet*). It's also possible to buy and print stamps (even stamps using your own photographs!) via the internet, but first you need to create an account.

La Poste actively promotes the use of pre-stamped envelopes (*enveloppes prétimbrées*) – a service known as *le prêt-à-poster*. Not surprisingly, these are rather expensive when purchased individually, although there are savings when buying in bulk. Stamped window envelopes (*avec fenêtre*) are also available, as are stamped envelopes with decorative designs (usually of local sights), stamped domestic postcards (*carte postale préaffranchie*) and international stamped envelopes (*enveloppe internationale*) for letters up to 20g. Blank pre-stamped envelopes are also sold at hypermarkets and supermarkets. It's no longer necessary to affix an airmail (*par avion*) label or use airmail envelopes for international post, as all post is automatically sent by air to distant locations.

Official fiscal stamps (*timbre fiscal*), used to legalise documents, pay government taxes and motoring fines, etc., must be purchased from a tobacconist or a tax office, and can't be bought at a post office.

Addresses

The international identification letter for French addresses is 'F', which precedes the postcode (*code postal*), although its use isn't obligatory. France uses five-digit post codes, where the first two digits indicate the *département* and the last three the town or commune or, in the case of Paris, Lyon and Marseille, a district (*arrondissement*); for example, 75005 indicates the fifth *arrondissement* of Paris. Paris addresses are often given with the *arrondissement* written, for example, 6ème/6e. To translate this into the postcode, simply add 7500 to make 75006.

All postcodes are listed by *commune* in alphabetical order in a yellow *Code Postal* booklet, available at any post office and via the post office website; they're also shown after commune names in telephone books. Small villages (*lieu-dit*) often use the postcode of a nearby village or town and the affiliated village/town name should be included in the address

```
Monsieur ROUGENEZ Jean
69 RUE DES ESCARGAUX
F-12345 GRENOUILLE VILLE
France
```

Traditionally, the street address is written with a comma after the house number (i.e. 69, rue du Vin), but the post office advises that no punctuation should appear in the address thus allowing them to be read by a machine. Similarly, the addressee's surname, the street name, the *lieu-dit* (if applicable) and the post town should all be written or typed in capital letters. A correct French address is shown above.

Many people include the department (or even region) name after the postcode, although this isn't necessary and the post office discourages it.

CEDEX (*Courrier d'Entreprise à Distribution Exceptionnelle*) is a special delivery service for business post and where applicable is included in addresses after the town, sometimes followed by a number, e.g. 75006 PARIS CEDEX 09. Post office (PO) boxes (*boîte postale/BP*) are shown in addresses as *BP 01*, for example and for some reason are usually given in addition to the street address. It's customary for the sender (*expéditeur*) to write his own address on the back of an envelope.

Post & Letter Boxes

Post boxes (*boîte aux lettres*) are yellow and are usually affixed to a pillar or set into (or attached to) a wall. There's always one outside post offices and railway stations and often one outside a tobacconist. It's best to post urgent letters at a main post office or railway station, as collections there are more frequent.

In cities and at main post offices, there's often a choice of boxes: for example, one for local post (within the town, *commune* or *département*) and another for other destinations (*autres destinations* or *départements étrangers*). There may be other boxes for economy post (*tarif réduit*) or packets/periodicals (*paquets – journaux périodiques*). In Paris, there are often separate boxes for the city (i.e. postcodes beginning 75) and the suburbs (*banlieue*).

French postmen/women (*facteur*) aren't obliged to deliver post to your front door unless it's on the street. If it isn't you must install a letter box at the boundary of your property on the street, which must meet specific requirements as to size, accessibility, and how and where they're mounted. Approved boxes can be purchased for around €10 in most DIY stores. See the La Poste website for details or ask at your local post office if you plan to install your own letter box.

If you live in an apartment block with a caretaker (*gardien/gardienne*), he/she may receive and distribute letters (and parcels) to tenants. Otherwise letters are put in your letter box in the foyer. Often letter boxes aren't large enough for magazines and packets, which are left in a common storage area. In some apartment blocks in main cities it isn't unusual for post to be stolen, therefore if possible you should install a letter box large enough to hold all your post or rent a post box at a main post office (see **Collections** below).

Deliveries

With the exception of the major cities there's usually only one post delivery a day, and in rural areas your postman may collect your outgoing post. If the postman calls with mail requiring a signature or payment when nobody is at home, he'll leave a collection form (*avis de passage*). Mail is kept at the post office for 15 days, after which it's returned to the sender, therefore if you're going to be away from home for longer than 15 days you should ask the post office to hold your post (see **Collections** below).

If a letter can't be delivered – e.g. because it's wrongly addressed or because the addressee has moved – it will be returned with a note stating *n'habite pas à l'adresse indiquée – renvoyer à l'expéditeur* (sometimes abbreviated to *NPAI*).

If you want your post to be redirected you must complete an *ordre de réexpédition temporaire* (temporary redirection) at least a week in advance or a permanent change of address card (*ordre de réexpédition définitif*) when moving house. Identification is required for each member of the household. Post can be redirected indefinitely and the service for domestic mail redirection costs €25.50 (€72 for international redirection) for up to six months or €46 for a year (€125 for international mail).

In addition ro 'real' mail you'll also receive heaps of junk mail (*courrier indésirable* or *publicité*), e.g. unsolicited letters, retail brochures and free newspapers. Before discarding it check that there isn't any important mail mixed in with it!

Collections

If you've received an *avis de passage* (see above), you must take it to your local post office, the address of which is written on the form. In large post offices there may be a window marked *retrait des lettres et paquets*. You usually need some form of identification (*pièce d'identité*), e.g. your passport, *carte de séjour* or French driving licence, although this may not be requested.

You can give someone authorisation to collect a letter or parcel on your behalf by entering the details on the back of the collection form in the box marked '*vous ne pouvez pas vous déplacer*', for which both your identification and that of the 'collector' is required. It's possible to set up a permanent authorisation (*procuration*) with the local post office granting permission for a spouse or other adult member of your household to collect registered or other post in your name using their own identity documents.

If you're going to be away from your home for a period you can have your post retained by the local post office (*garde du courrier* – see below) for €20.50 for up to two months. Alternatively, you can have mail redirected (see **Deliveries** above).

You can receive mail at any post office in France via the international *poste restante* service. If there's more than one post office in the town, include its name in the address to avoid confusion. Letters should be addressed as follows:

> **Marmaduke BLENKINSOP**
> **POSTE RESTANTE**
> **POSTE CENTRALE**
> **Post code CITY NAME [e.g. 75001 PARIS]**
> **FRANCE**

Post sent to a *poste restante* address is returned to the sender if it's unclaimed after 30 days. Identification is necessary for collection. There's a fee (equivalent to the standard letter rate) for each letter received.

You can rent a post office box (*boîte postale/ BP*) at most post offices for an annual fee. All your post will be stored there and the postman will no longer deliver to your home, but you can arrange to be informed when registered or express post arrives.

PARCELS

The Post Office provides a range of parcel (*colis*) services, both domestic and international, under the *Colissimo* brand. There's also an express international service called *Chronopost* (see below). Parcels must be securely packaged and must conform to certain size and weight limits (usually a maximum of 20kg and 2 metres in length, breadth or height). Although more expensive,

it's more convenient to use post office approved packaging (*emballage*) in the form of fold-flat cardboard boxes (each of which has a weight limit), rather than making up a parcel yourself.

Padded envelopes (*à bulles*) are also available in a range of sizes from post offices and stationery shops, along with special packages, e.g. for CDs or for one, two or three bottles. Minimal insurance is included in the postage fee but higher levels are available for an extra cost. For current tariffs ask at a post office or consult the La Poste website (www. laposte.fr). Domestic *Colissimo* parcels are usually delivered within 48 hours.

If you're using express post it's unnecessary to write on the envelope, as you must complete a form with giving your address and telephone number and those of the addressee, which is stamped and affixed to the parcel by post office staff. Parcels to addresses outside the EU must have an international green customs label (*déclaration de douane*) affixed to them.

When sending small parcels from a post office, use the window marked *Paquets* (if there is one). In larger branches there's usually an automatic coin-operated machine for sending packages.

International parcels: One of the fastest ways to send letters or parcels abroad (weighing up to 30kg) is via the *Chronopost International* service, called EMS in most other European countries, which serves around 220

 Caution

A parcel is anything other than an envelope containing sheets of paper or card. If you wish to send someone a CD or a small gift, it must be sent as a parcel, which involves going to a post office. Parcels can't simply be posted in a post box.

countries. *Chronopost* has an associate status with La Poste, which allows express parcels to be sent from La Poste offices. A range of domestic and international services is provided, depending on how urgent your parcel is and its destination. (Parcels are delivered the following day to the main European cities and in one or two days to other destinations in Europe.) Details and rates can be found at www. chronopost.fr/en.

DHL (www.dhl.com), UPS (www.ups.com) and other courier companies also provide domestic and international parcel services.

REGISTERED & RECORDED POST

The registered and recorded mail service is commonly used in France when sending official documents and communications, where proof of despatch and/or a receipt is required. You can send a registered letter (*lettre recommandée*) with (*avec*) or without (*sans*) proof of delivery (*avis de réception*). The sender's address must be written on the back of registered letters. A domestic recorded or 'tracked' service (*courier suivi*) enables you to check the progress (via the internet) of your post and when it's delivered. It's possible to combine the recorded service with registered post (*le prêt-à-recommander suivi*) if you need a signed receipt and also want to be able to track a letter.

You can insure your mail for an additional fee. It's also possible to insure a parcel under the *valeur declare internationale* scheme, whereby there's a fixed compensation amount based on the declared value up to a maximum of €5,000.

Registered letters require a signature and proof of identity on delivery – normally the person to whom they're addressed. If the addressee is absent when delivery is made, a notice is left and the letter must be collected from the local post office (see **Collections** above). When proof of delivery (*avis de réception*) is requested, a receipt is returned to the sender.

7.
COMMUNICATIONS

*F*rance has one of the largest telephone networks in the world and most French households have a fixed line telephone. Tariffs are reasonable and there's a range of providers to choose from, many providing telephone, internet and TV services. Following the ending of the France Telecom's (FT) monopoly in 2009 – rebranded as Orange (www.orange.fr) in 2013 – competition has been increased with a number of new entrants to the market.

France also has an efficient mobile telephone service, encompassing virtually the whole country, and a fast internet service in the major cities. Broadband (*le haut-débit*) via ADSL (*l'ADSL*) is available in most urban areas, although it's patchy in rural areas, while in Paris and other urban centres with cable television there are superfast fibre optic services (up to 100Mb/s), known as *le très haut-débit*.

If you need good mobile coverage and broadband internet you should check the availability **before** buying a home, as services and speeds vary considerably (see **Internet Services** on page 92).

EMERGENCY NUMBERS

The national emergency numbers (*services d'urgence et d'assistance*) in France are shown in the box below. If you aren't sure which emergency service you need (or can't remember which number to call), it's best to call the EU-wide emergency number (112), which will connect you to the emergency services switchboard for your department who will dispatch the appropriate service (ambulance, police or fire).

In some areas the 112 service may have English-speaking (or other language) operators, but you can't rely on this, particularly outside the Paris area, Therefore you should ensure that you know how to place an emergency call in French, stating your name, street address or location, and requesting the appropriate service.

The Fire service (*pompiers*) handle a wide range of emergency situations in France,

Emergency Numbers	
Number	**Service**
15	Ambulance (*Service d'Aide Médicale d'Urgence/SAMU*) or to contact a duty doctor out of hours
17	Police (*police-secours*)
18	Fire (*sapeurs-pompiers/feu centrale d'alarme*)
112	EU emergency number

including road accidents and natural disasters, and will notify the ambulance and/or police services if they think the situation warrants it. Calls to emergency numbers are free from public and private telephones.

In addition to the national emergency numbers shown in the box, you should make a note of the number of your local ambulance service (*ambulance*), police station (*gendarmerie*) and fire service (*pompiers*). Gas and electricity emergency numbers are also listed in telephone directories under *EDF/GDF*. Other numbers to note are the poison emergency service (*centre anti-poisons*), Samaritans (*SOS Amitié*) and various other help organisations that are listed at the front of telephone directories.

In Paris you can contact *SOS Médecins* (01 47 07 77 77, www.sosmedecins.fr) for an emergency doctor or *SOS Dentaire* (01 43 37 51 00, www.sos-dentaire.com) for emergency dental treatment. There are emergency telephone boxes at major junctions in Paris and other major cities, marked *Services Médicaux*, with a direct line to the emergency services, and there are also free SOS call boxes on motorways and other major roads throughout France for vehicle breakdowns.

INSTALLATION & REGISTRATION

Although the landline network is still largely in the hands of Orange, it's possible to change the subscription to another supplier, where your no longer required to pay Orange for your land line rental. The first thing you need to do before signing up to a telephone service is to determine whether your address is in a zone *dégroupée* (unbundling) or *zone non dégroupée*. In an area designated *zone dégroupée* the phone lines are open to competitors and you can (theoretically) get a phone number from any phone company

and avoid paying a monthly service charge (*abonnement*) to Orange. In an area designated as *zone non dégroupée* you must obtain a phone number from Orange and pay a service charge. You can then sign up with any vendor for ADSL or other digital services, but should bear in mind that it may take a few weeks to set up.

If you're planning to move into a property without an existing telephone line (*ligne fixe*), you'll need to have one installed. Bear in mind that if you buy a property in a remote area without a telephone line it can be very expensive to have a telephone installed as you must pay for an existing line to be extended to the property. Contact Orange (tel. 1014) for an estimate. To have an existing phone line connected visit your local Orange office where you'll need to provide proof of your identity – passport or residence permit (*carte de séjour*) – and proof of your address, e.g. a utility bill, confirmation of purchase (*attestation d'acquisition*) or a lease (*bail*).

When moving into a home with a telephone line, you must have the account transferred to your name and a telephone number issued. It isn't possible to take over the telephone number of the previous occupant of a property as the telephone number always changes when the ownership or tenancy of a property changes. A straightforward reconnection costs €55. You can buy a fixed-line telephone (*téléphone*) from Orange or any telephone retailer.

You'll also be asked whether you want a listed or unlisted number, where you want your bill sent (you can have it sent to an address abroad) and how you wish to pay for it. If you plan to pay by direct debit you'll need to provide your account details (*relevé d'identité bancaire/RIB*), so you'll need a French bank account.

If you'll be letting a property short-term (holiday lets) you can arrange to have outgoing calls limited to the local area or to regional or national calls only, but you can't limit the service just to incoming calls.

SERVICE PROVIDERS

Savings can be made on national as well as international calls (and other services) by shopping around for the best rates. French telecoms providers bundle their products into call packages to appeal to the French market – which include optional French TV deals – which may not appeal to foreigners (particularly if you can't understand or have no interest in French TV). There are a number of alternative telephone service providers to Orange in France, some of which provide English-language services (see **English-language Providers** below).

To help find your way through the maze of alternative French telephone providers you can compare tariffs via a comparison site such as BudgeTelecom (www.budgetelecom.com),

Comparatel (www.comparatel.fr) or Zone ADSL (www.zoneadsl.com).

There's a monthly line rental or service charge (*abonnement*) for a standard telephone line or ADSL. If you use an alternative provider (i.e. other than Orange), there may be a separate monthly fee in addition to your call charges, although most providers have dropped these.

English-language Providers

You can rent your telephone line and any call packages and broadband services from both French and specialist foreign telecom companies with services targeted at English-speaking expats, which include UK Telecom (UK 01483-477 100, freephone from France 0805 631 632, www.uktelecom.net) and Teleconnect (www.teleconnect.fr).

The services offered by companies are broadly similar and include everything from line installation to satellite broadband, VOIP (Voice Over Internet Protocol) phones and a range of call packages. Some advantages for British (and other English-speaking expatriates in France) include:

♦ Fast and reliable Broadband, lines and minutes in France.

♦ Free technical support in English.

♦ Free UKdirect2U number, so your friends and family can call you in France from as little at 3p per minute.

♦ Free catchup UK TV with a choice of packages.

◆ Payment online via Worldpay or from a French or English bank account.

UK Telecom also offers a free survey of broadband availability in France before you buy a property.

USING THE TELEPHONE

Using the telephone in France is simplicity itself. All French telephone numbers have ten digits, beginning with a two-digit regional code (01 for the Île-de-France, 02 for the northwest, 03 northeast, 04 southeast and 05 southwest), followed by another two-digit area code.

> If you're calling within France, you must dial all ten digits, even if you're phoning your next-door neighbour.

Monaco isn't part of France and has its own country code of 377. Numbers beginning 06 are mobile numbers and those beginning with 08 are premium (expensive) rate service numbers.

International direct dialled (IDD) calls can be made to most countries from both private and public telephones. A full list of country codes, plus area codes for main cities and time differences, is shown in the information pages (*les info téléphoniques*) of the Yellow Pages or can also be found online. To make an IDD call you must first dial 00, then the country code, the area code (**without** the first zero) and the subscriber's number.

One of the most difficult things to do in any foreign language is to understand telephone numbers given to you orally. This is particularly difficult in French, as telephone numbers are dictated in the same way as they're written, i.e. normally two digits at a time. For example, 04 15 48 17 33 is *zéro quatre, quinze, quarante-huit, dix-sept, trente-trois*. It's therefore wise to practise your French numbers (particularly

those from 70 to 100). Note that the French don't say 'double' when two digits are the same: for example, 22 is *vingt-deux*. Note also that some numbers aren't written in pairs, e.g. 0800 300 400; these are also spoken as written – in this case *zéro huit cents, trois cents, quat' cents.*

CALL RATES

Domestic call tariffs may be divided into peak times (*heures creuses*), which may be Mon-Fri 8am to 7pm and Sat 8am to noon and are charged at the 'normal' rate (*tarif normal*); calls at all other times, including all day on public holidays, are charged at a reduced rate (*tarif réduit*). Orange no longer publicises its rates, however, but offers instead an array of 'all-inclusive' packages (*forfait*). Packages require a fixed monthly payment (e.g. between €1.50 and €10) in return for reduced rates or in some cases 'free' calls, which makes it all but impossible (deliberately!) to calculate what you're paying for each call or to compare rates with those of other providers.

A recent comparison between rates charged by the five major providers showed price variations of up to five centimes (as the French refer to euro cents) for a three-minute, off-peak local call, and a much wider range for a ten-minute, peak rate local call, with FT's charges – not surprisingly – generally the highest, although if you're a telephone addict you may find their 'unlimited use' (*illimité*) packages good value.

Alternative telephone service providers (see above) also offer a variety of call packages, consisting of a combination of varying initial charges and lengths followed by different per-minute charges and, in some cases, a single rate for all times of day and all destinations.

Calls from fixed telephones to mobile phones are more expensive and include 'connection' charges plus higher per-minute rates compared with fixed-to-fixed or mobile-to-mobile rates. Note that special rate numbers (beginning with 08) and are charged at a high premium rate and cost even more when called from a mobile phone.

Orange's tariffs for international calls are listed on its website (www.orange.fr). Other telephone providers have different tariff structures for international calls. Most also offer a variety of discount plans such as half-price on all calls to a designated ('favourite') country or to a number of overseas phone numbers (e.g. your mum's).

Charges for equipment rental, credit card calls and (if you use the same provider) internet connection are included on your bill, as are any charges for custom and optional services (see below).

CUSTOM & OPTIONAL SERVICES

Orange – and most other service providers – provide a range of custom and optional telephone services, described as 'comfort services' (*service confort*). Almost all services can be ordered online from the Orange website (www.orange.fr), where you can also find a description of the services available, but have to be arranged beforehand either by phone (to your service provider) or by visiting a local Orange office. *Services confort* can be ordered individually or as part of a package and include:

♦ answering service (*top message*)

♦ call barring (*blocage d'appels*)

♦ caller identification (*présentation du numéro/nom*)

♦ call monitoring (*allofact*):

♦ call transfer (*transfert d'appel*)

♦ call waiting (*signal d'appel*)

♦ new number (*annonce du nouveau numéro*)

♦ reminder call (*mémo appel*)

♦ ring back (*autorappel*)

♦ three-way conversation (*conversation à trois*)

Some comfort services require an annual subscription charge, while others incur a fixed (per use) charge each time the service is used. As a result of increased competition, some services that were previously charged are now free. It pays to check with Orange or read the advertising material that comes with your telephone bill to find out about the latest offers. For details of all custom and optional services, call 1014.

Demandez, c'est trouvé !

Activité		Guid
	ex : garagiste, resto	
Nom		
Adresse		
	ex : 7 av de la cristallerie	
Localité		Guid
	ex : rennes, paris 9, 37100	
Département ou région		Guid
	ex : 92, finistère, aquitaine, idf	

Rechercher

DIRECTORIES

When you've a telephone installed, your name and number are usually automatically included in the next edition of your local telephone directory (*annuaire*), as well as the online telephone directory. Like most telephone companies, Orange sells its list of subscribers to businesses, but you can choose to have an unlisted number which may spare you from the dreaded telephone marketing that's increasingly prevalent in France. You can also have your mobile number, email address, postal address and profession included.

Telephone directories are published for each department (*département*), some of which have more than one volume (*tome*), e.g. the Paris White Pages (*Pages Blanches*) consist of five volumes and the Yellow Pages (*Pages Jaunes*) two. Yellow Pages, which contain only business and official (e.g. government) telephone numbers, are included with the White Pages in one volume or may be published in a separate volume or volumes. You should receive a copy of your local directories when you register for a phone line.

Subscribers are listed in the White Pages under their town or *commune* (or *arrondissement* in Paris, Lyon and Marseille) and not alphabetically for the whole of a department or city. For example, it isn't enough to know that someone lives in the department of Dordogne (you must know the town).

Telephone directories (both White and Yellow Pages) contain a wealth of information, including emergency information and numbers, useful local numbers, Orange numbers and services, tariffs, international country codes and costs, how to use the telephone (in English, French, German, Italian and Spanish), public telephone information, information about bills, directories and Orange products, administration numbers, town plans and maps of the department(s) covered by the telephone book.

You can call 118712 for directory enquiries in France (there are a number of services, all starting with 118), although it's expensive; the service is also available free online at www.118712.fr. Other free online directory enquiry services include http://phonebookoffrance.com, http://france.europe.numbers.tel, www.annuairetel247.com and www.lannuaire.com. White and Yellow Pages can also be accessed online at www.pagesjaunes.fr (yellow) and www.pagesjaunes.fr/pagesblanches (white).

MOBILE TELEPHONES

After a relatively slow start in introducing mobile telephones (*portable* or, increasingly, *mobile*), France is now one of Europe's largest markets. Mobile phones are now so widespread that some businesses (e.g. restaurants, cinemas, theatres, concert halls, etc.) ban them and some use mobile phone jammers that can detect and disable every handset within 100m. Like the rest of Europe, France uses a GSM network; all GSM-compatible phones should work there, but CDMA phones used in North America and parts of Asia, won't.

There are four mobile phone service providers in France: Bouygues Télécom, pronounced 'bweeg' (www.bouyguestelecom.fr), Free Mobile (http://mobile.free.fr), Orange (www.orange.fr) and SFR (www.sfr.fr). As in most other countries, the mobile phone market is a minefield. There aren't just four networks to choose from but a plethora of tariffs covering connection fees, monthly subscriptions, insurance and call charges. To further complicate matters, most providers have business ties to one or more of the fixed telephone services and offer various deals combining mobile and fixed line services (plus internet and TV services).

 Caution

There are many rural areas and *communes* in France where there's no mobile phone service and many thousands more with only partial coverage. See www.sensorly.com/map/2G-3G/FR/France#|coverage for information.

The first decision when buying a mobile phone is whether to take out a contract, whereby you pay a fixed monthly charge and obtain a certain amount of call time 'free' or use a 'pay-as-you-go' scheme, where you pre-pay for your calls using a phone card. Note that if you opt for pay-as-you-go there's usually a time limit of one or two months on the use of each card; if you don't make many calls you may be wasting money on cards you don't use.

The most popular contracts usually give you a set number of hours of outgoing calls (e.g. two, three or five) and a number of texts for a flat monthly fee. Hours included in the fee may be limited to evenings and weekends or split between peak and off-peak calling times. Fees are usually reduced if you agree to a contract of 12 months or more, or order certain add-on features or services. Note that contracts can be complicated and include hidden fees such as connection fees (*frais d'activation*) and disconnection fees (*frais de résiliation*); ideally you want a contract with no minimum period (*sans engagement*). The cost of text messaging (*envoyer des SMS/textos*) is limited by law in France.

New EU regulations came into force in June 2017 that abolished all 'roaming' charges – the extra fees charged by mobile phone companies when a phone is used abroad – in all European Union countries. All calls and texts when using a foreign registered mobile phone in France are now charged at the user's domestic rate.

All mobile phone numbers have the prefix 06 and calls to mobiles from a fixed phone in France are charged at higher rates than calls to another fixed line. Calls between mobile phones of the same company are generally discounted and most companies offer similar 'frequent caller' plans to those offered for fixed phone services.

Further information about mobile phone use in France can be obtained from the Association Française des Opérateurs de Mobiles (AFOM, www.afom.fr).

PUBLIC TELEPHONES

Despite the widespread use of mobile telephones (see below) public telephone boxes (*cabine téléphonique*) can be found in most towns and villages, post offices, bus and railway stations, airports, bars, cafés, restaurants and other businesses, and of course, in streets. Most telephone boxes are Perspex kiosks and most public telephones (*téléphone publique*) accept telephone cards (*télécarte* – see below), Cartes France Télécom, and bank debit and credit cards. Phones that accept coins are now extremely rare.

Calls to emergency services can be made free from any telephone box and all public telephones allow international direct dialling (IDD); international calls can also be made via the operator.

There are SOS (e.g. breakdown) telephones on motorways and at main junctions in Paris and other large cities (marked *Services Médicaux*), for use in the event of accidents or medical emergencies.

INTERNET SERVICES

Although the number has fallen in recent years there are still many internet service providers (*fournisseur d'accès/FAI* or *serveur*) in France offering a variety of services and products at varying prices. Most ISPs offer packages that include telephone (both fixed-line and mobile), internet and TV services (known as 'triple play'). The main telecoms provider Orange (formerly France Télécom) dominates the market for internet services in France, particularly in rural areas, although there are many competitors in urban areas where the best offers are to be found.

Broadband (*le haut-débit*) via ADSL (*l'ADSL*) is available in most urban areas and in Paris and other urban centres with cable television there are superfast fibre optic services (up to 100Mb/s), known as *le très haut debit*. However, ADSL is patchy in rural areas, many of which may never be connected as it's uneconomical. If you need good mobile

coverage and broadband internet you need to check the availability **before** buying a home in France, although it's possible to obtain a broadband connection via satellite (see **Satellite Broadband** below) or via a mobile phone.

You can check the internet speed and availability of broadband, fibre or ADSL via a number of websites – you'll need the commune post code or existing phone number – including Orange (http://boutique.orange.fr/internet/offres-fibre), www.degrouptest.com, www.zoneadsl.com, www.jechange.fr/telecom/internet and www.ariase.com/fr/haut-debit.

The major French internet service providers (ISPs) include the following:

♦ **Alice France**: www.aliceadsl.fr

♦ **Bouygues Telecom:** www.bouyguestelecom.fr

♦ **Free:** www.free.fr

♦ **Orange:** www.orange.fr

♦ **SFR:** www.sfr.fr

♦ **Teleconnect:** www.teleconnect.fr (see English-language Providers on page 87)

♦ **UK Telecom:** www.uktelecom.uk.net (English-language Providers on page 87)

For a comparison of ISP services and charges, consult one of the dedicated internet magazines (such as *Windows & Internet Pratique*) or visit the Comparatel (www.comparatel.fr) or Budgetelecom website (www.budgetelecom.com), which provides information on current offers.

One advantage of French internet services is that junk email is strictly controlled and therefore less of a nuisance than in many other countries. The leading French search engine (*moteur de recherche*) is called Voilà (www.voila.fr).

Internet cafés (*webcafé*) are popular in France, where over 1,000 communes have been awarded the appellation '*Villes Internet*' for providing public internet centres (for a complete list, see www.villes-internet.net).

> La Poste offers the facility to send and receive emails from around 1,000 post offices, as well as via its website (www.laposte.fr or www.laposte. net).

Satellite Broadband

As with many other parts of Europe, France's broadband performance varies from region to region, depending on how remote your home or business is and whether a fast ADSL service is available. Satellite broadband provides a fast and reliable service irrespective of your location (although it can be affected by inclement weather), allowing you to work from home, stream films and TV programmes, and keep in touch with friends and family via email from anywhere in France. (Many providers use the KA-SAT high throughput Ka-band satellite, the first European satellite designed exclusively for Internet access.)

In recent years the quality and range of satellite internet offers has improved considerably, both in the speeds available and low fees, and there's now a wide range of options available. The main suppliers include Sky DSL (www.skydsl.eu), Europa Sat (UK 01869-397292, www.europasat.com), Internet Satellite (www.internetsatellite.fr), Nordnet (www.nordnet.com) and Alsatis (www.alsatis. com).

Most providers have basic offers starting at around €30 per month, to which you need to add a fixed monthly sum for telephone calls starting at around €7 per month, (more if you wish to include mobile calls). However, if you choose the telephone option you don't need to take out a fixed telephone line subscription (*abonnement*) with Orange or another provider.

With most offers the satellite and equipment (satellite dish, etc.) costs around €350, but it may be possible to pay for it through a higher monthly charge. Most suppliers require you to take out a contract for a minimum of 12 months or longer.

Internet Telephony

If you've a high speed ADSL broadband connection, you can make long-distance and international phone 'calls' free (or almost free) to anyone with a broadband connection using VOIP (voice over internet protocol), which has revolutionised the international telecommunications market in recent years.

A leading company in this field is Skype (www.skype.com), now owned by Microsoft, with some 75 million users worldwide, while others include Ring Central (www.ringcentral. co.uk) and Vonage (www.vonage.co.uk). There are numerous other companies in the market (a web search for 'VOIP' will throw up dozens), some of which also allow you to call landline phone numbers.

All you need is access to a local broadband service and a headset (costing as little as €15) or a special phone and you're in business. Calls to other computers anywhere in the world are free, while calls to landlines are charged at a few centimes per minute.

8.
TELEVISION & RADIO

*F*rench television (TV) and radio broadcasting is in a combination of state and private ownership. France has five public free-to-air television stations and you can watch more with a 'free-to-air' set top box (similar to the UK's Freeview). If you want more choice, including English-language programmes, you need to subscribe to satellite and cable television services or watch it online via the internet. Cable TV is available in the main cities and towns, although it's less common than in many other western European countries. Nowadays, most households have a combined television, telephone and broadband subscription, which may be via a phone line, cable or satellite.

TV and radio programmes are listed in daily newspapers, some of which provide free weekly programme guides with reviews and comments, and there's also a number of weekly TV guides, including *Télé Poche* and *Télé Z*.

TELEVISION

French TV is generally no worse than that in most other European countries, i.e. largely a mixture of news, sport, talk and game shows, plus dubbed American films and sitcoms. Police detective series are universally popular and imports from the UK, US, Italy, Germany and other countries are regularly shown in dubbed form (French TV rarely shows foreign material in its original language). There are also interesting documentaries, French drama series and films.

Terrestrial TV

France has six terrestrial stations broadcasting throughout the country (although reception is poor in some areas): France 2, France 3 and France 5 (publicly-owned and operated by France Télévision), TF1 and M6 (commercial free-to-air) and Canal Plus (subscription).

As in most European countries, all television broadcasts (whether terrestrial, cable or satellite) are digital (*télévision numérique terrestrial*) and analogue broadcasts were switched off in 2011. As with Freeview in the UK, through digital TV you can receive many new channels with a 'free-to-air' set top box (in addition to free-to-air terrestrial TV stations).

Main evening news programmes start at around 8pm and last half an hour. These are usually followed by weather forecasts (*prévision météorologique* or simply *météo*), which often include a traffic forecast for the coming weekend. The news and weather are usually followed by a film, serial or feature documentary on most channels. Films and some programmes are coded 10, 12, 16 or 18 in order to indicate their suitability (or unsuitability) for children.

There's advertising (*publicité* or *pub*) on all French channels, although the government favours funding state-owned channels through increased license fees and has already reduced the number of hours per day that they can screen commercials.

TF1 (Télévision Française 1, www.tf1. fr) boasts around 23 per cent of the viewing audience and is France's most popular TV channel. Its programming is conservative, although it's usually of good quality (with some decent series), with the notable exception of mindless game shows and soaps. Its news reporting is generally weak, although popular.

DVDs

DVDs may be encoded with a region code, restricting the area of the world in which they can be played. The code for Western Europe is 2, while discs without any region coding are called all-region or region 0 discs. However, you can buy all-region DVD players and DVD players can be modified to be region-free, allowing the playback of all discs (see www.regionfreedvd. net and www.moneysavingexpert.com/shopping/dvd-unlock).

France 2 (www.france2.fr) is liberal and progressive in its programming. Programmes include event coverage and interviews. News coverage is fairly nondescript and similar to TF1's. France 2 shows several of the better American dramas and screens major films during the week.

France 3 (www.france3.fr) is a network of regional stations and shares much of its programming with France 2, augmented by regional news, documentaries and environmental programmes. The quality of programmes has improved in the last decade and they're generally more intellectual than TF1 and France 2.

France 4 (www.france4.fr) is a French public channel owned by France Télévisions and dedicated to entertainment, including theatre, opera and French-language and other European drama. Originally launched as Festival, the channel took its current name in 2005 to match that of the other France Télévisions channels.

France 5 (also known as *La Cinquième*, www.france5.fr) is a public television network that's part of the France Télévisions group. It principally features educational programming – its motto is *la chaîne de la connaissance et du savoir* or 'the knowledge network' – in contrast to the group's two main channels, France 2 and France 3. France 5 is a welcome cultural alternative to commercial broadcasting, its output consisting largely of documentaries (health, education, politics, etc.) and cultural transmissions, foreign films in VO (*version originale*) with French subtitles, English comedy and no game shows. Not surprisingly, it's considered by many to be excessively highbrow.

Canal Plus (or Canal+, www.canalplus.fr) is Europe's largest pay channel (*chaîne à péage*) and main movie channel (and funder of the French film industry), with some 15 million subscribers. Apart from a few free-to-air (*en clair*) programmes, indicated in newspapers and programme guides by a + or * sign, the signal is scrambled. To receive scrambled programmes you must pay a subscription, usually via a cable or satellite TV package.

Canal Plus specialises in films and sports programmes, particularly live soccer matches. It shows its share of second-rate films, although the selection includes many television premieres of hit films, both French and American.

M6 (www.m6.fr) – also known as Metropole Television – broadcasts mostly general entertainment programmes. It shows many American programmes and other mainstream shows plus soft-porn movies, although it also screens some surprisingly good programmes.

Foreign Stations: If you live close to a French border you may also be able to receive foreign stations. In the Nord-Pas-de-Calais region it's possible to receive British and Belgian stations; those in northern Lorraine can receive Luxembourg TV; in Alsace many people watch German and Swiss TV; those near the Spanish and Italian borders can usually receive programmes broadcast in those countries; and in certain parts of the Côte d'Azur you can receive Télé Monte Carlo (which is also available on most cable and satellite networks).

Cable TV

Cable TV in France is mostly provided by Numericable (www.numericable.fr), which has a near-monopoly. Their fibre-optic cable network includes 160 cities and towns, offering over 150 TV channels. Subscription packages include both fixed-line and mobile telephones and internet access from around €20 per month. Programme listings for cable services are included in French TV guides.

Satellite TV

France is well served by satellite TV (*télévision par satellite*), and the main source of English-language satellite TV is Sky Television (see below). The English language media in France is packed with ads for satellite TV equipment and installation, which also allows you to receive high speed broadband in areas where it would otherwise be impossible (see **Satellite Broadband** on page 93). Suppliers in France include Big Dish Satellite (www.bigdishsat. com), which works closely with Europasat in the UK.

If you've a standard broadband satellite service with a download speed of at least 2Mbps you can use this to access UK catch-up TV. This is provided free by the major British broadcasters – BBC 1 and 2, ITV and Channel 4 – who repeat programmes (usually for a limited period, e.g. 30 days) previously aired via digital distribution. You can use an HDMI cable to connect your PC to your TV to get the best sound and picture quality.

Sky Television

It's possible to receive Sky TV (www.sky.com) throughout France, which provides access to up to 350 channels, including all the BBC and ITV channels. Sky offers a number of packages, including films and exclusive live sports events.

In recent years Sky reduced the footprint (the area of coverage) and the further you are from the UK the larger the dish you'll require. In the north of France you can get away with a 90cm dish, but in the south you'll probably need a 1.2m satellite dish, depending on your exact location.

To receive Sky television you need a Sky digital receiver (digibox) and a Sky viewing card. It's possible to subscribe in the UK or Ireland (personally, if you've an address there, or via a friend) and then take your Sky receiver and card to France. Alternatively, you can buy a digibox and obtain a Sky card in France. A number of companies advertise in the expatriate press or you can locate them via the internet, including Sky in France (www.skyinfrance.co.uk), Sky Europe (www.skyeurope.tv/sky-subscription-france) and UK Telecom (UK 01483-477100, www.uktelecom.net/ker-pow).

TV Licence

A TV licence (*redevance audiovisuelle*) is required by TV owners, and cost €137 per year in 2016. The licence fee covers any number of TVs (owned or rented), irrespective of where they're located in France, e.g. in holiday homes, motor vehicles or boats, although you must pay for a separate licence for TVs in accommodation that's let, e.g. *gîtes*. Even if you only have a foreign TV that you use solely for watching videos you must have a licence.

> You can also watch TV via a computer and web browser, although most UK TV services are blocked outside the country. Catch-up services use your IP (internet protocol) address, making it impossible or difficult to watch catch-up TV, although it's possible to get around this using a virtual private network (VPN) or proxy server, which channels your network traffic so that it appears to be coming from a different country (e.g. the UK). This is illegal, although it's estimated that some 65 million people worldwide regularly access, for example, the BBC catch-up TV service this wayy.

If you import a TV capable of receiving French programmes you should inform your local Centre Régional de la Redevance Audiovisuelle (listed under *Les infos administratives/Impôts et taxes* in the Yellow Pages – or you can obtain the address from your local post office or online) within 30 days.

The licence fee is now levied in conjunction with the *taxe d'habitation* and is therefore payable in December each year, although it's possible to pay in monthly instalments. If you're aged over 65 (on 1st January of the relevant year), paid no income tax in the previous year and live alone (or with other people in the same situation), you're exempt (*exonéré*) from paying the licence fee. To obtain exoneration or to declare that you've no TV, apply to your regional Centre de la Redevance.

If you buy a TV in France the retailer must inform the relevant authority and the TV licence fee will be added to your next residential tax bill. You'll be fined if you're found to have a TV without a licence when an inspector calls. If you dispose of your TV and don't replace it, you must notify the authorities, otherwise you remain liable to pay the licence fee.

RADIO

Radio was deregulated in France in the '80s, since when scores of local commercial radio stations have sprung up, representing diverse ethnic groups, lifestyles and communities. Some English-language broadcasters have established radio channels in areas of with a large expatriate population. Local stations often have small catchment areas and low transmitting power, although many have been grouped into national networks. The largest is operated by NRJ, a popular Paris music station.

When it come to digital radio, France was slower to adopt it than most of the rest of Europe and digital radio is still in the early stages there. However, as it was a latecomer to the party it was able to adopt DAB+, the very latest specification for digital broadcasting, which unfortunately isn't compatible with most UK digital radios

A radio licence isn't required in France.

French Radio

French radio is dominated by the five stations (see below) run by state-owned Radio France (www.radiofrance.fr), which are available throughout France, although the frequencies may vary from region to region.

- ◆ **France-Bleu:** Mixes light music and 'easy listening rock' with regional features and interviews.

- ◆ **France-Culture:** Talks, debates and interviews on the arts and literature, much of it highbrow (some would say pretentious).

- ◆ **France-Info:** An all-news channel with detailed news broadcasts every half an hour, followed by interviews and discussions of major issues. News stories and some features are repeated several times throughout the day.

- ◆ **France-Inter:** The main channel, broadcasting news bulletins, current affairs, magazine programmes, discussions, light music and plays. During the summer it broadcasts news bulletins in English.

- ◆ **France-Musiques:** Broadcasts mostly classical music, but also some jazz and 'world' music as well as cultural discussion programmes.

English-language Radio

Apart from English-language songs, there's little French radio in English, although in a few areas there are English-language stations run by expatriates, e.g. World Radio Paris (www.worldradioparis.fr) and Riviera Radio (http://rivieraradio.mc, 106.5FM) in the south of France. France's answer to the BBC World Service is Radio France Internationale (RFI,

www.rfi.fr), which broadcasts in some 19 languages, including English.

If you've an internet connection you can listen to hundreds of radio stations via websites such as www.internetradiouk.com (for UK radio stations) – including all the main BBC stations – www.live-radio.net/us.shtml (US radio stations) and www.internet-radio.com, which has links to hundreds of music stations from around the world which you can choose via genre. A recent internet radio station targeted at British expats in France is Expat Radio (http://ex-patradio.com), offering a mixture of chat and music delivered entirely in English.

You can also access a comprehensive list of internet radio stations via Wikipedia (https://en.wikipedia.org/wiki/list_of_internet_radio_stations) or you can search for a station online simply by typing its name into a search engine such as Google.

9.
EDUCATION

*F*rance spends more per capita on education than most other developed countries and has traditionally been noted for its high academic standards. However, although it remains a world leader in certain fields, overall it's rated only average by the Organisation for Economic Co-operation and Development (OECD) compared to other developed countries, and standards in state schools have fallen in recent years.

In France, parents are obliged to school their children between the ages of 6 to 16, which includes the children of foreign residents. The free state-funded school system is supplemented by a comprehensive network of private schools, including many distinguished international schools. Around 18 per cent of all French children attend private schools, mostly co-educational day schools, which generally achieve much better exam results than state schools (hence their increasing popularity). Higher education standards in France are only average, with the notable exception of the elite *grandes écoles*, which are rated among the world's best tertiary educational establishments.

French schools place great emphasis on the French language (particularly grammar), arithmetic and the sciences.

Schools usually impose more discipline than most foreign children are used to (teachers may use any disciplinary method other than corporal punishment), as well as more homework (*devoirs du soir*), which increases with the age of a child and can become onerous, particularly for children used to a more lax education system. France has a highly competitive and selective examination system that separates the brighter students from the less academically gifted at around the age of 14.

Education in France is compulsory between the ages of 6 and 16, and state schools are entirely free from nursery school through to university (free state schools have existed in France for over a century). Most children start free nursery school (from the age of two or three) and over 50 per cent of 18-21 year olds remain in full-time education or follow a vocational training course. Some two-thirds of pupils complete their secondary education and take the high-school leaving certificate examination (*baccalauréat* or the *baccalauréat professionnel*).

The curriculum is broadly the same in all schools of the same level throughout France, which allows children to move between schools and continue their education with the minimum disruption. Regions (or rather *académies*) do, however, have a certain amount of autonomy in setting school timetables, and school holidays vary from region to region (see page 105).

INSURANCE

It's advisable that schoolchildren in France are covered by liability insurance for damage and injury to themselves and third parties while at school or travelling to and from school; insurance isn't obligatory except for school trips such as skiing holidays but is highly recommended. Basic school insurance (*assurance scolaire de base*) covering a child for all school-related activity costs as little as €10 per year, but for a few euros more (between around €12 and €25 per year) you can cover your child for all eventualities, whether school-related or not, known as a *contrat scolaire et extrascolaire*.

Some schools provide an insurance proposal form at the beginning of each school year, but you aren't obliged to take out a school's policy. Whatever cover you choose, the insurer must provide an *attestation d'assurance scolaire* which you present to the school authorities.

ADAPTING TO THE SYSTEM

Generally, the younger your child is when he enters the French education system, the easier he'll cope; conversely the older he is the more problems he'll have adjusting. Foreign teenagers often have considerable problems learning French and adjusting to French school life. In some schools, foreign children who can't understand the language may be neglected and are just expected to 'get on with it'. In your early days it's therefore important to check exactly what your child is doing at school and whether he's making progress (not just with the language but also with their other lessons).

As a parent you should be prepared to support your children through this difficult period. If you aren't fluent in French you'll be aware how frustrating it is being unable to express yourself adequately, which can easily lead to feelings of inferiority and inadequacy.

It's also important for parents to ensure that their children maintain their native language, as it can easily be neglected. See also **Language** below.

For many children, being educated and living in a foreign land is a stimulating challenge, providing invaluable cultural and educational experiences. Your child will become bilingual and a 'world' citizen, less likely to be prejudiced against foreigners and foreign ideas. This is particularly true if he attends an international school with pupils from different countries, although many state schools also have pupils from a number of countries and backgrounds.

> Before making any major decisions about your child's future education, it's important to consider his ability, character and needs.

LANGUAGE

For most children, particularly those aged under ten, studying in French isn't such a handicap as it may first appear. The majority of children adapt quickly and most become reasonably fluent within three to six months (if only it were so easy for adults!). However, not all children adapt equally well to a change of language and culture, particularly those aged over ten (at around ten children begin to learn languages more slowly), many of whom encounter difficulties during their first year. It will help if your child has some intensive French lessons before arriving. It may also be possible to organise an educational or cultural exchange with a French school or family before moving to France, which is a considerable help in integrating a child into the language and culture.

Children who don't speak French may initially be put in a class below their age group or made to repeat a year until their language skills have reached an adequate level, which can make the first few months quite an ordeal for foreign children. However, some state schools provide free intensive French lessons (*classes d'initiation/CLIN* or *Français Langue Etrangère/FLE*) for foreign children and have international sections for foreign pupils. It may be worthwhile inquiring about the availability of extra French classes before choosing where to live. Once a child has acquired sufficient knowledge of spoken and written French he's integrated into a regular class in a local school.

The only schools in France using English as the teaching language are a few foreign and international private schools (see page 114). If your children attend any other school, they must study all subjects in French. Many state schools teach regional languages, including Alsatian, Basque, Breton, Catalan, Corsican, Provençal and Occitan, which are usually optional and taught for around three hours a week, generally outside normal school hours. The exceptions are Breton, which is used exclusively in the early classes in some schools in Brittany, and Provence, where a small number of primary schools teach French and Provençal bilingually. See also **Learning French** on page 118.

INFORMATION

Information about French schools, both state and private, can be obtained from French embassies and consulates abroad, and from foreign embassies, educational organisations and government departments in France. The Fédération des Écoles, des Parents et des Educateurs (01 47 53 62 70, www.ecoledesparents.org) provides free advice for parents on all aspects of education and careers, as does the Office National d'Information sur les Enseignements et les Professions (ONISEP, www.onisep.fr), which has regional offices in France and publishes regional guides to education and careers.

The Association of American Wives of Europeans (01 40 70 11 80, www.aaweparis. org), a member of the Federation of American Women's Clubs Overseas (FAWCO), publishes the *AAWE Guide to Education*, which claims to be the definitive guide to educating English-speaking children in France, with information on over 120 English language and bilingual school programmes throughout the country.

Other useful websites include the French Ministry of Education's site (www.education. gouv.fr) and the Public Service site (www. service-public.fr), which has sections on education (*enseignement*) and training (*formation*). The French Ministry of Education provides a nationwide free information service through Centre d'Information et d'Orientation (CIO, www.uclouvain.be/cio.html) offices. For the address of your local CIO office contact your town hall (*mairie*), which can also provide local information.

STATE SCHOOLS

French state-funded schools are called 'public schools' (*école publique*), although the term 'state' has been used in this book in order to prevent misunderstandings (a 'public school' in the UK is a private, fee-paying school). The state school system in France differs considerably from the school systems in, for example, the UK or the US, particularly regarding secondary education.

The Ministry of National Education, Youth and Sport is responsible for most of France's state education system, which divides the country into academies (*académies*), which confusingly don't correspond to the 22 regions, each made up of a number of *départements* headed by a superintendent (*recteur*) and attached to at least one university. The *académies* set the curriculum and examinations (all schools in the same *académie* have the same exam questions), but a high degree of consultation ensures that standards vary little from *académie* to *académie*.

Children usually go to local nursery and primary schools, but attending secondary school often entails travelling long distances. One of the consequences of the depopulation of rural areas in recent years has been the closure of many schools, resulting in children having to travel further to school, although in most areas there's an efficient school bus service.

A general criticism of French state schools is the lack of extra-curricular activities such as sport, music, drama, and arts and crafts, and over half of pupils have no access to gymnasia, sports grounds or a swimming pool. State schools have no school clubs or sports teams and if a child wants to do team sports he must join a local club. On the plus side, children are taught calligraphy (French handwriting may be quite different from the style you're used to), grammar (every French child knows the difference between a direct object and an indirect object!), philosophy and ethics, environmental studies and civics.

Note that class numbering in French state schools differs considerably from the US and British systems. The French system is almost the exact reverse of the US system. Instead of rising from 1 to 12, the French start in the 11th form (grade) at the age of six and end in the first form, followed by the *classe terminale*, the last year of high school (*lycée*) at age 18 or 19. If pupils fall behind at secondary school they're often required to repeat a year (*redoubler*), although this is seldom the case in nursery and primary schools.

Having made the decision to send your child to a state school you should stick to it for at least a year to give it a fair trial. It may take a child this long to fully adapt to a new language, a change of environment and a different curriculum. If you wish to change your child's school, you must obtain a *certificat de radiation* from his current school.

Enrolment

Children must attend a state school within a certain distance of their homes, so if you've a preference for a particular school it's important to buy or rent a home within that school's catchment area (which may change periodically in accordance with demographic changes). Information about schools in a particular area can be obtained from the schools information service (*service des écoles*) at your local town hall.

You can request (*dérogation*) that your child attends a different school from the one assigned, but you must usually have good reasons for doing so, e.g. another of your children already attends your preferred school, the preferred school is close to your place of work or it teaches a unique course that you wish your child to follow, such as certain foreign languages. The transfer must be approved by the *directeurs* of both schools.

To enrol your child in a French school you must compile an 'enrolment file' (*dossier d'inscription*) at your town hall (for primary schools) or at the *rectorat* school service (for secondary schools) and provide documentation. This includes proof of residence (such as an electricity or telephone bill), a birth certificate (with an official French translation), proof of immunisation, evidence of insurance, plus – if a child is currently attending another French school – a *certificat de radiation* issued by his previous school.

School Hours

French state schools have abandoned the four-day week (*semaine de quatre jours*) with Wednesday remaining free and Saturday lessons. A standard five-day, Monday to Friday, week is now usual. Contact your local education department or town hall to check the school hours in your area.

School hours also vary depending on the type of school. Nursery school hours are from 8.30 or 9am to 11.30am or noon and from 1.30 or 2pm to around 4.30pm. There's a 15-minute break in the mornings and afternoons. Primary school consists of around 26 hours per week, usually from 08.30-11.30am and 1.30-4.30pm. In a secondary *collège*, students attend school for around 27 or 28 hours per week and in a *lycée* for 30 to 36 hours (depending on the type of *lycée*). The school hours for a *lycée* are usually from 8am to noon and 2-5pm, although some start at 9am and finish at 6pm.

Most schools provide (free) buses, which collect children from outlying regions and return them home at the end of the day, which often adds considerably to the school day. State schools and communities usually provide an after-school nursery (*garderie*) for working mothers.

Holidays

French children have the longest school holidays (*vacances scolaires*) in the world amounting to over 100 days (excluding weekends in term time and some public holidays). They generally attend school for 160 days a year only, from early September until late June, although they compensate with long school hours and abundant homework (from primary school onwards). Winter and spring school holidays vary from town to town according to a system of zones (see www. schoolholidayseurope.eu/france.htmltable) in order to allow ski resorts to cope with the flood of children during these periods. Term dates may be modified to take account of local circumstances. Schools are also closed on public holidays (see page 41) when they fall within term time.

The school year is made up of five terms, each averaging around seven weeks. Current and future term and holiday dates can be found on the Ministry of Education's website (www. education.gouv.fr – click on '*Le calendrier scolaire*'). Schools and local communities publish school holiday dates well in advance, thus allowing parents plenty of time to schedule family holidays.

Usually you aren't permitted to withdraw your children from classes during the school term except for visits to a doctor or dentist, when the teacher should be informed in advance. In primary school a note to the teacher is sufficient, while in secondary school an official absence form must be completed by the teacher concerned and submitted to the school office. For absences of over two days, a doctor's certificate is required.

Provisions

Education is free in France, but pens/pencils, stationery and sports clothes/equipment must be provided by parents. Most other provisions are provided in primary schools (ages 6 to 11) and in *collèges* (ages 12 to 15), although parents may need to buy some books; however, 'everything' must be purchased by parents of children attending a *lycée*. Secondary school students also require a number of passport-size photographs.

Primary school children require a school bag or satchel; a pencil case, pencils and crayons, stationery, etc.; gym shoes, shorts and a towel for games and exercise periods; and possibly a sports bag. You may be given a list of the items required (*liste des fournitures de rentrée*) at the end of the summer term or the beginning of the autumn term. Don't forget name tapes (*noms tissés sur ruban*) for coats and sports equipment, which can be ordered from a *mercerie* or you can simply use write on tape in indelible ink, but it's better to sew them into clothing rather than use iron-on tapes.

At nursery school children usually take snacks for breaks but at other schools they either go home for lunch or eat at the school canteen (*cantine*), where gourmet-style meals are available. The cost of lunch at a nursery or primary school varies with the area, the parents' income and whether they live within a school's catchment area. Lunch at secondary school costs around €100 per term. Children who have school lunches are called *demi-pensionaires* and those who go home for lunch

are *externes*. (Taking a packed lunch isn't usually considered an option and may even be forbidden.) Lunch may consist of five courses and can last up to two hours, and there may be no 'tuck shop' or even vending machines.

With the exception of a few 'exclusive' schools, school uniforms are non-existent in France, although there may be dress codes regarding what may and may not be worn. Pupils aren't permitted to wear any 'signs of religious affiliation' such as crucifixes or headscarves.

Nursery & Primary School Cycles

Nursery and primary schooling are divided into educational cycles (*cycles pédagogiques*), each of three years' duration as follows:

1. *Cycle des Apprentissages Premiers* comprising the three sections of nursery school from the age of three to six (*les petits, les moyens* and *les grands* – see **Nursery School** below).
2. *Cycle des Apprentissages Fondamentaux* comprising the final year of nursery school and the first two years of primary school (*cours préparatoire/CP* and *cours élémentaire 1/CE1*).
3. *Cycle des Approfondissements* including the primary school years *cours élémentaire 2/ CE2, cours moyen 1/CM1* and *cours moyen 2/CM2*.

Although each cycle normally lasts three years, it can be completed in two or four, depending on a child's progress. The decision whether a child is ready to progress to the next cycle is made jointly by a teachers' council (*conseil des maîtres de cycles*), the school director, the pupil's teachers and a psycho-pedagogical group. It's no longer possible to fail a year and have to repeat it, as the system allows pupils to progress at their own speed and doesn't require them to repeat the same work as in the previous year. A school record book (*livret scolaire*) is maintained for each child during the three cycles.

Pre-school

Children aged between two months and three years can be left at a *crèche*, usually on the condition that both parents work. There are four kinds of *crèche*: 'collective' crèches (*crèche collective*) run by the local community, which are the most popular choice and therefore oversubscribed; 'mini-crèches' (*mini-crèche*), which are similar to collective crèches, only smaller; parental crèches (*crèche parentale*) organised by groups of parents and limited to 16 children; and family crèches (*crèche familiale*) where you leave your children at the home of a 'maternal assistant' (*assistante maternelle*).

☑ **SURVIVAL TIP**

If you leave your child with an *assistante maternelle*, you should ensure that she's accredited (*agréée*) by the Protection Maternelle et Infantile (PMI).

Crèches are usually open between 7am and 7pm on weekdays. The cost of a *crèche collective* varies depending on the number of children accommodated, the parents' salaries and the commune. Contact your local Service de la Petite Enfance or Caisse d'Allocations Familiales (CAF) for details. To find out about parental crèches, contact the Association des Collectifs Enfants Parents Professionels (ACEPP, www.acepp.asso.fr).

If you need a crèche only occasionally (i.e. both parents don't work full-time) children between three months and six years old can be left for up to a day at a time at a *halte-garderie* or *jardin d'enfants* or a *multi-accueil* centre (limited to 20 children). If children need looking after for a short time before or after school, they can be accommodated by an *accueil péri-scolaire* or a *centre de loisirs sans hébergement* (minimum age three years), sometimes attached to a nursery school.

If you can afford it, you can employ a (tax-deductible) child-minder (*garde d'enfant à domicile*) or nanny (*nounou*), who must, however, be declared to the authorities as a salaried employee and be paid at least the minimum wage.

Nursery School

Nursery schooling between the ages of two and six years is optional. France has a long tradition of free, state-funded nursery schools (*école maternelle*) and has one of the best programmes in the world. Some 80 per cent of women with one child and around 50 per cent of those with two or three children work, and most make use of some form of nursery school.

In many areas facilities are in short supply and, although a place is theoretically available in nursery school for every three-year-old whose parents request one, you may need to enrol your child virtually at conception! (Normal enrolment takes place during the April before the start of the school year.) The place must be in a nursery school or an infant class (*classe enfantine*) in a primary school as close as possible to a child's home. Priority is given to children living in underprivileged areas, children with two working parents, children from families with three or more young children, and children who live too far from school to go home for lunch.

Nursery school hours are generally from 8.30 or 9am to 11.30am or noon and from 1.30 or 2pm to 4-4.30pm. Young children usually sleep for two hours after lunch. Children may have lunch at the school canteen by arrangement. For parents who are unable to collect their children when school is over, there's usually a supervised nursery (*garderie*) until around 6pm.

Nursery school has traditionally been divided into three stages, according to age: *les petits* – from two to four years, *les moyens* – from four to five years, and *les grands* – from five to six years. However, this isn't official terminology. The three years of primary school from age three to six are included in the first of the *cycles pédagogiques* and the last year is incorporated in the second cycle.

Nursery school is designed to introduce children to the social environment of school and to develop the basic skills of coordination. It encourages the development of self-awareness and provides an introduction to group activities. Exercises include arts and crafts (e.g. drawing, painting and pottery), music, educational games and perceptual activities, e.g. listening skills. During the final years the rudiments of reading, writing and arithmetic are taught in preparation for primary school.

Primary School

Primary school (école primaire or élémentaire) attendance is compulsory between the ages of 6 and 11 for around 26 hours per week. Schools are established and maintained

Primary School Structure

Age	Form/Grade	Course
6 to 7	11e	*cours préparatoire/CP*
7 to 8	10e	*cours élémentaire 1/CE1*
8 to 9	9e	*cours élémentaire 2/CE2*
9 to 10	8e	*cours moyen 1/CM1*
10 to 11	7e	*cours moyen 2/CM2*

by local communities, although overall responsibility lies with the state. Each primary school has a director (*directeur/directrice*), who presides over the school council (*conseil d'école*). The council makes decisions regarding school regulations, communication between teachers and parents, school meals, after school care (*garderie*), extra-curricular activities, security and hygiene.

The school council usually meets twice a year and comprises a teachers' committee (*comité des maîtres*), a parents' committee (*comité des parents*) and representatives of the local education authority and municipality. The parents' committee is the equivalent of the parent-teacher association (PTA) in many other countries.

The five years of primary school are structured as shown in the table below. The subjects taught at primary school are divided into three main groups: French, history, geography and civic studies; mathematics, science and technology; physical education and sport, arts and crafts, and music. Minimum and maximum numbers of tuition hours are set for each group of subjects, although teachers are allowed flexibility in determining the hours so they can place more emphasis on certain subjects for individual pupils, based on their strengths and weaknesses.

The main objectives of primary school are the learning and consolidation of reading, writing and mathematics. There are no examinations at the end of primary school, although a child's primary record is forwarded to his secondary school. However, all children are expected to be able to read and write French by the end of their first term in primary school and are tested to see whether they're up to standard.

Homework is required from the start of primary school and primary school children have a notebook (*cahier de texte*) that they bring home each day. Parents sign the book to verify that a child has done his homework and teachers use it to convey messages to parents, e.g. special items a child requires for school the next day. Some *assistantes maternelles* use a similar system, which provides a comprehensive record of a child's school years.

Secondary School

Secondary education is compulsory until the age of 16 and includes attendance at a *collège* until the age of 15. At age 15, continuing education is decided by examination: students with the greatest academic aptitude go to a *lycée* (high school) until they're 18 (*cycle long*) to study for the *baccalauréat*, while others follow shortened studies (*cycle court*) in a vocational course. These include the study for a *brevet d'enseignement professionnel* (BEP) or *certificat d'aptitude professionnelle* (CAP), which can lead to a *baccalauréat professionnel* in a 'professional' *lycée*.

At the end of *collège* a certificate of competence is issued for particular skills, provided a certain level of language ability has also been attained. Students can repeat a year until they pass the final examinations and few leave without a certificate.

The secondary school(s) your child attends is primarily determined by where you live. In some rural areas there's little or no choice, while in Paris and other cities there are usually a number of possibilities. As in all countries the schools with the best reputations and exam results are the most popular and are therefore the most difficult to gain entry to. Parents should plan well ahead, particularly if they want a child to be accepted by a superior *collège* or *lycée*. Some *collèges* are attached to *lycées*, with *collège* students granted preferential entrance to the *lycée*.

Collège

At the age of 11 all children attend a *collège* (formerly known as a *collège d'enseignement secondaire/CES*), headed by a *principal*. The school year is organised on a trimester basis (a period of three months equating to a term) and students are evaluated by teachers (*conseil des professeurs*) at the end of each trimester. This evaluation is particularly important as it determines the future studies open to a student and the type of *baccalauréat* that he may take (see below). It's common for school class councils (*conseil de classes*) to recommend that a student repeat a year of *collège*.

The four years of *collège* education are numbered from the 6th to the 3rd and are divided into two two-year cycles, described below.

Cycle d'Observation: The first two years of *collège* (sixth and fifth forms) are called the 'observation' cycle, where all students

follow a common curriculum. General lessons total around 25 hours per week and include French, mathematics, a modern foreign language, history, geography, economics, civics, physics and chemistry, biology and geology, technology, art, physical education and sport. A further three hours (*heure de soutien*) of lessons are set each week in subjects chosen by the *collège* (usually French, mathematics and a foreign language), depending on individual students' needs. At the end of the fifth form, students move to the orientation cycle (cycle d'orientation) or fourth form, or repeat the fifth form.

Cycle d'Orientation: The last two years of *collège* (fourth and third forms) are called the 'orientation cycle' as students are allowed some choice of subjects and can thus begin to decide the future direction (*orientation*) of their studies. Students follow a common curriculum of around 25 hours of lessons a week in the same subjects as in the sixth and fifth forms. In addition to the core subjects, there are compulsory lessons in a second foreign language chosen from a list of options (*option obligatoire*), and optional classes (*options facultatives*) in a regional language or a classical language, i.e. Greek or Latin.

Decisions regarding future studies are made at the end of the third form (at around the age of 14), when exams are taken to decide whether students will go on to a *lycée* and sit the *baccalauréat* (see below), attend a vocational *lycée* or take an apprenticeship.

Technology fourth and third forms offer a more practical educational approach for students suited to a less academic form of learning. Students who attain the age of 14 or 15 and haven't reached the necessary level to move on to the fourth form are taught in small pre-vocational classes (*Classes Préprofessionnelles de Niveau/ CPPN*). Here they receive extra lessons, particularly in French and mathematics, in order to enable them to continue their studies, while others continue with preparatory apprenticeship classes (*Classes Préparatoires à l'Apprentissage/CPA*).

At the end of their last year at *collège* students sit a written examination (*brevet des collèges*) in French, mathematics and history/geography. The *brevet* is the entrance examination to a *lycée*, although failure doesn't exclude students from going on to higher education.

Lycée

A *lycée* (headed by a *proviseur*) is roughly equivalent to a sixth form college in the UK and similar in standard to a grammar or high school (but higher than a US high school or two-year college), which provides an excellent education that's the equal of any school system in the world. It's the aim of all ambitious students to attend a *lycée*, where competition for places is fierce.

At a *lycée* students are treated more like university students and aren't required to remain in school if they don't have lessons.

However, the informal, often casual, air contrasts with the constant pressure of monthly tests (*interrogation*) and the writing of formal dissertations in most subjects. It goes without saying that unless a student is prepared to work hard it's a waste of time attending a *lycée*.

In rural areas *lycées* take students from a wide area and, because of the travelling distances involved, many offer boarding (*internat*) for four nights per week (Mondays to Thursdays) and a few accept boarders (*internes*) on Sunday nights.

There are two types of *lycée*, a general and technology *lycée* and a vocational *lycée*:

A **general and technology** *lycée* (*Lycée d'Enseignement Général et Technologique*) prepares students for the general or technology *baccalauréat* (see below) or the technical certificate (*brevet de technicien/BT*). There are also professional *lycées* (*Lycées Professionnels/LP*) and *Centres de Formation d'Apprentis* (*CFA*) offering courses leading to vocational certificates.

The course is divided into second (*seconde*), first (*première*) and final (*terminale*) years. Second form or *classe de seconde de détermination* is so called because it prepares students to choose the type of *baccalauréat* they'll take. Few second-form students specialise and work for a specific *baccalauréat*, with the exception of music, dance and certain technical subjects. During their second form students study French, mathematics, a modern foreign language, history, geography, physics, chemistry, biology and geology, and have physical education and sports lessons. It's possible to transfer from a practical to an academic course or vice versa by way of a transition class (*classe passerelle*).

Vocational *lycée* (*Lycée Professionnel/LP*) courses lead to vocational certificates. These include the *brevet d'études professionnelles* (*BEP*) and the *certificat d'aptitude* *professionnelle* (*CAP*). The *BEP* certificate covers the range of knowledge required in a particular trade or industrial, commercial, administrative or social sector, rather than a specific skill. The *CAP* is more specialised and is awarded for skill in a particular trade, e.g. carpentry, plumbing or dressmaking. In addition to school lessons, the *BEP* and *CAP* programmes include practical experience with companies that provide students with an introduction to the workplace.

After passing the *CAP*, students may be permitted to enter the 'special second form' (*seconde spéciale* or *spécifique*), where they undertake three years of technological studies leading to the *BT*. Students with a *BEP* or *CAP* can also take a technology or vocational *baccalauréat*, known as a *baccalauréat professionnel*, after a further two years' study (see below).

Baccalauréat

The *baccalauréat* (commonly called the *bac*) is taken at a *lycée* at the age of 18 or 19 and is an automatic entrance qualification to a French

MINISTÈRE DE L'ÉDUCATION NATIONALE

ACADÉMIE DE VERSAILLES

RÉPUBLIQUE

FRANÇAISE

DIPLÔME
DU BACCALAURÉAT GÉNÉRAL

Vu le procès-verbal de l'examen du baccalauréat général établi le 11 Juillet 2000 par le président du jury, enseignant-chercheur,

Le diplôme du baccalauréat général

en ECONOMIQUE ET SOCIALE AVEC LA MENTION ASSEZ BIEN

est conféré à

né(e) le   à FONTENAY AUX ROSES (092)

pour en jouir avec les droits et prérogatives qui y sont attachés.

FRANÇAISE

fait à ARCUEIL, le 01 Septembre 2000

Le recteur de l'académie de Versailles
Signé : D. BANCEL

N° 003137003451

university. Those who pass are known as *bacheliers*. There are over 30 *baccalauréats* to

choose from, but three main groups as shown below:

General *baccalauréat:* The general *bac* is an academic diploma and prepares students for higher education rather than for a trade or profession. It enables students to continue their studies at university, in preparatory classes for a *grande école* (see below), in a higher technicians' section (*STS*), in a university institute of technology or in specialised schools. There are three main types of general *bac*: literature and classics; science; and economic and social sciences.

Technology *baccalauréat:* This is awarded for general knowledge and for training in modern technologies. It's the first stage of higher technical training, usually at a university institute of technology or *STS*, and occasionally at a university or *grande école*. There are eight types of technology *bac*: industrial; science and technology; laboratory science; medical and social science; agriculture; environment; hotel and catering; and music and dance.

Vocational *baccalauréat:* Also known as the *baccalauréat professionnel*, this is chosen by an increasing number of students and has enjoyed huge success since its introduction. The majority of those who pass the exam go straight into employment, although it also entitles them to enter higher education. A major feature of the vocational *baccalauréat* course is that students spend a quarter of their time training in industry.

Within the above three basic groups there are four 'series' (*série*) of *bac*: A, B, C and D in ascending order of difficulty and importance. For example, those wishing to study medicine usually take *Bac* D, and *Bacs* C and D are the most common among those wishing to attend a *grande école* (see below). Among students planning to go to university, *Bacs* A and B are common.

European universities and most US colleges recognise the French *baccalauréat* as an entrance qualification, although foreign students must provide proof of their English language ability to study in the UK or the US. A US university may grant credits to a *bachelier*, allowing him to graduate in three years instead of four.

The international baccalaureate option (*option internationale du baccalauréat/OIB*) and international baccalaureate (IB) examinations are offered by some international *lycées* in France (and *lycées* with international sections).

Grandes Écoles Preparatory School

Grandes écoles preparatory schools (*classes préparatoires aux grandes écoles/CPGE* or *prépa* for short) are the first step for anyone with ambitions to attend a *grande école*, France's elite higher education institutions. Admission to a *prépa* is based on a student's grades in his final (*terminale*) year at *lycée* and the subjects chosen. For example, to attend a science *CPGE,* a student must take a C or D science *baccalauréat.* Usually, students require an average score of 14 (*mention bien*) to be accepted.

Applications must be made by 1st May, i.e. before actually sitting the *baccalauréat*, with provisional selection based on school reports for the final year of *lycée* and teachers' reports. Entrance to a *prépa* constitutes a first selection procedure before the competitive examination (*concours*) for the *grande école*, taken at the end of the two-year period. This exam has a failure rate of around 90 per cent!

PRIVATE SCHOOLS

There's a wide range of private schools (*écoles privées*) in France, including parochial (mostly Catholic) schools, bilingual schools, international schools and a variety of foreign schools, including US and British schools (see below). Together they educate around 18 per cent of French children, some 14 per cent in primary schools and 22 per cent in secondary schools.

Most private schools are co-educational, non-denominational day schools (Catholic private schools usually admit non-Catholics and aren't allowed to promote Catholicism). Most private schools operate a Monday to Friday timetable. There are few private boarding schools (*internat*) in France, although some schools provide weekly (Monday to Friday) boarding or accommodate children with 'host' families.

The cost of private schooling can be surprisingly reasonable – fees are typically €1,000-2,000 per year – particularly for those used to eye-watering UK school fees. Private education is increasingly popular in France (thanks in part to poor performing state schools) and many schools are oversubscribed.

Enrolment is often carried out on a first-come, first-served basis and prospective pupils (and their parents) may have to arrive very early on enrolment day to be sure of a place – for admission to some schools overnight camping is recommended!

For a list of private schools in a particular town or region, visit www.servicepublic.fr and search for '*Écoles privées*' or contact your local Centre d'Information et d'Orientation (ask at your *mairie* for details). The Office de Documentation et d'Information de l'Enseignement Privé (ODIEP, www.odiep.com) provides information about private schools, from nursery to university level. APEL (www.apel.fr) provides information about parochial schools, while the Centre National de

Documentation sur l'Enseignement Privé (www. enseignement-prive.org) publishes a list of all French private schools.

Bilingual, International & Foreign Schools

Some schools are classified as bilingual (*avec section bilingue* or *classes bilingues*) or international (e.g. *lycée international* or *avec section internationale*). Certain bilingual schools, such as the Ecole Active Bilingue in Paris, have US, British and French sections, while the Ecole Internationale de Paris teaches in both French and English. Most American and British schools are in the Paris area and on the French Riviera. Note, however, that the curriculum in most bilingual schools is tailored to children whose mother tongue is French. Places in bilingual and international schools are in strong demand and there are usually stiff entrance requirements.

> The only school in France teaching the UK curriculum is the British School of Paris (01 34 80 45 90, www.britishschool.fr).

There are international schools in Aix-en-Provence, Bordeaux, Cannes, Grenoble, Lille, Lyon, Nice and nearby Sophia Antipolis, Saint-Etienne, Strasbourg and Toulouse, as well as in Luynes in Alpes-Maritimes and in Monaco. The Lycée International at Saint-Germain-en-Laye (near Paris) has nine national sections (American, British, Danish, Dutch, German, Italian, Portuguese, Spanish and Swedish). Each section aims to teach children about the language, literature and history of the particular language/country selected, although all other lessons are taught in French. Where applicable, students who don't speak French are usually given intensive French lessons for three to six months.

Private schools in France teach a variety of syllabi, including the British GCSE and A Level examinations, American High School Diploma and college entrance examinations (e.g. ACT, SAT, achievement tests and AP exams), and the Option Internationale du Baccalauréat (OIB) and International Baccalaureate (IB). However, many schools offer bilingual children the French *baccalauréat* only. A number of private schools in France also follow unorthodox methods of teaching, such as Montessori nursery schools and Rudolf Steiner schools, plus schools for children with special language requirements.

There are two main types of private school in France: those with a contract with the French government (*sous contrat d'association*) and those without (*hors contrat* or *école libre*). A private school with a contract must follow the same educational programme as state schools, in return for which it receives government subsidies and is therefore less expensive than an *hors contrat* school. A private school without a contract is free to set its own curriculum, receives no state subsidies and is therefore more expensive.

Private school fees also vary considerably depending on the quality, reputation and location of a school and range from as little as €300 per year for a Catholic private school that's *sous contrat* to well over €15,000 per year for an independent (*hors contrat*) international senior day school. Fees aren't all-inclusive and there are additional obligatory charges (such as registration fees) as well as optional fees.

HIGHER EDUCATION

France has numerous higher education (*enseignement supérieur*) institutions, including over 75 traditional universities (13 in the Paris region) and around 250 *grandes écoles* and *écoles supérieures* (see below).

French Universities

Universities are the weakest part of the French education system and are obliged to accept anyone who passes the French baccalauréat examination – some 30 per cent of secondary students (around 1m) – resulting in overcrowding, under-funding and generally mediocre standards. Lecture halls are packed and students have no tutorial system and little supervision. These problems are exacerbated by the length of time it takes to obtain a degree in France, where the average leaving age is around 30! Most courses aren't tailored to specific careers and a huge number of students fail to obtain a degree.

Although still famous (particularly among foreigners), the Sorbonne is little more than a building housing part of the sprawling Université de Paris, and it has lost much of its eminence within France to the grandes écoles.

Entrance Qualifications

Anyone who passes the French baccalauréat examination is guaranteed entry to a university, but not necessarily to study the subject of his choice. Schools of medicine, dentistry and pharmacy are attached to certain universities, where entry is restricted to the top 25 per cent of students with a Baccalauréat C. Other restricted entry institutions include schools of economics and law.

Foreign students comprise around 10 per cent of the university intake, most coming from North Africa, although there's also large numbers from EU countries, South America and China. There are quotas for foreign students at certain universities and for particular courses. Foreign students are admitted to French universities on the basis of equivalent qualifications to the French baccalauréat. French universities accept British A Levels as an entrance qualification, but an American high school diploma isn't generally accepted, and American students must usually have spent a year at college or have a BA, BBA or BSc degree.

All foreign students require a thorough knowledge of French, which is usually examined if a baccalauréat certificate isn't

furnished. French language preparatory courses are provided.

Overseas students must complete an initial registration form (*dossier de demande de première admission en premier cycle*) and lodge their application by 1st February for entry the following October (the academic year runs from October to June). Application forms are available from the cultural sections of French embassies. Applicants must present a residence permit valid for at least a year or that of their parents if they have a residence permit. Application must be made to three universities, at least two of which must be outside Paris.

Curriculum & Exams

During their first two years at university (called Stage I), students study a core curriculum, and in their second year take the *diplôme d'études universitaires générales* or *DEUG*. There are nine types of *DEUG*: economic and social administration, law, literature and language, the arts, economics and management, science and technical studies, physical and sports studies, human and social sciences, and theology. The *DEUG* has a high failure rate; almost half of undergraduates failing to complete their degrees, although students may be given a third year in which to pass.

Those who pass the *DEUG* can take a degree (*licence*) in arts and sciences (equivalent to a BA or BSc) after a further year, or two years in the case of economics and law. The *licence* is classified as the first year of Stage II studies.   A *maîtrise*, roughly equivalent to an MA, is awarded after completion of the second year of Stage II studies, one year after gaining a *licence*. In certain subjects, e.g. science and technology, business studies and computer science, a *licence* isn't awarded, and after

obtaining a *DEUG*, students study for a further two years for a *maîtrise*. Students can study for a further three or four years after receiving their *maîtrise* for a doctorate (*doctorat*) or Stage III degree.

Recent reforms aim to 'harmonise' French higher education with that of other European countries by introducing a system known as *licence, master* and *doctorat* (*LMD*), and awarding students credits (*crédits*) for each course.

Fees & Grants

University students don't pay tuition fees and the costs for foreign students are minimal, depending on the options chosen. Between €200 and €300 is sufficient to cover registration fees, including obligatory fees for health insurance and social security. Students aged over 26 are required to take out health insurance in their country of origin or insurance under the French social security system on arrival in France. However, many universities charge 'illegal' course fees, which are usually quite modest but can run into , several thousand euros.

Government grants (*bourse*) are awarded to around 20 per cent of students. The maximum grant is €5,500 per year, although most grants are around €1,000. Grants are also available to students wishing to study abroad and scholarships are provided by international

organisations and foreign governments (see www.european-funding-guide.eu/articles/ scholarships/grants-and-loans-france for information).

> Note that students require numerous passport-size photographs (usually on a white background) and photocopies and translations of relevant documents.

Banks make long-term, low-interest loans for quite large amounts if they judge the applicant to be a high-calibre student, i.e. one who will earn enough to repay the loan! Parents are obliged by law to support their children at university until they're 20, after which age they're officially financially self-reliant. One in three students support themselves during their studies by working part-time during terms and over holiday periods.

Accommodation

Students are eligible for a room in a university hall of residence, although places are limited and accommodation is generally poor. Students should expect to pay around €150 to €200 per month for a room in a hall of residence and between €250 and €350 per month for a private room (more in Paris). Foreign students need around €750 to €1,000 per month to live in Paris (less in the provinces). Many students attend the nearest university to their home and treat university as an extension of school, particularly in Paris and other large cities where accommodation is expensive.

CROUS (see **Information** below) subsidise some university accommodation and student restaurants but not all, therefore you may wish to contact CROUS before choosing a university.

American Universities & Colleges

There are a number of American colleges and universities in France, including the American University in Paris (AUP), where all classes are taught in English and the 1,000-strong student body comes from over 70 countries. The AUP offers both BA and BSc degrees, and students can study for a BA in seven fields, including international business, art, history and European culture. Fees for a full academic year are around €15,000, excluding health insurance, accommodation and deposits.

A popular American college in Paris is the Parsons School of Design (a division of New York's New School for Social Research), where students take a four-year Bachelor of Fine Arts (BFA) degree. The Paris American Academy, which specialises in fine arts, fashion, languages and interior design, also has a good reputation. There are many other American colleges in Paris offering a range of subjects and degrees (from a BA to an MBA).

Information

The Centres Régionaux des Oeuvres Universitaires et Scolaires (CROUS, 01 44 18 53 00, www.crous-city.fr – replace 'city' with the name of the city, such as www.crous-paris. fr) are responsible for foreign students in France and provide information about courses, grants and accommodation. In Paris students can contact the Centre National des Oeuvres Universitaires et Scolaires (CNOUS, www. cnous.fr).

The French Ministry of Education's website (www.education.gouv.fr) provides information about the organisation of the French university system and also has a list of all state universities. All state universities are listed on the Education Ministry's website, which has another site aimed at making it easier for students with a *bac* to find a suitable course in France or abroad, obtain a grant and even find accommodation (www.etudiant.gouv.fr). The cultural section of French embassies also provides information about higher education.

FURTHER EDUCATION

Further education generally embraces everything except first degree courses taken at universities, *grandes écoles* and other institutions of higher education, although the distinction between further and higher education (see above) is often blurred.

Each year many thousands of students attend further education courses at universities alone, often of short duration and job-related, although courses may be full-or part-time

and include summer terms. France has many private colleges and other university-level institutions, some affiliated to foreign (usually US) universities, which include business and commercial colleges, hotel and restaurant schools, language schools and finishing schools.

Many educational institutions offer American MBA degree courses, including the European University in Paris and Toulouse. Among the most popular MBA subjects are banking, business administration, communications,

economics, European languages, information systems, management, marketing, public relations, and social and political studies. Tuition fees are high and study periods strictly organised. Although most courses are taught in English, some schools require students to be fluent in both English and French, e.g. the European Institute for Business Administration (INSEAD) at Fontainebleau, one of Europe's most prestigious business schools.

Over 30,000 students take part in correspondence courses taught through universities with distance learning centres and through the Centre National d'Enseignement à Distance (www.cned.fr), which prepares students for competitive exams and provides specific training.

General information about further education and training is available from town halls and libraries, and the French Ministry of Education provides a free information service through departmental Centre d'Information et d'Orientation (CIO) offices.

LEARNING FRENCH

If you want to make the most of your time in France, it's essential that you speak French or learn as soon as possible. For people living in France permanently, learning French isn't an option but a necessity. Although it isn't easy, even the most non-linguistic person can acquire a working knowledge of French. Your business and professional success and social life in France will be directly related to the degree to which you master French.

Most people can teach themselves a good deal through 'self-help' courses, which includes books, CDs, computer programmes and online courses.

French classes are offered by language schools, French and foreign colleges and universities, private and international schools, foreign and international organisations (such as the British Institute in Paris), local associations and clubs, and private teachers. Most universities provide language courses and many organisations offer holiday courses year-round, particularly for children and young adults (it's best to stay with a local French family). Tuition ranges from courses for complete beginners through specialised business or cultural courses to university level courses leading to recognised diplomas.

There are many language schools (*école de langues*) in cities and large towns. One of the most famous French language teaching organisations is the Alliance Française (AF, www.alliancefr.org), a state-approved, non-profit organisation with over 1,000 centres in 138 countries, including 32 centres in France, mainly in large towns and cities. The AF runs general, special and intensive courses, and can also arrange a homestay in France with a host family.

Most language schools run various classes and which one you choose will depend on your language ability, how many hours you wish to study a week, how much money you want to spend and how quickly you wish to (or think you can) learn. Language classes generally fall into the following categories: extensive (four to ten hours per week); intensive (15 to 20 hours); and total immersion (20 to 40 or more). Unless you desperately need to learn French quickly, it's best to arrange your lessons over a long period. However, don't commit yourself to a long course of study, particularly an expensive one, before ensuring that it's the right course. Most schools offer free tests to help you find the appropriate level and a free introductory lesson.

There are many things you can do to speed up your language learning, including watching television (if you can display sub-titles where the words appear on the screen as they're spoken, all the better) and DVDs (where you can select French or English subtitles), reading (especially children's books and product catalogues, where the words are accompanied by pictures), joining a club or association, and (most enjoyable of all) socialising with French friends.

 Caution

Don't expect to become fluent in a short time unless you've a particular flair for languages or already have a good command of French.

10.
PUBLIC TRANSPORT

*P*ublic transport (*transport public*) services in France vary considerably depending on where you live. They're generally excellent in cities, most of which have efficient local bus and rail services, often supplemented by metro, tram and light rail networks, and French railways provide an excellent and fast rail service, particularly between cities served by the *TGV*. France is also served by excellent international and domestic airline services, and extensive international ferry services, particularly along its northern coast.

However, bus and rail services are poor or non-existent in rural areas and it's essential to have your own transport if you live in a rural area. Paris has one of the most efficient, best-integrated and cheapest public transport systems of any major city in the world. In addition to its world-famous *metro* it boasts a comprehensive bus service and extensive suburban transport systems, including 'underground' (*RER* – see page 129) and overground rail networks, light rail and tramways.

Other cities have similar systems and many have reintroduced trams in the last few decades. Most cities are moving towards more 'ecological' public transport systems, with, for example, buses running on bio-fuel or batteries, and encouraging or even obliging people to use them by restricting the circulation of private vehicles. Thanks to government subsidies, public transport is generally inexpensive (although this doesn't stop the French from complaining about the cost) and a wide range of commuter and visitor discount tickets are available.

AIRLINE SERVICES

The state-owned national airline, Air France (www.airfrance.fr) is France's major carrier, flying to over 30 French, 65 European and 120 other destinations in over 70 countries. Air France and its various subsidiaries (including its recently acquired partner the Dutch airline KLM; they're known collectively as Groupe Air France) together have a fleet of over 200 aircraft and carry over 16 million passengers annually. It provides a high standard of service and, as you would expect, has excellent in-flight cuisine.

International Flights

All major international airlines provide scheduled services to Paris, and many also fly to other main French cities such as Bordeaux, Lyon, Marseille, Nice and Toulouse. Air France shares many international routes with just one foreign carrier and is thus able to charge high fares. The lack of competition means that Air France's international and domestic flights are among the world's most expensive. However, some competition is starting to appear and fares on some European and transatlantic flights have been reduced as a result of pressure by travel agents, e.g. Nouvelles Frontières, and no-frills airlines such as EasyJet, Flybe and Ryanair.

British visitors are especially well served by cheap flights, particularly from London's Gatwick, Luton and Stansted airports, to many regional French airports, although routes change with alarming frequency. Booking online is the norm, which permits airlines to change their prices constantly. Budget airlines levy surcharges for baggage and paying with a credit card, among other things, so aren't always as cheap as they at first appear.

Domestic Flights

Sadly, most of France's regional airlines have been swallowed up by Air France, which dominates the domestic flight market although there are still a few regional services, e.g. Corsair and Air Corsica. Air France operates domestic services between major cities such as Paris, Bordeaux, Lyon, Marseille, Mulhouse/Basel, Nice, Strasbourg and Toulouse, which connect with international arrivals in Paris.

Competition on major domestic routes from the TGV rail service, e.g. Paris-Lyon and Paris-Marseille (which carries twice as many passengers as the corresponding air route), has helped reduce air fares, and flying is

sometimes cheaper than travelling by train and quicker on most routes – provided you discount the time spent travelling from town centres to airports, queuing to check-in and security checks, and the time spent going from airport to the town centre after your arrival! Smoking is prohibited on all French trains.

Any destination in mainland France or Corsica can be reached from any other in less than 100 minutes by air, although stricter security now means that check-in times can be an hour or more before departure.

TRAINS

The French railway network extends to every corner of France and is the largest in western Europe, with over 32,000km (20,000mi) of track – of which 1,850km (1,150mi) are high-speed lines – serving around 5,000 passenger stations and carrying over 800 million passengers per year. The French railway system is operated by the state-owned Société Nationale des Chemins de Fer Français (SNCF) and is one of the most efficient in Europe.

French high-speed trains (see **TGV** below) compete successfully with road and air travel over long distances, both in cost and speed. However, despite huge government subsidies and recent price increases, SNCF still manages to run up an annual deficit.

Under new EU rules, from 2012 French railway tracks have been open to any EU railway company, which led SNCF to restructure its organisation to meet the new competition. There was outrage in France when a German carrier sought and won the use of the Channel Tunnel, but there was some corresponding satisfaction when it turned out that prospective services into France from Italy could not travel at TGV speeds because of the incompatibility of French and Italian rolling stock.

Nonetheless, competition is coming, although to what extent it will benefit passengers is unknown.

A knock-on effect of the SNCF reorganisation is a move to use the stations (still owned by the company) to better effect. There's a massive programme of redevelopment in which new designs employing the latest environmentally-friendly and carbon-saving techniques are employed. There's a greater concentration on making life easier and more comfortable for passengers, as well as opening their concourses to shops and other amenities attractive to the local populace in addition to travellers. This is already having the beneficial effect of generating further development in the often run-down areas traditionally found around main line stations. New services are being trialled throughout the network as well as new uses for station space, such as concerts, exhibitions and even sporting events.

Main Lines

Many things in France emanate from or are routed via Paris and this is also true of the railway system. (The Île-de-France region provides the SNCF with around two-thirds of its passengers.) There aren't many cross-country train routes, and it's often necessary to travel via Paris to reach a destination.

There are direct trains from French cities to many major European cities, including Amsterdam, Barcelona, Basle, Berlin, Brussels, Cologne, Florence, Frankfurt, Geneva, Hamburg, London, Madrid, Milan, Munich, Rome, Rotterdam, Venice, Vienna and Zurich. Some international services operate only at night, and daytime journeys may also involve a change of train.

Paris Stations

Paris has seven railway termini, each serving a main line (*grande ligne*) or a number, as shown in the table.

If you buy a ticket for a journey starting in Paris, the departure station is indicated on it. All the Paris stations are on the *métro* and some are also on the *RER* (see page 129). It's best to allow around a hour to travel between Paris stations, except between Gare Saint-Lazare, Gare du Nord and Gare de l'Est, which are close together (the Gare Saint-Lazare and the

Paris Train Stations	
Station	**Regions & Countries Served**
Gare d'Austerlitz	Central and south-west France (including Toulouse), except *TGV Atlantique* routes, Spain and Portugal
Gare de Bercy	Italy (Artesia), car berths (train auto-couchettes, TAC) and TER Burgundy
Gare de l'Est	East (Nancy, Strasbourg), Germany and Eastern Europe
Gare de Lyon	The south and south-east (Lyon, Marseille, Côte d'Azur), including *TGV Méditerranée*, *Rhône-Alpes* and *Sud-Est* routes, Switzerland, Italy, the Balkans and Greece
Gare Montparnasse	Brittany and *TGV Atlantique* routes, including Bordeaux
Gare du Nord	The north, via *TGV Nord Europe* (Lille and London), and *Thalys* (Belgium, Holland and Scandinavian countries) services
Gare Saint-Lazare	The north-west (Dieppe, Cherbourg-Octeville, Le Havre, etc.)

Gare du Nord are linked by a fast underground connection). The main stations in Paris also provide access to the city's comprehensive suburban rail service (*réseau banlieue*).

TGV

The SNCF operates high-speed trains (*train à grande vitesse*, abbreviated to *TGV*) on most of its main lines (see map in **Appendix B**). Launched in 1981, they're among the world's fastest trains and set a new rail speed record of 574.8kph (over 350mph) in 2007. Despite its rapidity, the *TGV* is as smooth and quiet as a conventional train (and has an excellent safety record). The TGV takes just three hours at an average speed of 300kph, to travel from Paris to Marseille.

The dedicated high-speed *TGV* rail network totals 1,850km (ca. 1,150mi), although TGV trains also run on conventional tracks at lower speeds, operating over 800 high-speed services per day carrying over 100 million passengers a year to more than 50 French cities. It has revolutionised domestic travel in France and air travel on *TGV* routes has fallen significantly, e.g. Paris-Lyon, on which route there are around 35 trains per day in each direction with over 75

per cent seat occupancy, carrying over 20,000 passengers daily.

Trains are often long with up to 20 air-conditioned carriages and four engines, so finding your seat can be a challenge, including first-and second-class carriages, a bar/relaxation area, a shop and sometimes a nursery. Carriages and compartments are colour-coded: red for first class, blue-green for second class and yellow for the bar. In second-class carriages seats are arranged in airline fashion and are comfortable with reasonable space, pull down trays and foot rests. First-class seats are naturally more comfortable and roomy – and not always a lot more expensive.

All seats must be reserved and no standing passengers are permitted. The basic fare on the TGV is the same as on ordinary trains, except that there's a 'booking fee' that varies depending on the day and time of travel, and the length of the journey, but averages around 10 per cent of the ticket price; the fee is included in the price quoted. Bookings can be made up to 90 days in advance; depending on the route and the time of travel, you may need to book weeks, days or just minutes before your departure. Tickets can purchased online

in English via Rail Europe (UK 08448 484 064, www.raileurope.co.uk) or in French at www.idtgv.com.

Eurostar

The Channel Tunnel – the world's most expensive hole in the ground – joins France with the UK by rail, surfacing at Coquelles (near Calais) in Pas-de-Calais and Folkestone in Kent. Thanks to a new high-speed line from Folkestone to London, opened in 2003, and moving the London terminal from Waterloo to St Pancras in 2007, the London to Paris journey time has been reduced to around 2hr 15m.

One way (*aller simple*) fares from Paris to London (late 2016) were from around €55 standard, €120 standard premier and €310 first class. Note that return fares aren't double the one way fares quoted, but depend on the day and time of travel and vary considerably. Generally the longer you book in advance, the lower the fare. Note that second class is very cramped and uncomfortable (worse than budget airlines) and you may find it pays to travel standard premier or first class.

You can obtain train information in English or make a booking by calling a UK number (01233-617575) or via the Eurostar (Le Shuttle) website (www.eurostar.com/fr-fr). Cars can be taken through the Channel Tunnel using the Eurotunnel (Le Shuttle) service (www.eurotunnel.com).

Other Trains

Standard French trains have either electric (*Corail*) or gas turbine (*Turbotrain*) locomotives, which, although not in the *TGV* league, are fast and comfortable. Some branch lines operate *express* and *rapide* diesel trains. The slowest trains are the suburban *omnibus* services (some with double-deck carriages), which stop at every station. An *express* or *train express régional* (*TER*) stops only at main stations

and is second in speed to the *TGV*. A *rapide* is faster than an *omnibus* but slower than an *express*. The SNCF also operates an extensive Motorail service.

Some non-*TGV* international trains, including *Trans-Europ-Express* (*TEE*) and *Trans-Europ-Nuit* (*TEN*), are first class only. Booking is necessary and a supplement is payable in addition to a first-class fare. Booking is recommended on all long-distance trains, particularly during peak periods, e.g. school and public holidays.

Tickets

Tickets (*billet*) can be purchased by telephone (08 92 35 35 35) and via the internet (www.voyages-sncf.com or uk.voyages-sncf.com), in addition to station ticket offices (at major stations staff may speak English or other languages, e.g. German, Italian or Spanish), via ticket machines (*billetterie automatique*) at stations, and from rail travel centres and appointed travel agents. A ticket must be purchased and validated before boarding a train.

Single tickets are *aller simple* and return tickets *aller-retour*. All tickets are valid for two months. There are two classes on most trains: first class (*première classe*) and second class (*deuxième classe*), with the exception of *TEE* and *TEN* international trains, which are first class only. Note that you must buy a half-fare, second-class ticket for a pet if it weighs over 6kg (13lb), which is also valid in first class. Dogs must be muzzled when travelling on trains.

You can also buy tickets via www.loco2.com and www.trainline.eu, www.raileurope.com (for US residents) or www.raileurope-world.com (all other countries).

Tariffs

There are two tariffs (*tarif*), depending on the day and the departure time of a journey:

♦ **Off-peak** (*tarif bleu*): usually from 10am Mondays to 3pm Fridays, 8am Saturdays to 3pm Sundays and 8pm Sundays to 6am Mondays;

♦ **Peak** (*tarif blanc*): all times not designated as off-peak and a few special days and public holidays.

The relevant period is indicated on timetables. A daily travel calendar (*Calendrier Voyageurs*) is published by the SNCF and available free at stations, which is updated every six months. Fares are determined by the tariff applicable at the start of a journey, e.g. a journey that starts in the off-peak period and runs into the peak period is charged at

the reduced ('blue') tariff. If you're discovered travelling in a peak ('white') period with a ticket that only entitles you to travel off-peak, you must pay the higher fare and a fine. Various discounts are available (see below). The above tariff periods don't apply to TGVs.

Discounts

Season and other discounted tickets are available for various types of traveller, including senior citizens (who can buy a *Carte Senior*); children aged 4 to 11 (who travel for half-fare); students and apprentices (aged up to 23 or 25); families (with three or more children under 18, who can purchase a *Carte Famille Nombreuse*); couples (any two adults travelling together); groups (of ten or more people); and commuters (a range of season ticket are available). There are also reduced holiday tickets (*billet séjour*) and advance purchase tickets when paying for tickets in advance.

Bookings

Disabled passengers are entitled to a range of reductions, depending on the extent of their disability. In certain cases a person accompanying a disabled person is entitled to travel free. Information is provided in the SNCF booklet *Guide Pratique du Voyaguer à Mobilité Réduite*.

Seats can be reserved on most trains (a nominal booking fee is included in the ticket price) and they must be reserved on TGVs. The fee for a TGV booking varies depending on the time and day of the week. However, you can travel on the train following or preceding the one that you booked without changing your ticket. When reserving a seat you can choose between first or second class, and a window (*fenêtre*) or corridor (*couloir*) seat. Seats can be reserved by telephone (08 92 35 35 35) and both reserved and paid for online (www.voyages-sncf.com). Eurostar bookings can be made by phone in English (08 92 35 35 39).

Seats can also be reserved via automatic ticket machines (*billetterie automatique*) at stations, where there are dedicated machines for main-line tickets, including those for *TGV*s (*billetterie automatique grandes lignes*). Payment can be made with a debit or credit card. At main stations bookings may need to be made at a particular window (marked *Locations*) and there may be a separate window for information (*Renseignements*).

With the exception of tickets purchased outside France and passes already marked with a validity date, all tickets are valid for up to two months and must be date stamped in a validating machine (*composteur*) before boarding a train. This includes booked TGV tickets (called *Resa*) and the return ticket of a day return. Insert one end of your ticket in the machine face up and a code number is stamped on the reverse (if you don't hear a satisfying 'chonk' or the stamp is illegible, try again).

Validating machines have a sign '*COMPOSTEZ VOTRE BILLET*' and are mounted on pillars at the entrance to platforms (*accès aux quais*); the SNCF is replacing the existing orange machines with more sophisticated blue ones in an effort to reduce ticket fraud.

If you break a journey and continue it the same day, your ticket remains valid. However, if you break a journey overnight (or longer), you must re-stamp your ticket before continuing your journey. There are ticket inspectors on most French trains and failure to validate your ticket will result in a surcharge or a fine.

Night Trains

A range of sleeping accommodation is provided on night trains, depending on your budget and the size of your party. These include reclining seats (*siège inclinable*), for which there's no charge but seats must be reserved; *couchettes* (*places couchées*) in four-berth compartments in first class and six-berth compartments in second class; and sleepers (*voiture-lits*), which provide sleeping accommodation for one to three people with a proper bed and private washing facilities.

 Caution

Beware of thieves and armed robbers on overnight trains, especially those running along the Mediterranean coast and across the Italian border.

After a spate of robberies a number of years ago security locks were fitted to sleeping compartments; however, you should still take care before opening the door, as crooks sometimes pose as attendants. There are dedicated compartments for women travelling alone. Bookings can be made at SNCF offices, travel agencies and motoring organisations abroad, and at railway stations, rail travel centres and SNCF-appointed travel agents in France.

Information & Timetables

All SNCF rail enquiries are centralised on premium-rate telephone number 3635; press 1 for details of delays or cancellations, 2 for recorded timetable information or 3 to speak to someone. The SNCF head office is at 10 place Budapest, 75009 Paris (01 53 25 60 00, www.sncf.com) and it also has offices in other countries including the UK (0870-241 4243, www.raileurope.co.uk). Rail information is also provided on the SNCF website (www. voyages-sncf.com). SNCF publishes a wealth of free brochures and booklets detailing its services, including *Le Guide du Voyageur*, available from French stations. It organises hotel accommodation, bus and coach services, boat cruises and package holidays.

At major stations, arrivals (*arrivées*) and departures (*départs*) are shown on large electronic boards. French timetables (*horaire*) are usually accurate, particularly timetables for TGVs and other fast trains. Rail timetables are published in national, regional and local versions, and also for individual routes or lines, but can be all but indecipherable. Some routes have separate timetables for each direction!

SNCF also publishes three regional timetables: for the *Nord Est*, *Atlantique* and *Sud Est et Corse*. There are separate timetables and guides (*Horaires et Guide Pratique*) for TGV routes and a *Lignes Affaires* (Mon-Fri) timetable is published containing times for a selection of the most popular trains linking major centres. In most regions, a *Guide Régional des Transports* is available from local railway and bus stations. Rail timetables are updated twice a year.

Many rail services operate only from Mondays to Saturdays (*semaine*) and not on Sundays and holidays (*dimanches et fêtes*), and some run at different times on different days of the week. Before planning a trip, check that your planned travel dates aren't 'special days' (*jour particulier*) such as a public holiday, when there are usually restricted services.

METRO

A number of French cities have metro (*métro*) networks – underground railways or subways – including Lille (which had the world's first driverless system), Lyon, Marseille, Paris, Toulouse and most recently Rennes, whose *Val* system claims to be the world's smallest

underground network. (The French will boast about anything!) In most cities public transport tickets and passes permit travel on all modes of transport, including the metro, buses, trams/ light rail and suburban trains. No smoking is permitted on underground trains or in stations.

Paris

The Paris *métro*, which dates from 1898, is one of the world's oldest and most famous 'underground' railways, although some of it runs overground. In the centre of Paris you're rarely more than five minutes' walk from a *métro* station.

Trains operate from 5.30am until around 1am the following day and there's a frequent service during the day with trains running every 40 seconds at peak times and every 90 seconds at other times. The *métro* is operated by the Régie Autonome des Transports Parisiens (RATP, www.ratp.fr) and a single all-purpose ticket is valid for all public transport in the capital (*métro*, *RER*, buses and suburban trains). A flat fare is charged for journeys irrespective of distance, although you aren't permitted to break your journey and can't make a round trip.

Tickets are sold at *métro* stations, bus terminals, tobacconists, RATP offices and from ticket machines. A ticket for a single journey costs around €1.80 and ten tickets (a *carnet*) cost €14.10. Children under four travel free and those under ten for half fare. *Métro* stations are easily recognisable by a huge 'M' sign.

Métro and neighbourhood maps (*plan de quartier*) are displayed outside and inside stations, and there are computerised maps (*système d'information de trajets urbains/SITU*) at many stations: simply enter the name of the street you want and you're given a print-out showing the quickest way to get there, including on foot.

Main lines are numbered from 1 to 13, and the two supplementary lines are numbered 3b and 7b. To make sure you take a train going in the right direction, note the name of the station at the end of the line (or lines) you intend to travel on and follow the signs indicating that direction, e.g. *Direction Porte d'Orléans*. If you need to change trains, look for *Correspondance* signs. Up to six lines may cross at an intersection. When changing lines, there's often a long walk, although some stations have moving walkways.

⚠ Caution

You should be wary of pickpockets when travelling on the *métro*, particularly when boarding trains, as they tend to 'strike' just as the doors are closing, leaving you bag-less or wallet-less on the train as it pulls away.

The RATP provides a range of discount and season tickets, including the *Carte Orange* which allows unlimited travel within the Ile-de-France. The cost varies depending on the number of zones you wish to include. Schoolchildren and apprentices under 26 can buy a *Carte Imagine-R*, which functions like a *Carte Orange*, while a *Carte Navigo Annuel* is an annual pass allowing unlimited travel on lines 1-5. It's also possible to buy a ticket covering any combination of lines, from two to five.

Visitors can enjoy unlimited travel by public transport, including the *métro* and *RER*, the SNCF Paris network, the bus network (including *Montmartrobus*, *Noctambus* and *Orlybus*) and the Montmartre funicular, by buying a *Paris Visite* ticket for zones 1 to 3, zones 1 to 5 or all eight zones plus Orlybus, Orlyrail, Roissyrail and Marne-la-Vallée-Chessy (for Disneyland Paris). Tickets can be purchased for one, two, three or five days.

Information for disabled travellers is provided on the RATP website (www.ratp.fr), and general information for disabled people in Paris is available from Pauline Hephaistos Survey Projects (PHSP, www.accessinparis.org), which publishes a useful book, *Access in Paris* (in English).

RER

The *RER* (*Réseau Express Régional*) is an express underground rail system that's independent of the *métro* and links most suburbs with the centre of Paris. It's much faster than the *métro* as there are fewer stops. There are four *RER* sectors (A, B, C and D), each comprising up to eight lines (e.g. A1, B2). Sectors A and B are operated jointly by the SNCF and RATP, and sectors C and D exclusively by SNCF. Operating hours are the same as the *metro*.

RER tickets must be machine-stamped before journeys commence and also, unlike *métro* tickets, when exiting an *RER* station.

Within the central area (*Ville de Paris*) a *métro* ticket is valid on *RER* trains. Outside this area the *RER* has a different ticket system from the *métro*, with prices increasing according to the distance travelled. *RER* tickets can be purchased only at *RER* station ticket offices. A ticket for the central zone costs around €1.80 (the same as the *métro*).

BUSES & TRAMS

There's a nationwide campaign in France for 'car-free' cities, and there are excellent bus services in Paris and other major cities and towns and many also have tram or light rail transit (LRT) networks. Trams go back to 1837 and at the start of the 20th century most cities had a tram network, although nearly all were replaced by bus services in the '30s or soon after the Second World War.

Today, France is at the forefront of the revival of light rail and tramways and since the mid-'80s many new systems have been installed in cities including Angers, Aubagne, Besançon, Bordeaux, Brest, Caen, Clermont-Ferrand, Dijon, Grenoble, Laon, Le Havre, Le Mans, Lyon, Marseille, Montpellier, Mulhouse, Nancy, Nantes, Nice, Orléans, Paris, Reims, Rennes, Rouen, Strasbourg, Toulon, Toulouse, Tours, and Valenciennes. There have also been major upgrades of existing tramways in Lille and St-Étienne (which have operated continually since the 19th century) and more LRT projects are under construction or planned. For more information, see www.trams-in-france.net.

The Paris tramway, which closed in 1957, reopened in 2006. It's actually called the Île-de-France tramway – only two lines operate in the Paris city limits, T3A and T3B – which extends to nine lines covering over 100km (the original tram network had over 1,000km of track!) with further lines planned.

In stark contrast to the cities, in rural areas buses are few and far between and the scant services that exist are usually designed to meet the needs of schoolchildren, workers and shoppers on market days. This means that buses usually run early and late in the day with little or nothing in between, and may cease altogether during school holidays. (Note that a city bus is generally called an *autobus* and a rural bus a *car* or *autocar*.) Smoking isn't permitted on buses.

The best place to enquire about bus services is at a tourist office or railway station. In large towns and cities, buses run to and from bus stations (*gare d'autobus/routière*), which are usually located next to railway stations. In rural areas bus services are often operated by SNCF and operate to and from a railway station. An SNCF bus, on which rail tickets and passes are valid, is shown as an *autocar* in rail timetables. Private bus services are often uncoordinated and operate from different locations, rather than a central bus station.

Some towns provide free or discount bus passes to senior citizens (aged over 60) on production of an identity card, passport or *carte de séjour* and proof of local residence.

There are no national bus companies in France operating scheduled services, although many long-distance buses are operated by foreign companies such as Eurolines (www.eurolines.com), which operates regular services from the UK to over 50 French cities, including Bordeaux, Cannes, Lyon, Montpellier, Nice, Orléans, Paris, Perpignan, Reims, Saint-Malo and Strasbourg. Discounts are available to students and young people on some routes.

Note that bus and coach passengers are required by law to wear seatbelts if they're fitted.

Paris

Paris has over 112km (70mi) of bus lanes, so buses move at a reasonable speed. Operating hours vary, although buses are in service on most routes from 7am to around 9pm, and on the main routes evening buses (*autobus du soir*) run until at least midnight. From Mondays to Saturdays, there's a bus every 10 to 15 minutes during peak hours on most routes and a reduced service after 9pm. On Sundays and public holidays services are severely restricted on most routes. Night buses ('*Noctambus*') provide an hourly service on ten routes (a night bus map is available from *métro* stations).

The *métro* (see above) and buses use the same ticket, which is valid for two bus sections or fare stages, marked *fin de section* at stops. Two tickets are needed for trips encompassing three fare stages and up to four tickets for trips to the suburbs.

Paris bus stops are indicated by a post with red and yellow panels marked with the name of the stop (e.g. a street or corner), as shown on route plans. Each stop displays the numbers of the buses stopping there, a map showing all stops along the route(s), and the times of the first and last buses. The route number and destination of buses is displayed on the front (of buses) and the route on the sides. Route maps are also displayed inside buses and stops may be announced as you approach them.

To stop a bus you signal to the driver by waving your arm. On boarding a bus you must stamp (*composter*) your ticket by inserting it in the stamping machine (*composteur*) next to the driver. A ticket inspector (*contrôleur*) may ask to see your ticket and if it isn't stamped you'll be fined. If you've a *Carte Orange* or other pass valid on Paris buses show it to the driver as you board. When you want a bus to stop in order to get off you signal to the driver by pressing a button or pulling a cord. A 'stop requested' (*arrêt demandé*) sign will be illuminated above the driver's cab. Buses usually have separate entrance (*montée*) and exit (*sortie*) doors.

TAXIS

Taxi ranks (*station de taxi*) are usually found outside railway stations, at airports, and at main junctions in towns and cities. At some taxi ranks a button is provided to call a taxi when none are waiting. You can hail a taxi in the street but it must be at least 50 metres (160ft) from a taxi rank where people are waiting. You can also call a radio taxi by telephone (usually provided at taxi ranks), but you must pay for the taxi's journey to the pick-up point. Drivers aren't usually permitted to accept fares outside their normal operating area (shown on the light on top of the vehicle), e.g. Île-de-France for Paris taxis.

Smoking isn't permitted in taxis. Drivers can refuse to carry animals (except guide dogs, which must be allowed), although most have no objection to small dogs; there's a set charge as there is for extra luggage, etc. Taxis adapted for use by the disabled are available in major cities, but must be booked (search online).

In many cities there are simply too many cabs and the situation is exacerbated by unlicensed operators and new challenges (see **Uber** below). Beware of illegal and unmetered cabs operating in main cities.

Parisian taxis are among the cheapest in Europe and are ordinary cars fitted with a meter and a light on top. Taxi ranks are indicated by blue and white 'taxi' signs and taxis for hire by a white light on the roof. An orange light means a taxi is engaged and no light at all (or the meter is concealed by a black cover) means the driver is off duty. Rates are displayed on

the meter inside a taxi and extra charges are shown on a notice in a rear window. Note that very few Paris taxi drivers accept credit cards.

A useful website for information about taxis in Paris is http://infotaxiparis.com (in English and French), which shows taxi rank locations, current fares, etc. You can book a Parisian taxi online via www.taxisbleus.com.

Uber

Uber (www.uber.com/en-gb/cities/paris/) operates an inexpensive taxi service in Paris (and other European cities) using private drivers operating private cars, which can be booked via a mobile phone using a special app. To start using Uber as a passenger, you must signup and create an account, after which you download and install an app on your mobile phone. Bookings are made via the app and payment is via a debit or credit card, so you don't need to pay (or tip!) the driver. You must be aged 18 to use Uber (or 21 to be a driver).

Needless to say regular taxi services (and private 'minicabs') have been hard hit by Uber – which is allegedly already worth some $60 billion worldwide! – and licensed taxi drivers have staged protests in Paris and other cities. A number of court rulings – for example regarding using unlicensed drivers – in France and Germany have gone against the company and it can expect more legal challenges.

Monet's garden, Giverny, Normandy

11.
MOTORING

*F*rance has an extensive motorway network of over 9,500km (6,000mi), supplemented by a network (around 30,000km/18,500mi) of trunk (primary routes) roads which vary from motorway standard dual-carriageways to narrow two-lane roads passing through a succession of villages. French motorways are among Europe's finest roads, but they're also among the world's most expensive, being mostly toll roads.

Whereas motorways are often virtually empty, trunk roads are often jammed in the tourist season by drivers who are reluctant to pay (or can't afford) the high motorway tolls. In rural areas a car is generally a necessity and driving can be enjoyable in remote areas, particularly outside the tourist season, where it's possible to drive for miles without seeing another motorist (or a caravan). On the other hand, if you live in a city, particularly Paris, a car is a liability and may be unnecessary.

Rush hours are from around 6.30-8.30am and 4.30-6.30pm Mondays to Fridays, during which hours town centres are best avoided. A recent phenomenon, known as *l'effet des 35 heures* (the effect of the 35-hour week) is an advanced rush hour on Friday afternoons – or before a public holiday – caused by workers knocking off early for the weekend. Paris, where traffic moves at around the same speed as a hundred years ago, is best avoided at any time. Lunch times – any time between noon and 3pm – can also be very busy in major cities.

Traffic jams (*bouchon/embouteillage*) are notorious at the start and end of holiday periods, particularly on roads out of Paris and other northern cities, as people flock southwards. The most important days to stay at home are the first weekends in July and August, which are

traditionally times when Parisians escape the city (*la départ*), and the first the last Sundays in August when they return (*la rentrée*).

As you may know, the French drive on the right-hand side of the road – it saves confusion if you do likewise! If you aren't used to driving on the right, take it easy until you're accustomed to it. Be particularly alert when leaving lay-bys, T-junctions, one-way streets, petrol stations and car parks, as it's easy to lapse into driving on the left. It's helpful to display a reminder (e.g. 'Think right!') on your car's dashboard.

Information about driving in France is available from many websites, including the UK's Automobile Association's (www.theaa. com/european-breakdown-cover/driving-in-europe/driving-in-france), Drive France (http://drive-france.com), Eurotunnel (www.rac.co.uk/drive/travel/country/france) and the UK's RAC (www.eurotunnel.com/uk/traveller-info/driving-in-france).

The above websites also provide up to date information regarding what you must carry in your vehicle when driving in France. These include your passport (proof of ID), driving licence, insurance details, vehicle registration document (the original, not a copy), a reflective jacket for each occupant, a warning triangle, a nationality sticker (e.g. GB) on the rear or an EU number plate bearing a sticker, and a breathalyser/alcohol tester. In addition your headlights must be adjusted for driving on the right or must be fitted with beam deflectors so that you don't blind oncoming traffic.

Paris has a serious pollution problem (apparently worse than London and Shanghai), which has led to the mayor imposing a Low Emission Zone where diesel and petrol lorries and buses made before 1997 are prohibited, and (since July 2016) petrol and diesel cars registered before 1997 are banned from 8am to 8pm on weekdays. By 2020, only vehicles constructed in 2011 or later will be allowed access. There are also other restrictions in place such as car-free routes on Sundays and public holidays and permanent traffic-free zones.

IMPORTING A VEHICLE

A new or used vehicle (including boats and planes) on which VAT (*TVA*) has been paid in another EU country can be imported free of French VAT by a French resident. If you buy a new car abroad on which VAT hasn't been paid (VAT should already have been paid on a secondhand car), VAT is due immediately on its arrival in France.

VAT is calculated on the invoice price if a vehicle is less than six months old or has covered less than 6,000km (3,728mi); otherwise a reduction is made depending on its age and VAT is payable on the balance. It's therefore advantageous to buy a tax-free car and use it abroad for six months before importing it. The VAT rate is 20 per cent for all cars and caravans and for motorcycles above 240cc.

In addition to VAT, customs duty must be paid on cars imported from outside the EU; there's no duty on cars imported from another EU country, provided you produce purchase and registration documents.

The rate of duty varies with the country of origin (some countries have reciprocal agreements with the EU resulting in lower duty rates) and, of course, the value of the vehicle in France, calculated using the *Argus* guide (www.largus.fr) to secondhand car prices. Tax and duty must be paid at the point of importation or at the local tax office (*Hôtel/Recette des Impôts*) where you live.

An imported vehicle must be registered in France within three months. However, before you can register it you must contact your local Direction Régionale de l'Environnement et de l'Aménagement (DREAL) listed in the Yellow Pages (and online), who will send you a checklist of the documentation required: it involves a lot of bureaucracy and you'll find it much easier to simply purchase a car in France! The documents required include a certificate from DREAL declaring that your vehicle conforms with EU standards; a declaration from your local Hôtel des Impôts that there's no tax to pay (or it has been paid); and a test certificate (see below) if it's over four years old.

You then take all the documents you've amassed to the local *préfecture* (not a *sous-préfecture*), where, if everything is in order, you'll be given a registration document (*carte grise* – see **Registration Document** below). You then need to obtain registration plates and insure the vehicle.

BUYING A CAR

Unlike people in most developed countries, the French generally drive cars manufactured in their own country. This isn't simply chauvinism, as French cars are relatively cheap and usually very good and, when they need servicing or break down, you can have them repaired at almost any garage in France. Japanese cars have become popular in recent decades, although Fiat and Audi/VW are the best-selling foreign makes. The availability of local service facilities is, of course, linked to the number of cars sold in France. Peugeot-Citroën and Renault dealers can be found in all large towns and there are also many Audi-VW, Fiat, Ford, Mercedes and Opel (General Motors/Vauxhall) dealers. Dealers for other makes are fewer and further between.

New Cars

New car prices are higher in France than in most other European countries, although lower than those in the UK, and many French people buy their cars in Belgium or Denmark, where most new cars are generally cheaper than in France. You should make sure, however, that the local French dealer of a car purchased abroad will agree to service it under the terms of the warranty.

Making comparisons between new car prices in countries that have adopted the euro currency is easy, but attention should be paid to the different levels of standard equipment and warranty levels. Most dealers will offer one or two extras free of charge, provide up to 10 per cent discount on the list price, and some offer 'cash back' deals (shop around for the best package deal). French manufacturers have 'open days' at their dealers at least once a year, where giveaways and other promotions encourage test drives and generous discounts are offered.

All new cars sold in France must be labelled with their energy efficiency (i.e. the amount of carbon dioxide their engines emit for every kilometre travelled), with colour codes ranging from dark green for the most environmentally-friendly models (emissions of less than 100g/km) to red for the most polluting (over 250g/km). There's a surcharge on the cost of a

registration document for high-emission cars (see **Registration Document** below).

Electric cars and hybrids (which combine an electric motor with a petrol engine) with low CO_2 emissions are popular in France and attract government subsidies towards the cost and no road tax. In 2016, France passed the milestone of 100,000 plug-in electric vehicles, making it the second largest plug-in market in Europe after Norway. France offers drivers of certain (polluting) diesel cars a €10,000 grant to switch to an electric car.

Used Cars

Used cars (*voiture d'occasion*) in France are expensive compared with new cars and generally more expensive than in the UK, for example. It's often best to buy a car that's around two years old, as depreciation in the first two years is considerable. If you plan to buy a used car in France, whether privately or from a garage, you must check that it has passed the official technical inspection, if applicable, and that the chassis number tallies with the registration document, which should be in the name of the vendor when sold privately.

Car dealers usually provide warranties of 3 to 12 months on used cars, depending on the age of the car and the model. Used car dealers, rather than franchised dealers, have the same dreadful (and well deserved) reputation as in other countries, and caution must be taken when buying from them. If you're buying a used car from a garage, try to negotiate a reduction, particularly when paying cash and not trading in another vehicle.

All national and local (including free) newspapers carry advertisements for used cars. Specialist journals for used-car buyers include the monthly *Auto Journal* (www.autojournal.fr), *La Centrale des Particuliers* (www.lacentrale.fr) and *L'Argus* magazine (www.largus.fr). *L'Argus* contains a used car price guide that's used throughout the industry, e.g. by dealers buying and selling cars and by insurance companies when calculating values for insurance premiums and claims. You should pay within around 10 per cent of the *Argus* value, depending on the condition and the kilometre reading. Secondhand prices vary with the region and are generally higher in remote areas than in Paris and other major cities.

VEHICLE REGISTRATION

When you import a car into France or buy a new or used car, it must be registered at the *préfecture* or *sous-préfecture* in the department where you're resident within 15 days (although the process is usually carried out by the dealer in the case of a new car purchase) or can be done online (www.carte-grise.org). Registration in Paris is done at the *préfecture de police* or the town hall (*mairie*) of your *arrondissement*. If you import a car you must obtain customs clearance and have it inspected by the DREAL before it can be registered (see **Importing a Vehicle** above).

Registration Document

A vehicle registration document is known as a 'grey card' (*carte grise*), which can be applied for at your local *prefecture*, by post or online. A *cartes grise* incorporates a tear-off portion, which must be completed by the vendor. You must present this and the sales certificate (*certificat de vente*), *certificat de non-gage* and *certificat de non-opposition* that you received from the vendor, technical inspection certificate, if applicable (see below), and a photocopy of your *carte de séjour* or passport, and complete a registration request form (*demande de certificat d'immatriculation*), available in some cases from your *mairie* or *hôtel de ville*.

If you move home in the same department you must inform your *préfecture* of your change of address. However, if you move to another department, you must re-register your car with the new *préfecture* within three months. You present the tear-off portion of your registration document, your *carte de séjour* (if applicable) and proof of residence; you may also be asked for a *certificat de résidence* obtainable from your local town hall. Since 2009 a vehicle has retained the same registration (as in the UK) when the owner moves (or there's a new owner) to a new French department.

The registration number shows the F (for France) and EU insignia in a blue band on the left, a seven-digit alphanumeric code (of two letters, three numbers and two letters in XX-NNN-ZZ format) in the centre and a departmental logo or coat of arms and department number on the right. You can now choose which department to show on your plate, irrespective of where you live. When you receive a registration document with a new registration number, e.g. after importing a car or moving to a new department, you must fit new registration plates within 48 hours.

Registration plates are made on the spot for around €25 a pair by supermarkets and ironmongers (*quincaillerie*), on production of your registration document. If you lose your registration document or have it stolen you must report it to the police, who will issue you with a certificate allowing you to obtain a replacement from your *préfecture*.

The fee for a registration document varies according to the size of a vehicle's engine, termed 'fiscal horsepower' (*chevaux fiscaux*), which isn't the same as the actual horsepower (*chevaux DIN*) produced by the engine. Fee scales vary with the region; for example, they're up to 50 per cent higher in Paris than elsewhere. The website www.carte-grise.org contains a calculator which shows the fees in all regions and for all models.

TECHNICAL INSPECTION

All cars over four years old are required to have a technical inspection (*contrôle technique* or CT) every two years, carried out at an authorised test centre.

Tests cover over 50 points, including steering, suspension, fuel tank, bodywork, seats, seatbelts, mirrors, tyres, windscreen, windscreen wipers and horn, all of which must be functional and in good condition, and the car's emission levels. The points covered by the CT are frequently updated and expanded and around 20 per cent of vehicles fail the test. Tested items are listed on a report (*certificat d'inspection/autobilan*).

Tests take around three-quarters of an hour and must usually be booked in advance. There's no fixed charge for a test and each centre can set its own rate, but the average is between €70 and €90. If your car passes the test you receive a badge (*macaron*), which you must affix to your windscreen next to your insurance tab (the test centre may do this for you). You usually have two months' grace at the end of each two-year period in which to submit your car for a test. After this period you can be fined for not displaying a valid badge on an increasing scale according to how overdue you are. If your car fails the test for minor reasons (e.g. non-working bulbs, worn tyres, etc.) it's noted on the report and you're given two months to correct the problems.

Cars over 25 years old can be classified as 'collectors' vehicles' (*véhicule de collection*), which means that they're exempt from the technical inspection under certain conditions

(e.g. they can only be used at weekends and on certain roads in certain parts of the country), although an initial test is required to obtain a registration document.

A green disc (*pastille verte*) is provided by car dealers for new cars with 'low' air pollution and can be obtained for older cars (petrol-driven vehicles manufactured since 1993 and diesel-engine vehicles manufactured since 1997) from a *préfecture*. The disc must be displayed inside the windscreen, and cars displaying it are the only vehicles allowed to circulate in cities such as Paris on 'bad air quality days' (level 3), known as *pics de pollution*. Discs should be renewed every two years.

ROAD TAXES

French-registered private vehicles no longer require a road tax certificate (*vignette automobile*), except certain camper vans. If you use a vehicle over 3.5 tonnes for your business it must be taxed, and if you run a business with over three vehicles you must pay tax on the fourth, fifth, etc. If you have vehicles that need taxing you must declare them to the tax authorities when you acquire them and before 10th December each year. Forms 2856 and 2857 must be completed; these, along with other relevant information, can be found on the Tax Office's website (www.impots.gouv.fr).

If your vehicle requires a *vignette*, keep the receipt with your other car papers, as this proves that you didn't acquire it illegally and also enables you to obtain a replacement if it's stolen. If you need to replace your *vignette*, visit any tax office (*Centre des Impôts*) and produce your receipt. If you lose the receipt you can obtain another from the issuing office, which keeps a record of payments.

Since January 2006, a tax has been added to the cost of a registration document for cars that emit more than a certain amount of carbon dioxide (see **Registration Document** above). The use of most motorways (*autoroute*) and certain bridges and tunnels is 'taxed' in the form of tolls (see **French Roads** on page 146).

DRIVING LICENCE

The minimum age for driving a car in France is 18 and those aged between 16 and 18 may follow an accompanied or 'anticipated' apprenticeship (*apprentissage accompagné* or *apprentissage anticipé de la conduite/AAC*, commonly known as *conduite accompagnée*) consisting of at least 20 hours' instruction by a qualified driving instructor. This culminates in a written test (*épreuve théorique générale/ ETG* or *code*) followed by 3,000km (1,875mi) of accompanied driving, which is a requirement for all learners irrespective of age.

The cost of a course of 20 hours' instruction, including the theory (*code*) and practical tests, is around €750, although 16-25 year olds can obtain an interest-free bank loan to cover the cost and impoverished ones can take a course for €1 per day. Almost 200,000 teenagers each year opt for the accompanied apprenticeship and 80 per cent of them pass, compared with just 50 per cent of those who start learning as adults.

 Caution

If you wish to accompany a learner driver you must obtain permission from your insurance company.

The practical test can't be taken until the age of 18. You've three years to pass the practical test after passing the written test and you may take it up to five times during this period; if you fail it on the fifth attempt or don't pass within the three-year period you must retake the theory test as well as the practical (or give up!).

RÉPUBLIQUE FRANÇAISE

F

PERMIS DE CONDUIRE

Permiso de Conducción ● Řidičský průkaz
Kórekort ● Führerschein ● Juhiluba
Άδεια Οδήγησης ● Driving Licence
Ceadúnas Tiomána ● Patente di guida
Vadītāja apliecība ● Vairuotojo pažyméjimas
Vezetói engedély ● Liċenzja tas-Sewqan
Rijbewijs ● Prawo Jazdy
Carta de Condução ● Vodičský preukaz
Vozniško dovoljenje ● Ajokortti ● Körkort

New drivers can run up fewer points on their licences and must observe lower speed limits than experienced motorists in the three years after passing their test (see below and **Speed Limits** on page 144). Drivers over 75 must pass a medical examination every two years in order to retain their licence.

A standard car licence (called a *permis B*) also entitles you to ride a motorcycle up to 125cc provided you've held the licence for at least two years, although you must retake the theory exam if you've held a licence for over five years without riding a motorcycle.

You must have a licence E(B), for which additional training is required, to tow a caravan or trailer weighing over 750kg (1,650lb) if it's heavier than your car or if the combined weight of the car and caravan/trailer is over 3.5 tonnes. If a caravan or trailer exceeds 500kg (1,100lb) it must be insured and have its own registration document (see above).

A French driving licence is pink and contains a photograph. It's issued for life and doesn't expire when the holder reaches the age of 70

(as in some other EU countries). You can drive in France for at least a year on most foreign driving licences or an International Driver's Permit (IDP). If you hold a French licence and want an IDP to drive in other countries, it can be obtained from your *préfecture* on production of your current licence and two passport-size photographs (an IDP is free and valid for five years).

When an EU citizen moves to France it's no longer necessary to obtain a local driving licence after one year. However, a resident who commits a motoring offence in France involving a loss of licence points is obliged to exchange his foreign licence for a French one so that the penalty may be applied (non-residents escape the penalty but must still pay fines).

Some non-EU countries and some US states have reciprocal agreements with France to waive the practical driving test, but applicants must take the written test. If you need to take a driving test, it's wise to take a course with a certified driving school, some of which have sections for English-speakers.

Driving penalties in France are based on a points system. Drivers normally start with 12 licence points and between one and six points are deducted for each offence, depending on its gravity. Points are automatically reinstated after three years but, if you lose all 12 points within this period, you're usually banned from driving for a minimum of six months. If a new driver accrues six points during his probationary period, his licence is suspended and he must wait six months before being able to retake the test. The points system is explained in a booklet, *Permis à Points*, available from police stations and via www. actiroute.com.

If you lose your French driving licence or it's stolen, you must report it to the police and obtain an acknowledgement (*récépissé de déclaration de perte ou de vol de pièces d'identité*), which is valid until a replacement licence is issued.

CAR INSURANCE

As in most other countries, car insurance is essential in France and driving without it is a serious offence for which you can be fined and imprisoned. If you arrive in France with a vehicle that isn't insured there, you can buy a temporary policy valid for 8, 15 or 30 days from the vehicle insurance department of the French customs office at your point of entry. However, vehicles

insured in an EU country, Liechtenstein, Norway or Switzerland are automatically covered for third party liability in France. The following categories of car insurance are available in France:

Third-party (*responsabilité civile, minimale, tiers illimitée* and *au tiers*): the minimum required by law in France, which includes unlimited medical costs and damage to third party property;

Third-party, fire & theft (TPF&T; *tiers personnes/restreinte/intermédiaire/vol et incendie*): known in some countries as part comprehensive – includes cover against fire, natural hazards (e.g. falling rocks), theft and legal expenses (*défense-recours*). TPF&T includes damage to (or theft of) contents and car stereo.

Multi-risk collision (*multirisque collision*): covers all risks listed under TPF&T (see above) plus damage caused to your own vehicle in the event of a collision with a person, vehicle, or animal belonging to an 'identifiable person';

Comprehensive (*multirisque tous accidents/tous risques*): covers all the risks listed under TPF&T and multi-risk collision (see above) and includes damage to your

vehicle, however caused, and whether a third party can be identified or not. Note, however, that illegally parked cars automatically lose their comprehensive cover. Comprehensive insurance is usually compulsory for lease and hire purchase contracts.

Driver protection (*protection du conducteur/ assurance conducteur*) is usually optional. It enables the driver of a vehicle involved in an accident to claim for bodily injury to himself, including compensation for his incapacity to work or for his beneficiaries should he be killed. Additional insurance can be purchased for valuable contents and accessories. High-value cars must usually have an approved alarm installed and/or the registration number engraved on all windows, in order to be insured against theft.

You should also check whether your insurance policy covers items stolen from your car. When motoring in France (or anywhere else), don't assume that your valuables are safe in the boot of your car, particularly if the boot can be opened from the inside.

French insurance companies provide an automatic green card (*carte internationale d'assurance automobile/carte verte*), which extends your normal insurance cover to most other European countries.

Premiums

Insurance premiums are high in France – an indication of the high accident rate, the large number of stolen and vandalised cars, and high car insurance tax. Premiums vary considerably according to numerous factors, including the type of insurance and car, your age and accident record and where you live. Premiums are highest in Paris and other cities and lowest in rural areas and for cars over three years old; drivers with less than three years' experience usually pay a 'penalty' and drivers under 25 also pay higher premiums. However, the maximum penalty for young drivers is 100 per cent or double the normal premium.

Some premiums are based on the number of kilometres (*kilomètrage*) driven each year, and a surcharge is usually made when a car isn't garaged overnight. Shop around and obtain a number of quotations. Value added tax (*TVA*) at 20 per cent is payable on insurance premiums.

☑ SURVIVAL TIP

You can reduce your premium by opting to pay a higher excess (*franchise*), e.g. the first €300 to €750 of a claim instead of the usual €125 to €250.

No-Claims Bonus

A foreign no-claims bonus is usually valid in France, but you must provide written evidence from your present insurance company, not just an insurance renewal notice. You may also need an official translation. A French no-claims bonus isn't as generous as those in some other countries and is usually 5 per cent for each year's accident-free driving up to a maximum

of 50 per cent after ten years. If you have an accident for which you're responsible, you're usually required to pay a penalty (*malus*) or your bonus (*bonus*) is reduced.

Your premium will be increased by 25 per cent each time you're responsible for an accident or 12.5 per cent if you're partly to blame, up to a maximum premium of three and a half times the standard premium. If you're judged to be less than 30 per cent responsible, you won't usually lose your no-claims bonus. However, if you've had the maximum bonus for three years, one accident won't reduce it even if you were at fault. All penalties are cancelled if you have no accidents for two years.

Claims

Claims are decided on the information provided in accident report forms (*constat amiable d'accident de voiture/constat européen d'accident*) completed by drivers, as well as reports by insurance company experts and police reports. You must notify your insurance company of a claim resulting from an accident within a limited period, e.g. two to five days. If your car is stolen you must usually wait 30 days before an insurance company will consider a claim.

If your car is damaged in an accident you may take it to any reputable repairer (*carrosserie*), where the damage must usually be inspected and the repair approved by your insurance company's assessor (*expert*), although sometimes an independent assessment may be permitted. Assessors normally visit different repairers on different days of the week, therefore you should arrange to take your car on the relevant day. For minor repairs an inspection may be unnecessary.

Breakdown Insurance

Breakdown insurance (*assurance dépannage*) is provided by car insurance companies and motoring organisations (see page 154). If you're motoring abroad or you live abroad and are motoring in France, it's important to have breakdown insurance (which may include limited holiday and travel insurance – see page 183), including repatriation for your family and your car in the event of an accident or breakdown.

Most foreign breakdown companies provide multi-lingual 24-hour centres where assistance is available for motoring, medical, legal and travel problems. Some organisations also provide economical annual motoring policies for those who frequently travel abroad, e.g. owners of holiday homes in France. If your car is registered outside France, you may be unable to obtain breakdown insurance from a French insurance company.

French insurance companies offer an optional accident and breakdown service (*contrat d'assistance*) for policyholders for an additional premium, which is adopted by some 90 per cent of French motorists. The breakdown service usually covers the policyholder, his spouse, single dependent children, and parents and grandparents living under the same roof. The 24-hour telephone number for the breakdown service is shown on the insurance tab affixed to your windscreen.

RULES OF THE ROAD

All motorists in France must be familiar with the highway code (*Code de la Route*), available from bookshops throughout France (around €15), when they take their test, but most promptly ignore it as soon as they've passed. In fact, there isn't a single official highway code, but numerous versions of it produced by different publishers, e.g. Ediser and Rousseau!

The Prévention Routière publishes a leaflet in English called *Keep Right*, which highlights the major rules and conventions, and a similar guide, entitled *Welcome on France's Roads*, including a list of common fines, can be downloaded from the Sécurité Routière website (www.securite-routiere.gouv. fr). These are both rather basic, however. For more detailed guidance, you should obtain the *Guide Pratique et Juridique de l'Automobiliste* (Editions Grancher), which explains the rights and obligations of car owners.

SPEED LIMITS

The speed limits in force throughout France are shown in the table below; limits are reduced in rain (*par temps de pluie*), when the second limit shown in the table applies. When visibility is less than 50m (162ft), e.g. in fog or heavy rain, speed limits are automatically reduced to 50kph on all roads. The speed limit in built-up areas (*agglomération*), such as small towns and villages, is 50kph and starts with

Speed Limits	
Road	**Speed Limits (normal/rain)**
Motorways	130/110kph (81/69mph)
Dual-carriageways	110/100kph (69/62mph)
Other roads	90/80kph (56/50mph)
Built-up areas/towns	50kph (31mph) or as signposted

a town or village's name sign and ends with same sign with a diagonal red line through it. The word *rappel* (reminder) is often displayed beneath speed restriction signs to remind motorists that a limit is still in force.

Speed limits also apply to cars towing a trailer or caravan, provided the trailer's weight doesn't exceed that of the car. If the trailer's weight exceeds that of the car by less than 30 per cent, you're limited to 65kph (39mph); if the trailer is over 30 per cent heavier than the car, you mustn't exceed 45kph (28mph). Cars towing trailers with restricted speeds aren't permitted to use the left (overtaking) lane of a three-lane motorway. Vehicles fitted with studded tyres or snow chains are restricted to 90kph (56mph) and a '90' plate must be displayed at the rear.

For two years after passing your driving test in France you're designated a 'young' driver (*jeune conducteur*), irrespective of your age, and must display a *disque réglementaire*, consisting of a red capital letter A on a white background, on the back of any car being driven. During this period you mustn't exceed 80kph (50mph) on roads where the limit is normally 90kph, 100kph (62mph) on roads with a 110kph limit, or 110kph (69mph) on motorways with a 130kph limit.

There's a minimum speed of 80kph (50mph) on motorways in the outside (overtaking) lane during daylight, in dry weather on level surfaces and in good visibility, i.e. perfect conditions. Sleeping policemen (*ralentisseur* or *dos d'âne*) are common on many major and minor roads and are often accompanied by a 30kph (18mph) sign; if you don't slow down you risk damaging your vehicle!

France employs radar speed detectors to identify and photograph speeding motorists (you can find camera locations at www.controleradar. org). If your car has a GPS system you can be 'caught' speeding by a Big Brother-style satellite surveillance system called '*Lavia*' (short for *Limitation s'adaptant à la vitesse autorisée*). Note also that motorway toll tickets are timed and you can be convicted of speeding if you complete a section of motorway in less than a certain time!

TRAFFIC POLICE & FINES

In France, the *gendarmerie nationale*, which is actually a branch of the army, is responsible for road patrols outside towns and cities, using both cars and motorcycles. In towns and cities, it's the *police nationale*.

The police can stop motorists and ask for identification and car papers at any time (and also check your tyres, lights, etc.). This is known as a *contrôle*, when you're routinely asked to produce your driving licence (French if held), vehicle registration document (*carte grise*) and insurance certificate. It's wise to make a copy of all these documents and keep the originals on your person (you should not leave them in the car). Police may accept copies, provided you present the originals at a *gendarmerie* within five days; if you don't the required documents (or copies) you can be fined.

Fines can be imposed for a range of traffic offences. For offences not involving third parties (e.g. exceeding the speed limit or failing to stop at a *Stop* sign), police can demand an on-the-spot fine. On-the-spot fines are commonly applied to non-resident foreigners, whose vehicles are usually impounded if they're unable to pay. It's well known that French traffic police target foreign vehicles, although it's naturally officially denied.

FRENCH ROADS

France has a good road system that includes everything from motorways (*autoroute*) to forest dirt tracks (*route forestière*). French motorways are excellent and most other main roads are also very good, although roads are generally poorer in areas with low traffic density (i.e. most of rural France) and the economic downturn has led to less frequent and thorough maintenance. Roads are identified by their prefix and colour-coded markers.

Motorways

France boasts one of Europe's best motorway (*autoroute*) networks, totalling over 9,500km (some 6,000mi). The network is being continually expanded, therefore you shouldn't use a motoring atlas that's more than a few years old. Good guides to French motorways and their services are *Bonne Route!* by Anna Fitter (Anthony Nelson) and Michelin's *autoroute* guide.

Because of the toll system (see below), many French consider driving on motorways to be something of a luxury and consequently they have the lowest traffic density of any European motorways and are France's safest roads. Your risk of dying on a motorway – with the notable exception of the Paris *Périphérique* – is around four times lower than on any other road.

Most motorways are toll roads (*à péage*), which have long been among the most expensive in Europe. In 2016 the toll for a car from Calais to Paris was €21.70 and Calais to Nice €106.30. There are five toll categories on most motorways (motorhomes and cars towing trailers or caravans are charged more than cars). Fees aren't standardised throughout the country and vary with the age of the motorway and the services provided. There are no tolls on the sections of motorways around cities.

Residents who are unable to pay fines on the spot are given 30 days to pay and fines are automatically increased (significantly) if they aren't paid on time, the penalties starting 45 days after the fine was imposed. A reduction is granted to residents who pay a fine on the spot or within 15 days. You can opt for your case to go to court rather than pay a fixed penalty, in which case you must usually pay a deposit (*amende forfaitaire*). The case can be dismissed (although extremely rare) or the fine confirmed or increased. You receive the verdict in the form of an *ordonnance pénale* and have 30 days to appeal against the judgement, should you wish to do so. If you receive a fine by post (e.g. having been caught speeding by a camera), you must pay it within seven days or the fine is increased.

Information is available from the Association des Sociétés Françaises d'Autoroutes (www. autoroutes.fr/en/key-rates.htm – in English and French), which includes a route planner that calculates both tolls and petrol costs.

If you use motorways regularly, it's worth paying via the Liber-t system, where you've a remote control 'box' fitted (attached to your windscreen just behind the rear-view mirror) that records your motorway use. This enables you to drive through the *Télépéage* (automated payment) lane without even having to wind down your window, tolls being registered automatically and payment deducted from your bank account. You pay an annual subscription depending on your usage plus a deposit of around €30, refundable when you return the control box (both added to your first bill).

If you use the motorway on your way to and from work you can also benefit from a reduction of up to 35 per cent in toll charges. *Télépéage* badges can be obtained from offices of your local motorway company (Société d'Autoroutes), which are usually situated near toll stations. You need to provide your bank details, proof of address and, to qualify for the work-use discount, confirmation from your employer that you drive to and from work.

UK residents can register for the Liber-t system online (www.saneftolling.co.uk), which includes a €20 refundable deposit for the transponder, a registration fee of €10 and an annual 'management' fee of €6. You receive a monthly invoice for toll fees, which is paid by direct debit.

Tolls are also levied for the use of major tunnels, e.g. Mont Blanc (Chamonix to Entrèves, Italy, 11.6km/7.2mi), Fréjus (Modane to Bardonecchia, Italy, 12.8km/8mi) and Bielsa (Aragnouet to Bielsa, Spain, 3km/1.86mi), and bridges, e.g. the Normandie, Saint-Nazaire, Tancarville and Millau Viaduct.

Other Roads

Unlike French motorways, main trunk roads in France are jammed by vehicles, including heavy goods vehicles, whose drivers are reluctant to pay (or can't afford) the high motorway tolls. If you must get from A to B in the shortest possible time there's no alternative to the motorways. However, if you aren't in too much of a hurry, want to save money and wish to see something of France, then the trunk roads are ideal.

The main non-motorway roads are classified as national roads (*routes nationales*), which are supplemented by some 365,000km of departmental roads (*routes départmentales*). National roads are often straight and many are dual carriageways, on which you can usually make good time at (legal) speeds of between 90 and 110kph (56 to 68mph). On the other hand, many also pass through towns and villages, where the limit is reduced to 50kph (30mph), which can make for slow progress. However, each year sees the construction of new bypasses to help speed the flow, particularly on the busiest routes.

In general, signposting is good, even in the most rural areas. However, only large towns or cities are usually signposted as you approach a ring road system, therefore you should plan your journey accordingly and make a note of the major route numbers and destinations along your route. In towns, only the town centre (*centre ville*) and 'all directions' (*toutes directions*) may be signposted. If you don't want the town centre, simply follow the *toutes directions* or 'other directions' (*autres directions*) signs until you see a sign for where you want to go.

On mountain roads, driving conditions can be treacherous or even prohibitive, and studded tyres or chains may be obligatory. Many mountain passes are closed in winter (check with a French motoring organisation).

Paris

Paris is a beautiful city but should be avoided at all cost when driving, especially if you need to park, which is usually difficult or impossible. If you can't avoid driving in Paris, at least give the *Place Charles de Gaulle/Étoile* (at the top of the *Champs-Elysées*) a wide berth; it's one of the worst free-for-alls in the whole of Europe – a vast roundabout where 12 roads converge, all with (theoretical) *priorité à droite*. Because of the impossibility of apportioning blame in this circus, if you have an accident responsibility is automatically shared equally between the drivers concerned, irrespective of who had right of way.

The *Place de la Concorde* is, if anything, even worse, and a road to avoid unless you've a death-wish is the *Boulevard Périphérique* (usually referred to simply as the *Périphérique*), an eight-lane race track around the city centre on which there's an average of one fatal accident a day! There's also an inner ring road, which is slower but safer.

Avoiding Congestion

In June each year, the French Ministry of Transport issues a 'wily bison' map (*Carte de Bison Futé*) showing areas likely to suffer congestion in summer, and providing information about alternative routes (*itinéraire bis*) indicated by yellow or green signs with the word *Bis*. The map is available free from petrol stations and tourist offices in France and from French Government Tourist Offices abroad, as well as via the internet (www.bison-fute. gouv.fr/index,langen.html). There are around 90 information/rest areas throughout France, indicated by a black '*i*' and an *Information Bison Futé* sign. Green-arrowed holiday routes (*flèches vertes*), avoiding large towns and cities, are also recommended.

Colour-coded traffic days and traffic jams (*orange* for bad, *rouge* for very bad and *noir* for 'stay at home') are announced via radio and television. Up-to-date information about roads can be obtained by phoning the information line of the Centres Régionaux d'Information et de Coordination Routières (08 06 02 20 22), by tuning in to *Autoroute Info* (on 107.7FM) or via the internet, e.g. www.info-autoroute.com. General information about motorways, tolls and driving in France can be obtained from French Government Tourist Offices abroad.

FRENCH DRIVERS

France has some of the most hairy drivers (*chauffard*) in Europe, who seem to use their brakes only when their horns or headlights don't work. The personality of many Frenchmen (and women, who can be very aggressive) changes the minute they get behind the wheel of a car, when even the gentlest person can become an impatient, intolerant and suicidal maniac, with an unshakeable conviction in their immortality. The French themselves, however, have a quite different opinion of their driving: according to a survey by the Association Française de Prévention des Comportements au Volant, no fewer than 98 per cent consider themselves to be 'courteous' and 'responsible' – a sad case of self-delusion.

The French revere racing drivers and many drivers are assailed by an uncontrollable urge to drive everywhere at maximum speed. To a French person, the racing line on a bend (which usually means driving on the wrong side of the road!) is *de rigueur* and overtaking is an obligation; me first (*moi d'abord*) is the French driver's motto. Even when not overtaking or cutting corners, the French have an unnerving tendency to wander across the centre line, threatening a head-on collision with anything coming in the opposite direction.

When following another vehicle (and even when they have no intention of overtaking it), French drivers sit a few metres (or even centimetres) from its rear bumper trying to push it along irrespective of traffic density, road and weather conditions or the prevailing speed limit. They're among Europe's worst tailgaters, despite a law forbidding driving within two seconds of the car in front (referred to as the *distance de sécurité*, sometimes shown on motorways by arrows marked on the road surface).

Beware of lorries and buses on narrow roads, as lorry drivers believe they have a divine right to three-quarters of the road and expect you to pull over. Don't, however, pull over too far, as many rural roads have soft verges and ditches! What makes driving in France even more hazardous is that for many months of the year French roads are jammed with assorted foreigners, including many (such as the British) who don't even know which side of the road to drive on, and whose driving habits vary from exemplary to suicidal.

Most French drivers have little respect for traffic rules, particularly anything to do with parking (in Paris, a car is a device used to create a parking space). French drivers wear their dents with pride and there are many (many) dented cars in France – particularly in Paris (a '75' Parisian registration number acts as a warning to other motorists to keep well clear!).

However, don't be too discouraged by the road hogs and tailgaters. Driving in France can be a pleasant experience (except in Paris), particularly when using rural roads that are almost traffic-free most of the time. If you come from a country where traffic drives on the left, rest assured that most people quickly get used to driving on the 'wrong' side of the road. Just take it easy at first, particularly at junctions, and bear in mind that there are other foreigners around who are just as confused as you are!

MOTORCYCLES

The French are keen motorcyclists and there are more bikers per head of population in France than in any other European country, which perhaps explains why the French aren't generally prejudiced against bikers (or cyclists).

☑ SURVIVAL TIP

Third-party insurance is necessary for bikes, as well as passenger insurance. All bikes must also be registered, have registration plates and carry a nationality sticker (*plaque de nationalité*). All motorcycle riders and passengers must wear approved crash helmets.

Nevertheless, motorcycling can be a dangerous pursuit: over 20 per cent of road casualties are motorcyclists and they're some 15 times more likely to have an accident than a car driver.

Some rules apply to all motorcycles (collectively known as *deux-roues*), while others apply to certain types of motorcycle only. Speed limits for all motorcycles are the same as for cars – although you wouldn't think so. Motorcycles over 50cc are permitted to use motorways, where tolls are lower than for cars (although the cost of a long journey can still be prohibitive). Dipped headlamps must be used at all times by riders of motorcycles over 125cc.

When parking a bike in a city, lock it securely and if possible chain it to an immovable object. Take extra care when parking in a public place overnight, particularly in Paris, where bike theft is rife.

From the age of 14, children can ride a moped (variously known as a *cyclomoteur*, *scooter*, *vélomoteur* or *Mobylette*, the last being a trade name), with an engine capacity below 50cc and capable of a maximum speed of 45kph (28mph). Mopeds aren't permitted on motorways, and riders must use cycle paths where provided. Bear in mind that mopeds are lethal in the wrong hands (most teenagers have as much road sense as hedgehogs and rabbits) and many young people are killed on them each year. If you've a child with a moped, it's important to impress upon him the need to take care (particularly in winter) and not take unnecessary risks, e.g. always observe traffic signs and signal before making manoeuvres.

ACCIDENTS

If you're unfortunate enough to be involved in a car accident (*accident d'auto*), you must stop immediately, call the emergency services by dialling 18 if anyone is injured or trapped, and complete an accident report form (*constat amiable*) provided by insurance companies. All

 Caution

If you witness an accident or its aftermath, it's a criminal offence not to try to assist anyone who's injured or in danger, at least by calling for help, and you can be fined up to €75,000 and imprisoned for up to five years for failing to do so.

drivers involved must complete a form and sign each other's forms. Always check exactly what the other driver has written before signing. It's particularly important to check the information entered on forms by other drivers against official documents, e.g. driving licence, car registration document and insurance certificate. If the police attend the scene of an accident, they'll make their own report.

France has a national fund, the Fonds de Garantie Automobile (FGA, www.fga.fr) that pays compensation to those who are injured and vehicles that are damaged by hit-and-run drivers.

Accident prevention is promoted by Prévention Routière (www.preventionroutiere. asso.fr). Other useful sites are those of the Fondation Anne-Cellier Contre l'Insécurité Routière (www.fondation-annecellier.org) and the Ligue Contre la Violence Routière (www. violenceroutiere.org).

DRINKING & DRIVING

The French are reluctant to use taxis when they go out for a meal or to a party or even to let a non-drinking person take the wheel, therefore it isn't surprising that some 40 per cent of accidents (i.e. over 2,000 deaths per year) involve 'drunken' drivers. The permitted blood alcohol concentration is 50mg of alcohol per 100ml of blood, but the amount you can drink and remain below the limit depends on whether you regularly imbibe, your sex and your weight. An 'average' man can generally drink a maximum of two small glasses of wine, two small glasses of beer or two 4cl measures of spirits; for most women the limits are lower.

Random breath tests (*Alcooltest*) are carried out by the police and motorists who are involved in accidents or who infringe motoring regulations are routinely tested for alcohol and drugs. If you're found to have over 25mg of alcohol per 100ml of air in your lungs, you're obliged to take a blood test.

Penalties usually depend on the level of alcohol in your blood and whether you're involved in an accident. If you've an accident while under the influence of alcohol your car and health insurance could be nullified and your car insurance premium will also be increased by up to 150 per cent.

CAR THEFT

Car theft is common in France, which has one of the highest rates of vehicle theft in Europe. If you drive anything other than a worthless heap, you should have theft insurance that includes your personal effects. It's particularly important to protect your car if you own a model that's desirable to car thieves, e.g. most new sports and executive cars, which are often stolen to order by professional crooks. In Provence, and on the Côte d'Azur in particular, stolen cars often find their way to Africa or the Middle East and may already be on a ferry by the time owners report them stolen.

When leaving your car unattended you should store any valuables (including clothes) in the boot or out of sight. Never leave the key in your car, even when you're paying for petrol, or leave your original car documents in your car. If possible, avoid parking in long-term car parks. Foreign-registered cars, particularly camper vans and motorhomes, are popular targets, especially when parked in ports. When

parking overnight or when it's dark, parking in a well-lit area may deter thieves.

If your car is stolen or anything is stolen from it, report it immediately to the police in the area where it was stolen and complete a statement (a copy of which will be required by your insurance company).

PARKING

Parking in most towns and cities (Paris excepted) isn't such a problem or as expensive as in many other European countries. Parking regulations may vary according to the area of a city you are in, the time of day, the day of the week, and whether the date is odd or even! In many towns, parking is permitted on the side of a street with odd-numbered houses for the first half of the month and on the 'even' side for the second half of the month. This is called *stationnement alterné semi-mensuel* and is shown by a sign. (Note that the French for 'parking' is *stationnement*; *parking* means 'car park'.)

Parking may also alternate weekly or daily; parking on alternate days is indicated by a sign stating '*Côté du Stationnement – Jours*

Pairs' (even) or *'Jours Impairs'* (odd). In Paris, signs may indicate that parking is forbidden on one side of the street at certain times, e.g. for street cleaning. On-street parking is forbidden in many streets in the centre of Paris and other cities, and also on main access routes designated as red routes (*axe rouge*). *'Stationnement interdit'* means parking is forbidden and may be accompanied by the sign of a 'P' with a line through it.

A 'Stationnement gênant' with a sign depicting a tow truck towing away a car may also indicate no parking or be indicated by yellow kerb markings. It's forbidden to park in front of a fire hydrant. In Paris, it's illegal to leave a car in the same spot on a public road for more than 24 hours and parking a caravan on roads is forbidden at any time (and some other towns and cities). Overnight parking in a lay-by isn't permitted anywhere in France, although you can stop for a rest if you're falling asleep at the wheel. On roads outside town limits, you must pull off the road to stop.

Legal parking areas in towns and cities include the following:

Blue Zones: In many cities and towns there are 'blue zones' (*zone bleue*), indicated by blue street markings. Here you can park free for one hour between 9am and noon and 2 or 2.30pm until 7pm from Mondays to Saturdays, with no limit outside these hours or on Sundays and public holidays. Parking isn't restricted between noon and 2pm, meaning you can park free from 11am until 2pm or from noon until 3pm. To park in a blue zone you must display a parking disc (*disque de contrôle/stationnement*) in your windscreen.

Ticket machines: In most French cities, parking meters have been replaced by ticket machines (*horodateurs*). If a parking sign has the word *'Horodateur'* beneath it or there's a *'Stationnement payant'* sign, perhaps with *'Payant'* also marked on the road, it means that you must obtain a ticket from a nearby machine. Paid parking is usually from 9am to 7pm, although it's free from noon to 2pm, when even traffic wardens stop for lunch. Buy a ticket for the period required and place it behind your windscreen.

Car Parks: The cost of parking in car parks (*parking*) in cities and towns varies considerably. Long-term parking, e.g. at railway stations, is available in most towns for around €10 for the first 24 hours with a reducing scale thereafter. Monthly tickets can be purchased at a discount if you park frequently.

In most cities, local residents pay reduced parking fees by obtaining a permit from the town hall, which is affixed to the right-hand side of your windscreen. Subscription cards for ticket machines are also available for residents and commuters. Disabled motorists are provided with free or reserved parking in most towns, shopping centres and at airports, but they must display an official disabled motorist's badge (*macaron*) inside their windscreen.

Fines for illegal parking are based on the severity of the offence and increase if they aren't paid within three months. If your car is given a ticket (*papillon*) and isn't moved within

an hour it will be given a second ticket, and after two hours a wheel clamp may be fitted or it may even be towed way.

FUEL

Leaded petrol is no longer available in France, where unleaded petrol (*sans plomb*) is available in two grades: 95 octane and 98 octane. Diesel fuel is *diesel* (pronounced 'dee-ezel') or *gazole/gasoil* (both pronounced 'gazwal'), and is available at all service stations. An increasing number of petrol stations (notably on *autoroutes*) also supply fuel containing biofuel. To help prevent errors, petrol pumps and hoses are colour coded; green for unleaded and black for diesel. Liquid petroleum gas (LPG) is also available and there are around 1,800 petrol stations offering LPG (*GPL* or *Gépel*), particularly on motorways (a free map is available from petrol stations).

The general word for fuel is *carburant* and petrol is *essence*; *fuel* (or *fioul*) is heating oil, and *pétrole* is paraffin or oil (the black stuff that comes out of the ground).

The cost of fuel has fallen in recent years, although prices vary considerably depending on the area, town and petrol station. The cheapest source is usually hyper/supermarkets, while rural petrol stations and those on *autoroutes* are the most expensive. The cost per litre in late 2016 was around €1.05 (diesel), €1.29 (95 octane unleaded) and €1.31 (98 octane unleaded). LPG costs around €0.70 per litre.

Self-service petrol stations (*libre service*) are common and include most motorway and supermarket stations. Manned petrol stations are more common in small towns and villages. To ask for a fill-up, say '*le plein s'il vous plaît*'. Service may include cleaning your windscreen

and checking oil and tyre pressures; tips aren't expected, although they won't be refused! When paying at self-service petrol stations, simply tell the cashier your pump number. Debit cards and major credit cards are accepted by most petrol stations.

There are 24-hour petrol stations on motorways and some other stations have automatic pumps that accept debit or credit cards, which can be used when the station is open (to save queuing) or closed. Insert your card (you may need to lift a flap – *Soulevez le volet*) and you'll receive instructions, sometimes on an LCD display, sometimes by recorded message. Some automatic pumps also have instructions in English as well as French.

GARAGES & SERVICING

Garages are required to display a list of their charges for routine repairs and servicing, and many also display their hourly rate for different types of work, e.g. mechanical, electrical or bodywork. The quality of work is usually of a high standard and charges compare favourably with those in other European countries (they're usually much lower than in the UK).

It's generally cheaper to have your car serviced at a village garage than at a main dealer, although the quality of work is variable. Note that when a car is under warranty it must usually be serviced by an approved dealer in order not to invalidate the warranty, although since 2002 dealers no longer have exclusive rights to servicing and the supply of spare parts, which were previously marked up by up to 400 per cent.

Most garages don't provide a free 'loan car' (*véhicule de remplacement*) while yours is being serviced or repaired, although the idea is beginning to catch on. Otherwise your insurance company may do so or you may be able to hire a car from a garage at a reasonable rate. Some garages will collect your car from your home or office and deliver it after a service, or will drop you off at a railway or bus station or in a local town and pick you up when your car is ready for collection.

CAR HIRE

Car hire (rental) companies such as Avis, Eurodollar, Europcar, Hertz and Thrifty have offices in most cities and large towns in France and at major airports. Look under *Location de voitures* in the Yellow Pages or search online. If you're a visitor, it's wise to book a hire car before arriving, although this is no guarantee that you'll get the car you book and won't save you having to queue to complete the paperwork when you collect it. French railways (SNCF) offer inclusive train and car-hire deals. You can hire an Avis car from some 200 SNCF stations and leave it at any station operating the *Train + auto* scheme.

Car hire in France is expensive, particularly for short periods, although rates have fallen in recent years. Prices, which include VAT (*TVA*) at 20 per cent, start at around €100 for a one-day rental of a small car such as a Peugeot 106 or Renault Twingo, but can vary widely from one company to another, so it pays to shop around. Rates also vary depending on your age and the number of years you've been driving. You may see small hire-cars marked '*Louez-moi de €55 par jour*' ('Hire me from €55 per day'); In fact, this is not a brilliant price for a day out, but rather a rate that applies only to hire contracts of at least a year!

Rates usually include 100km 'free', above which you pay a (high) rate per km. Reduced rates are available at weekends, usually from noon on Friday to 9am on Monday, and rates fall considerably over longer periods, e.g. from €260 per week. There may, however, be a large excess (*franchise*), e.g. €2,500, and you may be charged extra (as much as €20 per day) for collision damage waiver (CDW), which reduces or cancels the excess. It's possible to take out an annual insurance policy against having to pay an excess on hire, for example with via Insurance 4 Car Hire (UK 0344-892 1770, www.insurance4carhire.com), although you're covered only for trips of up to 31 days.

Local hire companies are usually cheaper than the nationals, although cars must be returned to the pick-up point. Older cars can be hired from many garages at low rates. If required, check in advance that you're permitted to take a car out of France (usually prohibited).

To hire a car you must be a minimum of 18 years old, although most companies have increased this to 21 or even 25, and most also have an upper age limit of 60 or 65. Drivers must have held a full licence for at least a year. International companies require payment by credit card and you may also need to produce a residence permit or passport.

MOTORING ORGANISATIONS

There are a number of motoring organisations in France, although membership isn't as large as in many other European countries. Breakdown insurance is provided by French insurance companies and most motorists take advantage of their low rates. Motoring organisations offer membership for individuals, couples and families and many offer 'premium' levels of membership that include additional services.

Other services provided by motoring organisations include vehicle pre-purchase serviceability checks, health and legal assistance, insurance and financial services, tourist services (e.g. a camping carnet and petrol coupons) and expert advice. Motoring organisations, like insurance companies, don't usually operate their own breakdown rescue vehicles but appoint approved garages to assist members.

The principal French motoring organisation is the Automobile Club de France (www. automobileclubdefrance.fr).

PEDESTRIAN ROAD RULES

As in many other countries, being a pedestrian in France is almost as dangerous as being a motorist; over 10 per cent of those killed on French roads are pedestrians. Pedestrian crossings (*passage à piétons*) are usually indicated by black and white or red and white stripes on the road, but can be shown merely by a different kind of paving and unlike in many 1other countries they aren't usually illuminated, e.g. by flashing or static lights. Many have humps to encourage motorists to slow down, although you shouldn't assume that they will.

In towns, pedestrian crossings are incorporated with traffic lights. At a crossing with lights pedestrians must wait for a green light (or green man) before crossing the road, irrespective of whether there's any traffic. You can be fined for crossing the road at the wrong place or ignoring pedestrian lights and crossings.

Pedestrians in France are generally better disciplined than those in many other countries and they usually wait for the green light, although where there's no crossing they're prone to wander across (and along) the road without even looking. Pedestrians must use footpaths where provided or may use a bicycle path where there's no footpath. Where there's no footpath or bicycle path, you should walk on the left side of the road (facing the oncoming traffic).

An increasing number of towns and cities have central pedestrian areas (*secteur piétonnier* or *zone piétonne*) barred to traffic, while other roads are often barred to pedestrians (indicated by an '*Interdit aux Piétons'* sign).

2 PASSAGES SURÉLEVÉS

⚠ Caution

Under a recent law, motorists are required to stop for pedestrians who indicate their intention to cross whether there's a pedestrian crossing or not; however, old habits die hard and many drivers haven't yet taken this on board, so it pays to be extremely cautious. If you're within 50m of a pedestrian crossing you must use it and can be fined for not doing so.

12.

HEALTH

*T*he quality of healthcare in France is generally excellent and the country was ranked number one in the world in a recent survey by the World Health Organization. By law all residents must have some form of health insurance, whether private or the French national health insurance scheme. The standard of hospital treatment is second to none and there are virtually no waiting lists for operations or hospital beds. Public and private medicine operate alongside one another and there's no difference in the quality of treatment provided by public hospitals and private establishments. However, local hospital services, particularly hospitals with casualty departments, are limited in rural areas.

The average life expectancy is amongst the highest in the world at 85.4 for women and 82.4 for men (source: www.worldlifeexpectancy. com). In fact people are now living so long that a new 'category' of people has been created, *le quatrième âge*, which refers to those aged over 75 – those in *le troisième âge* are now positively wet behind the ears! The infant mortality rate is around 3.3 deaths per 1,000 live births before the age of one year, which ranks France around 9th in the world (the same as life expectancy).

France has long been a nation of hypochondriacs (famously satirised by Molière in *Le Malade Imaginaire*), and the French visit their doctors more often than most other Europeans and buy large quantities of medicines, health foods and vitamin pills – in fact they're the European pill-taking champions. Part of the reason for their addiction to medicine is that healthcare has always been free (and the French are obsessive about their digestive systems).

France devotes a greater proportion of its GDP (around 11 per cent) to healthcare than to defence or education, around half of which

is spent on hospitals, a quarter on doctors' salaries and a fifth on medicines. A wide-ranging reform of the health service aimed at 'treating you better while spending less' has been approved by parliament, but has had little impact. While most people recognise the need for reform, they're reluctant to lose their abundant access to doctors, specialists and hospitals, the right to unlimited second opinions and an endless supply of free pills.

In general, French healthcare places the emphasis on preventive medicine rather than treating sickness. Alternative medicine (*médecine douce*) is popular, particularly acupuncture and homeopathy (in which France is the world leader). These treatments are recognised by France's medical council (Ordre des Médecins) and homeopathic products are reimbursed by the national health service when prescribed by a doctor at a rate of 35 per cent off the normal *tarif de convention* (set price).

You can safely drink tap water – unless it's labelled as non-drinking (*eau nonpotable*) – although the wine (especially Pétrus 1982) is more enjoyable.

EMERGENCIES

France's emergency medical services are excellent but may operate in a slightly different way from those you're used to. The action to take in a medical emergency depends on the degree of urgency. In a life-threatening emergency such as a heart attack, poisoning or serious accident, you should dial 15 for your nearest Service d'Aide Médicale d'Urgence (SAMU) unit.

SAMU is an emergency service that works closely with local public hospital emergency and intensive care units, whose ambulances are manned by medical personnel and equipped with resuscitation equipment. SAMU has a central telephone number for each region and the duty doctor decides whether to send a SAMU mobile unit, refer the call to another ambulance service, instruct you to make your own way to hospital, or call a doctor for a home visit. In the most critical situations, SAMU can arrange transport to hospital by aeroplane, helicopter or, if appropriate, boat. If you call the fire brigade or police services, they'll request a SAMU unit if they consider it necessary.

You can also call the local fire brigade (*sapeurs-pompiers* or *pompiers*) in an emergency by dialling 18. The fire brigade and public ambulance services are combined and the fire brigade is equipped to deal with accidents and emergency medical cases. It operates its own ambulances equipped with resuscitation equipment and doctors.

If you need an ambulance but the emergency isn't life-threatening you should call the local public assistance (*assistance publique*) or municipal ambulance (*ambulance municipale*) service. There are also private ambulances in most towns providing a 24-hour service, while in small towns and villages the local taxi service also provides an 'ambulance' service.

You're billed for the services of *SAMU*, the fire service or the public ambulance service, although the cost is reimbursed by social security and your complementary insurance policy (see **Mutuelles** on page 180) if you have one, in the same way as other medical costs (see below). In an emergency any hospital must treat you irrespective of your ability to pay.

There are 24-hour medical and dental services in major cities and large towns (numbers are listed in telephone directories). For medical emergencies you can contact SOS Médecins (tel. 3624 nationwide, www.sosmedecins-france.fr), while in Paris you can call SOS Dentaire (01 43 37 51 00, www.sos-dentaire.com) for dental emergencies. In Paris and other main cities there are emergency medical telephone boxes at major junctions marked 'Services Médicaux', with direct lines to emergency services. If someone has swallowed poison you should call your local 'anti-poison centre' (*centre anti-poison*), listed at the front of telephone directories.

Emergency Numbers		
Organisation	**Number**	**Emergency**
Ambulance (SAMU)	15	Serious medical emergencies
Police	17	Police emergencies
Fire Service	18	Fire, rescue and medical emergencies
General emergency	112	Pan-European emergency number
Doctor (out of hours)	116/117	Out of hours doctor

If you're unsure whom to call, your local police service will tell you or call the appropriate service for you. Whoever you call you should provide the age of the patient and if possible, specify the type of emergency. Keep a note of the telephone numbers of your doctor, local hospitals and clinics, ambulance service, poison control, dentist and other emergency services (e.g. fire, police) next to your home telephone and on your mobile phone.

If you're able to you can go directly to a hospital emergency or casualty (A&E or ER) department (*urgences*). Note that not all hospitals have paediatric units, particularly private hospitals and, if a child needs emergency treatment you should take him to a hospital catering for paediatric emergencies. Check in advance which local hospitals are equipped to deal with emergencies and the quickest route from your home, which may be of vital importance in the event of an emergency.

NATIONAL HEALTH SYSTEM

France has an excellent national health system funded partly by obligatory social security (*sécurité sociale*) contributions (*cotisations sociales*), paid by both employees and employers. It's also funded by central government and patients pay a small contribution towards costs when they use the system.

In 2016, the French government implemented a new healthcare system for foreigners called the Protection Universelle Maladie (PUMA, see http://travailleurs-sociaux-cpam75.fr/la-protection-universelle-maladie-puma or www.ameli.fr), which replaced the previous Couverture Maladie Universelle (CMU, www.cmu.fr) system. The reform is aimed at simplifying the healthcare system and reducing paperwork, as well as guaranteeing that everyone who works or lives permanently in France for longer than three months has access to basic healthcare. You usually need to pay social security contributions (*cotisations sociales*) to cover comprehensive healthcare in France, although some people are exempt from making payments.

By the end of 2017, doctors and certain other medical personnel won't be permitted to charge up front and will be paid directly by the government or a health insurer (unlike the present system whereby some patients pay up front for their healthcare services and claim a reimbursement later).

NHS Benefits

Practitioner/Treatment	Reimbursement
Maternity-related care	100 per cent
Hospitalisation	80 per cent
Doctor, dentist and midwife services; consultations as an out-patient; basic dental care; miscellaneous items, e.g. laboratory work, apparatus, ambulance services	70 per cent
Spectacles	65 per cent
Services of medical auxiliaries, e.g. nurses and therapists	60 per cent
Medicines	0 to 100 per cent

Benefits

If you qualify for healthcare under the national health system, you and your family will be entitled to subsidised or (in certain cases) free medical and dental treatment. Benefits include general and specialist care, hospitalisation, laboratory services, medicines, dental care, maternity care, appliances and transportation. If you don't qualify for health treatment under the national health system, you'll need to take out private health insurance (see page 180).

Under the national health system, health treatment is assigned a basic monetary value (*tarif de convention*), of which the healthcare system pays a proportion, usually around 70 per cent (as shown in the table). The figures shown are intended only as a guide and should be confirmed with social security and practitioners, as they can vary depending on your circumstances and social security 'status'. For example, certain patients who need serious long-term treatment, e.g. diabetic, cancer and cardiac patients, receive 100 per cent reimbursement for all treatment. The cost of buying or hiring medical equipment such as walking sticks, wheelchairs, and special pillows and mattresses, is also reimbursed up to specified limits.

The reimbursement you receive from social security applies to the *tarif de convention*, which isn't necessarily the same as the amount you pay. For example, if a blood test costs €75 and the *tarif de convention* is €60, you're reimbursed 70 per cent of €60 (€42), leaving you with a bill of €33. The balance of medical bills, called the *ticket modérateur*, can usually be reclaimed from a complementary health insurance scheme to which most people subscribe (see **Private Health Insurance** on page 180).

A charge of €1 is added to all consultation fees as part of the government's effort to reduce the social security debt and this isn't reimbursed except in the case of treatment for children and women over six months pregnant.

Registration

If you've lived in France longer than three months (and are applying under PUMA – see above) you can register for French healthcare via your local *Caisse Primaire Assurance Maladie* (CPAM, www.ameli.fr) office. However, if you're employed your employer will register you with French social security after which you can register for French healthcare. Your employer may also arrange your healthcare registration but isn't required to, therefore you should ensure that CPAM has been informed. If you're self-employed you'll need to contact the *Regime Social des Indépandants* (RSI, www. rsi.fr).

You'll need to produce certain documents, which include your passport or national ID card, proof of your long-term residence, your marriage or birth certificates (and translations) if family members are to be included, evidence of income, bank account details and proof of your address in France. You'll also need to choose a primary doctor (*médecin traitant*) – see **Doctors** below – and provide a declaration (*Declaration de Médecin Traitant*).

The CPAM office handles your reimbursements (see above), although it's the URSSAF (www.urssaf.fr) that handles your social security contributions (*cotisations sociales*).

Carte Vitale

When you register with the French health system you're issued with a green plastic membership card called a *Carte Vitale* which facilitates your reimbursements and prevents you having to pay up front for your health care. Bear in mind that you may have to request the card and wait some time before it's issued (many people wait months).

The *Carte Vitale* has your name and your social security number (*No. d'Immatriculation de l'Assuré*) printed on the front and a photo, and contains a smart chip (*puce*) with additional Information needed to process any claim for reimbursement or services. The card is linked to a computerised system known as a *dossier médical personnel* (DMP), containing all your medical records and vital information such as your blood group and allergies.

Along with a *Carte Vitale*, you receive a certificate (*attestation*) containing a list of those entitled to benefits on your behalf (*bénéficiaires*), i.e. your dependants, and the address of the office where you must apply for reimbursement of your medical expenses. Dependants include your spouse (if she isn't personally insured), dependent children under the age of 16 (or under the age of 20 if they're students or unable to work through illness or invalidity), and ascendants, descendants and relatives by marriage supported by you and living in the same household. Ensure that you keep your certificate in a safe place as you may be required to show it if you require services from a medical practitioner or chemist who isn't linked to the card system (or whose computer is out of order).

You may need to ask for documentary evidence that shows you're covered by the French health system (*attestation de couverture sociale*) and entitled to state

complete form Cerfa 60-3406 *Declaration en vue de l'immatriculation d'un pensionné* in France (provided by French social security). You're also required to produce evidence of your pension, birth certificate (with a French translation), passport and proof of residence.

Early retirees can also access **healthcare in France** under the PUMA scheme (see page 159) after three months of residence in France, although they're usually liable to pay social security contributions on their early retirement pension (there are a number of exceptions). If you're retired and under the state pension age you'll need to take out private medical insurance until you reach retirement age when you can get an S1.

 Caution

If you're planning to take early retirement in France, check whether you'll be covered under the national health system before making the move or that you can obtain (and afford) private health insurance.

Whatever your circumstances you'll be liable for the specific social charges on investment and rental income, business income and capital gains.

Visitors

If you're an EU/EEA or Swiss national visiting France you can take advantage of reciprocal healthcare agreements (in France and other EU countries) by obtaining a free European Health Insurance Card (EHIC) from your country's social security provider. You should apply for an EHIC (by post, phone or internet) at least a month before you're planning to travel to France (British residents see www. ehic.org.uk/Internet/startApplication.do). Each family member needs their own card and

parents need to apply for a card for each child under the age of 16 and in full-time education. The card's validity varies depending on the country of issue (in the UK it's valid for five years). However, you must continue to make social security contributions in the country where it was issued and, if you become a resident in another country (e.g. France) it becomes invalid in that country.

The EHIC covers 'any necessary medical treatment arising during a temporary stay in another EU member state', although it doesn't entitle you to 100 per cent reimbursement of all medical expenses, but gives you the same cover as a French resident, which is usually around 70 per cent of routine healthcare and treatment costs (see **National Health System** on page 159). You can still receive a large bill from a French hospital, as the national health service assumes only a percentage of the cost! It's therefore advisable to enquire about the availability of 'top-up' insurance covering the balance of costs.

Note that the EHIC isn't a substitute for standard travel insurance (which includes comprehensive health insurance), as it doesn't offer the same level of cover, and neither will it cover you for private medical care. If you aren't an EU/EEA national you should have travel insurance or private health insurance when visiting France.

If you incur medical costs in France, you must obtain a treatment confirmation (*feuille de soins*) and go to the local CPAM, the authority which deals with health insurance to apply for reimbursement, which will be sent to you or credited to your UK bank account. Details of the procedure are included in the booklet that comes with the EHIC form. Note that it can take months for medical expenses to be reimbursed and there are also reports of medical practitioners and hospitals in some countries, including France, refusing to accept the EHIC.

DOCTORS

There's an abundance of excellent doctors (*médecins*) in France, although they can be thin on the ground in rural areas where the depopulation of many villages has created what have become known as 'medical deserts'. If you don't speak French finding a doctor who speaks English can be a problem, as most doctors' English tends to be limited to the names of medical conditions (most of which are the same in both languages). Doctors may be in single or group practices, although there are also healthcare centres (*centres médical et social*) which offer services that are usually unavailable at doctors' surgeries, e.g. health screening, vaccinations, dental care (*soins dentaires*) and nursing care (*soins infirmiers*).

When choosing a medical practitioner, it's important to verify whether he has an agreement (*convention*) with social security –

the vast majority do. If he has an agreement, he's known as *conventionné* and will charge the set *tarif de convention*. If he has no agreement, he's termed *non-conventionné* and the bill may be two to five times the *tarif de convention*; some *non-conventionné* practitioners are 'approved' (*agréé*) by social security, but only a small proportion of their fees are reimbursed.

Town halls and chemists maintain a list of local practitioners or your employer, colleagues or neighbours may be able to recommend one. If you're covered by the French healthcare system you need to register with a general practitioner or family doctor (*médecin généraliste*) as your attending or primary doctor (*médecin traitant*) in order to claim a full reimbursement from the French healthcare system.

Your family doctor holds and maintains your medical records and will refer you to other healthcare practitioners and specialists as necessary. If you don't get a referral to see a medical auxiliary or specialist, you won't be able to claim full reimbursement from the French healthcare system. However, you don't require a referral to see a gynaecologist, paediatrician or ophthalmologist but can consult them directly. Many French doctors are specialists in acupuncture and homeopathy, both of which are reimbursed by social security when performed or prescribed by a doctor.

Surgery hours vary considerably, but if your doctor is unavailable his surgery will give you the name of a standby doctor (there may be a recorded message giving this information out of hours). If you need a doctor or medicines in a non-urgent situation and are unable to contact your doctor, your local police station (*commissariat de police*) will give you the telephone number of a duty doctor or the address of a pharmacy that's open. Alternatively you can dial 15 (there may also be a local 'emergency' number) and ask for the number of your nearest duty doctor. If you're unable to attend a surgery, your doctor may make a house call (although many don't).

☑ SURVIVAL TIP

A list of local doctors on duty on Sundays and public holidays is displayed in chemists' windows and can be obtained from police stations. Local newspapers also contain lists of doctors (and vets) who are on call over the weekend (under the heading *Urgences*).

When you visit a doctor in France you must pay a fee for the consultation if you don't present a *carte vitale* (see above). Most doctors have a contract with the **French healthcare system** to provide medical services at nationally agreed rates, which must be posted in the surgery, where you're automatically reimbursed a percentage of the medical fee by social security (see table on page 160). The balance is payable by you or your complementary health insurance or *mutuelle* (see page 180).

A routine visit to a doctor costs €24 from April 2017, rising to €25 in December 2017, of which €16.50 is reimbursed by the French healthcare system and €7.50 by a *mutuelle*. The final €1 is a 'participation fee' (*participation forfaitaire*), which isn't reimbursed by social security. The cost of visiting a specialist prescribed by your GP will rise to €50 in 2017 (from €46).

MEDICINES

The French take a lot of medicines (*médicaments* – *drogues* are narcotics!) and are Europe's largest consumers of sleeping pills, tranquillisers and antidepressants such as Prozac and Valium. Medicines prescribed by doctors represent over 80 per cent of sales, and doctors habitually prescribe a number of different remedies for each ailment.

The cost of prescription medicines is controlled by the government, with some important exceptions such as Viagra or equivalents. Prices are reviewed twice a year, although there are no price controls on non-prescription medicines. The healthcare system pays the whole cost of essential medication for certain illnesses or conditions, e.g. insulin and heart pills (labelled '100 per cent'), 65 per cent of medicines designated as important (with white labels) and 35 per cent for *médicaments de confort* (with blue labels).

Information (in French only) about medicines commonly prescribed in France can be found on the website of the Association Française de Sécurité Sanitaire des Produits de Santé (AFSSAPS, www.afssaps.fr). If you must pay for your own medicines it can be expensive, e.g. €100 or more for a course of antibiotics. Note that social security reimbursement is based on the generic equivalent of branded medicines (if one exists).

The brand names for medicines often vary from country to country, so if you regularly take a particular medicine you should ask your doctor for the generic name. If you wish to match a medicine prescribed abroad you need a current prescription with the medicine's trade name, the manufacturer's name, the chemical composition and the dosage. Pharmacies may suggest an alternative if the medicine you want isn't available. Most foreign medicines have an equivalent in France, although particular brands may be difficult or impossible to obtain.

Doctors can't prescribe for periods of longer than three months, therefore patients requiring regular repeat prescriptions usually visit their GPs once a quarter. Consequently, prescriptions for continuous-use conditions, e.g. high blood pressure or cholesterol, are usually packaged in one-month or three-month supplies.

CHEMISTS

Prescription and non-prescription medicines are obtained from a chemist or pharmacy (*pharmacie*), denoted by the sign of a green cross on a white background (which is usually illuminated when it's open). A chemist must own and run his own shop in France (chain chemists are illegal) and their numbers are strictly controlled, although there's at least one in every town and most villages (a total of over 20,000!).

Most chemists are open from around 8.30am to 7.30pm from Mondays to Saturdays, although in smaller towns they many close for lunch between noon and 2pm. Some may be closed on Mondays and/or Saturday afternoons. If you need medicine outside normal opening hours (including on Sundays) a notice giving the address of the nearest duty chemist (*pharmacie de garde*) is displayed in the chemist's window (the telephone numbers of local doctors on call may also be shown). This information is also available online at www.3237.fr or by calling 3237, and is also published in local newspapers and listed in monthly bulletins issued by town halls.

Several chemists are open in most cities until late evening or early morning and in Paris a 24-hour service is provided by the Pharmacie Les Champs, 84 avenue des Champs-Elysées, 75008 Paris (01 45 62 02 41, https://pharmaciedeschampselysees75.pharminfo.fr). There are also American and British chemists in the capital, stocking familiar American and British medicines.

Chemists are trained (and obliged) to give first aid and they can also perform procedures such as blood pressure tests. They can supply a wider range of medicines over the counter without a prescription than is available in the UK and the US, although some medicines sold freely in other countries require a doctor's prescription in France.

French chemists are trained to distinguish between around 50 species of edible and poisonous fungi (*champignon*) and will tell you whether those you've picked are delicious or deadly. They're also trained to identify local snakes to enable them to prescribe the correct antidote for bites. Crutches (*béquilles* or, oddly, *cannes anglaises*), wheelchairs and other medical equipment can be hired from chemists, although they're often provided by hospitals, e.g. after operations.

Chemists shops aren't cluttered with the non-medical wares found in American and British chemists, although many sell cosmetics and toiletries (these are called *parapharmacies*, where you can't buy certain medicines such as painkillers) and most stock animal medicines and baby products, e.g. feeding bottles. Chemists are cheaper than a *parfumerie* for cosmetics but more expensive than a supermarket or hypermarket, where only a limited range of non-prescription medicines can be purchased. A *droguerie*, which is a sort of hardware store selling toiletries, cleaning supplies, a wide range of general household goods, paint, garden supplies, tools and DIY supplies, shouldn't be confused with an American drug store.

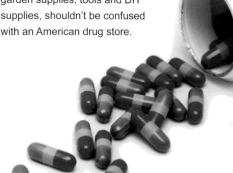

HOSPITALS & CLINICS

All cities and large towns have at least one hospital (*hôpital*) or clinic (*clinique*) – which may be public or private – which are indicated by a sign showing a red 'H' on a white background. Hospitals are listed in the Yellow Pages under *Hôpitaux* and can also be found online. France boasts more hospital beds in proportion to its population than most other European countries, although a shortage of doctors and nurses (particularly in the provinces) has led to the closure of wards in recent years.

Like doctors (see page 163), hospitals are either *conventionné* or *non-conventionné*. Every large town has at least one *hôpital conventionné*, which may be public or private, usually with a direct payment agreement with social security. Private hospitals and clinics that are *non-conventionné* may also have an agreement (*agréé*) with social security, whereby around 30 per cent of fees are usually paid by social security. For non-urgent hospital treatment, check the level of reimbursement made by social security and, if applicable, the amount your complementary insurance policy or other private health insurance will pay.

Unless you need emergency treatment you're usually admitted or referred to a hospital or clinic for treatment only after a recommendation (*attestation*) from a doctor or a specialist. Normally you're admitted to a hospital in your own *département*, unless specialist surgery or treatment is necessary which is unavailable there. If you wish to be treated in hospital by your own doctor you must check that he's able to do so.

Basic hospital accommodation that's reimbursed at 80 per cent by social security is in a two-or three-bed room (*régime commun*). A supplement must be paid for a private room (if available), although it may be paid in part or in full by your complementary or other private health insurance. The best hospital accommodation is similar to five-star hotels, with food and wine (and prices!) to match. Catering in basic accommodation varies from good to adequate.

You can usually rent a radio, TV or telephone for a small daily fee if they aren't included in the hospital room fee. A bed is also usually provided for relatives if required. You must usually provide your own pyjamas, robes, towels and toiletries.

Children aged 15 and under are usually treated in a paediatric unit well stocked with games, toys and books (and other children). However, not all hospitals have paediatric units, particularly private hospitals. Children who require long-term hospitalisation may, depending on their health, be given school lessons in hospital. Many hospitals permit a parent to stay with a child and some allow children to attend hospital during the day and return home at night if their health permits.

Patients covered by social security are charged a fixed daily fee (*forfait journalier/ indemnité journalière*) for meals of €18, unless hospitalisation was due to an accident at work or you're exempt on the grounds of low income. This fee is usually reimbursed by complementary health insurance or a *mutuelle*.

If a medical bill is expected to be above a certain amount (which is increased annually in line with inflation) you can apply to social security for a *prise en charge*, which means that the full bill will be sent directly to social security. Otherwise, you must pay the bill when you leave hospital unless you've made prior arrangements for it to be paid by your insurance company. You must pay for hospital outpatient treatment in the same way as a visit to a doctor or specialist.

Public Hospitals

There are generally three categories of public hospital: hospital centres or short-stay hospitals (*hôpital de court séjour*), medium-stay centres (*centre de moyen séjour*) and long-term treatment centres (*centre et unité de long séjour*). Hospital centres include general hospitals, *assistance publique* (*AP*) hospitals in Paris, specialist hospitals and regional centres (*centre hospitalier régional/CHR* or *centre hospitalier universitaire/CHU* when associated with a university). Public hospitals must accept all patients in an emergency irrespective of their ability to pay.

Medium-stay hospitals are usually for patients who've previously been treated in a short-stay hospital centre. They contain facilities for convalescence, occupational and physical therapy, and recuperative treatment for drug and alcohol abuse and mental illness. Long-term treatment centres are for those who are unable to care for themselves without assistance and include psychiatric hospitals and nursing homes for the aged (*maisons de retraite médicalisées*).

There are over 35 *CHU*s in France (12 in Paris), where medical students do their training. *CHU*s are rated among the best hospitals in France (indeed in the world), and professors and senior staff must undergo intensive training to secure their appointments. Rural community

hospitals are classified as hospital centres, although they're usually less well equipped than other short-stay hospitals.

Note that not all hospitals have accident and emergency (*urgences*) departments and you should check where your nearest A&E centre is to be found.

Private Hospitals & Clinics

Most private hospitals (*hôpital privé*) and clinics (*clinique*) specialise in in-patient care in particular fields of medicine, such as obstetrics and surgery, rather than being full-service hospitals (the American Hospital in Paris is a rare exception). The cost of treatment in a private hospital or clinic is generally much higher than in a public hospital, where a large proportion of costs are reimbursed by social security. However, some private hospitals participate in the French social security system and operate in the same way as public hospitals.

If your French is poor, you may prefer to be treated at a private hospital or clinic with English-speaking staff, as most public hospitals make little or no allowance for foreigners who don't speak French. There are a number of expatriate hospitals in the Paris area, including the American Hospital in Paris (01 46 41 25 25, www.american-hospital.org) and the Hertford British Hospital, also known as the Hôpital Franco-Britannique (01 46 39 22 22, www.british-hospital.org), which specialises in maternity care. Most staff at all levels in these hospitals speak English. Fees at the American hospital are much higher than at French hospitals, although they can usually be reclaimed through the French social security system and most *mutuelles*, and are accepted by most American medical insurance companies.

CHILDBIRTH

Childbirth in France invariably takes place in a hospital, where a stay of at least five days and as many as 12 is normal, depending on factors such as the number of beds available and the mother's and baby's health. Most hospital maternity units are equipped with single and double rooms. You can choose to have a baby at home, but it's unlikely you'll receive support from doctors or other medical staff or from social security.

As soon as your pregnancy is confirmed (by a blood test), your doctor will provide general information about the progress of your pregnancy and issue a document declaring the pregnancy (*déclaration de grossesse*). This is sent to your local health insurance fund (Casse d'Assurnace Maladie/CAM) and the family allowance fund (Caisse d'Allocations Familiales/CAF), who will issue you with a reference number to allow claims for family allowances.

You may be 'allocated' to a maternity hospital or clinic, although if you live equidistant from two or more you may be given a choice. You should continue to see your doctor or a midwife at your chosen hospital each month. At the end of your 11th, 22nd and 33rd weeks of pregnancy you're given an ultrasound scan (*échographie*) to check on the progress of the foetus. After the first scan, you'll be asked to take an additional blood test to check for the likelihood of Down's syndrome (*syndrome de Down* or *Trisomie 21*).

> If you don't wish to know the sex of your child, you should say so before each scan is made.

A midwife normally supervises expectant mothers. It's possible to consult an obstetrician, but he'll usually become closely involved in a birth only if complications are expected or when it's classified as high-risk. You can engage a private obstetrician to attend you before, during and after giving birth, although this won't be paid by social security (but may be covered by private health insurance). In any case you should register at the hospital, when a bed will be provisionally reserved for you at the appropriate time.

Social security pays 100 per cent of most medical expenses relating to a pregnancy, including medical examinations and tests, antenatal care and the delivery. However, it's expensive to have a child in a hospital if you aren't covered by social security or don't have private medical insurance, in which case it may be cheaper to have your child abroad (or at home).

To qualify for social security maternity benefit (*allocation pour jeune enfant*), mothers-to-be must undergo at least four antenatal examinations, during their third, sixth, eighth and ninth months of pregnancy. After your first examination you receive a certificate (*attestation de premier examen prénatal obligatoire*) that must be sent to your CAF to ensure that you receive social security benefits.

Registration

Births must be registered within three working days at the town hall of the district where they take place. In fact, this is done automatically if you don't do it yourself, but then your signature won't appear on the birth certificate. Registration applies to everyone irrespective of their nationality and whether they're resident in France or just visiting. When registering a birth you must produce a certificate signed by a doctor or midwife and the parents' passports or identity cards.

You should receive copies of the complete birth certificate (*acte de naissance – copie intégrale*) as well as 'summaries' (*extrait de l'acte de naissance*), which are required by various bodies, e.g. the tax office (see below). The hospital will issue you with a health record book (*carnet de santé*) for your child (see below). Children born to foreign nationals should be registered at the local consulate or embassy in order to obtain a national birth certificate and passport for a child, which may take several weeks.

Note than whenever someone born in France is required to produce his birth certificate, what's actually required is an extract (*extrait*) from the local record book, which contains details not only of his birth but also of his current status (*état civil*). Any such extract must be no more than three months old.

If you've private health insurance, don't forget to notify your health insurance company about the birth of a child. Also notify the tax office and ensure that your income tax payments are adjusted accordingly.

You may give your child any name that isn't 'prejudicial' (whatever that means) and may be given either his father's surname or his mother's (maiden) name or both the parents' family names (hyphenated, in either order). Parents are asked to complete a *déclaration conjointe de choix de nom* at the time of registering a birth, but if you fail to complete a declaration the child is given the father's surname only.

Information & Support

Midwives (*sages-femmes*), who are qualified nurses with special training, handle most routine pregnancies and play an important part in childbirth. They're also responsible for educating and supporting pregnant women and their families. Midwives can advise women

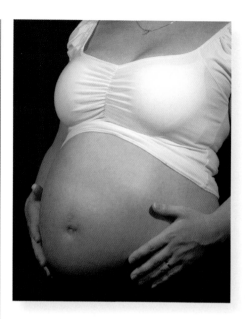

before they become pregnant, in addition to providing moral, physical and emotional support, both during pregnancy and after a birth.

All public hospitals and many private clinics offer childbirth classes, although these may take the form of discussions rather than instruction. French social security also pays for physiotherapy (*kinésithérapie*) after childbirth.

Your family doctor or obstetrician will advise you about postnatal examinations and check-ups. In some areas there are mother and child protection centres (Centre de Protection Maternelle et Infantile/PMI) providing free services to pregnant women and children under the age of six, covered by social security. A list of local PMI centres is available from your town hall.

A number of organisations provide counselling services for pregnant women, including SOS Bébé (01 42 47 08 67, www.sosbebe.org) and the Message Mother Support Group's website (01 58 60 00 53, www.messageparis.org).

CHILDREN'S HEALTH

The French healthcare system provides a comprehensive programme of preventive treatment for children and offers a range of dedicated medical facilities. All children are required to have monthly check-ups during infancy and three health checkups during their school years.

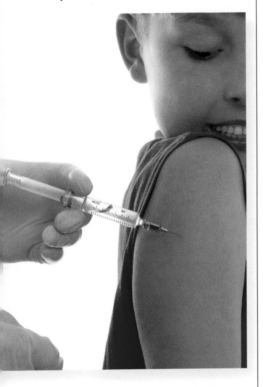

Children born in France are issued with a health record book (*carnet de santé*), in which is recorded every medical occurrence in their pre-adult lives, including vaccinations, childhood illnesses, general medical check-ups and surgery. It should always be taken with you on a medical visit with your child and must be produced when a child starts school. You can obtain a *carnet de santé* for children who weren't born in France from your local town hall on production of their passport, which is provided free if you're covered by social security.

When you arrive in France, you should bring proof of your child's immunisations with you. Vaccinations against diphtheria (*diphtérie*), polio (*polio*) and tetanus (*tétanos*), collectively called *DPT*, and whooping cough (*coqueluche*) are given between the third and fifth months after birth (via three injections at monthly intervals). *DPT* boosters are administered at 12 to 15 months and again at five to six years and are repeated thereafter at five or six-year intervals.

All children must be vaccinated again tuberculosis (*tuberculose*) by means of a BCG (*BCG*) before the age of six years, but the vaccination isn't recommended before the age of two. Note that without these compulsory vaccinations your child may not be admitted to school. Although it isn't compulsory, a multiple vaccination called ROR (or *rudirouvax*) against measles (*rougeole*), mumps (*oreillons*) and German measles (*rubéole*) is recommended between the age of 12 and 15 months. Vaccinations are provided free..

Mothers can obtain a 'health kit' (*kit de santé*) from a Centres d'Information et de Documentation Jeunesse (www.cidj.com). Information and help for parents of sick children is available from the Association Sparadrap (www.sparadrap.org – available in English), which publishes numerous books and leaflets.

DENTISTS

There are excellent dentists (*dentiste*) throughout France, although most don't speak fluent English ('Aaargh!' is the same in any language!). Your colleagues or neighbours may be able to recommend someone and town halls maintain lists of local dentists, which are listed in the Yellow Pages under *Dentistes* and can also be found online. Many dentists are qualified to perform non-routine treatment, e.g. endodontics (*endodontie*) or periodontics (*paradontie*), carried out by specialists in many other countries, but some treatment is available only from a 'surgeon dentist' (*chirurgien dentiste*). Dentists usually carry out routine teeth cleaning themselves in France, where specialist hygienists are rare.

Dentists' surgery hours vary considerably but are typically 9am to noon and 2-7pm from Monday to Friday (some dentists also have Saturday morning surgeries). You must make an appointment and shouldn't expect to receive a reminder you're due for a checkup. Many dentists provide an emergency service and there are also emergency services in most major cities. In Paris, there's a 24-hour home emergency dental service called *SOS Dentaire* (01 43 37 51 00, www.sos-dentaire.com).

As with doctors you should check whether a dentist is *conventionné* if you want costs to be reimbursed. Social security pays 70 per cent of the standard cost (*tarif de convention*) of dental care and prosthetic treatment, e.g. crowns and bridges. For orthodontic work, which is generally restricted to children under 12, you must obtain a written description of the treatment required and an estimate of the cost for social security prior to starting treatment (you should be reimbursed 100 per cent of the cost). If applicable (and possible), a dentist will charge the cost to the French health system using your *carte vitale*, otherwise you must pay the dentist and apply for a reimbursement.

OPTICIANS

There are no free eye tests for children or elderly people in France, where to obtain reimbursement (at 70 per cent) from social security it's necessary to have your eyes examined by an ophthalmologist (*ophtalmologue*), although you may have to wait weeks or even months for an appointment.

An ophthalmologist is a specialist medical doctor trained in diagnosing and treating disorders of the eye, performing sight tests, and prescribing spectacles and contact lenses. As with doctors, some ophthalmologists are *conventionné*, meaning that they charge the basic rate for a specialist consultation, whereas others (roughly half) aren't, which means that they charge more, although you're reimbursed only at the basic rate. Treatment, including surgery, is reimbursed at 65 per cent.

If glasses are necessary an ophthalmologist will write a prescription that you take to an optician. It isn't necessary to register with an optician or optometrist (*opticien*). To be reimbursed you must choose an optician who's approved (*agréé*) by social security. Social security pays 60 per cent of the cost of lenses and a 'basic' frame if you require new glasses or your spectacles are broken beyond repair (the balance may be reimbursed by a *mutuelle*). Note that although some opticians perform sight tests (as in many other countries, such as the UK) as well as providing glasses, you won't be reimbursed by social security if your eye test wasn't performed by an ophthalmologist (although some *mutuelles* cover the cost of optician-prescribed glasses).

The cost of spectacles (and contact lenses) isn't controlled in France and may be higher than in some other European countries, so it's wise to shop around and compare costs. Opticians are listed in the Yellow Pages under *Opticiens* and ophthalmologists under *Médecins: ophtalmologie* (or search online).

COUNSELLING

Counselling and help are available throughout France for various health and social problems including drug and nicotine addiction, alcoholism, compulsive gambling, obesity, teenage pregnancy, rape, AIDS, attempted suicide and psychiatric disorders, as well as problems related to homosexuality, adolescence, marriage and relationships, child abuse and family violence.

There's a 24-hour information/assistance telephone number (113) for problems associated with drugs, alcohol and smoking (*Drogue/ Alcool/Tabac Info-Service*). There are also self-help groups in all areas for problems such as alcoholism, gambling and weight control,

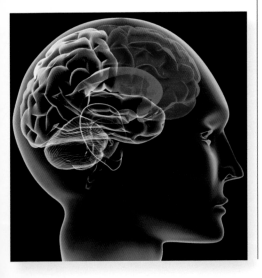

e.g. Weight Watchers. There are psychologists (*psychologue*), psychiatrists (*psychiatre*) and psychoanalysts (*psychanalyste*) in public as well as private practice, and consultations with those in public practice may be reimbursed by social security.

The telephone numbers of various local counselling and help services (*Services d'Assistance*) are listed at the front of telephone books and include numbers for *SOS Amitié* (www.sos-amitie.com), the French equivalent of the Samaritans, which provides a free counselling service in times of personal crisis. To find the number of your nearest *SOS Amitié*, telephone 01 40 09 15 22. SOS Help is an English-speaking Paris-based telephone crisis line in operation from 3 to 11pm daily (01 46 21 46 46, www.soshelpline.org).

DEATHS

When someone dies in France, the attending doctor completes a death certificate (*acte de décès*), but the medical cause of death is treated as confidential and doesn't appear on death certificates. (You should make at least six copies of the *acte de décès*.) This can lead to problems if the body is to be sent abroad for burial, when a foreign coroner may require a post mortem examination. If a death takes place at home in Paris, a coroner (*médecin de l'état civil/médecin légiste*) must be called, although elsewhere a family doctor can complete the death certificate. An inquest (*enquête judiciaire*) must be held when a death occurs in a public place or when it could have been caused by a criminal act.

A death must be registered within 24 hours at the town hall in the district where it took place. Anyone can register a death but you must present your own identification and that of the deceased. If the deceased was a foreigner the town hall will require his passport or *carte de séjour*. The family record book (*livret de famille*) is required for a French citizen. Deaths of foreign nationals in France should also be registered at your local consulate or embassy.

Within a week of a death you should inform banks and other financial instututions, employer, retirement fund, insurers and *notaire*, as appropriate, as well as the next of kin – who may all require a copy of the death certificate. Within a month, a surviving spouse should apply for any pension refund (*réversion*) and within six months of a death you should complete a *déclaration des revenues* (on form 2042N) for the tax office showing the income of the deceased's household between 1st January last and the date of death. See also **Wills** on page 204.

Further information about funerals can be obtained from the Association Française d'Information Funéraire (www.afif.asso.fr). Information about what to do in the case of the death of a British national in France is provided on the Gov.uk website (www.gov.uk/guidance/death-of-a-british-national-in-france).

Burial & Cremation

Dying in France is expensive, although since the state lost their monopoly on funerals at the end of the '90s the cost has fallen and there are now 'supermarkets for the dead' such as the Roc-Eclerc chain (www.roceclerc.com). Always obtain several quotations (*devis*) for a funeral and make sure that you aren't paying for anything you don't want.

Cemeteries (*cimetière*) are secular and are usually owned by local authorities, who license a local undertaker (*pompes funèbres*) to perform burials. Before a burial can take place, the town hall must issue an 'act of death' (*acte de décès*) and a burial or cremation permit (*permis d'inhumer/de crémation*), as well as a permit to transport the body if it's to be buried outside the commune. You also need the mayor's permission to be buried in the commune where you've a second home. Bodies are normally buried or cremated within six days of death.

Until recently there were few crematoria (*crématoire*) in France, although they're now found in most large cities. You're permitted to scatter ashes anywhere in France except on a public right of way.

13.
INSURANCE

*M*ost residents in France are covered by French social security, which offers higher benefits than in most other EU countries. Nevertheless, you would be unwise to rely solely on social security to meet your insurance needs. It's your responsibility to ensure that you and your family are legally insured in France and the law is likely to differ from that in your home country or your previous country of residence, so don't assume that it's the same. There are a few occasions where insurance (*assurance*) for individuals is compulsory, including third party car insurance, third party liability insurance for tenants and homeowners, and mortgage life insurance if you've a mortgage. If you lease a car or buy one on credit, a lender will insist that you have comprehensive car insurance.

Voluntary insurance includes third party liability insurance for schoolchildren, supplementary health insurance and pensions, disability, health, household, dental, travel and life insurance (all covered in this chapter). If you fancy hunting in France, you can even take out insurance against being shot or having a leg chewed off by a *sanglier!*

If you're planning to take up residence in France, you should ensure that your family has full health insurance during the interval between leaving your last country of residence and obtaining health insurance in France. This is particularly important if you've an existing health problem that won't be covered by a new policy.

When buying insurance, obtain recommendations from friends, colleagues and neighbours and compare the costs, terms and benefits provided by a number of companies before making a decision. Nowadays it's easy to compare policies online using comparison sites, e.g. www.assurland.com and www. lelynx.fr/comparaison/assurances.

Further information can be found on the Service Public website (www.service-public.

fr) and from the Fédération Française des Sociétés d'Assurances (www.ffsa.fr).

INSURANCE COMPANIES & AGENTS

Insurance is one of France's major business sectors, with over 500 French insurance companies and mutual benefit organisations to choose from, many providing a range of services while others specialise in certain fields only. The major insurance companies have offices or agents throughout France, including most large towns. Most insurance companies provide a free appraisal of your family's insurance needs.

Many of the largest companies, such as Groupement d'Assurances Nationales and Assurances Générales de France, which were previously government-owned, have now been privatised, although the government maintains regulatory control over the insurance industry. The insurance sector is governed by regulations set out in the 'insurance code' (*code des assurances*) and insurance companies are supervised by the Direction Générale des Assurances.

It's possible to take out certain kinds of insurance in another country, e.g. property insurance, although the policy must usually be written under French law. The advantages are that you've a policy you can fully understand (apart from all the legal jargon!) and can make claims in your own language. This is usually a good option for the owner of a holiday home in France. However, although theoretically EU residents are entitled to obtain insurance from any EU insurance company, they must be licensed to sell insurance in France and there are numerous obstacles (surprise, surprise).

Insurance companies and *mutuelles* (see page 180) sell their policies in a number of ways. There are 'general agents' (*agent général*), which is a misleading term for agents who represent a single company and sell the policies of that company only, and brokers (*courtier*), who sell policies from a number of insurance companies and *mutuelles* (see below). Most *mutuelles* and some insurance companies also sell their policies direct to the public, transactions often taking place by telephone, post and online.

Note that it can be difficult to obtain impartial insurance advice, as brokers may be 'influenced' by the high fees offered for selling a particular policy. (Regrettably, you can't sue an insurance agent for giving you bad advice or insure yourself against being uninsured!) Read all insurance contracts carefully before signing them. If you don't understand anything, get someone to check it and explain the terms and the cover provided. Policies often contain 'traps' in the small print and, like insurance companies everywhere, some companies will do almost anything to avoid honouring claims. You're usually issued with a provisional contract and, several weeks later, a definitive contract (the French love paperwork).

If you wish to make a claim, you must usually inform your insurance company in writing by registered letter within two to five days of the incident (e.g. for accidents) or 24 hours in the case of theft. Thefts should also be reported to the local police within 24 hours, as you must provide proof that you've filed a police report (*récépissé du dépôt de plainte*) when making a claim.

Always check the notice period required to cancel (*résilier*) a policy. Insurance policies are normally automatically extended (*tacite reconduction*) for a further period (usually a year) if they aren't cancelled in writing by registered letter two or three months before their expiry date. If you don't cancel a policy you must pay the next year's premium even if you no longer require the insurance!

However, you can cancel an insurance policy before the term has expired without penalty if the premium is increased, the terms are altered (e.g. the risk is reduced), an insured object is lost or stolen, or (in the case of home insurance) you move home. In certain circumstances you may cancel without penalty if your personal circumstances change, e.g. you change jobs, are made redundant or retire, get married or divorced, or a member of your family dies. A cancellation for any of the above reasons must still be made in writing and sent by registered post.

SOCIAL SECURITY

France has a comprehensive social security (*sécurité sociale*) system covering healthcare, injuries at work, family allowances, unemployment insurance and old age, invalidity and death benefits. France spends more on 'welfare' than almost any other EU country: over 30 per cent of GDP. Not surprisingly, social security benefits are among the highest in the EU (the average household receives around a third of its income from social support payments such as family allowances and pensions), as are social security contributions. Total contributions per employee average around 60 per cent of gross pay, some 60 per cent of which is paid by the employer (an impediment to hiring staff).

The self-employed must pay the full amount (an impediment to self-employment!), although the self-employed who operate a small business under the *auto-entrepreneur* system (see page 32) only pay contributions as and when they have income. However, with the exception of sickness benefits, social security benefits aren't taxed; indeed they're deducted from your gross taxable income. No surprisingly the public are highly resistant to any change that would reduce benefits, while employers are pushing to have their contributions lowered. Despite the high contributions paid in the French social security system is under severe financial strain due to an ageing population, which has contributed to a huge increase in spending on healthcare and pensions in recent years.

The Caisse Nationale d'Assurance Maladie (CNAM), which is part of the Ministry of Health and Social Security, is the public authority responsible for ensuring that social security policy is carried out on a national level, and for negotiating conventions and agreements with medical professions. Sixteen regional sickness insurance fund offices (Caisse Régionale d'Assurance Maladie/CRAM) deal with questions regarding accidents at work and retirement. They also coordinate the actions of local social security offices (Caisse Primaire d'Assurance Maladie/CPAM), of which there are around 130 throughout the country (at least one in each department) which deal with everyday matters and reimbursements.

Information about social security is available online in English from www.securite-sociale. fr/the-french-social-security-system-www-cleiss-fr?type=presse and www.cleiss.fr/docs/regimes/regime_france/an_index.html. Information is also available from the Service Public site (www.service-public.fr) and the Assurance Maladie site (www.ameli.fr – it stands for *Assurance Maladie en ligne*), where some information is available in English (click on 'Qui sommes nous?' on the home page).

Eligibility & Exemptions

Your entitlement to health and other social security benefits depends on your nationality, your work status (e.g. whether you're employed, self-employed or retired) and your residence status. Unless you're covered by a reciprocal social security agreement, you must normally contribute to French social security for a certain period before bring eligible for benefits. For example, you must contribute for three months before being entitled to family allowances, and you must contribute for at least a year before you can claim maternity benefits.

Different periods of salaried employment are required to qualify for either cash benefits

(*prestations en espèces*), e.g. disability payments, or benefits 'in kind' (*prestations en nature*), e.g. free medicines. For example, for *prestations en espèces* you must have been in salaried employment for at least 120 hours in the last quarter, while for *prestations en nature* you must have been salaried for at least 200 hours. Full details are available from your local social security office.

If you no longer meet the qualifying conditions, your benefits are extended for a maximum of a year from that date. (Benefits are extended indefinitely for the long-term unemployed, provided they're actively seeking employment.) If you don't qualify for social security benefits and don't have private health insurance and your annual income is below €9,654 (2016), you may be entitled to the most basic of state healthcare, known as Protection Universelle Maladie (PUMA, see http://travailleurs-sociaux-cpam75.fr/la-protection-universelle-maladie-puma or www.ameli.fr), provided you've lived in France continuously for three months. PUMA is intended to ensure that all French residents have at least some social security cover.

If you're working in France your employer will usually complete the necessary formalities to ensure that you're covered by social security. If he doesn't you must obtain confirmation that you're employed in France (*déclaration d'emploi*) and register at your local CPAM. Your town hall will give you the address or you can find it under *Sécurité Sociale* in your local Yellow Pages or online.

If you're a student following a standard course at a French state-supported institution, you're usually covered by French social security. However, if you're attending a private institution, e.g. the American University of Paris, or are following a non-standard programme such as French language classes, you must have (and must produce evidence of) private health insurance. Those coming to France under an exchange scheme must be covered for healthcare by the exchange authorities.

Contributions & Benefits

Social security contributions (*cotisations sociales* or *charges sociales*) are calculated as a percentage of your taxable income, although for certain contributions there's a maximum salary level. Contributions start as soon as you're employed or start work in France and not when you obtain your residence permit (*carte de séjour*) or proof of residence certificate.

Contributions are paid directly to the Union de Recouvrement des Cotisations de Sécurité Sociale et d'Allocations Familiales (URSSAF), which has around 100 offices throughout France. URSSAF offices collect contributions for their area and send them to the central social security agency (Agence Centrale des Organismes de Sécurité Sociale/ACOSS) which distributes funds to the various benefit agencies, e.g. CNAF, CNAV and CRAM.

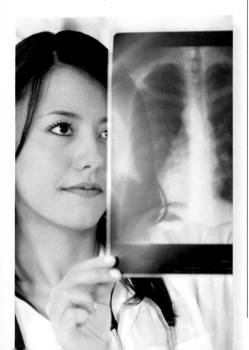

It's possible to pay contributions monthly (actually, you pay ten monthly instalments from January to October) based on an estimated total contribution; any necessary adjustment is made in November or December); you must apply before 1st December for monthly payments from the following 1st January.

Salaried employees come under the general regime for salaried workers (*régime général des travailleurs salariés*). There are special regimes for agricultural workers (*régime agricole*) called MSA or GAMEX, and for miners, seamen, railway workers and various other state employees. All these are termed obligatory regimes (*régimes obligatoires*).

Under French social security you're entitled to health, sickness and maternity, work injury and invalidity, family allowance, unemployment, and old age, widow(er)'s and death benefits. With the exception of health benefits (see page 160) these are known as 'cash' payments (*prestations en espèces*). Health benefits are known as payments 'in kind' (*prestations en nature*), e.g. free medicines. Most social security benefits (*allocations*) are paid as a percentage of your salary rather than at a flat rate, subject to minimum and maximum payments.

For detailed information about French social security benefits (in English) see www.securite-sociale.fr/the-french-social-security-system-www-cleiss-fr?type=presse and www.cleiss.fr/docs/regimes/regime_france/an_index.html.

PENSIONS

There's a crisis in state pension funding in France (and most of Europe), which has the largest proportion of inactive people over 55 in the EU, high unemployment, one of Europe's highest life expectancies, and around 40 per cent of 18 to 25-year-olds in full-time education. In 2010, the government extended the number of years some people are required to work in order to qualify for a full state pension on retirement (see **Retirement & Pensions** on page 44).

The French pension system is largely unfunded, which means that the active population pays the pensions of those who are retired or otherwise inactive, known as a *régime de répartition*. As in many other countries, there are plans to transfer the burden from the public to the private sector, although this is creating controversy and social unrest.

The state pension schemes (the principal one for employees in business and industry, and supplementary schemes for various government employees, small businessmen, shopkeepers and farmers) comprise both basic and supplementary pensions. Contributions are made by both employers and employees and vary according to income. Certain non-employed people can contribute voluntarily to the state pension scheme in order to qualify for a pension.

Retiring in France

If you move to France after working in another EU country, or move to another EU country after working in France, your state pension contributions can be exported to France (or from France to another country). French state pensions are payable abroad and most countries pay state pensions directly to their nationals resident in France. If you're salaried in France before your retirement there, following previous salaried employment in the UK, your local CRAM or CNAV office will handle your application for a UK state pension. They'll need your UK National Insurance number when you apply for your French state pension.

 Caution

Americans who retire in France can receive their pensions (and other benefits) via the Social Security department of the French Embassy in Paris.

If you plan to retire to France you should ensure that your income is (and will remain) sufficient to live on, bearing in mind possible devaluations if your pension or income isn't paid in euros, rises in the cost of living (see page 187), and unforeseen expenses such as medical bills or anything else that may reduce your income, e.g. stock market crashes.

Comprehensive information about retirement in France is contained in our sister publication, *Retiring in France* (Survival Books).

PRIVATE HEALTH INSURANCE

By law all residents in France must have some form of health insurance, whether private or the state health insurance scheme. If your stay in France is short you may be covered for emergency medical treatment by a reciprocal agreement between your home country and France or the visitors' EHIC scheme (see page 162) for EU/EEA nationals, but this may not cover you for routine treatment for which you may need to take out private health insurance. This could take the form of a holiday and travel policy (see below) or a comprehensive international health policy. It's essential to ensure that your family is adequately insured in France, otherwise you could be faced with some *very* high medical bills.

If you spend a lot of time in different countries you may wish to take out an international health policy (sometimes referred to as private medical insurance or PMI), which should provide immediate emergency healthcare, immediate access to a doctor, referral to a specialist if required and routine treatment, including dental treatment.

Once you become resident in France you must register with social security (see page 160) which covers most of your medical expenses, although you may wish to take out a complementary health insurance or *mutuelle* (see below) which pays the portion of medical bills that isn't paid by social security.

Mutuelles

A *mutuelle* (mutual benefit organisation) is an association made up of individuals who are grouped together, e.g. by profession or area, in order to insure themselves for a favourable premium. There are two kinds of *mutuelle*: one is a sort of provident society or sick fund, which is a non-profit organisation that ploughs its profits back into the fund, and the other a profit-making insurance company. A provident *mutuelle* provides fixed tariffs irrespective of the number of claims and is greatly preferable to an insurance company.

Most French residents are covered for most of their medical expenses under French social security, although this doesn't pay 100 per cent of bills. To cover the portion of bills not paid by social security, most French people take out a complementary health insurance (or 'top-up') policy (*assurance complémentaire maladie*, commonly called a *mutuelle*). A complementary scheme may also provide a supplementary pension, and the *Loi Madelin* allows you to deduct your contributions from taxable income provided you join the *mutuelle*, which costs (depending on your age) from around €15 per month.

Most trades and occupations have their own *mutuelle* commonly providing supplementary health insurance and pensions, of which there are some 400 in France. If you're self-employed (*travailleur independent* or *profession libérale*) you must take out a health insurance policy (known in this case as an *assurance au premier franc*) through your social security office or through the relevant professional organisation. Information about insurance for the self-employed can be obtained from offices of the Caisse d'Assurance Maladie des Professions Libérales.

If you aren't employed in France but have a social security card (*Carte Vitale*), you can join a complementary fund of your own choosing. Premiums are normally quoted as a flat rate per person covered, therefore unlike social security health cover, insuring a large family costs considerably more than insurance for a single person.

Many *mutuelles* base their reimbursements on those of social security and reimburse a patient only after social security has paid a proportion of the fee. Therefore, in a case where social security doesn't contribute, e.g. when a medical practitioner isn't part of the national health system (*non-conventionné, non-agréé* – see page 163), a complementary fund may also pay nothing. However, some *mutuelles* pay the whole cost or part of the cost of treatment or items that aren't covered or which are barely covered by social security, such as false teeth and spectacles.

Reimbursement applies only to the standard medical charges (*tarif de convention*). For example, if a blood test costs €50 and the *tarif de convention* is €40, your complementary fund will normally pay only the 30 per cent of the €40 that isn't refunded by social security. You must pay the €10 charged in excess of the *tarif de convention* yourself. However, for a higher premium you can insure yourself for actual charges (*frais réels*). Most policies offer different levels of cover. It's sometimes necessary to have been a member of a complementary fund for a period before you're eligible to make a claim, e.g. three months for medical claims and six months for dental claims.

When choosing a complementary fund, ask friends, colleagues and neighbours for recommendations, and compare the costs, terms and benefits provided by a number of funds before making a decision. Further information about *mutuelles* can be obtained from the Fédération Nationale de la Mutualité Française (www.mutualite.fr), which provides links to regional offices.

A few foreign insurance companies offer top-up policies for expatriates living in France, such as Aetna International (UK 0866-320 4023, www.aetnainternational.com) for UK nationals.

DENTAL INSURANCE

It's unusual to have full dental insurance (*assurance dentaire*) in France, as the cost is prohibitive. Basic dental insurance is provided under social security (see **Dentists** on page 170) and by *mutuelles* (see above). A *mutuelle* may offer additional cover for a higher premium.

Most private health insurance companies offer dental cover (or more comprehensive cover) for an additional premium, although there are many restrictions and cosmetic treatment is excluded. Where applicable, the amount payable by a health insurance policy for particular treatment is fixed and depends on your level of dental insurance. It's often

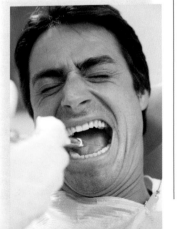

necessary to request 'pre-approval' for certain dental treatment and services, such as crowns, caps or bridge work. A list of specific refunds is available from insurance companies.

HOUSEHOLD INSURANCE

Household insurance in France generally includes third party liability (*responsabilité civile*), building and contents insurance, all of which are usually contained in a multi-risk household insurance policy (*assurance multirisques habitation*). Nine out of ten homeowners have a multi-risk policy but not all policies cover the same risks. For example, while over 90 per cent of policies cover water damage, fewer than 90 per cent include third party liability, only around 75 per cent include theft and just over half cover glass breakage.

All buildings under construction and major renovation or repair work on existing buildings must be covered by damage insurance (*assurance de dommages*) which guarantees work for ten years after completion. It's the builder who's responsible for taking out this cover, but during the first ten years of the building's life it passes automatically to a new owner and will pay for damage caused by faults in the original construction.

THIRD PARTY LIABILITY INSURANCE

It's customary to have third party liability insurance (*assurance responsabilité civile*) in France for all members of your family. This covers you for damage done or caused by you, your children and even your pets, e.g. if your dog (or child) bites someone, although where damage is due to negligence benefits may be reduced. Check whether insurance covers you against accidental damage to your home's fixtures and fittings.

Third-party liability insurance is usually combined with household insurance (see above), which is usually adequate for modern domestic requirements. When not included in household insurance it's normally designed for businesses where cover may be necessary for the activities of a number of employees and, perhaps, the uses of power tools, vehicles, etc. Consequently the costs would probably be prohibitive for domestic purposes. Rates typically start in the hundreds of euros per year, rising to many thousands for large-scale needs; even then policy holders may need to pay an excess for each claim. If you're self-employed or run a business, you must also have third party liability insurance for 'managers' (*assurance responsabilité civile chef d'entreprise*), the cost of which depends on your field of work.

☑ SURVIVAL TIP

If you've children at school, they must also be covered for third party liability (assurance scolaire – see Insurance on page 102).

If you're letting a property, you should ensure that you're covered for third party liability in respect of your tenants, as most home insurance policies exclude such 'commercial' liability.

HOLIDAY & TRAVEL INSURANCE

Travel insurance (*assurance voyage*) is available from many sources, including travel agents; insurance agents; motoring organisations; charge and credit card companies; household, car or private medical insurers; and transport companies. Package holiday companies also offer insurance policies. However, most don't provide adequate cover, although you should take advantage of what they offer. For example, car insurance

may include personal accident and health insurance (e.g. through Mondial Assistance) even if you don't use your car, but won't cover you for belongings or the cancellation of flights.

LIFE INSURANCE

There are two kinds of life insurance in France: life assurance (*assurance vie*) and death insurance (*assurance décès*). A life assurance policy is valid until you die and is essentially the same as a pension scheme, whereas a death insurance policy pays out only when you die. A life assurance policy benefits you, whereas a death insurance policy benefits your survivors.

A death insurance policy can be useful as security for a bank loan and can be limited to cover the period of the loan; companies will usually place an age limit, eg. 80, beyond which cover is no longer provided. A life assurance policy can be a useful tax planning tool, reducing your tax rate on investment income. The term 'life insurance' is used for both types of insurance in this section, but you should ensure that you know which type of insurance you're buying.

Many companies provide free life insurance as an employment benefit, although it may be accident life insurance only, i.e. if you die as the result of an accident. If your employer doesn't provide life insurance (or if the cover provided is inadequate), you should consider taking out a private policy. You can take out a private life insurance or endowment policy with numerous French or foreign insurance companies, although a life insurance policy that complies with and is intended to take advantage of French law is best taken out in France. You're entitled to a 30-day 'cooling off' period with a French life insurance policy, during which you may cancel it without penalty.

New laws have removed many of the tax exemptions previously accorded to life assurance policies. In certain cases, however, premiums and dividends are tax-deductible and income from a life assurance policy is taxed at a low rate provided the policy is allowed to mature for at least four years and the fund is redeemed as a lump sum. Even if you make withdrawals during the investment period, only the growth element of the withdrawal is taxable. Because a life assurance policy reduces your income tax liability, it may also reduce your wealth tax liability (see page 202).

You can choose the beneficiaries and the amount to be paid to them in the event of your death, which will obviously affect the amount you pay, as will your age and state of health, e.g. non-smokers are usually offered a reduction. You may pay as little as around €10 per month at the age of 30 for a benefit of €30,000, but premiums increase with age and there's a maximum age for taking out most policies, e.g. 45, 55 or 60.

Instead of taking a lump sum on retirement, you can opt for life annuities (*rente viagère*), whereby you're 'paid' a fixed amount each year for the rest of your life, but payments are subject to income tax (on a sliding scale according to your age). Note also that, when you die, payments stop and your spouse can't continue to benefit from your pension, unless you make the annuity 'reversible' (*reversible*), in which case you receive a lower annuity but your spouse (if she survives you) continues to receive either all or part of the annuity for the rest of her life.

Related beneficiaries (your spouse and children) aren't liable for French gift or inheritance tax, but unrelated beneficiaries are liable for inheritance tax at 60 per cent (see page 202), although they may be able to delay paying the tax until they're 70.

Finally, it's wise to leave copies of all life insurance policies with your will and with your lawyer. If you don't have a lawyer, keep copies in a safe place but make sure your dependants know where they are! A life insurance policy must usually be sent to the insurance company upon the death of the insured, with a copy of the death certificate (see **Death** on page 172).

Villefranche-sur-mer, Côte d'Azur

14.
FINANCE

*F*rance is one of the world's most sophisticated countries when it comes to financial services and has the world's sixth-largest economy (see page 18), with GDP per head of US$38,653 (source: www.statista.com). Financial services are provided by numerous banks, the post office, investment brokers and various other financial institutions.

Compared with many other developed countries, particularly the UK and the US, France isn't a credit economy and the French prefer to pay in cash or by debit card rather than by credit card. Nevertheless, they're getting increasingly into debt (*surendettement*) as they spend beyond their means – so much so that the government changed the law to make personal bankruptcy possible.

If you plan to live permanently in France, you must ensure that your income is and will remain sufficient to live on, bearing in mind exchange rate fluctuations (if your income isn't paid in euros), rises in the cost of living, and unforeseen expenses such as medical bills or anything else that may reduce your income (such as stock market crashes and recessions!). Foreigners, particularly retirees, often underestimate the cost of living in France (see below) and some are forced to return to their home countries after a few years. France is one of the highest taxed countries in the European Union (EU) when both income tax and social security contributions are taken into consideration.

COST OF LIVING

No doubt you would like to estimate how far your euros will stretch and how much money (if any) you'll have left after paying your bills. Anyone planning to live in France, particularly retirees, should take care not to underestimate the cost of living, which isn't as low as is commonly supposed.

France is an expensive country by American standards, and in recent years many US visitors have found it difficult or impossible to remain within their budgets. (Americans will be particularly shocked by the price of gasoline, electricity, clothing, paper products and books, not to mention social security contributions and income tax.) Even by British standards, France is an expensive place to live, with the notable exception of property prices (Paris excepted, although property there is cheaper than London). Social security costs are extremely high, particularly for the self-employed, and the combined burden of social security, income tax and indirect taxes make French taxes among the highest in the EU.

Your food bill will depend on whether you adapt to French eating habits or buy imported foods. Food in France costs around 25 per cent more than in the US but prices are similar overall to most other western European countries. From €400 to €600 should feed two adults for a month, excluding fillet steak, caviar and alcohol (other than a moderate amount of inexpensive beer or wine). Shopping abroad (e.g. via the internet) for selected 'luxury' items, such as electronics and computers, can result in significant savings. English-language books can also be bought cheaply from the UK.

In the Mercer 2016 Cost of Living Survey (www.mercer.com/costofliving) of 209 cities worldwide – one of the most respected annual surveys – Paris was ranked 44th, well below London in 17th place. Hong Kong topped the list of most expensive cities for expatriates, followed by Luanda (Angola), Zurich, Singapore, Tokyo, Kinshasa (Democratic Republic of the Congo), Shanghai, Geneva, N'Djamena (Chad), and Beijing.

> The fundamental flaw with most cost of living surveys is that they convert local prices into $US, which means that ranking positions are as much (or more) the result of currency fluctuations than price inflation. Therefore in the last few years, the Eurozone, Australia, Switzerland, China and Japan, with their harder currencies, have become more expensive in dollar terms, while the UK and the US have become cheaper.

It's also possible to compare the cost of living between various cities via websites such as the Economist Intelligence Unit (www.eiu.com/home.aspx), for which a fee is payable. There are numerous websites that provide an idea of costs in France, such as Numbeo (www.numbeo.com/cost-of-living/country_result.jsp?country=france), Expat Forum (www.expatforum.com/articles/cost-of-living/cost-of-living-in-france.html) and International Living (https://internationalliving.com/countries/france/cost-of-living-in-france). However, you need to take cost of living data with a pinch of salt, as it often isn't up to date, and price comparisons with other countries are frequently inaccurate (and include irrelevant items which distort the results).

It's difficult to estimate an average cost of living, as it depends very much on where you live and your lifestyle. There are also large differences in prices (and above all rents)

between the major cities and rural areas. If you live in Paris, drive a Porsche and dine in expensive restaurants, your cost of living will be much higher than if you live in a rural area, drive a Renault Twingo and eat mostly at home. You can live relatively inexpensively by buying local produce and avoiding expensive imported goods.

However, even in the most expensive cities, the cost of living needn't be astronomical. If you shop wisely, compare prices and services before buying, and don't live too extravagantly, you may be pleasantly surprised at how little you can live on.

FRENCH CURRENCY

Back in January 2002 the euro (€) replaced the French franc; a euro is divided into 100 cents (nostalgically called *centimes* by the French). Coins are minted in values of 1, 2, 5, 10, 20 and 50 cents, and €1 and €2. The 1, 2 and 5 cent coins are brass-coloured (and virtually worthless!), the 10, 20 and 50 cents copper-coloured, while the €1 coin is silver-coloured in the centre with a brass-coloured rim and the €2 coin has a brass-coloured centre and silver-coloured rim. The reverse ('tail' showing the value) of euro coins is the same in all euro-zone countries, but the obverse ('head') is different in each country. French coins carry traditional designs (e.g. Marianne), the letters RF (*République Française*) and the date of minting. All euro coins can, of course, be used in all eurozone countries.

Euro banknotes (*billets*) are identical on both sides throughout the euro-zone and depict a map of Europe and stylised designs of buildings. Notes are printed in denominations of €5, €10, €20, €50, €100, €200 and €500, the last being available only on request (and approval!) from your bank. The size of notes increases with their value. Money is *argent* in French and *monnaie* means currency or change (*change* means exchange, as in *bureau de change*). To pay 'in cash' is either *en espèces* or *en liquide*, although the word *cash* is increasingly used.

The euro symbol (€) may appear before the amount (as in this book), after it (commonly used by the French, who are used to putting F after the amount) or even between the euros and cents, e.g. 16€50. Values below one euro are usually written using the euro symbol, e.g. €0,75, rather than with a US-style cent symbol.

IMPORTING & EXPORTING MONEY

There are no limits on the import or export of funds in France and a French resident is permitted to open a bank account in any country and to export an unlimited amount of money from France. However, if you're a French resident, you must inform the French tax authorities of any new foreign account in your annual tax return. Sums in excess of €10,000 (since 2007) deposited abroad, other than by regular bank transfers, must be reported to the Banque de France.

Similarly, if you enter or leave France with €10,000 or more in French or foreign banknotes or securities (e.g. travellers' cheques, letters of credit, bills of exchange, bearer bonds, giro cheques, stock or share certificates, bullion or gold or silver coins quoted on the official exchange), you must declare it to French customs. If you exceed the €10,000 limit and are discovered, you can be heavily fined.

When you arrive in France to take up residence or employment+ you should ensure that you've sufficient cash (preferably deposited in a French bank account), travellers' cheques or deposit/credit card funds to last at least until your first pay day, which may be some time after your arrival. If you're planning to invest in property or a business that's financed with funds in a foreign currency (e.g. GB£ or US$), it's important to consider both present and possible future exchange rates (don't be too optimistic!). On the other hand, if you'll be earning your income in euros, this may affect your financial commitments abroad.

If you need to borrow money to buy property or for a business venture in France, you should carefully consider where and in what currency to raise finance. Note that it's difficult for foreigners to obtain business loans in France, particularly for new ventures, and you shouldn't rely on doing so.

It's possible to 'fix' the exchange rate to guard against unexpected fluctuations by buying a 'forward time option' from your bank or through a specialised currency exchange firm; the further in advance you buy, the more you pay. Note, however, that you may regret doing so if there's a big swing in your favour! Transferring large amounts of money to (or from) France can be done by bank draft (*chèque de banque*), bank transfer (*virement*) or a SWIFT transfer. The cost of transfers varies considerably; not only commission and exchange rates but also transfer charges.

If you plan to send a large amount of money to France or abroad for a business transaction such as buying property, you should ensure that you receive the commercial rate of exchange rather than the tourist rate, and shop around for the best rate. Always check charges

and rates in advance and agree them with your bank (you may be able to negotiate a lower charge or a better exchange rate).

Smaller amounts of money can be sent by international money order from a post office or by telegraphic transfer, e.g. via Western Union (the fastest and safest method, but also the most expensive). Post cheques can be cashed at any post office in France and most credit and charge cards can be used to obtain cash advances. Don't rely entirely on a card to obtain cash, however, as they're sometimes 'swallowed' by cash machines and it can take some time to retrieve them or obtain a replacement. Some machines refuse to recognise foreign cards for no apparent reason (if this happens try another bank).

It isn't wise to close your bank accounts abroad, unless you're certain that you won't need them in the future. Even when resident in France it's cheaper to keep money in local currency in an account in a country that you visit regularly, rather than pay commission to convert euros. Many foreigners living in France maintain at least two accounts: a foreign bank account (possibly in an offshore tax haven) for international transactions and a local account with a French bank for day-to-day business.

BANKS

There are two main types of bank in France: commercial and co-operative. The largest commercial banks with branches in most large towns and cities are the Banque Nationale de Paris (BNP Paribas) and Société Générale. Village branches are rare, although in many villages there are bank offices (*permanence*) that usually open one morning a week.

The largest co-operative banks are Crédit Agricole (CA), Crédit Mutuel and Banque Populaire (BP). These began life as regional, community-based institutions working for the mutual benefit of their clients, but most are now represented nationally and offer a full range of banking services. Unlike commercial banks, each branch office of a co-operative bank is independent and issues its own shares. Anyone can become a member and invest in their shares, which is usually mandatory if you wish to take out a mortgage or loan, but isn't necessary to open a current account.

Crédit Agricole is the largest co-operative bank – in fact it's the largest retail bank in Europe, with around 10,000 branches and some 17 million customers. (It's also the largest landholder in France.) The Banque de France is the authority that sets interest rates and regulates other banks.

There are also savings banks in France, the largest of which is the Caisse d'Epargne (*caisse d'épargne* is also French for 'savings bank'), with some 4,700 branches. Savings banks are similar to British building societies and US savings and loan organisations, and offer savings schemes and loans for property and other purchases, although general banking services are limited compared with commercial and cooperative banks.

There are some 200 foreign-owned banks in France, more than in any other European country except the UK, although they have a relatively small market share. Most major foreign banks are present in Paris, but branches in the provinces are rare.

Post Office Banking

As in many other countries, one of the most popular banking services in France is operated by the post office (*La Poste*), which also offers some of the 'cheapest' banking available. La Poste (*la Banque Postale*) is the country's largest bank in terms of the amount of money handled, number of customers and size of branch network. In rural areas, where the nearest bank branch is often many kilometres away, many people use the post office as their local bank. Another advantage of the post office is that branches are often open for longer hours than banks and also open on Saturday mornings.

Post office accounts provide the same services as bank accounts, including international money transfers (by post and telegraph to many countries) and payment of bills. However, the amount you can withdraw from La Poste without prior notice is generally lower than other banks, and international transfers are more expensive. Post office account holders are issued with a cash (debit) card for withdrawals from cash machines located at main post offices.

Opening Hours

Normal bank opening hours are from 9am to 5.30 or 5.45pm, Mondays to Fridays, although banks may open any time between 8.30 and 9.30am and some close between 4 and 5pm. Larger branches may stay open until 6.30 or 7pm on certain days or every day in cities. Banks at main railway stations in Paris are open from 9am until between 8 and 11pm, although they usually have long queues. In small towns, banks close for lunch from noon or 12.30pm until 1.30 or 2pm.

Some banks open on Saturdays (e.g. 9am to 4pm) or just Saturday mornings, although when a bank in a rural area opens on Saturdays it may close on Mondays. Banks are closed on public holidays; when a public holiday falls on a Tuesday or Thursday banks usually also close on the preceding Monday or the following Friday respectively.

Opening an Account

You can open a bank account whether you're a resident or non-resident. It's best to open a bank account in person than by correspondence from abroad. Ask your friends, neighbours or colleagues for their recommendations and go to the bank of your choice and introduce yourself. You must be aged at least 18 and provide proof of identity, e.g. a passport (although you may need more than one form of identification) and proof of your address in France if applicable, e.g. a utility bill.

You can open an account with a French bank while you're abroad, either by telephone or online. A number of French banks offer an English-language service, including the Crédit Agricole, who operate 'Britline' which is based in Caen (02 31 55 67 89, www.britline. com).

Any account holder can create a joint account by giving his spouse (or anyone else) signatory authority. A joint account can be for two or more people. If applicable, you must state that cheques or withdrawal slips can be signed by any partner and don't require all signatures.

Non-Residents: If you're a non-resident (i.e. spend at least six months per year outside France), you're only entitled to open a non-resident account (*compte non-résident*). However, there's little difference between non-resident and resident accounts and you can deposit and withdraw funds in any currency without limit, although there may be limits on the amount you can transfer between accounts (an anti-money-laundering measure). You can have documentation (e.g. cheque books, statements, etc.) sent to an address abroad.

Residents: You're considered to be a resident of France if you have your main centre of interest there, i.e. you live or work there for at least half the year. To open a resident account you must usually have a residence permit (*carte de séjour*), proof of residence from your town hall or evidence that you've a job in France.

Current Accounts

The normal account for day-to-day transactions is a current or cheque account (*compte courant* or *compte de chèques*) – despite the widespread use of bank cards, the French retain a fondness for cheques – which doesn't accrue interest on the balance. Most people deposit their 'rainy day' money in a savings account. However, banks will automatically transfer funds above a specified sum from a current account into an interest-bearing savings account. When opening a cheque account, you should request a bank card,

which can be used to pay bills throughout France (see **Cash & Debit Cards** below).

Your bank usually provides a number of slips showing your essential bank details (*relevé d'identité bancaire* or *RIB*, pronounced 'reeb'), which you can send to anyone who requires them. Most employers pay their employees' salaries into a bank or post office account by direct transfer (*virement*), so make sure that you give your employer your account details or you won't be paid!

There are no monthly charges on a current account, unless you want an overdraft facility, and no charges for transactions such as direct debits or (usually) standing orders, except when made overseas. However, banks normally charge a fee for a bank card and may charge you if your account is left 'inactive' for a period.

Account statements (*relevé de compte*) are normally sent on a monthly basis, although you can usually choose to receive them weekly or quarterly. It's also possible to obtain 'mini-statements' (showing your last few transactions) via cash machines (a facility known as *guichet automatique bancaire/*GAB).

CASH & DEBIT CARDS

Most banks offer customers a combined cash and debit card called a *carte bancaire* or *carte bleue* (both of which are abbreviated to CB), widely accepted throughout France. Confusingly, the term *carte bleue* is often also applied to credit and charge cards. Banks normally charge around €35 per year for a CB (€15 for a second card on a joint account). Although it's integrated with both the Visa and MasterCard/Eurocard networks, a CB isn't a credit card.

However, for around an extra €10 you can have a *carte différée*, from which debits are made at the end of each month rather than immediately after each purchase (although

for an old or disabled person; the installation of a condensing gas boiler; and capital invested in a business.

The parents of a married dependent child may be able to claim an allowance against income tax. There are further allowances for those aged over 65 (on 31st December of the relevant tax year) who are still working and for those receiving an invalidity pension. The figure you arrive at after deducting all allowances is your net taxable income (*revenu net imposable*).

There are also a number of tax breaks that allow you to reduce your liability to income tax, which may take the form of either tax relief (*réduction d'impôt*) or a tax credit (*crédit d'impôt*).

Family Quotient

Families are taxed as a single entity, although you can elect for a dependent child's income to be taxed separately if this is advantageous. The French income tax system favours the family, as the amount of income tax paid is directly related to the number of dependent children. Tax rates are based on a system of 'parts' (*parts*), reflecting the marital status of the taxpayer and the number of dependent children, as shown in the table below. The number of parts is known as the 'family quotient' (*quotient familial/QF*).

The above 'parts' increase proportionately for each additional child).

French law distinguishes between living with someone on an 'unofficial' basis (*en union libre*) and cohabiting with a spouse or 'official' partner (*en concubinage*). A partner can be made 'official' by entering into an agreement called a *pacte civil de solidarité* (PACS). If you live *en union libre*, you're treated for tax purposes as two single people, whereas if you're '*pacsés*' you're treated as a couple and are entitled to a number of tax advantages.

If you're living *en union libre* with someone and no longer have any dependent children living with you, the tax advantages of a *pacs* agreement should be considered.

Those with dependent children are allocated parts as shown in the table above. The first two children count half a part each, while each subsequent child is a full part. Dependent children are usually classified as those aged under 18 and unmarried, or disabled children of any age. However, if children aged 18 to 25 are divorced or widowed and without children of their own, they can be claimed as dependants; a form requesting dependent status must be signed by the child and must be sent with the parents' tax return.

Family Quotient

Dependent Children	En Union Libre	No. of Parts Allocated Single/Divorced	Married/En Concubinage/ Widowed
0	2	1	1
1	2.5	2.5	2
2	3	3	2.5
3	4	4	3.5

The above 'parts' increase proportionately for each additional child).

Tax Rates

The tax year runs for the calendar year, i.e. from 1st January to 31st December. The income tax rates for 2015 income (2016 tax return) are shown in the table below.

Note that taxable income is income after the deduction of social security contributions and other allowances. If your taxable income is below the thresholds (*seuil de nonimposition*) shown in the table, you pay no income tax. Once you've calculated your tax 'base', you may be eligible for reductions (*réductions*) or credits (*crédits*) to this amount.

Tax Rates (2015 income)		
Taxable Income	**Tax Rate**	**Cumulative Tax**
Up to €9,700	0%	€0
€9,701 to €26,791	14%	€2,392.74
€26,792 to €71,826	30%	€15,903.24
€71,827 to €152,108	41%	€48,818.86
Over €152,108	45%	

In addition to the basic rates of income tax, those fortunate few with a taxable income of upwards of €250,000 per annum are liable to pay a special tax called *contribution exceptionnelle sur les hauts revenus*. This tax is 3 per cent on income up to €500,000 and 4 per cent on income above €500,000. Married couples and those in a civil partnership are exempt up to €500,000, when they then become liable at the rate of 3 per cent to €1 million and 4 per cent above this figure. The tax is imposed on net income after determination of the tax liability under the standard scale rates.

The government website (www.impots.gouv. fr) contains a facility that allows you to estimate the tax payable on your previous year's income simply by entering the income figures for your household, your marital status and number of dependent children.

Self-employed

Those who qualify as self-employed in France include artisans or craftsmen (*professions artisanales*) such as builders, plumbers and electricians; those involved in trading activities such as shopkeepers and anyone buying and selling goods; and agents, brokers and property dealers. If you're a professional (*profession libérale*) such as an accountant, doctor, lawyer or a freelance worker (*travailleur indepéndent*), such as an artist or writer, you may complete a *déclaration contrôlée* (form 2035) requiring you to keep accounts of income and expenses, including all related receipts and documents.

If you're a professional or artisan whose earnings are below €32,900, i.e. a *micro-entreprise* or *micro-BNC* (*Bénéfices non Commerciaux*) you must declare all earnings and qualify for a 50 per cent tax reduction. Those in commercial enterprises, e.g. shopkeepers, should complete a normal tax return, unless their earnings are below €82,200, in which case they may complete a micro-BIC (*Bénéfices Industriels et Commerciaux*) declaration.

The self-employed don't qualify for the employee 10 per cent allowance, although they can claim a 25 per cent reduction by joining their local Association Agréée des Professions Libérales. The self-employed can also claim payments made to a *mutuelle*, provided the contract is drawn up according to the *loi Madelin*.

If you run a business from home, you must also pay *taxe professionelle*, although you can claim a reduction on your property tax.

Income Tax Return

You should be sent an annual tax return (*déclaration des revenus*) by the tax authorities in late February or early March of each year. If you aren't sent a form, you can obtain one from your local town hall or tax office (search online for *Impôts, Trésor Public*). The standard return is the 2042 and there are supplementary forms for non-commercial profits (forms 2035, 2037), property income (2044), foreign-source income such as a pension or dividends (2047), capital gains on financial investments (2074) and other capital gains (2049).

There's no 'head of a household' in France (at least, not as far as the tax office is concerned!), and either spouse or partner may complete and sign a tax return including all family members' income, although it's possible for children aged under 18 with their own income, e.g. income from an inheritance or their own earnings, to be independently assessed. An unmarried couple living together 'unofficially' (*en union libre*) are treated as two single people for tax purposes. If they enter into a *PACS* (see **Family Quotient** above), they're taxed as a couple from the year after making the agreement. A divorced couple continue to be taxed jointly at least until receipt of an *ordonnance de non-conciliation* (ONC).

French tax returns are complicated, despite attempts to simplify them in recent years, and the language used is particularly difficult for foreigners (and many French) to understand. Local tax offices (*Centre des Impôts*) will usually help you complete your tax return, either in person or via the telephone, but in French only. You can make an appointment for a free consultation with your local tax inspector at your town hall, although if your French isn't excellent you'll need to take someone with you who's fluent. Alternatively you can employ a tax accountant (*expert comptable/conseiller fiscal*) to complete and submit the necessary forms (and take the blame for any errors!).

Tax declarations can be made online, except for the first time you make a declaration; once you've been issued with a taxpayer number you can use the online facility, which is free and allows you an extension of one to three weeks on the filing deadline.

If you pay income tax abroad, you must return the form uncompleted with evidence that you're domiciled abroad. Around a month later you should receive a statement from the French tax authorities stating that you've no tax to pay (*Vous n'avez pas d'impôt à payer*). The French tax authorities may request copies of foreign tax returns.

Although you're permitted to 'accidentally' under-declare by up to 5 per cent, you must pay the difference; penalties for grossly understated or deliberately undeclared income and unjustified deductions range from 40 to 80 per cent, plus interest on the amount owed. Note also that you may be liable for penalties if you display 'exterior signs of wealth' (*signes extérieurs de richesse*), so don't drive to the Centre des Impôts in your new BMW to deposit your tax return!

Tax returns must be filed by late May for employees, or one month later for the self-employed. Late filing, even by one day, attracts a penalty of 10 per cent of the amount due. Changes in your tax liability may be made by the tax authorities up to three years after the end of the tax year to which the liability relates. Therefore you should retain all records relating to the income and expenses reported in your tax returns for at least three years, even if you've left France.

Payments

Sometime between August and December you'll receive a tax bill (*avis d'imposition*). There are two methods of paying the bill: in three instalments (*tiers provisionnels*) or in ten equal monthly instalments (*mensualisation*).

The most common method of payment is in three instalments. The first two payments, each comprising around a third (*tiers*) of the previous year's tax liability, are provisional (*acompte provisionnel*) and are payable by 15th February and 15th May respectively each year. The third and final instalment, the balance of your tax bill (*solde*), is payable by 15th September. The tax authorities adjust your third payment to take into account your actual income for the previous year. Payment dates are officially 31st January, 30th April and 31st August, but the tax

authorities allow you an extra two weeks (or 15 days) to pay bills. If you pay your tax bill late you must pay a penalty equal to 10 per cent of your annual tax bill.

During your first year in France you won't have a previous year's tax liability in France. Therefore the income tax computed with the information contained in the tax return filed at the end of May of the following year is payable in full by 15th September of the same year. In the following year the normal procedure applies. The 'end May' file date for tax returns is recent. In previous years it was the end of March. Check the *Date limite de Dépôt* (deadline date for filing your return) when you receive your *Déclaration* form.

You can choose to pay your tax in monthly instalments (*mensualisation*) by direct debit, in which case you need to write to the collector of taxes in your tax region requesting this method of payment. If you make your request before 10th May, monthly payments will begin immediately (with an adjustment for any instalments already paid). If you apply after 10th May they won't begin until the following January. Once started, monthly payments continue automatically each year unless you cancel them in writing.

Monthly payments are a good budgeting aid, particularly if you're prone to rushing out and spending your salary as soon as you receive it! However, most people prefer to pay in three instalments, with the advantage that you can invest the amount set aside for tax until each payment is due.

PROPERTY TAXES

There are two main types of local property tax (*impôt local*) in France: *taxe d'habitation* (residential tax) and *taxe foncière* (property tax). These pay for local services, including rubbish collection, street lighting and cleaning, local schools and other community services, and include a contribution to departmental and regional expenses. You may be billed separately for rubbish collection.

Both *taxe d'habitation* and *taxe foncière* are payable whether a property is a main or a second home and whether the owner is a French or a foreign resident. Taxes are calculated according to a property's notional 'cadastral' rental value (*valeur locative cadastrale*), which is reviewed every six years. If you think a valuation is too high you can contest it.

Property and residential taxes vary from area to area and are generally higher in cities and towns than in rural areas and small villages, where few community services are provided. They also vary with the type and size of property and will be significantly higher for a luxury villa than for a small apartment. If you're renting a property, check whether you're required to pay part of the *taxe foncière* as well as the *taxe d'habitation*.

Note that there's no reduction in either tax for a second home (*residence secondaire*); in fact your *taxe d'habitation* is likely to be higher, as there's a reduction for principal residences (*maison principale*).

Forms for the assessment of both *taxe d'habitation* and *taxe foncière* are sent out by local councils and must be completed and returned to the regional tax office (*Centre des Impôts*) by a specified date, e.g. 15th November or 15th December for residential tax. They will calculate the tax due and send you a bill. You may be given up to two months to pay and a 10 per cent penalty is levied for late payment. It's possible to pay residential tax monthly (in ten equal instalments from January to October) by direct debit from a French bank account, which helps to soften the blow.

Taxe Foncière

Taxe foncière is a property tax paid by owners of property in France and is similar to the property tax (or rates) levied in most countries. It's payable even if a property isn't inhabited, provided it's furnished and habitable. Property tax is levied on all 'shelters' for people or goods, including warehouses and house boats (fixed mooring), as well as on certain land. The tax is split into two amounts: one for the building (*taxe foncière bâtie*) and a smaller one for the land (*taxe foncière non bâtie*). Tax is payable on land whether or not it's built on. Property tax isn't applicable to buildings and land used exclusively for agricultural or religious purposes, nor to government and public buildings.

The amount of property tax payable varies by up to 500 per cent depending on the region, and even between towns or villages within the same region, and may be as little as €300 or as much as €1,500 per year, although there are plans to make the application of the tax 'fairer'.

Taxe d'Habitation

Taxe d'habitation or residential tax is payable by the occupier of any habitable – i.e. furnished – property on 1st January, whether as an owner, tenant (subject to the letting agreement) or rent-free. If you own a property that isn't let but are absent from it on 1st January, you're still liable to pay the residential tax. Residential tax is levied by the town where a property is located and can vary by as much as 400 per cent.

Even if you vacate or sell a property on 2nd January, you must pay residential tax for the whole year and have no right to reclaim part of it from a new owner. Residential tax is usually payable in autumn of the year to which it applies.

Residential tax is payable on residential properties (used as main or second homes), outbuildings (e.g. accommodation for servants, garages) located less than a kilometre from a residential property, and on business premises that are an indistinguishable part of a residential property. The calculation is based on the living area of a property, including outbuildings, garages and amenities, and takes into account factors such as the quality of construction, location, renovations, services (e.g. mains water, electricity and gas) and amenities such as central heating, swimming pool, covered terrace and garage. Properties are placed in eight categories ranging from 'very poor' to 'luxurious'. Changes made to a building, such as improvements or enlargements, must be notified to the land registry within 90 days.

Premises used exclusively for business, farming and student lodging are exempt from residential tax, as are residents whose income is below a certain threshold.

WEALTH TAX

A wealth tax (*impôt sur la fortune/ISF*) is payable by each 'fiscal unit' (*foyer fiscal*), e.g. a couple or family, when the assets exceed €800,000 (2016). If you're resident in France there's a 30 per cent allowance against the value of your principal home (this concession doesn't apply to second homes). Tax rates apply on a sliding scale of as shown in the table.

If you're domiciled in France (see **Liability** on page 195), the value of your estate is based on your worldwide assets. If you're resident in France but not domiciled there, the value of your estate is based on your assets in France only. Wealth tax is assessed on the net value of your assets on 1st January each year and is payable by the following 15th June by French residents, 15th July by other European

Wealth Tax Bands (2016)	
Wealth	**Tax Rate**
€0- 800,000	0
€800,001-€1,300,000	0.5%
€1,300,001-€2,570,000	0.7%
€2,570,001-€5,000,000	1%
€5,000,001-€10,000,000	1.25%
Above €10,000,000	1.5%

residents and 15th August by all others. The taxable estate doesn't include such things as works of art and antiques; pensions and life annuities; artistic and literary rights and commercial copyrights; rural property let on a long-term basis; and 'professional assets' (*biens professionnels*), which may include shares in a company in which you're active provided they total at least 25 per cent of the equity;

Newcomers to France benefit from a five-year exemption from wealth tax on assets located outside France.

CAPITAL GAINS TAX

Capital gains tax (*impôt sur les plus-values*) is payable on the profit from sales of certain assets in France including antiques, art, jewellery, shares and property, but a principal residence is exempt. Gains net of capital gains tax (CGT) are added to other income and are liable to income tax.

Note that if you move to France permanently and retain a home abroad you may be liable for CGT in that country. EU tax authorities co-operate in tracking down capital gains tax dodgers.

INHERITANCE & GIFT TAX

Dying in France doesn't free your assets from the clutches of the taxman, as the government imposes both inheritance and gift taxes. Inheritance tax – or estate tax or death duty – (*droits de succession*) is levied on the estate of a deceased person, while gift tax (*droits de donation*), which is calculated in the same way as inheritance tax, depends on the relationship between the donor and the recipient and the size of the gift.

The country where you pay inheritance tax is decided by your domicile (see **Liability** on page 195). If you're living permanently in France at the time of your death you'll be deemed to be domiciled there by the tax authorities, which means inheritance tax will apply to your worldwide estate (excluding property), otherwise it applies only to assets in France. It's important to make your domicile clear so that there's no misunderstanding on your death.

Inheritance Tax Bands (2016)	
Estate Value	**Tax Rate**
up to €8,072	5%
€8,073-12,109	10%
€12,110-15,932	15%
€15,933-552,324	20%
€552,325-902,838	30%
€902,839-1,805,677	40%
above €1,805,677	45%

When a person dies, an estate tax return (*déclaration de succession*) must be filed within six months of the date of death (within 12 months if the death occurred outside France). The return is generally prepared by a *notaire*. Inheritance tax is paid by individual beneficiaries, irrespective of where they're domiciled and not by the estate.

The rate of tax and allowances vary according to the relationship between the beneficiary and the deceased. There are no inheritance taxes for legacies between spouses and PACS (see page 197) partners, but lifetime gifts are taxed. French succession laws are quite restrictive compared with the law in many other countries. Children and parents have a €100,000 allowance – other beneficiaries have much smaller allowances – above which tax is payable on a sliding scale up to a maximum of 45 per cent as shown in the table.

For further information see the Service Public website (www.service-public.fr/particuliers/vosdroits/N31160) or http://droit-finances.commentcamarche.net/contents/1018-droits-de-succession-calcul-et-bareme-2016.

Gift Tax

France has a gift tax (*droits de donation*) which is calculated in the same way as inheritance tax (see above), i.e. according to the relationship between the donor and the recipient and the size of the gift.

The definition of a 'gift' for the purposes of gift tax excludes gifts ordinarily made in the course of daily life, such as wedding and birthday gifts, provided they're reasonable by the living standards of the donor. A gift may be in the form of cash, but it may equally take the form of the transfer of real estate, e.g. the transfer of all or part of the family home to your children. A gift can be made manually or via the auspices of a *notaire*, which is always required where real estate is being transferred.

There's no inheritance tax between married couples or those in a civil partnership and there are reasonable inheritance tax allowances for children, therefore the use of gifts as a tax planning strategy is probably only of importance to those with substantial wealth or those who don't benefit from family allowances. However, there are strict rules regarding the rights of children (see **Wills** below), so gifts remain important for those who wish to obtain greater freedom in the disposal of their estate.

Gift Tax Thresholds

Recipient	Gift Tax Exemption Threshold
Spouses/Partners	€80,724
Children	€100,000 (from each parent)
Grandchildren	€31,865 (from each grandparent)
Brother/Sisters	€15,932
Nieces/Nephews	€7,967

Before gift tax is payable, there's an allowance depending on the relationship between the donor and the beneficiary, as shown in the table below.

Allowances are cumulative so that, for example, a child may receive gifts from both parents and grandparents, without one affecting the exemption limits of the other. If you're gifting real estate, then the situation can be made easier by gifting your children a 'reversionary interest' in property, while you retain its 'life use'.

The allowances can be used every ten years, therefore a gift made every ten years is free of gift tax, provided it doesn't exceed the threshold limits. The limits on the amount that can be gifted free of tax depends on the relationship between the parties and, in some cases, the age of the donor. Any gifts made within six years of the death of the donor (en avancement d'horie) must be included in the inheritance tax return and are valued at the time of death rather than at the time of the donation. The payment of gift tax can be spread over a number of years, except in the case of the donation of a business.

WILLS

It's an unfortunate fact of life that you're unable to take your hard-earned assets with you when you take your final bow. All adults should make a will (testament) irrespective of how large or small their assets. The disposal of your estate depends on your country of domicile.

As a general rule, EU law permits a foreigner who isn't domiciled in France to make a will in any language and under the law of any country, provided it's valid under the law of that country. If you're domiciled in France you should make a French will.

Whatever type of will you wish to make, 'immovable' property (immeubles) in France, i.e. land and buildings, must be disposed of (on death) in accordance with French law. All other property in France or elsewhere (defined as 'movables' – meubles) may be disposed of in accordance with the law of your country of domicile. Therefore, it's important to establish where you're domiciled under French law.

French law is restrictive regarding the distribution of property and the identity of heirs and gives priority to children, including illegitimate and adopted children, and the living parents of a deceased person. Under French law, you can't disinherit your children, who have first claim on your estate even before a surviving spouse, although you can delay their inheritance. However, foreigners resident in France can specify that they wish to apply the standard inheritance laws of their country of residence, therefore (for example) if you're British you can leave your assets to whoever you wish without restrictions. Note that this has no impact on French inheritance tax rules and if you die while a French resident or if you own French property, you'll be liable to French inheritance taxes.

If you take up residence in France and decide to have only a French will, check that it covers any assets that you have in another country. It's possible to make two wills, one relating to French property and the other to foreign property. Opinion differs on whether you should have separate wills for French and foreign property, or a foreign will with a codicil (appendix) dealing with your French property (or vice versa). However, most experts believe it's better to have a French will for winding up your French estate and a will for any country where you own immovable property. If you've French and foreign wills, make sure that they don't contradict one another, or worse still, cancel each other out, e.g. when a will contains a clause revoking all other wills.

You should keep a copy of your will(s) in a safe place and another copy with your solicitor or the executor of your estate. Don't leave them in a bank safe deposit box, which in the event of your death is sealed for a period of time under French law. You should keep information regarding bank accounts, pensions and benefits, investments and insurance policies with your will(s), but don't forget to tell someone where they are! You should also make a separate note of your last wishes (e.g. regarding funeral arrangements) where your next-of-kin can find it immediately after your death, along with your social security number, birth, marriage, divorce and spouse's death certificates (as applicable), and the names and whereabouts of any children or other beneficiaries.

French inheritance law is complicated and it's important to obtain professional legal advice from someone familiar with the laws of all relevant countries when writing or altering your will(s).

Forms of Will

There are three kinds of legal will in France: holographic (*olographe*), notarial or authentic (*authentique*) and secret (*mystique*).

A **holographic** (*olographe*) will is the most common will in France, which must be written by hand by the person making the will (i.e. it can't be typewritten or printed) and be signed and dated by him. No witnesses or other formalities are required. It can be written in English or another language, although it's preferable if it's written in French (you can ask a *notaire* to prepare a draft and copy it in your own handwriting). A holographic will should be given to a *notaire* for filing.

An **authentic** (*authentique*) will is used by around 5 per cent of people and must be drawn up by a *notaire* in the form of a notarial document, and can be handwritten or typed. It's dictated by the person making the will and must be witnessed by two *notaires* or a *notaire* and two other witnesses.

A **secret** (*mystique*) will is rarely used and is a will written by or for the person making it and signed by him. It's sealed in an envelope in the presence of two witnesses. It's then given to a *notaire*, who records on the envelope that the envelope has been handed to him and that the testator has affirmed that the envelope contains his will.

15.

LEISURE

*W*hen it comes to leisure, few countries can match France for the variety and excellence of its attractions – from its outstanding natural beauty to the sophistication and grandeur of its cities and the abundant charm of its rural towns and villages. France is the world's most popular tourist destination, and tourism is the country's most important industry (the third-largest tourist industry in the world), earning the country over €40bn a year and employing around a million people. Some 85 million people visited France in 2015, over 15 million of them going to Paris, where the Eiffel Tower is the most visited admission-charging monument in the world. The following year however the number of visitors, particularly to Paris, did fall somewhat in the wake of terrorist attacks.

France is one of the most beautiful countries in Europe and has the most varied landscape, offering something for everyone: magnificent beaches, spectacular countryside, mountains, rivers, lakes and seas. France also boasts vibrant nightlife, particularly in Paris, some of the world's finest wines, *haute cuisine*, an abundance of cultural activities and rural tranquillity. The pursuit of *la bonne vie* is a serious business – most French rate the pursuit of pleasure and style way ahead of success and wealth – and even bons viveurs (*bons vivants* in French!) are spoilt for choice.

Paris is one of the world's great cities and is packed with national monuments. It's also one of the cleanest major capitals in the world (on the negative side, watch out for pickpockets, bag snatchers and canine waste). There's much to be enjoyed that's inexpensive or even free, not least its beauty and the extravagant street entertainment, both cultural and sartorial. Paris dominates the cultural scene in France, even more so than the capital cities in most other European countries.

Many provincial towns have a cultural centre (*maison de la culture*), where exhibitions, plays,

music festivals, debates and art classes are held. There are many excellent provincial art galleries and museums, and art and music festivals are staged in all regions and major towns. Traditional folk festivals are held throughout the country, most notably in Brittany and the south; in fact, France boasts more festivals than any other European country.

Holders of a *carte famille nombreuse* (family rail card) can benefit from discounts at over 30 national museums and certain theme parks, including Parc Astérix and Futuroscope.

TOURIST INFORMATION

Information regarding local events and entertainment is available from tourist offices and can also be found in local and foreign publications. In most cities there are magazines and newspapers devoted to entertainment, and free weekly or monthly programmes are published by tourist organisations in major cities and tourist centres. Many city newspapers publish weekly magazines and supplements containing a detailed programme of local events and entertainment, particularly during the high season.

Most towns have a tourist office (*office de tourisme*) or, in some smaller towns, a *syndicat d'initiative*, although the latter term is dying out. The official tourist websites are uk.france.fr for the UK or us.france.fr for the US, while another equally comprehensive website is France Tourism (www.francetourism.com). Around 45 major cities and tourist areas have a *Loisirs Accueil France* office (www.loisirsaccueilfrance.com) open every day of the year, which makes hotel bookings for personal callers anywhere in France. Most tourist offices will also find you a hotel or hostel room locally, usually for a small fee.

Each department and region of France has a tourist authority, and many regions have tourist offices in Paris. The main tourist office in Paris is the Office de Tourisme de Paris, 127 avenue des Champs Elysées, 75008 Paris (08 92 68 30 00, http://en.parisinfo.com – both in English). There are also tourist offices at the Gare de Lyon and the Eiffel Tower and international airports in Paris (and other cities), where you can make hotel bookings.

Tourist offices in major cities are open daily, including Saturdays and Sundays (telephone to check the exact opening hours). In major towns reduced opening hours are in operation during winter, while in smaller towns and resorts offices close for lunch and may be open only during the summer (or winter, in ski resorts).

HOTELS

There are tens of thousands of hotels in France (although *hôtels de ville*, *hôtels dieu* and *hôtels de police* **aren't** hotels!), with some 1,500 in Paris alone, catering for all tastes and pockets – from 'five-star palaces' (the French classification system has introduced a new 'palace' category) and *châteaux* to small family hotels, offering good food and accommodation and excellent value.

Hotels are classified from one to five star de luxe by the French Ministry of Tourism, depending on their facilities and the type of hotel. This provides a guarantee of standards related to the price. Note, however, that stars are based on facilities, e.g. the ratio of bathrooms to guests, rather than quality, and you can often find excellent ungraded and one-star hotels. Two-star hotels are usually small family-run hotels, although nowadays many are linked to one another through independent hotel groups, such as Contact Hotels (www.contact-hotel.com), with central booking arrangements.

The backbone of the hotel network is the Logis et Auberges de France, the world's largest hotel consortium, whose trademark is a green and yellow sign of a fire burning in a hearth. Logis members include over 3,500 privately run hotels/restaurants in the countryside (none in Paris). Members must conform to strict standards of comfort, service, hygiene, safety, quality of food and price. Most are one-or two-star hotels in popular locations, with prices ranging from around €50 to €100 per night for

a double room. A Logis guide is available from French Tourist Offices.

A number of Logis hotels can be booked through the '*Logis Stop*' service offered by Gîtes de France (www.gites-de-france.com). Contact the Fédération Nationale des Logis et Auberges de France (www.logishotels.com/en) for information. A *Logis de France* handbook is available from bookshops and French Tourist Offices, as well as via the Logis website.

There are a number of dedicated French hotel guides, including the venerable *Michelin Red Guide* which is the most comprehensive hotel (and restaurant) guide, including both the humblest and poshest of establishments. Others include the *Charming Small Hotel Guides France* by Fiona Duncan (Duncan Petersen) and *French Chateaux & Hotels* (Alastair Sawday). An excellent online guide is the Les Routiers (www.routiers.co.uk) recommended hotels, which were originally designed for long-distance truck drivers but are now widely used by travellers in general who've discovered the excellent value they offer. Other online hotel guides include www.france-hotel-guide.com and www.goodhotelguide.com/hotels-in-france.

Last but not least, there are numerous online hotel booking sites, which offer price comparisons and reviews – such as www.trivago.co.uk/france-31029/hotel, www.booking.com/country/fr.en-gb.html and www.france-hotel-guide.com.

Chain Hotels

In addition to thousands of small family-run hotels, France has its share of soulless 'business' hotels, such as Ibis, Mercure, Novotel and Sofitel, although many have been refurbished and updated in recent years. International chains including Hilton, Holiday Inn and Intercontinental are represented in Paris and other major cities. One advantage

of staying at chain hotels is that the standards and facilities are consistent, and any hotel can book you a room at any other in the chain.

If you wish to indulge yourself you need look no further than the Relais et Châteaux (www.relaischateaux.com) chain of over 250 independently owned elegant three-and four-star hotels (many occupying *châteaux* and other former stately homes) and exquisite restaurants (*relais*). An excellent association of privately owned two to four star hotels where you're assured of peace and tranquillity is Les Relais du Silence (http://en.relaisdusilence.com).

At the other end of the scale are a number of budget hotel chains such as Hotel F1 (www.hotelf1.com), which are common on the outskirts of towns and cities. From around €22 per night (breakfast costs around €6 per person) you don't get private facilities but there are shared toilets and showers available in the corridors. You can arrive at any time of day or night; if you arrive late you can obtain the number of your room and the entry code by inserting the credit card used to book the room in the automatic reception machine (instructions are available in English). Competitors include Mister Bed (www.misterbed.fr) and Première Classe (www.premiereclasse.com/fr).

BED & BREAKFAST

France has numerous bed and breakfast (*chambres d'hôtes*) establishments, particularly in villages and on farms; look for signs such as *ferme auberge, ferme de découverte/ pédagogique/équestre* and *goûter à la ferme*. Many *chambres d'hôtes* operate under the sponsorship of Gîtes de France (see **Self-catering** below) and are classified according to their comfort and environment with one to four ears of corn (*épi*). The cost is usually from around €50 per night for a room (possibly with a private bath or shower) for two people including breakfast.

Many *chambres d'hôtes* provide accommodation for families and most serve meals (*table d'hôtes*). The standard is usually high and the home-cooked food delicious, owners being required to use fresh local produce. Note that when staying in bed and breakfast accommodation, it helps if you speak some French as your hosts may not speak any English.

There are numerous online guides to French B&Bs, including www.airbnb.co.uk/s/france, www.bedandbreakfast.com/france.html, http://gitelink.com/bandb-in-france and www.bedandbreakfast.eu/en/bed-and-breakfast-france.

SELF-CATERING

France has an abundance of self-catering accommodation and you can choose from literally thousands of properties. The most luxurious dwellings have private swimming pools, tennis courts and acres of private parkland. Self-catering serviced apartments are provided in Paris and other major cities. Rates vary considerably and may be per person per night or a fixed rate per night irrespective of the number of guests. Rates are usually lower for longer stays. Unless somewhere has been highly recommended, it's best to book through a reputable organisation such as Gîtes de France (www.gites-de-france.com).

The word *gîte* means simply 'home' or 'shelter' but is nowadays widely used to refer to any rural self-catering holiday accommodation. A typical *gîte* is a small cottage or self-contained apartment with one or two bedrooms (sleeping four to eight and possibly including a sofa bed in the living-room), a large living-room/kitchen with an open fire or stove, and a toilet and shower room. There are usually shutters on the windows, stone or wooden floors with a few rugs and possibly bare stone walls. There's usually a garden with garden furniture and possibly a swimming pool (which may be shared).

Properties are generally well equipped with cooking utensils, crockery and cutlery, although you're usually required to provide your own bed linen and towels (they can be rented for an extra charge). Equipment and facilities may include central heating, a washing machine, dishwasher and microwave, covered parking and a barbecue. Some owners provide bicycles and badminton and table tennis equipment. If you need a cot or a high chair, mention it when booking.

by owners. The largest and most reputable self-catering organisation is Gîtes de France. Properties (called *gîtes ruraux*, as they're mostly in rural areas) are classified according to their comfort and environment, and are awarded one to four ears of corn (*épi*). For more information contact the Fédération Nationale des Gîtes Ruraux de France (www.gites-de-france.com), which publishes *Les Nouveaux Gîtes Ruraux*.

Clévacances is another major national organisation. Unlike Gîtes de France, Clévacances handles urban as well as rural properties. Properties are graded with one to five keys (*clés*), a similar system to GdF's *épis* or tourist board stars. Further information is available from the Fédération Nationale des Locations de France Clévacances (www.clevacances.com).

A handbook listing over 2,500 *gîtes* is published by the French Tourist Office in the UK, while tourist offices in most French *départements* publish a list of local *gîtes*. One of the most popular guides to self-catering accommodation in France is the *Guide des Locations Vacances Loisirs*, published annually.

The cost is usually calculated on a weekly basis (Saturday to Saturday) and depends on the standard, location, number of beds and facilities provided. The rent is higher for a *gîte* with a pool. The year is sometimes divided into low, mid and high seasons, although many owners offer accommodation from June to September only. If you're making a late booking try to negotiate a lower price, as it's often possible to obtain a large reduction if the owner is keen to fill a week or two.

Electricity, gas and water charges aren't always included, particularly outside the high season (June to August), and may be charged at high rates. There's usually a charge for cleaning, but this may be waived if you leave the place spotless. Heating (if necessary) is also usually extra and can be expensive. You may need to pay a small local tax (*taxe de séjour*).

Information

Gîtes can be booked from abroad through French Tourist Offices, Gîtes de France or a travel agent. Many properties are let by holiday companies and associations, often as part of a holiday package. Properties are also let directly

HOLIDAY VILLAGES

Holiday villages and club resorts (such as Club Méditerranée) are increasingly popular among holidaymakers and are usually self-contained with everything available on site, including shops, restaurants, swimming pools, and a wide range of sports and entertainment facilities. Many also have children's clubs.

Inexpensive holiday village accommodation is available through Villages-Vacances-Familles (www.vvf-vacances.fr), a non-profit organisation created in 1958 to provide holidays for low-income families. Villages-Vacances-Familles holiday villages provide child-minding and entertainment for children and are open to foreign visitors.

Holiday parks are similar to club resorts, except that sports and leisure facilities may be housed in a temperature-controlled plastic dome; Center Parcs (www.centerparcs.com), one of the best-known of these, has five parks in France. Guests stay in villas set in attractive countryside or by the sea.

There are also many mobile home holiday centres in France, usually located on campsites

HOSTELS

There's a variety of inexpensive hostel accommodation in France, although fewer than in many other European countries, including youth hostels (auberge de jeunesse) and other hostels such as hôtels de jeunesse, which are a cross between a hotel and a youth hostel.

There are two French youth hostel associations: the Fédération Unie des Auberges de Jeunesse (FUAJ, www.fuaj.fr), operating over 200 youth hostels, and the Ligue Française pour les Auberges de Jeunesse (LFAJ, www.auberges-de-jeunesse.com), both affiliated to HI.

Youth hostels are open to members of national hostelling associations affiliated to Hostelling International (HI, www.hihostels.com) and, despite their name, have no age restrictions. HI membership must be taken out in your home country and costs around €15 per year or €10 if you're under 26. One-night membership of HI is available for around €3.

French hostels are classified under three grades, with accommodation usually in single-sex rooms with two to eight beds. The cost is generally from around €10 to around €20 per night (there may be cheaper rates for groups), plus an additional hire charge for a sheet sleeping bag if you don't provide your own. Some hostels allow you to use your own sleeping bag. Breakfast costs from around €5.

The main advantage for budget travellers is that most hostels provide cooking facilities or inexpensive cafétérias. Hostels fill early in July and August, when you should book in advance, although some hostels don't accept bookings and restrict stays to four nights or less. All hostels have a curfew at 10 or 11pm (between midnight and 2am in Paris) and most are closed between 10am and 5pm, although some are flexible. There are restrictions on smoking and alcohol consumption and guests may be required to help with chores.

In major cities there are hôtels de jeunesse, which are a cross between a hotel and a youth hostel, and Foyers des Jeunes Travailleurs/Travailleuses, which are residential hostels for students and young workers. Ethic Etapes (formerly the Union des Centres de Rencontres Internationales de France, www.ethic-etapes.fr) links foyers throughout France and publishes a list of members and services. Room rates are usually from around €15 to €25 per night for singles and €30 to €40 for doubles. Foyers usually have an inexpensive cafétéria or canteen. In many areas there are guesthouses providing dormitory accommodation from around €10 per night.

In rural areas there are unmanned hostels or shelters providing dormitory accommodation called gîtes d'étapes (www.gitesdetape.be). They're listed in footpath guides and marked on IGN walkers' maps, and are usually reserved for walkers, cyclists, horse riders and skiers. The rate per night is usually from €10 to €15. An even more basic form of shelter, common in remote hill and mountain areas, is a mountain hut called an abri. Information about these can be obtained from local

Bureaux des Guides or tourist offices. The *Guide Gîtes d'Etapes et Refuges France et Frontières* (www.gites-refuges.com) lists over 1,600 establishments providing inexpensive accommodation.

CAMPING & CARAVANNING

The French are Europe's keenest campers (although most never leave France) and have elevated *le camping* to a high level of sophistication and chic. There are over 11,500 campsites in France, including over 2,000 rural and farm sites, and France is Europe's largest camper van (*camping-car*) market, with around 18,000 vehicles sold annually.

You can also camp on a farm (*camping à la ferme*), although there are generally no facilities. A maximum of six camping spaces are permitted on farmland or in a park near a *château*. Off-site camping (*camping sauvage*) is restricted in many areas, particularly in the south of France, due to the danger of fires. You need permission from the local Office des Eaux et Forêts to camp in state forests (*forêts domaniales*).

Campsites vary considerably from small municipal sites (*camping municipal*) with fairly basic facilities to luxury establishments with a wide range of facilities and amenities. Many sites are situated in popular hiking and climbing areas. Campsites are classified from one star (basic) to four stars (luxury). Many campsites have tents, caravans, mobile homes and bungalows for hire, and some provide (heated) winter accommodation. Some also provide fully-furnished luxury canvas 'houses' (termed 'glamping' in the UK) with all modern conveniences, including sprung mattresses, refrigerators, four-burner stoves and electric lighting. Some sites have facilities for the disabled, which are usually noted in guide books.

Most sites have different rates for high season (*haute saison*) and low season (*basse saison*). Prices can vary considerably between campsites with the same star rating and some sites charge extra to use showers, sports facilities (e.g. tennis courts) and other amenities, such as ironing facilities or a freezer. Booking is often possible at three-and four-star sites and is essential during the summer, particularly for sites on the coast and near lakes and waterways (or if you require an electricity hook-up). Outside peak periods you can usually find a campsite without difficulty on the spot, but don't leave it too late in the day if you're in a popular area.

The Fédération Française de Camping et de Caravanning (FFCC, www.ffcc.fr) publishes a *Guide Officiel* describing in detail the facilities at around 11,500 sites, including naturist and farm sites. It's available direct from the FFCC and from bookshops and camping, caravanning and motoring organisations. The FFCC also provides insurance for campers and caravanners and an international camping carnet.

Many sites are members of other associations or groups, which include Camping Qualité (www.campingqualite.com), Sites et Paysages de France (www.sites-et-paysages. co.uk), Club Airotel (www.airotels.com) and

Castels et Camping Caravaning (www.les-castels.com). Camping and caravanning guides are published for all areas and are available from local regional tourist offices. There are also many national camping guides, including *Camping à la Ferme* published by Gîtes de France (see above), and *Michelin Camping France* and *Camping Car Europe* (http://travel.michelin.co.uk/camping-guides-91-c.asp).

If you're a newcomer to camping and caravanning, you may wish to join a camping or caravan club. The foremost clubs include the Camping & Caravanning Club in the UK (0845-130 7632, www.campingandcaravanningclub.co.uk) and the Camping Club de France (www.campingclub.asso.fr). Further information about camping and caravanning in France can be obtained from www.campingfrance.com/uk and numerous other websites.

NATURISM

France is the naturist capital of Europe, with many naturist beaches, villages and over 60 holiday centres, including a huge number of superbly equipped naturist camping centres. Topless bathing is accepted almost everywhere, even in Paris along the banks of the Seine, but nude bathing should be confined to naturist beaches and resorts.

The main naturist areas include Aquitaine, Brittany, Corsica, Languedoc, Provence and the Midi-Pyrénées. Cape d'Agde on the Languedoc coast is the largest naturist resort in the world, with a population of 40,000 from Easter to September. Naked day trippers are allowed in most resorts, although single male visitors aren't usually admitted.

Information about naturist holidays can be obtained from the French Tourist Office, which publishes *France, a Land for all Naturisms*. If you aren't a member of a naturist association in another country you must join the Fédération Française de Naturisme (http://ffn-naturisme.com/en) or pay a fee in proportion to the length of your stay. You must be aged 18 and require a colour (head and shoulders only!) photograph for your naturist 'passport' or carnet.

THEME PARKS

France has over 300 theme parks and similar attractions of varying size and scale, which have increased in popularity at the expense of traditional attractions such as *châteaux* – even in the Loire valley!. Details of the major theme parks and attractions in France are provided by numerous websites, including http://guide-parc-attractions.fr, www.parc-attraction-loisirs.fr and www.lesparcsdattractions.com/france.

The most famous French theme park is Disneyland Paris, which is one of the world's most-popular visitor attractions. Its 23ha (56 acres) contain five themed 'lands', each with around 40 attractions, as well as shops, restaurants, hotels and an 18-hole golf course. Information is available from the Disneyland Paris website (www.disneylandparis.com) and a surfeit of Disneyland Paris guides.

☑ SURVIVAL TIP

The best way to get to Disneyland from Paris is via the RER express suburban railway (see Chapter 10) on Line A terminating at Marne-la-Vallée/Chessy, a station specially built for Disneyland.

Other major theme parks in France include Aventure Parcs (www.aventure-parc.fr), Bioscope (www.lebioscope.com), Cap Découverte (www.capdecouverte.net), Cité de la Mer (www.citedelamer.com), France Miniature (www.franceminiature.com), Futuroscope (www.futuroscope.com), Micropolis (www.micropolis.biz), Nausicaä (www.nausicaa.fr), Parc Astérix (www.parcasterix.fr), Vulcania (www.vulcania.com) and Walibi (www.walibi.com).

Funfairs and circuses are common in all areas and sound and light (*son et lumière*) shows are held at historic sites during summer, including Les Invalides in Paris, the Palais des Papes in Avignon, and at many *châteaux* and stately homes, particularly in the Loire valley. The *son et lumière* at the ruined Château du Puy du Fou (www.puydufou.com) in Les Epesses (between Nantes and La Roche in Vendée) from June to September is considered to be one of the most spectacular in Europe.

MUSEUMS & GALLERIES

France has around 7,000 museums and many important historical collections. There are over 100 museums and some 500 historic monuments in and around Paris alone, ranging from the Musée National du Louvre (www.louvre.fr), one of the largest museums and galleries in the world, to some of the smallest and most specialised. One of Paris's most popular art venues is the Centre National d'Art et de Culture Georges Pompidou (known as the Centre Pompidou), housing the Musée National d'Art Moderne, the Public Reference Library, with over a million French and foreign books, the Institute of Sound and Music and the Industrial Design Centre. Other important Paris museums and galleries include the Musée Rodin, Musée Picasso, Musée d'Orsay (superb!) and the Cité des Sciences et de l'Industrie.

Other members of the capital's museum and gallery collection include the Orangerie near the Place de la Concorde (housing Monet's grandest water-lily paintings), the Petit and Grand Palais just off the Champs-Elysées, the Cité de la Mode et du Design, the Musée du Quai Branly near the Eiffel Tower (dedicated to the art and culture of Africa, Asia, Oceania and the Americas), and the Musée de l'Erotisme in Pigalle – the only museum in Paris open until 2am!

In addition to its national galleries Paris boasts around 300 commercial galleries where admission is free. You can also visit many provincial museums, manor houses (*manoir*) and *châteaux,* gardens and businesses (particularly those connected with the food and drink industry), and even hydroelectric dams and nuclear power stations.

National museums are usually open six days a week; the most common day for closing is Tuesday, but it's wise to check before you go. Most museums close on public holidays. Most *châteaux* and other stately homes are open during the high season only, from May or June to September. Many are closed one day a week and most close from noon until 2pm for lunch. Most museums offer free entry to those under 18 and a 50 per cent reduction for those aged 18 to 25 and 60 and over. Entrance

Centre Pompidou, Paris

to provincial museums is free for those aged under 7 and over 60 at all times.

A museums and monuments card (*Carte des Musées et Monuments*) providing entry to over 50 museums and monuments in the Paris area (for 2, 4 or 6 days) is obtainable online (http://en.parismuseumpass.com) and from participating museums, the Paris tourist office, *métro* stations and French Tourist Offices abroad. The *Carte* allows you to bypass queues as well as saving you money.

Current museum and gallery exhibitions in Paris are listed in weekly entertainment magazines such as *Pariscope* and *l'Officiel des Spectacles*. Useful websites for museum information include www.museums-of-paris.com and the Réunion des Museés Nationaux (www.rmn.fr), which operates some 20 museums across France.

CINEMA

French cinema has resisted the threat of television far better than the cinema in most other developed countries.

> The French are huge film fans, and Paris is the cinema capital of the world, with some 350 cinemas, most of which are packed every day (Parisians buy some 80 per cent of all cinema tickets sold in France).

Many cinemas in Paris show old films or reruns (*reprises*) of classics and some hold seasons and festivals featuring a particular actor, director or theme. Film lovers shouldn't miss the 'cinema days' (*journées du cinéma*) in summer, when films are shown non-stop for 24 hours at low prices.

Most old cinemas have been replaced by modern multiplexes with ten or more screens and state-of-the-art technology. Cinemas listed as *grande salle* or *salle prestige* have a large screen (*grand écran*), comfortable seats, and high quality projection and sound standards. Some cinemas in Paris and larger towns are equipped to show films in 3D. Smoking isn't permitted in cinemas, some of which are air-conditioned (a relief in summer). There are also private *ciné-clubs* in most cities.

France has a dynamic and prosperous film industry and some 200 French films are made each year. However, foreign (especially American and British) films are widely screened, sometimes before their general release in the UK or US! In Paris and other major cities, foreign films are shown in their original version (*version originale/VO*) with French subtitles (*sous-titres français*). Dubbed films are labelled *VF* (*version française*). You may also come across *VA* (*version anglaise*), denoting an English-language film made by a French-speaking director (beware!). Films are classified and entrance may be prohibited to children under 18, 16 or 12 – listed as *interdit aux moins de 18/16/12 ans*; some form of identification (with a photo) may be required.

The time listed for each performance is usually ten minutes before the film starts. The last performance usually commences around 10pm from Sundays to Thursdays and at midnight on Fridays and Saturdays. In Paris, performances are usually continuous from 2pm until around midnight or 1am.

Cinema chains such as Gaumont and UGC offer season tickets (*cartes privilèges*) for frequent customers; the Gaumont also operates a membership scheme. Cine-addicts can also obtain a *carte cinéma*, entitling them to discounts at most cinemas. Screenings on Mondays and/or Wednesdays are often cheaper in many cinemas. Reduced price tickets are available for students, senior citizens, the unemployed, military personnel and families with three or more children. Children and students must produce a student card and senior citizens (those over 60) a passport, identity card or *Carte Senior* rail card.

Europe's largest and most important film festival is the Cannes Film Festival, although access to films is limited to those in the film industry (or with the right contacts). Major film festivals open to the public include the American Film Festival (Deauville in Calvados), the Comedy Film Festival (Chamrousse in Isère) and the Science-Fiction Film Festival (Avoriaz in Haute-Savoie).

There are many French magazines devoted to films, including *Première* and *Positif*. English-language film magazines are also available from international news kiosks. An excellent website for film information is www.cinefil.com, where you can find details (in French) of films showing in every department in France, including whether they're *VO* or *VF*.

THEATRE, BALLET & OPERA

High quality theatre, opera and ballet performances are staged in all major cities, many by resident companies. Parisian theatres include the famous Comédie Française (showing classics, i.e. plays by Molière, Racine, Corneille, Feydeau, etc.), founded by Louis XIV, and the Théâtre National Populaire (contemporary). Other than the classics, most French-language shows are translated hits from London and New York. There are also many café-theatres, where performances may not always be memorable but are usually

enjoyable. Children's theatres in Paris and other cities perform straight plays, pageants and magic shows. There are also a number of English-language theatre venues in Paris, including the Théâtre Marie Stuart, ACT, Theatre Essaion, Voices and the Sweeney Irish Pub.

Cinema le Grand Rex, Paris

In the provinces, performances are often held in theatres which are part of a cultural centre (*maison de la culture* or *centre d'animation culturelle*), and the only national theatre outside the capital is the Théâtre National de Strasbourg. In addition to the large and luxurious state-funded theatres, there are many good medium-size and small theatres. Performances aren't always top quality, but there's plenty of variety. Performances usually start at 8.30 or 9pm and theatres close one day a week. Smoking isn't permitted in theatres.

Ticket prices vary considerably depending on whether you go to a national or a private theatre. If you subscribe to www.theatreonline. com you can obtain half-price tickets. Midweek

Opera Garnier, Paris

international dance companies. Many small dance companies perform in small theatres and dance studios.

Opera: The Opéra de la Bastille (08 92 89 90 90) is France's major opera venue. Paris also boasts the celebrated Opéra Garnier in the 9th *arrondissement* (details of both Paris operas can be found at www.opera-de-paris.fr – tickets can be booked online or via 08 92 89 90 90) and the Théâtre du Châtelet (see above) also stages opera productions. France also has 12 regional opera companies, most notably those of Bordeaux, Lille, Lyon and Toulouse.

matinee subscriptions are available at reduced rates and just before a show starts seats are often available at huge discounts. Students can obtain reduced price tickets from the Centre Régional des Oeuvres Universitaires et Scolaires/CROUS (www. crous-paris.fr).

Obtaining theatre tickets in advance can be difficult, as many theatres allow booking only one or two weeks in advance or only use ticket agencies. However, bookings for certain shows can be made up to three weeks before a performance via the website www. theatreonline.com.

Ballet: The Paris Opéra Ballet has a history going back three centuries. Tickets are cheaper than their equivalents in London and New York, but they're difficult to obtain as most seats are sold by subscription months in advance. For information and booking details, see **Opera** below. Paris also boasts the Théâtre du Châtelet (www.chatelet-theatre.com) in the 1st *arrondissement*, where a variety of shows are staged, including ballet productions. Modern and contemporary dance thrives in France and the Centre Pompidou stages some 'interesting' avant-garde programmes by French and

MUSIC

The French are great music lovers, although their tastes may differ from what you're used to in your home country. France has (surprisingly) no world-renowned orchestras and few internationally famous performers, yet there's no shortage of classical music concerts, particularly in Paris, which boasts several major concert halls, including the Salle Pleyel, the Théâtre des Champs-Elysées, the Théâtre du Châtelet (see above), the Salle Gaveau and the Maison de Radio France. These feature leading foreign orchestras and soloists as well as performances by the Orchestre de Paris, the Orchestre Philharmonique de Radio France and various other national and provincial orchestras (among the best are those of Bordeaux, Lille, Lyon and Toulouse).

The Parisian concert season runs from October to June. Students at the Conservatoire

National perform regularly in the Paris *métro* and on the city's streets, as well as at the Cité de la Musique in northeast Paris, where there's a fascinating musical instrument museum. Recitals of organ and sacred music are often held in churches and cathedrals, including Notre Dame de Paris, and many churches sponsor concerts with fine soloists and excellent choirs. Paris also has a number of music halls where top international artists regularly perform. There's also plenty of classical music outside the capital, although much of it is poorly advertised.

Popular Music: French popular music is something of an acquired taste, being based on the traditional *chanson*, in which the words are far more important than the music. Even French rock music is rooted in this style and therefore, to American and British ears, generations out of date. Foreign bands are much better known to French fans than any French group. Most pop venues can be divided into those where you sit and listen, and dance clubs. The former (in Paris) include Bataclan, Bercy, Bobigno, Olympia, the Palais des Congrès and Zénith, although none of these is an automatic stop on a world tour.

Jazz: Paris is Europe's leading jazz centre and attracts the world's best musicians, while France as a whole hosts many excellent jazz festivals including the Festival de Jazz in Paris in autumn, the Antibes-Juan-les-Pins Festival and the Nice Jazz Festival in July, one of the most prestigious jazz and blues festivals in Europe. France even has a nationally-funded National Jazz Orchestra. Most jazz is performed in cellar clubs, where you'll normally encounter a cover charge and expensive drinks. Music starts at around 10pm and lasts until around 4am at weekends, and includes everything from trad to be-bop, free jazz to experimental.

Music Festivals: Open-air music festivals are common and popular in summer throughout the country, many of them staged in spectacular venues such as cathedrals and *châteaux*. Music festivals embrace all types of music, including classical, opera, chamber music, organ, early music, piano, popular, jazz and folk, many of which are listed in a booklet, *Festive France*, available from French Tourist Offices. Each year in May in some 40 towns, the bandstand (*kiosque à musique*) is given over to the performance of music of the Belle Epoque and 21st June is a national Fête de la Musique, when every French town becomes an open-air concert venue.

Two publications provide a guide to what's on in Paris: *L'Officiel des Spectacles* and *Pariscope*, the latter with an English supplement. The main agency for tickets to almost any concert or cultural event in Paris is FNAC, 136 rue de Rennes, 6e (08 92 68 36 22, www.fnac.com) and in the Forum des Halles, Level 3, 1–5 rue Pierre-Lescot, 1er (08 92 68 36 22).

SOCIAL CLUBS

There are many social clubs and organisations in France, including Ambassador Clubs, American Women's and Men's Clubs, Anglo-French Clubs, Kiwani Clubs, Lion and Lioness

Clubs and Rotary Clubs, along with clubs for business people and others.

Paris is home to a number of clubs and societies founded and run by groups of expatriates, including national groups, e.g. American Citizens Abroad, the American Club of Paris and the Association of American Residents Overseas, the Association Franco-Écossaise, The Clan MacLeod Society of France, The Caledonian Society of France, The Paris Welsh Society and The Royal Society of Saint George.

University-based groups include the Alumnae Club of Paris, the Alumni of the University of Edinburgh in France, the Cambridge Society of Paris and the Oxford University Club, while professional associations include the Association of British Accountants in France, the Chartered Management Institute, the Institute of Directors, the Institution of Civil Engineers and the Institution of Electrical Engineers. There are also many women's clubs, including the American Women's Group of Paris, the British and Commonwealth Women's Association, the International Women's Club, WICE and MESSAGE – the Mother Support Group). Miscellaneous societies include the Association France Grande-Bretagne, the British Freemasons in France, French branches of British Guides in Foreign Countries and the Scouts, the English-speaking Union France, the Royal British Legion for ex-servicemen, the Salvation Army and the TOC H Association for elderly people.

During October, many organisations hold 'open houses' or other events to welcome new expatriates, including the popular 'Bloom Where You Are Planted' programme, organised by the American Church in Paris (see **Finding Help** on page 59).

There are also a number of English-speaking sports clubs in the Paris region, including the British Rugby Club of Paris in Saint-Cyr-

l'Ecole (78), the Standard Athletic Club in Meudon-la-Forêt (92) and the Thoiry Cricket Club in Château-de-Thoiry (78), plus several arts groups, including The English Cathedral Choir of Paris, The International Players (an amateur drama group), the Paris Decorative and Fine Arts Society and The Royal Scottish Country Dance Society. There's also an English Language Library for the blind in the 17th *arrondissement*.

Outside the capital there are Anglophone clubs and societies in a number of areas, including Dordogne, Bordeaux and the Côte d'Azur, although most are in Ile-de-France. A free *Digest of British and Franco-British Clubs, Societies and Institutions*, published by the British Community Committee, is available from the British Embassy in Paris. Other sources of information about English-speaking clubs are *The Connexion* (www.connexionfrance. com) and its various regional publications, and the English-speaking church (see **Religion** on page 278).

For French speakers, the Accueil des Villes Françaises (AVF, http://avf.asso.fr/fr/welcome), a French organisation designed to welcome newcomers to an area, is an option (see page 61). And many local clubs organise activities such as chess, bridge, art, music, sports activities and theatre, cinema and local history outings. Ask your local town hall (*mairie*) for information.

NIGHTLIFE

French nightlife varies considerably with the town or region. In small towns you may be fortunate to find a bar with music or a *discothèque*, while in Paris and other major cities you're spoilt for choice. Paris by night is usually as exciting and glamorous as its reputation, and it offers a wide choice of entertainment, including jazz and other music clubs, cabarets, discos, theme bars, nightclubs and music halls. The liveliest places are the music clubs, which are infinitely variable and ever-changing, with a wide choice of music, including reggae, jazz, funk, rock and techno. High-tech discos are popular, where lasers and high decibels (not to mention drugs) combine to destroy your brain. Note that drunkenness and rowdy behaviour are considered in bad taste and bouncers are often over-eager to flex their muscles. The most popular clubs change continually and are listed in newspapers and entertainment magazines.

The action starts around 11pm or midnight and goes on until dawn (5 or 6am). The admission fee to Parisian clubs is usually high, e.g. from €15 to €30, and generally includes a drink. Some clubs offer free entry but drinks are expensive.

A traditional and entertaining night out in Paris is to be had at one of the city's many cabaret venues, which include the Crazy Horse Saloon, the Folies Pigalle, the Lido and the Moulin Rouge. The entertainment doesn't come cheap and runs to between €80 and €170 per head, depending on whether you just see the show or have champagne or dinner as well.

For those who prefer more sober entertainment, 'tea dancing' halls (*guinguette*) can be found throughout France. Old-style dance halls (*bal musette*), where dancing is to a live orchestra, are making a comeback in Paris and are popular with both young and old.

The French have taken to the art of making fools of themselves in public through karaoke (*karaoké*), which is becoming increasingly popular in Paris and other cities; venues are easy to find through an internet search

for 'karaoke' and the name of the city you are looking in.

GAMBLING

French law forbids gambling for money... but exceptions are made for the stock market, national lottery, horse racing and casinos, all of which are state-controlled (and taxed!). Over 20 million people regularly play LOTO, France's national lottery (*loterie nationale*). The LOTO and a plethora of scratch card systems are run by a company called La Française des Jeux (www.fdjeux.com). Tickets and cards can be purchased at tobacconists.

Gambling on horse racing is also popular, with betting on the tote system controlled by the Pari Mutuel Urbain (PMU, www.pmu.fr), which has branches at cafés throughout France. The most popular bet is the *tiercé*, which entails forecasting the first three horses to finish in the correct order; you can also choose four (*quarté*) or five (*quinté*) horses. Sunday is the most popular day for race meetings; the country's major races include the Prix de l'Arc de Triomphe, the Prix du Président de la République and the Prix d'Amérique.

There are over 170 French casinos, the largest being at Aix-les-Bains, Biarritz, Cannes, Deauville, Divonne and Evian. The most famous casino of all is that of Monaco (which is almost

French). Gamblers must be aged over 18 and be smartly dressed. Blackjack and roulette are the most popular games. Details of all casinos can be found at www.journaldescasinos.com, which is partly in English. In recent years French casinos have been losing out to online gambling – some 4 million people are reckoned to use 'cybercasinos'.

BARS & CAFES

There's at least one bar or café in virtually every town and village in France, although the number has fallen from over 500,000 at the turn of the 20th century to around 60,000 today. In major towns and cities, watering holes include wine bars, café/bars, brasseries, bar-brasseries and tea-rooms (*salon de thé*). Although they don't have a reputation as hard drinkers, the French spend a lot of time in bars and cafés, perhaps nursing a single drink and playing games, such as *belote* (a mixture of bridge, rummy and solo, played with a standard card pack minus all cards below nine). French café culture changed radically in 2008, when all eating and drinking establishments became smoke-free.

A bar (*bar* or *bar-comptoir* – also known as a *zinc*, after the traditional zinc counters) sells alcoholic drinks and perhaps coffee and snacks, but doesn't usually serve meals. Bars have been rapidly disappearing throughout France, especially in Paris, and many more have been 'modernised' by the installation of TVs, video games, pinball machines (*flipper*) and piped music. There are also 'English' and 'Irish' pubs in Paris and other cities serving a range of British and other imported beers and 'authentic' (foreign) pub food. There are also wine bars in Paris and some other cities, where fine wines are served by the glass and snacks are available, although they're expensive and aren't common or popular. A bar-brasserie or brasserie serves a wider selection of food than a café and is more like a restaurant.

Cafés (or café-bars) and bistros serve alcoholic drinks, soft drinks, and hot drinks such as tea and coffee. They usually serve snacks (e.g. sandwiches) and ice-cream all day and may serve meals at lunchtime. If you just want a drink, don't sit at a table with a tablecloth, which indicates that it's reserved for customers wishing to eat. Most cafés have outside tables or terraces on the street, depending on the season and the weather.

Cafés are an institution and have been called the life support system of French culture. They aren't simply places to grab a cup of coffee or a bite to eat, but are meeting places, shelters, sun lounges, somewhere to make friends, meet lovers, talk, write, do business, study, read a newspaper or just watch the world go by. As in other countries, there's a trend towards theme cafés, such as *cafés sports* (where you can watch top sports events on giant screens), and *cafés philos* (where you can indulge in a little philosophical debate over your absinthe).

A *salon de thé* is a tea-room serving tea and coffee, sandwiches, cakes and pastries, but no alcohol. Tea-rooms are fashionable in Paris (e.g. Angelina and Ladurée) and other major cities, but are more expensive than cafés or brasseries. Afternoon tea (*goûter* or *collation*) isn't usually served in France.

There are no licensing hours in France, where alcohol can be sold at any time of the

day or night, although an official permit is required. In general a bar or restaurant closes when the *patron(ne)* decides it will. Most bars and establishments selling alcohol open some time between 6 and 11am and close between midnight and 2am. Many Parisian cafés open at 7 or 8am and close at around 2pm. Most brasseries and cafés open at around 11am and remain open until 11pm or later, while cafés and bars near markets often keep the same hours as the market. Like restaurants, most bars and cafés close on one day a week (*jour de repos*), usually shown on the door.

The legal age for drinking in public establishments in France is 16, although children aged 14 to 16 may drink beer or wine when accompanied by an adult. Officially, unaccompanied children under 16 aren't allowed into establishments serving alcohol. However, there's virtually no enforcement.

RESTAURANTS

No other country is as devoted to its cuisine as France and the French are among the world's most enthusiastic diners (the French rarely snack but eat civilised meals). They like nothing more than to talk about food and wine (sex and even politics lag way behind). Good French food is noted for its freshness, lack of artificial ingredients and preservatives (the French are fighting a rearguard action against the onslaught of GM food and crop spraying), and exquisite presentation. French cooking is an art form and master chefs are national heroes, although French food reflects not only the expertise of its chefs but also the attitude of the customers, who are among the most discerning – and most conservative – in the world.

Almost everyone can afford to eat out, and culinary treats await you around every corner. However, not all restaurants offer good value (*rapport qualité-prix*) and it's possible to eat

☑ **SURVIVAL TIP**

If you want good French food without breaking the bank, look for establishments awarded a single knife and fork and marked with a red 'R' (repas) in the Michelin Red Guide.

badly in France. One simple rule is to frequent establishments packed with local residents.

Top-class restaurants are classified by Michelin (which awards them one to three stars/*étoiles*) and Gault-Millau (up to four chef's hats/*toques*). Ratings are reviewed annually and there are usually fewer than 20 restaurants in the whole of France with three Michelin stars. Paris is widely recognised as the gastronomic capital of the world and has more restaurants than any other city in the country, although Lyon has more Michelin-starred chefs and the southwest claims to be France's gastronomic heartland. Every region of France has its specialities, which it proudly offers and jealously guards.

Surprisingly, many restaurants (including expensive ones) are lacking in what might be assumed to be a quintessentially French quality: ambience. In particular, it isn't unusual for restaurants to be brightly lit, so it pays to check before booking a 'candle-lit dinner' for two. Since 2008 all French restaurants have been entirely non-smoking.

Given the quality and variety of French cooking (and the strength of French chauvinism), it's little surprise that most restaurants serve French food, and foreign restaurants are somewhat thin on the ground (except in Paris), although the choice is gradually widening. In Paris, the abundance of African, Middle Eastern, Vietnamese and West Indian restaurants reflects the colonial history of France, although foreign restaurants rarely make the top grade. In the provinces,

Italian restaurants are the most common (many serving mainly pizzas), followed by Chinese and, increasingly, Greco-Turkish kebab restaurants. Indian restaurants are scarce. If you're used to spicy foreign food, however, you may find familiar dishes disappointingly bland in France.

Many restaurants close on one day a week, often on Sundays or Mondays. Most restaurants also close for one or two months a year for a holiday (*fermeture annuelle*). Those in winter holiday resorts may close for part or the whole of the summer, while those in summer resorts generally close in winter. Many top-class Paris restaurants close for the whole of August.

Always book for popular restaurants, inexpensive restaurants offering exceptional value, and any restaurant in a holiday resort, especially for Sunday lunch. Top-class restaurants (particularly those that are Michelin or Gault-Millau rated) are often booked up months ahead. If you're eating at one of these gastronomic temples you should reconfirm your booking a few days before.

There are innumerable publications relating to French restaurants. Two invaluable books are the *Michelin Red Guide* and the *Gault-Millau Guide de la France*. The *Gault-Millau* (published only in French) is primarily a restaurant guide but includes a selection of hotels. It isn't as comprehensive as the *Michelin Red Guide* but makes up for it with its mouth-watering descriptions of the gastronomic delights on offer. The annual *Guide des Relais Routiers* is essential for those touring in France, while free guides to local restaurants are published in all areas and available from tourist offices.

Types of Restaurant

Eating houses encompass a wide range of establishments, including the following:

Auberge: An *auberge* (or *hostellerie* or *relais*) was originally a coaching-inn or hostelry. Today it's generally an alternative name for a restaurant and may no longer provide accommodation. An *auberge de jeunesse* is a youth hostel.

Brasserie: A brasserie (or bar-brasserie) is a down-to-earth café-restaurant serving meals throughout the day (unlike a restaurant) and often remains open until the early hours of the morning, particularly in Paris. See also **Bars & Cafés** on above.

Bistro: A bistro (*bistro* or *bistrot*) is generally a small, simple restaurant (or café-restaurant), although they can be trendy and expensive, particularly in Paris and other cities. The hallmark of a bistro is basic French cuisine at reasonable prices. They also provide a place to meet and talk and a stage for musicians. Unfortunately, like cafés, bistros have long been in decline and their numbers have fallen dramatically in the last few decades.

Buffet & Fast Food: A *buffet* is a self-service restaurant, usually found in railway stations and airports. A *libre-service* (or a *self*) establishment is a self-service cafétéria often found in department stores, hypermarkets and shopping centres, in motorway service stations and in city centres. There are many US-style fast food outlets in Paris and other

French cities, including McDonald's (which has around 1,000 outlets and has even invaded the Champs Elysées in Paris and the Promenade des Anglais in Nice) and Quick (the Belgian competitor to McDonald's with around 325 outlets and entertaining 'Franglais' menus), as well as pizzerias and pancake stalls (*crêperies*).

Relais Routier: A *relais routier* is a transport café, although these are nothing like the 'greasy spoon' establishments found in other countries and are usually excellent good value restaurants (mostly on trunk roads) patronised by all travellers, particularly truck drivers (a car park full of trucks outside any establishment is usually an excellent sign).

Restaurant: A restaurant is a serious eating place that serves meals at normal meal times and isn't somewhere for just a drink or snack, unless it's a café-restaurant. Note that you can expect to spend two to three hours or more over a meal in a top-class restaurant.

Rôtisserie: A rôtisserie specialises in grills, although it may serve a wide range of other dishes.

French Cuisine

French cooking (*cuisine*, which also means 'kitchen') is divided into a range of categories or styles, including the following:

◆ *Cuisine bourgeoise* (or *cuisine paysanne/traditionelle*) consists of plain fare such as meat or game stews and casseroles made with wine, mushrooms and onions, with a liberal dose of garlic and herbs. *Cuisine bourgeoise* is commonly found in *relais* (see above) and middle-class restaurants and, although sometimes lacking in imagination, is universally popular, particularly among those with hearty appetites.

◆ *Cuisine minceur* is gourmet food for slimmers (invented by Michel Guérard) and is the most delicious slimming food in the world. It's similar to *nouvelle cuisine*

(see below) but with the emphasis on the avoidance of fat, sugar and carbohydrates.

◆ *Cuisine régionale* (or *cuisine des provinces/campagnarde*) is cooking that's particular to one of the 22 regions of France (see map in **Appendix B**), each of which has its own style of cooking and specialities, often influenced by that of a neighbouring country. *Cuisine régionale* was traditionally based on the availability of local produce, although many well known regional dishes are becoming increasingly difficult to find in restaurants, while others have become ubiquitous.

◆ *Haute cuisine*, the cream of French cooking and naturally the most expensive, although it isn't as popular as it once was. It comprises a vast repertoire of rich and elaborate sauces made with butter, cream and wine, and a variety of exotic ingredients such as truffles, lobster and wild boar.

◆ *Nouvelle cuisine* is a healthier version of *haute cuisine* with the emphasis on freshness and lightness, i.e. pretty food in small portions artfully arranged on large plates. The accent is on minimal cooking to retain natural flavours, with sauces designed to enhance rather than mask the taste of the main ingredients. Chefs are encouraged to experiment and create new dishes; indeed, if master chefs wish to retain their ratings in the gastronomic bibles, it's mandatory. *Nouvelle cuisine* has become less fashionable in recent years.

Menus & Prices

Menus with prices must be displayed outside restaurants, with the exception of small village restaurants, where you're offered whatever is being served on a particular day. All restaurants must offer a fixed-price menu (*menu à prix fixe, menu conseillé, menu formule* or simply *menu* – the word for 'menu' is *carte*) with from three to seven courses (commonly four), and many offer a choice of fixed-price menus.

A fixed-price menu may offer a choice of between two or three dishes for each course, although in humble village restaurants there's usually no choice, but the price may include wine. The more expensive the menu, the wider the choice of dishes and the larger the number of courses (see below). You can also order separate dishes from the *carte* (the French don't use the term *à la carte*!), which may not be an option in basic restaurants, although it invariably works out much more expensive. Watch out also for the words *en supplément* (sometimes abbreviated to *en suppt*) after ites on a menu, as you'll be charged extra!

A *menu dégustation* or *menu gastronomique* is often served in a top-class restaurant and can cost hundreds of euros. It consists of many small portions of the specialities of the house designed to display the chef's expertise, each of which may be served with a complementary (but not complimentary!) wine.

The sign of good food, a frequently changed menu and an unpretentious establishment, is often a hand-written menu (possibly on a blackboard outside).

Most restaurants are more than happy to cater for children. Some have a children's menu (*menu d'enfants*) and many local restaurants provide a free (or low-priced) place setting (*couvert*) for a young child eating from his parents' order.

Fixed menu prices range from as little as €10 per head in a village café/restaurant up to €150 or more at a two-or three-star Michelin gastronomic shrine. Although menu prices are low compared with those in many other countries, the cost of wine, coffee and other drinks may be high (wine is often three or four times supermarket prices). Those on a tight budget and with limited time may prefer to eat in a self-service restaurant (*self*), where you can eat well for around €10. Holders of a *carte famille nombreuse* can benefit from discounts

at a number of restaurant chains, including Buffalo Grill.

Menu prices are legally required to include tax and service, although some restaurants still add 15 per cent for service (see **Tipping** on page 283). VAT on restaurant meals in France has been 10 per cent since 2014.

Wine

In France, wine is regarded as a necessary accompaniment to even the humblest of meals. The French value quality rather than quantity and will gladly stretch a good bottle between four people rather than guzzle a bottle of cheap wine each.

If wine is included in a fixed-price menu it's shown on the menu (*vin compris*) and includes, within reason, as much (table) wine as you want. You must pay for drinks other than wine (except tap water). When drinks are included (*boisson comprise*), you can usually choose between wine, beer and mineral water, but must usually pay for anything more than a quarter of a litre of wine or a small bottle of beer or water per head.

In restaurants serving good food, the cheapest house wine (*vin de la maison/vin du patron*) is often good. In cheaper eating places, house wine may be undistinguished but can be ordered by the glass (*verre*) or carafe (*carafe*), which usually come in litre, half-litre (50cl) and quarter-litre (25cl) sizes. Wine may also be served in a jug or pitcher (*pichet*). If there's no house wine or wine by the carafe, wine will probably be expensive,

Children under 14 aren't permitted to drink alcohol in a restaurant.

LIBRARIES

France isn't well provided with libraries (*bibliothèque – une librairie* is a bookshop). Most French people don't do a lot of reading and consequently libraries aren't popular.

Paris is better served than most cities and also boasts the Bibliothèque d'Information Publique in the Centre Georges Pompidou and the Bibliothèque Nationale, both of which are free (although the latter is open only to graduate students and bona fide researchers), as well as the new Bibliothèque de France, which isn't free. The Bibliothèque Nationale (www.bnf.fr) contains a copy of every book published in France. The Bibliothèque de France is the world's largest library and is open from 10am to 7pm on Tuesdays to Saturdays and from noon to 6pm on Sundays.

In addition to public libraries there are private libraries in Paris and other major cities. The American Library in Paris (01 53 59 12 60, www.americanlibraryinparis.org) is open Tuesdays to Saturdays from 10am to 7pm and houses the largest collection of English-language books in France. Other English-language libraries in Paris include the Benjamin Franklin Documentation Centre and the Canadian Embassy Special Library. Many other libraries are reference (consultation sur place) rather than lending libraries, and don't allow members to borrow books.

As in many other countries, traditional libraries are being replaced by médiathèques, where as the name suggests the coverage extends much beyond books as such. Some even include small art galleries, performance areas, etc.

DAY & EVENING CLASSES

Adult day and evening classes on a plethora of subjects are run by various organisations in all cities and large towns, and even in many small towns and villages. These include expatriate organisations such as the Women's Institute for Continuing Education (WICE 01 45 66 75 50, www.wice-paris.org), which provide classes for children (e.g. English), particularly during school holidays. French universities run non-residential language and other courses during the summer holiday period.

Among the most popular classes with foreigners are those related to cooking (and eating) and wine. A full list of companies offering cookery courses and gastronomic breaks is included in the Reference Guide to Travellers in France available from the French Tourist Office. The most famous French cookery school is the École Cordon Bleu (www.cordonbleu.edu).

Many famous French chefs have founded cookery schools, including Auguste Escoffier, Michel Guérard, Roger Vergé and Paul Bocuse, the 'English' version of whose website (www.bocuse.fr) includes the following description of the Restaurant Bocuse: 'Located at 4km in the north of Lyon on the edges of Saône not far from the bridge of Collonges, this house of family became the road of all the greedy ones.' Stick to cookery, Paul.

Adult further education programmes are published in many cities and regions, and include courses organised by local training and education centres. Local newspapers also contain details of evening and day courses. See also **Further Education** and **Learning French** on page 118.

16.
SPORTS

*S*ports facilities in France are generally good, although they can be lacking in some rural areas. Recreational sports don't play an important part in most French lives, and school and university sports participation is low compared with many other countries. When they do participate in sports, the French generally prefer individual to team sports. Among the most popular participation sports are *boules*, cycling, fishing, hiking, horse riding, hunting, swimming, tennis and skiing. On the other hand, the French (especially men) are as keen spectators of sports as the people of most other countries.

When the French decide to take a sport seriously, they do it with a vengeance, as is the case with skiing and tennis, where France has unrivalled facilities. The latest sport to get the treatment is golf which, although still exclusive, is one of the fastest growing sports in France. Many less well-known sports are popular in the summer in the French Alps and the Pyrenees including rock climbing, white water rafting, glacier skiing, mountain biking, grass skiing and off-road driving.

The French Government Tourist Office and local tourist offices are excellent sources of information about sports events and facilities. The sports daily newspaper *L'Équipe* is essential reading for sports fans and publishes fixtures, results and details of all sporting events in France, plus major international events.

Many indigenous and foreign sports are played in France, where groups of expatriates play American football, baseball, boccia, cricket, croquet, pelote (pelota/jai-alai), polo and softball. For information about local expatriate sports facilities and clubs, enquire at tourist offices, town halls, embassies and consulates.

AERIAL SPORTS

France has a historical and abiding passion for aviation and the love affair extends to all aerial sports, including light-aircraft flying, gliding, hang-gliding, paragliding, parachuting, sky-diving and ballooning.

The Alps and Pyrenees are excellent venues for aerial sports, particularly hang-gliding (*delta plane*) and paragliding (*parapente*). The Pyrenees are reckoned to be the best mountains in Europe for paragliding. There are flying clubs at most airfields, where light aircraft, including microlights (*ULM*) and gliders can be hired. Parachuting and freefall parachuting (sky-diving) flights can also be made from many private airfields.

The south of France is an excellent place to learn to fly as it's rarely interrupted by bad weather. For further information contact the Aéro-club de France (www.salons-aeroclub.com) or the Fédération Française de Vol à Voile (http://ffvv.org).

Ballooning is also popular, and there are balloon meetings throughout France, particularly in summer. It's an expensive sport, however, and participation is generally limited to the wealthy, although you can enjoy a flight in someone else's balloon for around €200.

BOULES

There are three principal games of *boules*: *boules lyonnaise*, *pétanque* and *le jeu provençal* (or *La Longue*), from which *pétanque* is derived. It's generally recognised that *pétanque* is easier to play, as no special playing area is required and the rules are simpler.

For most people, *pétanque* is a pastime or social game rather than a serious sport. It's played throughout France but particularly in the south, where most village squares have a pitch (*piste*) and many towns have a special arena called a *boulodrome*. It isn't unusual, however, to find people playing on almost any patch of ground – even in the middle of the road! The more uneven the surface the better, although grass is totally unsuitable. The other essential requirement is an unlimited supply of *pastis*.

The Fédération Française de Pétanque et de Jeu Provençal (FFPJP, www.petanque.fr) has over 500,000 members.

CLIMBING & CAVING

France has the best rock-climbing and some of the best mountaineering 'facilities' in Europe. The French have always been avid climbers and France has some of the world's leading exponents. If you're an inexperienced climber it's advisable to join a club and learn the ropes (literally!) before heading for the mountains. You'll need a guide when climbing in an unfamiliar area, particularly when climbing glaciers. The main climbing areas include Briançon, La Chapelle, Embrun, La Grave and Pelvoux in the high Alps; Chamonix and St-Gervais in Savoie-Dauphiné; Gavarnie, Luchon and Saint-Lary in the mid-Pyrenees; and Bastia in Corsica.

Guides can be hired from mountaineering schools and in many smaller resorts and should be members of the International Federation of Mountain Guides Associations (IFMGA, known in French as the UIAGM and in German as the IVBV, www.ivbv.info/en/home.html), which has strict standards.

A number of climbers lose their lives each year in France, many of whom are inexperienced and reckless (or just plain stupid). Many more owe their survival to rescuers who risk their own lives to save them. Mont Blanc, Western Europe's highest peak at 4,800m (15,780ft), has seen a record number of deaths in recent years and over 1,000 in the last 20 years. Needless to say, it's highly dangerous to venture into the mountains without proper preparation, being in excellent physical condition and haviong adequate training, the appropriate equipment *and* an experienced guide.

Information about climbing clubs is available from the Club Alpin Français, officially called the Fédération Française des Clubs Alpins et de Montagne (FFCAM, www.ffcam.fr).

CYCLING

France is one of Europe's foremost cycling countries, where cycling is both a serious sport and a relaxing pastime. Bicycles aren't expensive and can be purchased in supermarkets and hypermarkets. Mountain biking (VTT) is also a serious sport in France with sponsored events and even professional races. There are VTT trails in many areas, although bikes aren't permitted on hiking trails.

Cyclists must use cycle lanes (*piste cyclable*) where provided and mustn't cycle in bus lanes or on footpaths. You should wear reflective clothing, protective head gear, a smog mask (in cities) and a crucifix in Paris! Cycles must be roadworthy and fitted with a horn or bell and front and rear lights. A cyclists' safety manual, *Premiers Trajets de l'Enfant à Vélo*, specifically aimed at children, is available from La Prévention Routière (www.preventionroutiere. asso.fr).

Bicycles can be rented from over 200 SNCF stations in principal tourist regions, particularly on the coasts, which generally offer three types of bicycle. Payment can be made in cash or by credit card and bikes can be returned to any participating station. Some *métro* and RER stations in Paris also rent bikes, as do many bicycle shops (*marchand de vélos*) in Paris and other cities and towns, but the fee is around double the rate charged by SNCF.

The *Tour de France* is the ultimate challenge on two wheels and is probably the toughest sporting event in the world. It's also France's and the world's largest annual sporting event, watched by some 20 million people along the route. The *Tour de France* is held in July and consists of three weeks of cycling on the toughest roads in France and its neighbouring countries (even occasionally in the UK). The route and length of the race changes each year, with towns paying handsomely to be a 'stage town', but it always finishes on the Champs-Elysées in Paris. France stages other important road races, including the Paris-Nice in March. Professional track racing is also popular and includes the *Six Jours Cycliste de Paris*.

Chris Froome

Keen cyclists may wish to join the Fédération Française de CycloTourisme (FFCT, www.ffct.org) or the Fédération Française de Cyclisme (FFC, www.ffc.fr). There are cycling clubs in all medium to large towns and tours are arranged in most cities and many tourist areas. Less committed cyclists may be more interested in the UK's largest French cycling holiday company, Cycling for Softies (www.cycling-for-softies.co.uk).

Among the best maps for cycling are the Michelin yellow maps (scale: 1cm = 2km).

FISHING

There's excellent fishing in rivers, lakes and ponds throughout France, many of which are stocked annually with trout, grayling and pike. Fishing is permitted on beaches and other public areas of seafront but not in ports, and there are restrictions on the type of equipment you may use and the kind of fish you may catch (e.g. you aren't allowed to catch young fish); the amount of shellfish (especially sea urchins and oysters) you may gather is also strictly limited.

Almost all inland waters, from the tiniest stream to the largest rivers and lakes, are protected fishing areas, where fishing rights may be owned by a private landowner, a fishing club or the state. Wherever you fish, however, you must have a fishing permit and you must pay a fishing tax (*taxe piscicole*) by means of a *timbre fiscal* (obtainable from tobacconists). Permits are sold by fishing tackle shops, whose staff can advise you on the best local fishing spots, and in some cases also by local cafés. Always carry your fishing permit with you, as wardens (who patrol most waters) may ask to see it. Information about the types of permits available from the Associations de Pêche en France (http://en.cartedepeche.fr/52-liste-des-cartes.htm).

> To obtain a permit to fish state-controlled waters, you must in effect join a recognised fishing association, which will issue a *carte de pêche* with your annual membership. For a list of associations, ask at a tackle shop or contact the Fédération Nationale de la Pêche en France (FNPF, www.unpf.fr).

Signs such as *pêche réservée/gardée* are common and denote private fishing. Many of the best fishing waters are in private hands, although it may be possible to obtain permission to fish from the owners.

The fishing season varies with the area and type of fish, but is typically from around 1st March to 15th September for category 1 waters and from 15th January to 15th April for category 2. Fishing regulations vary from department to department. Boats can be hired on inland waters and from sea ports, where deep-sea fishing expeditions are organised. Sea fishing is better in the Atlantic than the Mediterranean. Further information can be obtained from the Office National de l'Eau et des Milieux Aquatiques (ONEMA, formerly the Conseil Supérieur de la Pêche, www.csp. ecologie.gouv.fr) or the Union Nationale pour la Pêche en France (see above).

Various websites offer information about fishing in France, including www.peche-direct. com and (for trout fishers) www.pechetruite. com. Information about local fishing areas and fishing permits is available from local tourist offices and town halls.

FOOTBALL

Association football or soccer (*le foot* – pronounced to rhyme with the English word loot) is generally reckoned to be France's national sport, with over 7 million players. The French soccer league has four divisions and teams also take part in a national cup competition (*coupe de France*). The first division has 18 teams, with top clubs including Auxerre, Bordeaux, Lille, Lyon, Marseille, Paris Saint-Germain and St Etienne (and Monaco). Football takes a break from Christmas Eve until the end of January, in common with many other European countries. Amateur football is widely played and there are clubs and leagues in all departments.

Further information is available from the Fédération Française de Football (www.fff.fr) and, at local level, from town halls and *mairies*.

GOLF

Golf is one of the fastest growing sports in France. The largest numbers of golf clubs are found in Normandy, Brittany, the southwest, the Côte d'Azur and the Paris region. Many courses have magnificent settings (seaside, mountain and forest), often linked with property developments. Properties on or near golf clubs, which may include life membership, are becoming increasingly popular with foreigners seeking a permanent or second home in France.

There are courses to suit all standards, and green fees are low in comparison with many other European countries (particularly the UK), although they may vary with the season;

service can be found at www.golfinfrance.f9.co.uk; comprehensive information is also available from the website of *Golf Magazine* (www.francegolf.fr) and the European Tour (www. europeantour.com). Another useful website for French golfers is www.golf.com.fr. The Institut Géographique National (IGN) publishes a general golf map of France (ref. 910).

fees are higher at weekends and on public holidays than during the week. In fact, most golfers prefer to pay and play than to pay an annual membership fee. Most courses require a minimum handicap.

Golf holidays are popular and are a major source of revenue for golf clubs. Most courses welcome visitors and some clubs have special rates for groups. A golf pass is available in some areas, allowing visitors to play at a number of courses in a particular area.

Most clubs have driving ranges (known as *practices*), practice greens, bunker practice areas, a clubhouse (possibly a *château*), restaurant and bar. Many clubs are combined with country or sporting clubs boasting a luxury hotel, restaurant, swimming pool, gymnasium, tennis courts, billiards, croquet and *boules*. You can hire golf clubs and a trolley at all clubs, and possibly also a buggy. In major cities, there are indoor driving ranges where membership can be obtained on a monthly or annual basis.

France hosts a number of international golf tournaments that are part of the European tour, including the French Open, the Mediterranean Open, the Cannes Open and the Lâncome Trophy.

For more information about golf in France contact the Féderation Française de Golf (www. ffgolf.org). A full list of golf courses in France, together with photographs and an online booking

GYMNASIUMS & HEALTH CLUBS

There are gymnasiums (*gymnase*) and health clubs (*club de forme*) in most towns. Most have swimming pools, saunas, Jacuzzis and steam baths, as well as the usual expensive bone-jarring, muscle-wrenching apparatus. Most clubs permit visitors, although there's usually a high hourly or daily fee. Some clubs are small and extremely crowded, particularly during lunch hours and early evenings. Gym, training and exercise classes are provided by sports centres and clubs throughout France, which usually charge reasonable rates. Many first-class hotels also have gyms and fitness rooms.

HIKING & RUNNING

France has some of the finest hiking (*tourisme pédestre*) areas in western Europe. Spring and autumn are the best seasons for hiking, when the weather is cooler and the trails less crowded, although the best time for mountain flowers is between May and August. There are pleasant walks in all regions but most serious walkers head for the Alps, Pyrenees, Vosges, Auvergne and Jura mountains. France has six national parks, all with an inner zone where building, camping and hunting are prohibited, plus 85 state-run nature reserves that were created to preserve the most-threatened areas of national heritage, which are ideal for hikers.

France has the finest network of walking trails in Europe, including some 30,000km (18,600mi) of footpaths known as the *Grande Randonnée* (GR) network. Started in 1947, the network has expanded into every corner of France under the guidance of the Fédération Française de la Randonnée Pédestre (FFRP, www.ffrandonnee.fr). The FFRP issues permits and provides insurance, although these aren't compulsory. A *GR de pays* is a country walk and a *Promenade Randonnée* (PR) a one-day or weekend excursion from a GR.

In mountain areas there are refuge huts on the main GR routes, although these are usually open only in summer. They're basic but much better than being stranded in a storm. The cost is around €10 per night or less if you're a member of a climbing association or a club affiliated to the Club Alpin Français (www.ffcam.fr). More comfortable accommodation is provided by France's 130 *Rando Plume* (www.rando-accueil.com/Label/randoplume.htm) establishments – B&Bs conveniently located for hikers. There are hiking clubs in most areas, all of which organise local walks, usually on Sundays. Local footpaths include forest paths

(*routes forestières*) and 'little walks' (*petites randonnées*), usually between 2 and 11km.

The basic source of information for the GR network is the Institut Géographique National (IGN) map number 903 (*Sentiers de Grandes Randonnées*), showing all GR trails. The FFRP (see above) publish a series of topographic guides (*Topo-guides*) which are available in English and French and cover all of France's long-distance footpaths, and also has an annual *Rando Guide*. The Michelin 1,100 orange series maps (scale 1:50,000 or 1cm = 500m) are good for walking, although for the ultimate in detail you need the IGN *Rando* series of 2,000 maps. A route-planning CD ROM is available from retailers or the IGN website (www.ign.fr).

HUNTING

France has over 1.6 million registered hunters (*chasseurs*), more than all other European countries combined. Hunting is a key part of the masculine culture (only a few women join in). Hunting rights are jealously guarded and hunters pay €1,500 per year or more for the privilege of hunting in some areas.

A licence isn't required for a shotgun and French hunters are notoriously bad marksmen; around 50 people (often other hunters) are killed by hunters each year. Many are inexperienced and some are downright dangerous, especially if they've been on the bottle before taking to the land. Although they won't deliberately shoot you (unless you're a conservationist or *garde-chasses*), it's advisable to steer clear of the countryside during the hunting season.

The minimum age for hunting is 15 (although those under 18 must have parental consent) and a permit (*permis de chasser*) is necessary. Hunters must pass a practical as well as a theoretical exam set by each Fédération Départementale des Chasseurs (FDC, www.

fdc[number of department].com, e.g. www.
fdc14.com for Calvados) to obtain a permit.

It's possible to apply to the Association
pour la Protection des Animaux Sauvages
(www.aspas-nature.org) for your land to be
designated a 'refuge', although this won't
do much for your local popularity! Note that
hunting within 150m (500ft) of a house is
forbidden, although some hunters ignore this
rule. Where hunting is forbidden it's usually
shown by a sign ('chasse interdite/gardée').
Certain areas are denoted as réservé pour
repeuplement, which means that hunting
access is prohibited in order to allow wildlife
to reproduce; red public notices are attached
to the perimeter.

 Caution

Before buying a property you should
be aware of any hunting rights on
or adjacent to your land and check
before planning any fencing or walling
that this won't raise objections.
Although hunters don't have the right
to hunt on private land (propriété
privée) without permission, where land
has traditionally been used by hunters
they won't bother to ask.

For further general information about
hunting in France contact the Office Nationale
de la Chasse (www.oncfs.gouv.fr). Local
information, including the dates of the hunting
season, can be obtained from your Direction
Départementale de l'Agriculture et de la Forêt
or Fédération Départementale des Chasseurs
or mairie. There are many magazines devoted
to hunting in France.

RACKET SPORTS

Tennis is by far the most popular racket sport
in France; squash and badminton are also
played, but facilities are often poor. There are
two main kinds of racket club: sports centres
open to all, and private clubs. Sports centres
require no membership or membership fees
and anyone can book a court. Clubs tend to
have little or no social aspect and there may
not even be club nights or competitions. Most
towns and villages have municipal courts
that can be rented by the hour. Some hotels
have tennis and squash courts and organise
coaching holidays throughout the year.

Local information about racket sports
facilities is available from mairies, travel agents
and tourist offices.

Tennis

Tennis's popularity has grown tremendously
in the last few decades and there are courts
in most towns and villages, although in small
villages there may be only one court and it
may be in poor repair. One of the reasons for
the popularity and high standard of tennis in
France is that there are hundreds of covered
and indoor courts, enabling tennis to be played
year round.

Tennis was long regarded as an elite sport
in France and remains that way in many
private clubs, which are usually expensive and
exclusive and rarely accept unaccompanied
visitors. Membership runs to several hundred
euros per year and most clubs have long
waiting lists.

France has many tennis schools and resorts,
and in Paris and other cities there are huge
tennis complexes with as many as 24 courts
open from 7am to 10pm daily. Many tennis
clubs provide saunas, whirlpools, solariums
and swimming pools, and most have a
restaurant.

Further information about tennis can be
obtained from the Fédération Française de
Tennis (www.fft.fr).

Squash & Badminton

There are squash clubs in most large towns, although many have only one or two courts. There are also many combined tennis and squash clubs. The general standard of squash is relatively low due to the lack of experienced coaches and top competition, although it's continually improving, encouraged by the recent success of France's top male players. Rackets and balls for racket-ball (a 'simplified' version of squash played with a larger, bouncier ball and shorter rackets) can also be hired from most squash clubs. Some tennis centres also provide badminton courts and there are around 600 badminton clubs, although facilities generally tend to be poor.

Further information can be obtained from the Fédération Française de Squash (www. ffsquash.com) and the Fédération Française de Badminton (www.ffba.org).

RUGBY

Most rugby in France follows the rugby union code (15 players a side), although rugby league (13 players a side) is also popular, particularly in Carcassonne and Perpignan. The national rugby union team (*les tricolores*) competes in the annual Six Nations championship along with England, Ireland, Italy, Scotland and Wales, home games being staged at the Parc des Princes or the Stade de France in Paris.

French rugby owes its popularity (and existence) to clubs rather than schools or universities. It has its stronghold in the southwest of the country (the Midi), where every town has a team. Among the most famous clubs are Agen, Bayonne, Béziers, Brive, Narbonne and Toulouse. French clubs compete in an annual European Cup competition with British clubs. There's even a British Rugby Club in Saint-Cyr-l'Ecole in Yvelines near Paris.

Further information is available from the Fédération Française de Rugby website (www. ffr.fr), where you can find a list of clubs in your region.

SKIING

Both downhill skiing (*ski alpin*) and cross-country skiing (*ski de fond/ski nordique*) are hugely popular in France, although downhill skiing is greatly preferred. Most resorts have a range of ski lifts, including cable cars, gondolas, chairlifts and drag lifts. Drag lifts are usually 'Pomas' for single riders, rather than the two-person T-bars, common in Austria. Lifts are marked on *piste* plans, as are all runs, which are graded green (for beginners), blue (easy), red (intermediate) and black (difficult).

France is Europe's number one destination for serious downhill skiers and some 15 per cent of the French population ski regularly. France boasts over 3,000km^2 (over 1,150mi^2) of skiing areas spread over six mountain ranges, which between them have the largest number of resorts and the most extensive network of ski lifts in the world (over 4,000).

Ski resorts provide a variety of accommodation, including hotels, self-catering apartments and chalets. Accommodation is more expensive during holiday periods (Christmas, New Year and Easter), when lift queues are interminable and runs overcrowded. During public and school holidays (see pages 41 and 105) the crowds of school children may drive you crazy, both on and off piste.

Cross-country skiing (*ski de fond/ski nordique*) doesn't have the glamorous and exciting image of downhill skiing, but it's nevertheless a popular sport in France. It appeals to both young and old, the fit and the unfit, as it can be enjoyed at any pace and over any distance and a variety of terrains. Trails, usually consisting of two sets of specially prepared tracks (*pistes de ski de fond*), are well signposted. Some resorts have floodlit trails for night skiing.

If cross-country skiing is too much like hard work and downhill skiing old hat, you may wish to try something more exciting such as freestyle, off-piste, speed, heli-or 'extreme' skiing or snow-boarding (*surfing*). Snow-boarding is particularly popular in France and is taught in most resorts. The French invented 'extreme' skiing, which involves negotiating slopes steeper than 60 degrees. Other activities may include paragliding, parasailing, hang-gliding, snow-shoe walking, dog-sledding, tobogganing, snowmobiling and, for the seriously suicidal, snow-joering (being towed on skis by a horse!), bob-sleighing and ice-diving.

Most winter resorts have heated indoor swimming pools, gymnasiums, fitness centres, saunas and solariums, along with a variety of other indoor activities, including tennis, squash, ice-skating, curling, indoor golf and tenpin bowling. There's an excellent choice of restaurants and bars in most resorts, although they can be expensive. Other entertainment includes discos, cinemas, nightclubs and casinos.

Summer skiing is available in Alpe d'Huez, Les Deux Alpes, La Plagne, Tignes, Val d'Isère and Val Thorens, and can be combined with other sports such as tennis, swimming, golf, horse riding, grass skiing, fishing, water-sports, hiking, climbing and a range of other activities.

Always abide by the International Ski Federation's (FIS) Safe Skiing Code, which can be found at www.boardsure.com/safety_information/isfssc.php. Further safety guidelines are contained in the booklet *Pour Que la Montagne Reste un Plaisir*, available from tourist offices and ski hire shops in

resorts. General information about health and safety for skiers can be obtained from the Médecins de Montagne website (www.mdem.org).

For further information about skiing and other winter sports, contact the Club Alpin Français (www.ffcam.fr), the Fédération Française de Ski (www.ffs.fr) or the Association des Maires des Stations Française de Sports d'Hiver (also known simply as SkiFrance, www.skifrance.fr). The latest weather and snow conditions are available via telephone (08 92 68 08 08), the internet (e.g. the France Météo website, www.meteofrance.com), daily newspapers and direct from resorts.

SWIMMING

Swimming (*natation*) is one of the country's favourite sports and pastimes. Beaches vary considerably in size, surface (sand, pebbles, etc.) and amenities. Most resorts provide beach clubs for the young (*club des jeunes*) and all but the smallest beaches have supervised play areas where you can leave young children for a fee. Otherwise, most beaches are free.

French beaches are generally noteworthy for their cleanliness. Officially, some 95 per cent of French beaches are 'clean' and over a third have been awarded an EU 'blue flag' (*pavillon bleu*) for the quality of their water, although some that fail the tests are dangerously polluted. The dirtiest beaches are on the northern coast between Calais and Cherbourg, the cleanest around Nice (although not all). The pollution count must be displayed at the local town hall: blue = good quality water, green = average, yellow = likely to be temporarily polluted, and red = badly polluted.

A list of blue flag beaches can be found on the Blue Flag website (www.blueflag.org) and a list of 'black flag' beaches on that of the Surfrider Foundation Europe (www.surfrider-europe.org – the 'English' version of the site is 99 per cent in French!), which draws attention to what it considers to be unacceptably high levels of pollution.

Sea swimming is dangerous at times, particularly on the Atlantic coast, where some beaches have very strong currents. Most beaches are supervised by lifeguards who operate a flag system to indicate when swimming is safe; always observe flags and other beach warning signs. When a beach is closed or swimming is prohibited, it's shown by a sign ('*baignade interdite*'). There are stinging jellyfish in parts of the Mediterranean and along the Atlantic coast but no dangerous sharks.

Swimming pools (*piscine municipale*) can be found in most French towns. Paris now boasts around 35 public pools, including a floating pool on the river Seine (opened in 2006 to complement the annual 'Paris-Plage' initiative, which transforms 3.5km of the Seine river bank into a sandy beach for five weeks of the summer).

Most swimming pools and clubs provide swimming lessons (all levels from beginner to fish) and run life-saving courses. All French children are required to follow a 'learn to swim' programme and take swimming tests at regular intervals.

France also has a number of huge water-sports centres with indoor and outdoor pools, slides, flumes, wave machines, whirlpools and waterfalls, plus sun-beds, saunas, solariums, Jacuzzis and hot baths.

WATER SPORTS

Popular watersports include sailing, windsurfing, waterskiing, jet-skiing, rowing, canoeing, kayaking, surfing, barging, rafting and sub-aquatic sports. Wetsuits are recommended for windsurfing, waterskiing and sub-aquatic sports, even in summer. Rowing and canoeing are possible on most lakes and rivers, where canoes and kayaks can usually be hired.

Scuba diving and snorkelling are popular, particularly around the coasts of Brittany, the French Riviera and Corsica. There are clubs for most water-sports in all major resorts and towns throughout France, where instruction is usually available. France has over 8,500km (5,300mi) of inland waterways, controlled by Voies Navigables de France (VNF, www.vnf.fr), and it's possible to navigate from the north coast to the Mediterranean along rivers and canals. Canals aren't just for pleasure craft, and millions of tonnes of freight are transported on them annually. Except for parts of the

Moselle river, all French waterways provide free access.

France has Europe's best surfing beaches, on the extreme southwest Atlantic coast, including Biarritz (the capital of European surfing), Capbreton, Hossegor and Lacanau.

French residents must obtain a certificate of competence to pilot power boats of 9 to 50hp; separate certificates are required for inland waters (*permis fluvial*) and coastal waters, including rivers within five nautical miles of a harbour (*permis mer*). You must have an International Certificate of Competence (ICC), valid for five years, to hire a boat over 15m (50ft) long.

Be sure to observe all warning signs on lakes and rivers. Take particular care when canoeing, as even the most benign of rivers have 'white water' patches that are dangerous for the inexperienced. Some rivers have strong currents and require considerable skill and experience to navigate. It's sensible to wear a lifejacket, regardless of whether you're a strong swimmer. On some rivers there are quicksand-like banks of silt and shingle where people have been sucked under.

France has literally hundreds of harbours and sailing is a popular sport with over 750,000 yacht owners and numerous sailing clubs and schools. Boats of all shapes and sizes can be hired in most resorts and ports, from motorboats to barges and houseboats (*pénichette*) accommodating 10 to 12 people. In contrast, many inland waters are devoid of sailing boats and inland sailing clubs are few and far between. If you prefer to let someone else do the work there are hotel barges, some with heated swimming pools, air-conditioning, and even suites with four-poster beds!

If you wish to berth a boat in France, you must find a caretaker (*gardien/ne*) to look after it. The cost of keeping a yacht on the Atlantic coast is much lower than on the Mediterranean, although even there it needn't be too expensive provided you steer clear of the most fashionable ports. Mooring fees vary considerably depending on the size of boat, the time of year and the location.

Further information about inland waterways can be obtained from Voies Navigables de France (VNF, www.vnf.fr).

Galeries Lafayette, Paris

17.
SHOPPING

*F*rance is one of Europe's great shopping countries, where shops are designed to seduce you with their artful displays of beautiful and exotic merchandise. Paris is a shoppers' paradise where even the shop windows are a delight, although it isn't the place for budget shoppers. One of France's main attractions is its markets, which are held regularly in most towns, selling everything under the sun in a uniquely French atmosphere.

Most towns have a supermarket or two and there are usually huge shopping centres with hypermarkets, do-it-yourself (DIY) stores and furniture warehouses on the outskirts of large towns. In many city centres there are pedestrian streets (*rue piétonne*), where you can walk and shop without fear of being mown down by cars and motorcycles – although you're still be at the mercy of skateboarders and rollerbladers.

The French don't usually make good servants, and shop staff are often surly and unhelpful, particularly in department stores, where you can wait ages to be served while staff chat among themselves (in France the customer often comes last). On the other hand, one of the delights of French life is the art with which even the simplest purchase is wrapped – especially if you say it's a gift (*pour offrir*).

In Paris and other cities and tourist resorts you need to be wary of pickpockets and bag-snatchers. Never tempt fate with an exposed wallet or purse or by flashing your money around.

PRICES

French retailers are among the world's most competitive and have smaller profit margins than those in many other countries. Price fixing isn't permitted, except on books, although the

Loi Lang (named after Culture Minister Jack Lang) allows up to a 5 per cent discount off manufacturers' 'recommended retail prices'. Prices of bread and pharmaceuticals are government controlled.

Some products are particularly expensive in France and are worth importing. These including electronic and audio equipment, cosmetics, furniture, books, paint and similar products, and almost anything that's manufactured outside the EU. Among the best buys in France are pottery, decorative glass, kitchenware, quality clothes (including children's), fashion accessories, toys, domestic electrical equipment, wines, spirits (but not imported ones), luxury foods and perfumes.

SALES & BARGAINS

There are relatively few bargain shops in France (certainly compared with the UK or US), although there's usually at least one cheap 'bazaar' in each town. The French generally don't go in for secondhand goods and charity shops are virtually non-existent, apart from the those of Emmaüs (www.emmaus-france.org), an international charitable organisation with around 120 shops in France, and a few *dépôts-vente*, where you can leave unwanted clothes (or other articles) and receive 50 per cent of the price when they're sold.

On the other hand 'boot sales' (known as *foire à tout* in the north and *vide grenier* in the south) are becoming increasingly common (see **Markets** on page 247). There are also secondhand bookshops in most large towns and cities.

It's possible to buy goods direct from factory shops with discounts of between 30 and 70 per cent, although they aren't nearly as common as in the US. Most are to be found in the north and east of France, although the factory-shopper's Mecca is Troyes in Aube, where there are around 230 'factory' outlets.

You should be wary of fake goods as some 70 per cent of all fake products are copies of French brands, reckoned to cost the country 30,000 jobs and some €6 billion in lost sales annually. Perfumes are a favourite target, but counterfeit goods include leather products, CDs and DVDs, household goods and food – French truffles, which can cost hundreds of euros per kilo, have been 'counterfeited' by the Chinese in recent years. If you're buying a designer item (i.e. a handbag) in a market and the price seems too good to be true – then it almost certainly is!

SHOPPING HOURS

Shopping hours vary considerably depending on the city or town and the type of shop. Food shops can't legally open for more than 13 hours a day and other shops are limited to 11 hours per day. Food shops such as bakeries outside Paris are open from as early as 6.30 or 7am until noon or 12.30pm, and again from between 3 and 4pm until 7 or 8pm. Non-food shops usually open from 9 or 10am to noon and from 2pm until 6.30-7.30pm. Small shops tend to tailor their opening hours to suit their customers rather than their staff.

Large shops and super/hypermarkets remain open at lunchtime, although smaller stores usually close, except perhaps on Fridays and Saturdays. Most hypermarkets are open from 9am until between 8 and 10pm, Mondays to Saturdays.

France is generally closed on Sunday although some village shops, particularly *boulangeries*, *charcuteries* and *pâtisseries*, open on Sunday mornings. There's widespread opposition to Sunday trading from unions and small shopkeepers, although French shops are permitted to open on five Sundays a year and those in designated 'tourist' areas (e.g. coastal and ski resorts) may open on any Sunday. Many shops (and some other businesses) are closed on Monday mornings or all day Mondays, particularly those that open on Sundays.

In many cities and towns shops have a late-opening day (*nocturne*) once a week, e.g. Wednesdays in Paris, until between 8 and 10pm. It's generally best to avoid shopping on Wednesdays if possible, as many children are off school and are taken shopping on that day.

Paris and some other cities have food shops that stay open until 10pm or midnight and a few that are open 24 hours. Many small Parisian boutiques open at around 10 or 10.30am until 7 or 7.30pm. Some shops close for the whole of August or for another month in the year.

Shops and restaurants often indicate the days they're open or closed, e.g. every day (*tous les jours* or *TLJ*), every day except Monday (*sauf lundi*), and Saturdays, Sundays and holidays (*samedis, dimanches et fêtes* or S, D & F). Most shops close on public holidays (see page 41) and most (except some newsagents') shut on 1st January, 1st May, 14th July and 25th December.

SPECIALIST FOOD SHOPS

Buying food is a serious business in France, where the range and quality of fresh food is without parallel. The French have a passion for eating, and shopping for food is a labour of love and not to be rushed. When they have time, people usually shop in small specialist food shops and markets rather than in large, soulless supermarkets and hypermarkets. Despite intense competition from supermarkets, traditional family-run shops still thrive in villages and small towns and enjoy some 60 per cent of the general retail trade and around 50 per cent of the food trade. Although their numbers are decreasing – more as a result of the depopulation of rural areas than competition from supermarkets – they survive by offering personal service (advice, tastings, etc.) and high quality, as well as serving as a meeting place for locals.

When living in France, one of the best ways to integrate with the local community is to support local businesses. The quality and range of food provided by small shops varies considerably, so shop around to find those that you like most and become a regular customer. In many rural villages there are mobile shops

(*marchands ambulants*) selling bread, meat, fish, dairy products, fruit and vegetables, which usually visit once or twice a week. Ask your neighbours what days they call and listen for their horns. Despite the availability of almost any fruit and vegetable at almost any time of year (from somewhere in the world), the French tend to eat only what's in season locally (i.e. in France) and generally avoid imported produce.

> Food is sold by the kilo or by the 'piece' (*pièce*). *Une livre* (not to be confused with *un livre*, meaning 'book') means 'pound' (either in weight or in money) and is equivalent to half a kilo or 500g.

Farmers and producers sell their produce direct to the public and you'll often see signs such as '*produits de la ferme – vente directe*' in country areas for fruit, vegetables, wine (and other drinks), cheese, pâté, honey, eggs and other foods. You can also pay in advance, usually annually, for a weekly or monthly supply of fresh fruit and vegetables direct from a local producer, where the grower makes up a basket of seasonal produce, which you must usually collect. There's also a growing trend to pick your own fruit and vegetables. (If you're tempted to pick mushrooms in the forest, take them to a chemist and check that they aren't poisonous!)

Boucherie

Most villages and all towns have a butcher's shop (*boucherie*) selling all kinds of meat, including pork, although generally speaking pork is the preserve of the *charcuterie* (see below). A *boucherie* doesn't sell horse meat (*cheval*), which is sold by a specialist horse butcher (*boucherie chevaline*), denoted by a sign with a horse's head (it's also sold in some supermarkets and hypermarkets) and is similarly priced to beef; many people believe it's the best of all meats, although its popularity has waned in recent years. A butcher may also sell poultry, although this is sold exclusively by specialist poultry shops (*volailler*) in some towns. Butchers will often cook meat purchased from them at little extra cost and many also sell spit-roasted chickens and other cooked meats.

> Butchers often open on Sundays but close all day on Mondays or just in the morning, whereas supermarkets (which have a meat counter) are open on Mondays.

The French are voracious carnivores and are second in Europe only to the Belgians in the quantity of meat they consume per capita. When the French kill an animal for food, nothing is wasted, not even the ears and tail, not to mention its innards and private parts (offal), which are highly prized. The French are puzzled by many foreigners' aversion to eating certain parts of an animal. However, since the 'mad cow disease' (*maladie de la vache folle*) epidemic, butchers must display details of the life and manner of slaughter of all bovines (including the country or area of origin) on a *ticket de pesée* attached to the joint or carcass. Unless your French is particularly good, you're better off buying your meat pre-packed from a supermarket. However, if your French is up to the task, your local butcher is a better choice and is usually an excellent source of cooking tips.

Boulangerie

Thanks to a 19th-century law all towns and villages above a certain size must have a baker (*boulangerie*) or an outlet selling bread (*dépôt de pain*), e.g. a café, newsagent's, supermarket or petrol station. The French love their daily bread (many old country homes have a bread oven) and won't keep bread for more than a few hours (let alone freeze it – heaven forbid!), although consumption has fallen from some 84kg per head per year in 1965 to less than 40kg today (or from 230g to around 110g – half a *baguette* – per day).

When foreigners refer to French bread, they usually mean a *baguette*, although there are many other varieties of loaf. *Pain* (or *pain parisien/gros pain*) is the thickest and longest, while the narrowest and shortest is the *ficelle* (literally a 'piece of string'). Other common types of loaf are *flûte* and *bâtard*. Note also that otherwise identical loaves are often cooked in different ways, e.g. in a mould (*moulé*) or on a flat baking tray or tiles (*pavé*) and you should specify which you prefer.

French bakers are producing an increasingly wide variety of non-standard breads, including wholemeal bread (*pain complet/intégral*), *pain de campagne* ('country' bread, made with a blend of white, wholemeal and rye flour), *pain de seigle* (rye and wheat bread) and *pain au son* (with added bran). Unlike a *baguette* or *pain*, these can be kept for a few days. Wholemeal or mixed-grain *baguettes* are sometimes available. *Pain de mie* is a tasteless sandwich loaf used for toast (or feeding ducks), although *pain de mie complet* is a slight improvement.

A *boulangerie* also sells *croissants*, chocolate *croissants* (*pains au chocolat*), *brioches* (a type of bun), special breads made with raisins and nuts (e.g. almonds, hazelnuts or walnuts) and a limited range of cakes and biscuits, although for fancy cakes you need to visit a *pâtisserie* (see below). Bakers sometimes also sell sandwiches and other snacks, such as quiches and mini-pizzas. Like bread, *croissants* vary considerably in quality and taste, and it's well worth shopping around for the best (avoiding those in packets).

Bakeries usually close on one day a week, although in a town with more than one they won't all close on the same day. When the only baker in a village closes, bread (usually *baguettes* and *pains* only) is usually available from another outlet, such as the village café.

Charcuterie

A *charcuterie* (literally pork butcher's) is a delicatessen selling mostly cooked meats, plus pâtés, pies, quiches, omelettes, pizzas, salads and prepared dishes. Each region has its own pork specialities, as does each *charcutier*. A *charcuterie* may also have a *rôtisserie*, where meat and poultry is spit-roasted. A *charcutier* may also be a caterer (*traiteur*), who can create delicious dishes for two or a banquet for 100.

Confiserie

A *confiserie* is a high-class confectioner, not to be confused with a common sweet shop (which don't exist in France). Each town has a *confiserie*, where you can buy hand-made chocolates and confectionery made with every fattening (and expensive) ingredient under the sun. They may also make excellent home-made ice-cream. A *confiserie* isn't the place to buy children's mass-produced sweets, best bought in bulk at a supermarket, but confectionery to win somebody's heart. A *confiserie* may be part of a cake shop (*pâtisserie* – see below).

Crémerie

A *crémerie* ('dairy shop') sells butter, cream, cheese, eggs, yoghurt, ice-cream, and a variety of other foods, many with nothing to do with milk. Surprisingly, *crémeries* don't usually sell fresh milk. They're mainly found in rural areas where there are lots of cows, such as Normandy and the Jura.

Both salted (*demi-sel*) and unsalted (*doux*) butter (*beurre*) is available, made from both pasteurised and unpasteurised (*cru*) milk. (Low-fat, margarine-like spreads are available in supermarkets, although they aren't normally used as a substitute for butter.) A *crémerie* usually sells dozens of cheeses, many of which can't be found elsewhere. If it doesn't, there's probably a cheese shop (*fromagerie*) nearby (see below).

Épicerie/Alimentation Générale

A grocers or general store (*épicerie/ alimentation générale* – *épicerie* is literally a 'spice shop') sells most everyday foods, including butter, cheese, coffee/tea, fruit, vegetables, wine and beer, plus a range of preserved and packaged foods. Many general stores are now self-service (*libre-service*). Prices are usually considerably higher than in supermarkets; you pay for the convenience and personal service. In Paris and other cities, many grocers stay open late.

Fromagerie

France produces around 400 varieties of cheese, including many made with unpasteurised milk (*lait cru*). This practice is under threat from Brussels' eurocrats, although under the French *AC* system it's illegal to make cheeses from pasteurised milk! Many thousands of cases of food poisoning are attributed to cheese each year, although nobody knows for

sure whether the cheese is infected before, during or after it's made.

Imported cheeses are rare, although the French make their own 'foreign' cheeses, particularly Emmenthal. Goat's milk cheese (*fromage de chèvre*) is popular and comes in many varieties, as does sheep's milk cheese (*fromage de brebis*).

When buying a soft cheese such as brie or camembert, you should state whether you want it ripe (*fait*) or unripe (*pas fait*). A sell-by-date of around three weeks ahead of the purchase date on pre-packaged camembert is a good indicator for *pas fait*.

Patisserie

A *pâtisserie* is a cake shop, selling wonderful (but expensive) home-made pastries, fruit tarts and chocolate éclairs, and perhaps home-made ice-cream. It's possible to buy just one or two slices (*une part*, not *tranche*) of a fruit tart or flan or a whole one. Every town and region tends to have its own specialities. Cakes are made to order for special occasions. All creations are beautifully wrapped, even when you buy just a single *tartelette*.

Poissonnerie

Fishmongers' (*poissonnerie*) are rare in inland France compared with other food shops, although fish stalls are common in markets. Fish isn't an cheap alternative to meat and is often more expensive, although it's reasonably priced in fishing ports – even more so if you buy directly off the fishing boats – and mussels (*moules*) can be purchased for around €3-4 per kilo.

Most foreigners find it difficult to identify the myriad types of fish sold in France, which vary from region to region. The most common species include anchovy (*anchois*), bass (*basse*), bream (*acarne*), eel (*anguille*), haddock (*aiglefin* – haddock is smoked

haddock), mackerel (*maquereau*), monkfish (*baudroie/lot*), mullet (*barbeau*), octopus (*pieuvre*), plaice (*carrelet*), salmon (*saumon*), sardine (*sardine*), sea bass (*bar/loup*), skate (*raie*), sole (*sole*), squid (*calamar*), trout (*truite*), tuna (*thon*), turbot (*turbot*), whitefish (*blanc*) and whiting (*merlan*). Fish are cleaned, scaled and 'topped and tailed' free on request.

Common shellfish (*coquillage*) include clams (*clovisse/flie/palourde/vernis* according to size), cockles (*bulot/coque*), crab (*crabe*), crayfish (*langoustine*), lobster (*langouste* or *homard*), mussels (*moules*), oysters (*huîtres* – see below), prawns (*crevette rose*), scallops (*coquille Saint-Jacques*) and shrimps (*crevette*). The 'queen' of mussels, *moules de bouchot* from Normandy's Mont St Michel bay was the first seafood to be awarded an AOC.

France is by far Europe's largest producer of oysters, which aren't just for millionaires and cost as little as €5 per kilo in fishing ports, although they can cost twice as much in markets and supermarkets. Oysters are, however, usually sold by the dozen and not by weight, and the price varies with the category or size. They're 'properly' eaten raw (despite periodical 'scares'), although they're equally tasty when cooked.

All fish must be labelled with its source (e.g. wild or farmed), the location of the catch (if wild), and its commercial and scientific names. There are three quality grades: *Label Rouge* (top quality, like meat), *Certification de Conformité Produit/CCP* (medium quality) and *Qualité Aquaculture de France* (basic quality).

Foreign Food Shops

French supermarkets sell few foreign foods, with the exception of biscuits, coffee and tea, confectionery, preserves, Italian pasta, Chinese and Vietnamese foods, delicatessen foods (e.g. *charcuterie*) and perhaps a few cheeses, particularly Dutch (many French people are unaware that there are any British cheeses!). You may also find American hamburger buns and British-style (sliced) bread, marmalades and sauces, e.g. HP and Worcester. There may be wider ranges, even including curry-making products, in supermarkets in areas where there are many foreign residents or tourists, sometimes in a 'tastes of the world' (*gouts du monde*) section.

Foreign food shops are common in Paris and some other cities (notably Toulouse). In Paris, Galeries Lafayette features a British Food Hall and the Grande Épicerie de Paris is an international grocery store selling foods from the UK, the US and other countries. Other American food shops in the capital include Thanksgiving (4th *arrondissement*) and The Real McCoy (7th). Marks & Spencer Food have a store at 6 Rue de la Pépinière (8th). There are also a number of enterprising expats in France selling British food, such as Brittain's Stores (04 93 42 0170, www.brittains-stores.com).

Foreign foods can be also ordered from abroad via the internet, although prices are inevitably high. If you can't live without you daily fix of American or British specialities you can order them from My American Market (www.myamericanmarket.com), the Brit Super Store (www.britsuperstore.com) or the British Corner Shop (www.britishcornershop.co.uk).

MARKETS

Markets are a common sight in towns and villages and are an essential part of French life, largely unaffected by competition from supermarkets and hypermarkets. They're colourful, entertaining and an experience not to be missed, even if you don't plan to buy anything. There are generally three kinds of market in France: indoor markets, permanent

street markets and travelling open-air street markets that move from neighbourhood to neighbourhood on different days of the week or month. Many small towns hold a market or fair once a month, usually on the same day each month.

The *raison d'être* of the French market is fresh food – meat, fruit, vegetables, fish, cheese, bread, etc. – mostly produced locally, although it's generally more expensive than in supermarkets. In many markets a wide range of live 'food' is available, including snails (the best quality snails for festive occasions can cost around €1 each), lobster, crab, duck, chicken, guinea fowl, pigeon and rabbit. Most rural food markets have a selection of stalls run by organic farmers. A variety of other goods are commonly sold in markets, including flowers, plants, clothes and shoes, ironmongery, crockery and hardware.

Specialist markets (particularly in Paris) include antiques, books, clothes, stamps/postcards, flowers, birds and pets. Antique and flea markets (*marché aux puces*) are common throughout France; the largest regular market is held at Saint-Ouen in Paris, with 7km (4mi) of shops selling secondhand goods, antiques and curios (*brocante*). It's open every Saturday, Sunday and Monday from 7.30am until 7pm. Paris also has a number of smaller flea markets. However, don't expect to find many bargains in Paris, where anything worth buying is snapped up by dealers.

Elsewhere, Lille stages the *Grande Braderie de Lille* on the first weekend in September, which is the largest flea market in Europe with 100km of stalls! In the provinces there are also

foires à tout or *vide-grenier* (a cross between a flea market and a car boot sale), where you can turn up some real bargains, particularly fine china, e.g. Limoges. There are numerous online guides to French flea and antiques markets, including www.brocantesfrance. com, www.day-tripper.net/shopping-markets-braderie-france.html, www.fleamarketinsiders. com/best-flea-markets-in-france and https://vide-greniers.org.

The most popular days for markets are Wednesdays and Saturdays, although they can be found somewhere every day of the week except Mondays. In the provinces markets are often held in the mornings only, from around 6am until noon or 1pm (shrewd shoppers get there before 9am). You need to get up with the birds to shop at some wholesale markets (e.g. in Paris), open from around 4-8am. Each district (*arrondissement*) in Paris has at least two or three weekly street markets, some of which close for lunch, e.g. from 1-4pm, and continue until 7 or 8pm. There are Sunday morning markets in many towns.

To find out when local markets are held, ask at your local tourist office or town hall. Market days may be listed on a sign when entering a town, which may also indicate any parking restrictions).

DEPARTMENT & CHAIN STORES

Among the most famous department stores, most of which are in Paris, are Au Bon Marché (the first department store in France, founded in 1852), Printemps (best for perfumes), Galeries Lafayette (famous for high fashion) and La Samaritaine, the largest department store in the capital.

Fashion is the forte of most Parisian department stores, many of which stage regular fashion shows. Most also specialise in cosmetics and provide money-changing services, export discounts (i.e. VAT refunds), a travel agency, and theatre and concert tickets. Many department stores also have a food (*alimentation*) department.

Department stores don't close for lunch and usually open from 9.30am until around 7pm, Mondays to Saturdays, with late-night shopping on one day a week until around 9.30pm. Most deliver goods within a certain radius and also ship goods overseas (for a fee).

Chain stores are rarer than in most other European countries. French chain stores include Bally and Eram (shoes), and FNAC (audio, books and video). Department stores such as Printemps, Au Bon Marché, Trois Quartiers, La Samaritaine and Nouvelles Galeries are also chain stores, with branches in several towns. Chain stores such as Monoprix and Prisunic (subsidiaries of Galeries Lafayette and Printemps respectively) and Uniprix are budget department stores known as *magasins populaires* and have outlets throughout France.

There are also a number of British and other foreign chain stores operating in France, including The Body Shop, Brentanos, Burton, Espirit, Gap, Habitat, Ikea, Jaeger, Toys 'R' Us, WH Smith and Zara.

SUPERMARKETS & HYPERMARKETS

There are supermarkets (*supermarchés*) and hypermarkets (*hypermarchés*) – both often referred to as 'large areas' (*grandes surfaces*) – in or just outside most towns. Among the leading supermarket and hypermarket chains are Auchan/ATAC, Carrefour, Casino, Intermarché, E. Leclerc, Prisunic and Super U/Hyper U. The last ten years has seen a steady increase in the number of low-price supermarkets known as *supermarchés hard discount*, e.g. Aldi, Lidl and ED. They sell the usual range of foodstuffs and household goods you find in traditional supermarkets and

hypermarkets, but without the frills of attractive presentation and shelving. Savings on a mixed-bag shopping basket can be as much as 20 per cent.

Hypermarkets are often located in a shopping or commercial centre (*centre commercial*) housing many smaller shops, cafés and restaurants (often including a self-service restaurant), toilets, a huge free car park, and a petrol station (usually the cheapest local source for fuel). Large supermarkets and hypermarkets are generally open all day from 8am until around 7.30pm (some hypermarkets stay open later). However, some small supermarkets close for lunch, although not usually on Saturdays. Some supermarkets are open on Sunday mornings.

 Caution

When you enter a supermarket or hypermarket, there's often a counter, called a *consigne*, where you must leave goods purchased elsewhere, large bags and crash helmets (you receive a receipt). If there's no *consigne*, a security guard may heat seal your previous purchases in a plastic bag, which you can then take into the store with you.

One thing you won't find in supermarkets or hypermarkets in France is much in the way of medicines, which can only be purchased at a chemists (see **Medicines** on page 164), and tobacco products which are sold by a *tabac* (see **Tobacconists** on page 252).

The French are keen on DIY (*bricolage*) and there are numerous DIY superstores, some of which (e.g. Castorama, Leroy Merlin) offer free telephone advice and DIY courses. There are also supermarkets for furniture (e.g. But, Monsieur Meuble) and electrical goods (e.g. Darty, Boulanger). France even has funeral supermarkets (Roc-Eclerc), where you can choose your coffin and headstone at your leisure.

The French are keen gardeners, and many hypermarkets have extensive garden departments, often selling plants as well as gardening equipment. There are also dedicated garden centres (*jardinerie*) and nurseries (*pépinerie*) in or on the outskirts of most towns.

At many supermarkets and hypermarkets, plastic bags aren't provided except for fruit and vegetables, and are now banned, although you can buy a biodegradable bag at checkout tills for a few cents. Checkout staff don't bag your purchases or take them to your car for you. It's usually essential to have a returnable €1 coin (or similar size token/*jeton*) to use a trolley (*caddie*).

Food

The range of food sold by French supermarkets and hypermarkets is similar to that in the UK. Most supermarkets and hypermarkets have separate counters for meat, fish, bread and cheese. The French generally don't like to buy pre-packaged meat, fish, fruit or vegetables. Supermarkets sell few foreign foods, although some have sections (usually hidden) where imported products can be found (see **Foreign Food Shops** above). Some supermarkets also have a salad bar.

Fruit and vegetables may be sold individually (*la pièce*) or by the kilo (*le kg*). In the latter case, they may be weighed by an assistant or you weigh them yourself on scales with buttons depicting the various produce, although some supermarkets still weigh produce at the checkout. (If you're supposed to weigh produce and forget, you'll be sent by the checkout assistant to do so, while frustrated shoppers in the queue behind fume!).

As in other countries, perishable items have a sell-by date (*date limite de vente*) or use-by date (*date limite d'utilisation optimale/DLUO*), which may also be described as a 'consume-by-date' (*date limite de consommation/DLC*) or 'expiry date' (*date de péremption*). You should always check this as it's common for out-of-date products to be left on the shelves.

ALCOHOL

Drinking alcohol is an integral part of everyday life in France, where many people have a daily tipple. There's also plenty of choice among non-alcoholic drinks.

Wine

France is, of course, world-famous for its wines, and one of the essential features of a civilised home is a large cellar (*cave*), where wines are left to mature for years (often far longer than is good for them). Despite its renown the French wine industry is in crisis as more and more foreigners switch to 'new world' wines and the French themselves, although inseparably wedded to their own wines, drink less and less.

Indeed, the popular view of the French as great drinkers could hardly be further from the truth: their alcohol consumption per head is relatively low (wine consumption has reduced by a third in the last 25 years) and there's a growing anti-alcohol lobby.

As even teetotallers are no doubt aware, there's more to wine than its colour, which may be red, white, pink or even yellow (e.g. *vin jaune* from the Jura and most dessert wines), and it's a well-known fact that the more you know about wine, the more you'll enjoy it (it also make your more eloquent and a better driver!). There are numerous excellent books about French wine, and information about wine-related tours and holidays can be found at www.winetourisminfrance.com.

Merchants

France doesn't have the equivalent of a British off-licence, and there are few specialist wine merchants (*marchand de vins/caviste/négociant*), although there's usually at least one in most large towns. There are, however, a few chains of wine shops (such as Nicolas – www.nicolas.com)', where prices are fixed throughout the chain, and independent wine shops and local chains in Paris, such as Le Repaire de Bacchus. Most wine shops will deliver if you buy more than a few bottles. A good *épicerie* or *charcuterie* usually also sells wines, although they're generally considerably more expensive than supermarkets.

Most people buy their wine from supermarkets and hypermarkets, although the quality and range isn't usually outstanding. If you buy wine from your local supermarket, keep an eye open for their *Foire au Vin* special offers.

Nowhere are French stores more parochial and nationalistic than when it comes to selling wine. Most supermarkets and hypermarkets stock a wide selection of local wines, but may offer little from other regions of France apart from Bordeaux and, to a lesser extent, Burgundy. You're likely to find few (if any) non-French wines in your local supermarket, where they're normally segregated from French wines (e.g. hidden behind a pillar) and overpriced.

Buying Direct

Buying direct is the best way to buy wine in France, where many wine lovers buy the bulk of their wine direct from growers, either by making an annual visit to vineyards or by mail-order. Vineyards selling wine direct usually have signs inviting you to free tastings (*dégustation gratuite* or *dégustation et vente*), with the hope of selling you a few bottles or cases. Most vineyards and distillers are geared to receive visitors, particularly the great Bordeaux, champagne and cognac houses, which usually make a small charge for a conducted tour and tasting. Appointments must be made to visit some smaller vineyards and most are closed during lunchtimes.

Beer

French beer (*bière*) is usually of the 'lager' variety and comes mainly from the northeast, e.g. Alsace, Lorraine, Picardie and Nord-Pas-de-Calais. As well as the well-known brands, there are many excellent, strong beers (e.g. top-fermented *bières de garde*) brewed by farmhouse breweries. The French also drink Belgian beer but rarely beer from any other country. Beer is usually sold in packs of 6 to 24 x 25cl or 33cl bottles and is much cheaper than in most

other European countries. Supermarkets have frequent offers on beer, although the practice of selling beer in returnable bottles (*bouteilles consignées/verres consignés*), which works out even cheaper than small bottles, has practically died out.

Spirits & Other Alcoholic Drinks

Spirits are cheaper in France than in many other European countries, although more expensive than in Italy and Spain. Among the many popular spirits in France are Cognac, Armagnac, Marc (a grape brandy made from the residue of wine production in wine-growing regions), Calvados (apple brandy from Normandy), Kirsch (cherry brandy from Alsace) and a wide variety of liqueurs, such as Bénédictine, Chartreuse, Cointreau and Grand Marnier. Imported gin and, especially, Scotch, Irish, American and Canadian whiskies are also popular.

Brandy is classified by age, i.e. *vieux* or *réserve* (three years old), *vieille réserve* (four years old), *VSOP* (an abbreviation of the English 'very special old pale', indicating five years' ageing), and *hors d'âge* (literally 'ageless' but meaning over six years old).

> France is the world's largest whisky market after Spain and the French buy 12 times as much whisky as brandy, whose sales are suffering as a result.

Aniseed liqueurs (*pastis*) such as Pernod and Ricard are brewed in the south, and Alsace is home to Fleur de Bière – distilled malt beer. Absinthe, long banned (and for good reason), has recently been legalised.

Among the many other popular alcoholic drinks in France are apple and pear cider from Brittany and Normandy, and fortified wines, drunk as aperitifs. Alcohol flavoured with fruit and other things is common throughout France, every region having its own variations such as *crème de cassis* (which is added to white wine to make *kir*), *crème de menthe* and *crème de cacao*, Pineau des Charentes (grape juice and cognac), Floc de Gascogne (grape juice and Armagnac) and pommeau (apple juice and calvados).

TOBACCONISTS

The tobacconist (*bureau de tabac*, commonly called simply *tabac*) is a unique French institution. They're identified by a vertical orange sign representing a carrot (which dates back to when slices of raw carrot were put in tobacco to keep it moist). Not only are *tabacs* the sole authorised vendors of cigarettes and other tobacco products, they're also mini-stationers. A *tabac* sells postage stamps, postcards, single envelopes and writing paper, as well as gifts and souvenirs, cigarette lighters and other odds and ends. They also sell lottery tickets and may be agents for PMU off-track betting.

Oddly, a *tabac* is also the source of government forms and the official outlet for fiscal stamps (*timbre fiscal*) used to pay fines (e.g. parking tickets), government taxes and official fees such as those required for a residence permit (*carte de séjour*). Stamps are sold in denominations of €0.50, €1, €2, €5, €8, €10, €20, €30 and €90, although few *tabacs* stock the whole range of fiscal stamps and you may need to try a few to get the stamp you need. A *tabac* is usually combined with a bar or newsagent, and there's often a post box (*boîte aux lettres*) outside. They're usually open late (some Parisian *tabacs* never seem to close).

CLOTHING

Clothing outlets range from street bazaars selling cut-price clothes to elegant boutiques offering the ultimate in chic. The flagship of the French fashion industry is *haute couture*: made-to-order clothes employing the best designers (some of them British!), craftsmanship and materials. Garments are outrageously expensive (costing from €3,000 to €8,000 or more). Not surprisingly, the worldwide clientele for *haute couture* clothing is estimated to be no more than a few thousand people, with just a few hundred regular customers.

Everyday clothes are expensive compared with those in other Western countries, mainly due to a lack of imports. As with other things in life, the French generally prefer quality to quantity, and 'classic' clothes are made to last and never go out of fashion. One of the best value ready-to-wear labels is Tati, who have their flagship store at boulevard Rochechouart in Paris and branches in a number of other cities.

Bargains can be found in cities if you're willing to hunt around or wait for the sales. Last season's designer labels are usually sold at half-price, i.e. ridiculously instead of outrageously expensive. Most shops hold sales in January and at the end of June, and bargains can be found year round in Alésia, the major discount shopping district in Paris' 14th *arrondissement*. The Forum des Halles in Paris is a giant subterranean shopping centre where you can find every kind of clothing at bargain prices. There are also 'label villages' (*ville de marques*), where designer clothes and other luxury goods can be purchased at discounts of up to 30 per cent.

Popular women's ready-to-wear shops include Benetton, Cacharel, Caroll, Franck et Fils and Infinitif, while top men's shops include 100,000 Chemises, Alain Figaret, Cacherel, Cerrutti 1881, Charles Le Golf, Kenzo and New Man.

There are also many secondhand shops selling clothes, euphemistically referred to as 'twice twice' (*bis bis*), especially in Paris, e.g. the Magasin du Troc, which sells slightly used *haute couture* clothes and accessories, perhaps worn only by models. Here you can pick up a Chanel suit for as little as a third of the new price. Secondhand clothing stores for men are also becoming increasingly popular among Parisians. Costume and formal wear hire is possible from many stores in Paris and other cities.

There are many excellent women's fashion magazines in France, including *Modes et Travaux* and *Vogue*.

NEWSPAPERS, MAGAZINES & BOOKS

There are over 200 daily, weekly and monthly newspapers and magazines in France, not including trade magazines and reviews. However, there are few, if any, national newspapers as the French generally prefer local news. Most daily newspapers are published for a region, such as *Le Progrès de Lyon*, *La Voix du Nord* (Lille), *Sud-Ouest* (Bordeaux) and *Ouest-France* (published in Rennes and France's largest-selling daily paper, with a circulation of over 1 million). *Le Parisian* is the capital's daily newspaper (and the nearest France comes to a 'tabloid'), with regional editions named *Aujourd'hui*.

There are only three French newspapers that can claim to be national. The most famous is *Le Monde*, the most intellectual and respected, as well as the best-selling 'national' daily. It's centre-left and similar in prestige

to the English *Times* (which is centre-right), and published in Paris in the afternoon and given the following day's date (which can be confusing!). Next in pecking order is *Le Figaro* (moderate right, conservative – similar to the UK's *Daily Telegraph*) and lastly *Libération* (known colloquially as *Libé*), an intellectual and one-time fashionable tabloid of the centre-left (it was co-founded by Jean-Paul Sartre).

Other popular newspapers include *l'Humanité* (known as *l'Huma* – the French will abbreviate anything), the recently revamped official organ of the French Communist Party, *L'Equipe*, a daily newspaper devoted entirely to sport, and *La Croix*, a right-wing Catholic newspaper. There are also a number of financial newspapers, including *Les Echos* and *La Tribune* (France's answer to the *Financial Times* or *Wall Street Journal*). Surprisingly, specialist Sunday newspapers are almost unknown apart from the undistinguished *Le Journal de Dimanche* and *L'Humanité Dimanche*, although many daily newspapers are also published on Sundays. As elsewhere, weekend papers often carry extra supplements, e.g. travel, fashion and TV programmes, and cost more than weekday issues.

Many newspapers provide excellent weekly magazines (see below) and reviews, and free local weekly newspapers full of advertisements are delivered to homes in many areas. A 'tabloid press' is virtually non-existent, as scandal-mongering is largely the preserve of magazines. France has strict laws regarding personal privacy, although this hasn't prevented the publication of a number of scandal sheets in recent years, including *Minute* and *Voici*, and there are two weekly satirical papers, *Le Canard Enchaîné* (similar to the UK's *Private Eye*) and *Charlie Hebdo* (more juvenile), both published on a Wednesday.

Where the French excel is in the field of magazines and they produce a larger number than any other European country, with the possible exception of the UK, where the diversity of technical and trade magazines is unmatched, even in the USA. French publishers produce over a thousand monthly and even more weekly and quarterly titles. Popular weekly current affairs magazines include the best-selling *Paris Match* (largely 'celebrity' news), *Le Nouvel Observateur* (left), *Le Point* and *L'Express* (middle-of-the-road conservative), *Marianne* (left, tabloid-like) and *VSD* (semi-serious).

Business and financial titles include *Enjeux les Echos*, *L'Expansion* and *Le Nouvel Economiste*. Among the many women's magazines are *Biba*, *Elle*, *Femme Actuelle*, *Marie Claire* and *Marie France* and there are French versions of men's magazines such as *FHM* and *Men's Health*. Other popular magazines include *Figaro Magazine*, *Madame Figaro* and *Jours de France*.

Newspapers and magazines are sold at tobacconists (*tabac*), newsagents' (e.g. the Maison de la Presse chain) and railway station kiosks, and in supermarkets. Many are also available online, e.g. www.lecanardenchaine. fr, www.figaro.fr, www.liberation.fr, www. lemonde.fr, www.marianne2.fr and www. mondediplomatique.fr (or http://mondediplo. com for the English version).

It used to be cheaper to buy bestselling books, such as Michelin guides, from hypermarkets. However, the French government introduced fixed prices to protect small bookshops, thus restricting the availability of most books, although the *Loi Lang* allows a maximum 5 per cent discount off manufacturers' recommended retail prices.

In small towns there are usually a few small shops selling a limited selection of books rather than one large bookshop (note that the French for bookshop is *librairie*; a library is a *bibliothèque*). There are secondhand bookshops in larger towns and cities. Secondhand and rare bookshops and markets are fairly common in Paris, notably the *bouquinistes* along the banks of the river Seine, although these tend to stock specialist books (at specialist prices).

English-language Publications

Major international newspapers are available on the day of publication in Paris and a day or two later in the provinces. Some English-language daily newspapers are printed in Europe and widely available on the day of publication, including *USA Today*, the *International Herald Tribune* (edited in Paris), the *Wall Street Journal Europe* and the *European Financial Times* (printed in Frankfurt). Foreign newspapers are much more expensive than in their home countries (the price is stated in the newspaper, usually on the front or back page) and usually don't include many (if any) of the supplements normally carried in weekend issues (such as the *Sunday Times*). You can access most newspapers via the internet, which may be free, although some such as the *Times/Sunday Times* require a subscription.

Many British and foreign newspapers produce weekly editions, including the *Guardian Weekly*, *International Express* and the *Weekly Telegraph*, which are available on subscription. *Le Monde* publishes a supplement in English on Saturdays. A number of other English-language publications are available in Maisons de la Presse, major supermarkets and on subscription.

Most French bookshops don't stock English-language books. There are, however, English-language bookshops in most large towns and cities, as well as in resort towns. English-language bookshops in Paris include the Abbey Bookshop (5th *arrondissement*), Berkeley Books (6th), Galignani (1st), San Francisco Book Co. (6th), Shakespeare & Company (5th) and WH Smith & Son (1st). However, imported English-language books are expensive (except for this one, which is an absolute bargain!), usually costing around double their 'recommended' home country price. Americans in particular will be appalled. It's cheaper to buy them from Amazon via their UK website and to stock up when visiting the UK or USA.

Many expatriate organisations and clubs run their own libraries or book exchange schemes, and some French public libraries keep a small selection of English-language books (see **Libraries** on page 226). Some bookshops also sell secondhand books, which may also be available from market stalls.

FURNITURE & FURNISHINGS

Furniture (*meubles*) is generally quite expensive in France compared with many other European countries and the choice is usually between basic functional furniture and high-quality designer furniture, with little in between. Exclusive (i.e. expensive) modern and traditional furniture is available everywhere, including bizarre pieces from designers such as Gaultier for those with money to burn and a need to impress.

If you're looking for antique furniture at

affordable prices, the best bargains are to be found at flea markets (*foire à tout*) in rural areas. However, you must arrive early and drive a hard bargain, as the asking prices are often a joke. You can often buy good secondhand and antique furniture at bargain prices from a *dépôt-vente*, where people sell their old furniture and courts sell repossessed household goods. Look under *Dépôts-vente*, *meubles* and *équipement pour la maison* in your local Yellow Pages or search online. There are also companies selling furniture that has been repossessed from bankrupt businesses at bargain prices.

Modern furniture is popular and is often sold in huge stores in commercial centres (inexpensive chain stores include But, Conforama and Fly) and hypermarkets, some of which provide the free loan of a van. Pine

furniture is inexpensive. Beware of buying complicated home-assembled furniture with indecipherable French instructions (translated from Korean) and too few screws. If you want reasonably priced, good quality, modern furniture, you need look no further than Ikea, a Swedish company manufacturing furniture for home assembly with a 14-day money-back guarantee. (The price of Ikea furniture varies with the country and most items are much cheaper in France than, for example, in the UK.) If you're buying a large quantity of furniture, don't be reluctant to ask for a discount, as many stores will give you one if you ask.

When buying furniture for a home in France don't forget to take the climate into consideration. Note also that, if you plan to furnish a holiday home with antiques or expensive furniture, you'll need adequate security and insurance.

HOUSEHOLD GOODS

Household goods are generally of good quality and the choice, although not as wide as in some other European countries, has improved considerably in the last decade. Not surprisingly for a nation that spends much of its time in the kitchen (the rest is spent in the dining room), French kitchenware is among the best in the world. Prices are also competitive, with bargains to be found at supermarkets and hypermarkets. Apart from hypermarkets, one of the best stores for household appliances is Darty, which has outlets in most towns.

Bear in mind when importing household appliances not sold in France that it may be difficult or impossible to get them repaired or serviced locally. If you bring appliances with you don't forget to bring a supply of spares and refills, such as bulbs for a refrigerator or sewing machine, and bags for a vacuum cleaner. Similarly, the standard size of kitchen appliances and cupboard units in France isn't the same as in other countries, and it may be difficult to fit an imported dishwasher or washing machine into a French kitchen. Check the size and the latest French safety regulations before shipping these items to France or buying them abroad, as they may need expensive modifications.

If you already own small household appliances it's worth bringing them to France as all that's usually required is a change of plug or an adapter. However, if you're coming from a country with a 110/115V electricity supply, such as the US, you'll need a lot of expensive converters or transformers, and it's better to buy new appliances in France. Small appliances such as vacuum cleaners, grills, toasters and electric irons aren't expensive and are of good quality (the label 'NF' indicates compatibility with French safety standards). Don't bring your TV without checking its compatibility first, as TVs from many countries don't work in France (see **Chapter 8**).

Subject to electricity supply compatibility, foreign computers will work. If you need to buy a computer while in France but don't want it to have a French operating system or an AZERTY keyboard, you can order one from an international supplier or buy one in the UK or USA. It's possible, however, to 'convert' a French computer to work with a QWERTY keyboard (although the on-screen instructions will still be in French).

If you need kitchen measuring equipment and can't cope with decimal measures you'll need to bring your own measuring scales, jugs, cups and thermometers. Pillows and pillowcases aren't the same size in France as, for example, in the UK or US.

LAUNDRY & DRY CLEANING

Thanks to the French obsession with their appearance, all large towns have laundries (*blanchisserie*) and dry cleaners (*nettoyage à sec/pressing*), most of which also do minor repairs, alterations and dyeing. (There are more dry cleaners and laundries in Paris than in the whole of many other European countries!). Dry cleaning is expensive, however, and you must usually pay in advance. Cleaning by the kilo with no pressing is possible in some places, and you can also save money by having your clothes brushed and pressed, rather than cleaned. Note also that 'express' cleaning may mean a few days rather than hours, even at a dry cleaners where cleaning is done on the premises.

Except in Paris, there are few self-service launderettes (*laveries automatiques*), as the French prefer not to wash their dirty linen in public. Launderette machines are usually operated by tokens (*jetons*) marked with the price and purchased from an attendant. Machines usually take around 7kg (15lb) of washing, although there are often machines of different sizes. Washing powder and softeners are available from vending machines, although it's much cheaper to provide your own. Launderettes have heavy-duty spin dryers (*super essorage*) that reduce the time required to dry clothes but may make them impossible to iron! Dryers can be very hot, so take care with delicate items requiring little drying.

ONLINE & MAIL-ORDER SHOPPING

Shopping by mail-order (*vente par correspondance* or *vente à domicile*) and by telephone has long been popular in France and shopping online has now taken off, accounting at the end of 2016 for over 10 per cent of retail sales with a value of some €70 billion. TV shopping (*téléachat*, 'abbreviated' to TVHA) is also popular.

When ordering goods from outside France, ensure that you're dealing with a bona fide company and that the goods will work in France (if applicable). If possible, always pay by credit card when buying by mail-order or over the internet, as the credit card issuer may be jointly liable with the supplier if there's a problem. Also take into account shipping costs, duty and VAT. If you purchase a small item by post from outside the EU, you'll need to pay French VAT (TVA) on delivery or at the post office on collection. Mail-order shopping and online shopping is regulated in France by the Fédération du e-commerce et de la Vente à Distance (www.fevad.com).

The French mail-order catalogue business is the third-largest in Europe after Germany and the UK, and most French catalogue companies have an up-market, modern image, particularly when compared with the rather old-fashioned image of mail-order in some countries. The leading companies include Camif (www.camif.fr); Cyrillus (www.cyrillus.com/en), La Redoute (www.laredoute.fr), specialising in fashion with around 9 million customers; 3Suisses (www.3suisses.fr), with an extensive clothing range; and Vert Baudet (www.vertbaudet.fr). Most of the aforementioned also have stores in major cities and collection points throughout the country.

DEPOSITS, RECEIPTS & CONSUMER RIGHTS

Under the French Civil Code, all products sold in France must be suitable for the use for which they're intended. If they aren't, you're entitled to exchange them or obtain a refund and it's illegal for traders to use 'small print' (*clauses abusives*) to try to avoid liability.

You've the same legal rights whether goods are purchased at the recommended retail price or at a discount during a sale. Despite all this, obtaining an exchange, let alone a refund, can be a difficult, long-winded and frustrating experience, although most supermarkets and hypermarkets now have an automatic refund policy within a limited period (e.g. two weeks), provided you produce your receipt, and may even exchange goods or provide a voucher (*bon*) if you don't have a receipt.

You should always insist on a receipt (*quittance/ticket/reçu*) and retain it. It's wise to keep receipts and records of all major purchases made while you're resident in France, particularly if your stay is short. This may save you both time and money when you leave France and may be required to declare your belongings in your new country of residence.

If you're asked to pay a deposit for an item,

> The INC (see above) publishes a monthly magazine, *60 Millions de Consommateurs*, containing comparative product tests, practical and legal information, loan calculations and details of insurance surcharges. It's available on subscription, from newsagents or via is website (www.60millions-mag.com).

check whether this is an *acompte* or *arrhes*. With *arrhes* you've the right to cancel your order, although you'll lose your deposit (if the vendor cancels the agreement, he must return twice the amount of the deposit), whereas an *acompte* constitutes the first instalment payment for the item as part of a binding contract to pay the full amount. If you break something in a shop, you're legally liable to pay for it, although the shopkeeper may not wish to enforce the law.

CONSUMER PROTECTION

There are strict consumer protection laws (*code de la consummation*) in France, where the price of goods and services must be clearly displayed and indicate whether tax and service is included (as applicable). Refunds must be made for faulty or inadequate goods returned within seven days (or if a refund is requested within ten days in the case of goods installed in the home); after this period, a credit note, replacement or alternative product can be offered.

Each French department has a Direction Départementale de la Protection des Populations (DDPP) or Direction Départementale de la Cohésion Sociale et de la Protection des Populations (DDCSPP) – a departmental agency for competition, consumption and fraud repression – whose job is to prevent dishonest vendors from cheating consumers, although it deals only with 'minor' complaints.

The national body for consumer rights and protection is the Direction Générale de la Concurrence, de la Consommation et de la Répression des Fraudes (DGCCRF, www.economie.gouv.fr/dgccrf). Some model complaint letters (*lettre type*) are provided on the DGCCRF website, although the mere threat of an official complaint often has the desired effect.

The Institut National de la Consommation (INC) is the umbrella organisation for all French national consumer associations. Its website (www.conso.net) provides links to regional consumer organisations, government agencies and other consumer sites, and contains around 100 model letters. It can provide you with the name of an appropriate consumer association if you require information or have a particular complaint or problem. Another consumer associations is the Union Fédérale des

Consommateurs Que Choisir (www.quechoisir. org), who publish a monthly magazine similar to *Which?* In the UK.

Lavendar fields, Provence

18.
ODDS & ENDS

*T*his chapter covers miscellaneous information. Although not of vital importance, most of the topics covered are of general interest to anyone living or working in France, including everything you ever wanted to know about tipping and toilets (but were afraid to ask).

CITIZENSHIP

There are three ways you can acquire French citizenship: by being born in France, through marriage and through naturalisation:

Birth: France operates the *droit du sol*, whereby anyone born on French soil automatically becomes a French citizen at the age of 18 (unless he wishes not to), provided that he has lived in France for at least five years between the ages of 11 and 18. However, children born of foreign parents acquire their nationality until the age of 13, when they can choose to become dual nationality, provided they've lived in France continuously from the age of 8 to 13.

Marriage: The marriage of a non-French citizen to a French citizen entitles him or her to French citizenship after four years of marriage, unless they have a child in France, in which case naturalisation is immediate. In the case of a non-French citizen who hasn't lived regularly in France for at least three years since their marriage, the post-marriage qualifying period for naturalisation is five years.

Naturalisation: To obtain French citizenship through naturalisation, as opposed to acquisition through marriage, you must have lived in France for at least five years, be at least 18 and satisfy the authorities that you're of good character and have an adequate knowledge of the French language. The period of residence may be reduced (e.g. to two years) if you've attended certain French institutions of higher education or have rendered special services to the country.

An application for naturalisation takes between around 12 months and two years to be processed and must be made to the *préfet* of your local *département*. Around 20 per cent of applications are rejected or postponed (usually because of inadequate language skills), although many applicants – after battling forlornly with the daunting French bureaucracy for years – simply give up.

A passport can be obtained, within two to six weeks, from the local town hall and costs around €100. French passports are valid for ten years (with a possible extension for a further five years) at a time and can be renewed free of charge. *Cartes d'identité*, which are obligatory but free, are also valid for ten years and also available from your local town hall.

CLIMATE

France is the only European country that experiences three distinct climates: continental, maritime and Mediterranean. It isn't easy to generalise about the weather (*temps*), as many regions and areas are influenced by two distinct climates as well as by micro-climates

coastal area, below Brittany, has experienced some exceptionally severe storms and unusually high tides (with inland flooding) in the last few years.

The Massif Central (which acts as a weather barrier between north and south) and eastern France have a moderate continental climate with cold winters and hot, stormy summers. However, the centre and eastern upland areas have an extreme continental climate with freezing winters and sweltering summers. The northern Massif is prone to huge variations in temperature and it was here that a record 41°C (106°F) minimum/maximum temperature difference occurred in one day (on 10th August 1885). In Paris, it's rare for the temperature to fall below minus 5°C (24°F) in winter or to rise above 30°C (86°F) in summer.

created by mountains, forests and other geographical features.

Generally the Loire river is considered to be the point where the cooler northern European climate gradually begins to change to the warmer southern climate. If you're planning to live in France and don't know whether the climate in a particular region will suit you, it's advisable to rent accommodation there until you're absolutely sure, as some people find the extremes of hot and cold in some areas unbearable. Spring and autumn are usually fine throughout France, although the length of the seasons vary with the region and altitude.

The west and northwest (principally Brittany and Normandy but also parts of Poitou-Charentes) have a maritime climate tempered by the Atlantic and the Gulf Stream, with relatively mild winters and warm summers, and most rainfall in spring and autumn. The area around La Rochelle in the west enjoys a pleasant micro-climate and is the second sunniest region of France after the Côte d'Azur. Many people consider the western Atlantic coast to have the best summer climate in France, with the heat tempered by cool sea breezes, although the wind can be less pleasant at other times of the year. The Atlantic

The Midi, stretching from the Pyrenees to the Alps, is hot and dry except for early spring, when there's usually heavy rainfall; the Cévennes region is the wettest in France with some 200cm (79in) of rain a year. Languedoc has hot, dry summers and much colder winters than the French Riviera, with snow often remaining until May in the mountainous inland areas. The Riviera enjoys mild winters, daytime temperatures rarely dropping below 10°C (50°F), and humid and very hot summers, the temperature often rising above 30°C (86°F). The average daily sunshine on the French Riviera is five hours in January and 12 hours in July. Note, however, that it isn't always warm and sunny on the Riviera and it can get quite cold and wet in winter.

The higher you go, the colder it gets. The Alps and Pyrenees experience extremes of weather with heavy snow in winter and hot summers, although the western Pyrenees have

Temperature Guide				
Location	Spring	Summer	Autumn	Winter
Bordeaux	17/6 (63/43)	25/14 (77/57)	18/8 (64/46)	9/2 (48/36)
Boulogne	12/6 (54/43)	20/14 (68/57)	14/10 (57/50)	6/2 (43/36)
Lyon	16/6 (61/43)	27/15 (81/59)	16/7 (61/45)	5/-1 (41/30)
Nantes	15/6 (59/43)	24/14 (75/57)	16/8 (61/46)	8/2 (46/36)
Nice	17/9 (63/48)	27/18 (81/64)	21/12 (70/54)	13/4 (55/39)
Paris	16/6 (61/43)	25/15 (77/59)	16/6 (57/43)	6/1 (43/34)
Strasbourg	16/5 (61/41)	25/13 (77/55)	14/6 (57/43)	1/-2 (34/28)

surprisingly mild winters. The Alpine range disrupts normal weather patterns and there are often significant local climatic variations. Central and eastern France have the coldest winters.

France experiences many strong, cold and dry winds (*vent violent*) including the Mistral and the Tramontane. The Mistral is a bitterly cold wind that blows down the southern end of the Rhône valley into the Camargue and Marseille. The Tramontane affects the coastal region from Perpignan, near the Pyrenees, to Narbonne. Corsica is buffeted by many winds, including the two aforementioned plus the Mezzogiorno and Scirocco. There are over 800 other named winds in France – from the A de Pargues, a cold easterly wind felt in the northeast of France, to the Zéphyr, a warm westerly wind felt in the west – listed and described in the *Petite Encyclopédie des Vents de France* (J C Lattès).

France occasionally experiences extreme and unpredictable weather, particularly in the south, where flash floods can be devastating. Wherever you live, if you're anywhere near a waterway you should ensure that you have insurance against floods.

Weather forecasts (météo) are broadcast on TV and radio stations and published in daily newspapers. You can also obtain weather forecasts by telephone or via the internet, e.g. www.meteo.fr or www.meteoconsult.fr.

Average daily maximum/minimum temperatures for selected cities in Centigrade and Fahrenheit (in brackets) are shown in the table below.

CRIME

France has a similar crime rate to most other European countries and in common with them, has experienced an increase in crime in the last decade. However, violent crime is relatively low, with a murder rate of around 1 per 100,000 of population, which is average for Europe and around a fifth of the US rate (although the figures have been distorted in recent years by terrorist attacks). Property crime accounts for around half of all crime and is most prevalent in Paris and the Mediterranean coastal cities of Marseille and Nice. Car theft and theft from cars is rife in Paris and other cities. In stark contrast, crime in rural areas remains low, and it's still common for those in villages and small towns not to lock their homes or cars.

The worst area for crime is the Mediterranean coast (one of the most corrupt and crime-ridden regions in Europe), particularly around Marseille and Nice, where most crime is attributable to a vicious underworld of racketeers and drug dealers. Marseille is notorious as the centre of organised crime such as drug-trafficking, money-laundering, robbery and prostitution.

Paris is generally a safe destination, although street crime is a concern, most notably in areas frequented by tourists. Pickpockets and bag-snatchers have long been a plague in Paris, where the 'charming' street urchins (often gypsies) are highly organised and trained. They will surround and distract you, and when your attention is diverted pick you clean without your noticing. Keep them at arm's length, if necessary by force, and keep a firm grip on your valuables.

Always remain vigilant in tourist haunts, queues and on the *métro*. Don't tempt fate with an exposed wallet or purse or by flashing your money around, and hang on tight to your bags. One of the most effective methods of protecting your passport, money, travellers' cheques and credit cards is with a money belt worn under your clothes. The Paris Police Prefecture publishes a pamphlet entitled *Paris in Complete Safety* which provides practical advice and useful telephone numbers for visitors (dial 117 in an emergency). See also www.worldnomads. com/travel-safety/europe/france/crime-in-france.

In most cities you can usually safely walk almost anywhere at any time of day or night and there's no need for anxiety or paranoia about crime. However, you should be 'street-wise' and take certain elementary precautions. These include avoiding high-risk areas at night, such as suburbs that are inhabited or frequented by drug addicts, prostitutes and pickpockets.

Street people (*clochards*) in Paris and other cities may occasionally harass you, but they're generally harmless. You can safely travel on the Paris *métro* (and other *métros* in France) at any time, although some stations are best avoided late at night. When you're in an unfamiliar city, ask a police officer, taxi driver or other local person whether there are any unsafe neighbourhoods – and avoid them!

GEOGRAPHY

France, often referred to as *l'hexagone* on account of its hexagonal shape (the French are sometimes known as *les hexagonaux*), is the largest country in western Europe. Mainland France (*la métropole*) covers an area of almost 550,000km² (212,300mi²), stretching 1,050km (650mi) from north to south and almost the same distance from west to east (from the tip of Brittany to Strasbourg). Its land and sea border extends for 4,800km (around 3,000mi) and includes some 3,200km (2,000mi) of coast.

France is bordered by Andorra, Belgium, Germany, Italy, Luxembourg, Spain and Switzerland. Its borders are largely determined by geographical barriers, including the English Channel (*la Manche*) in the north, the Atlantic Ocean in the west, the Pyrenees and the Mediterranean in the south, and the Alps and the Rhine in the east.

Mainland France is divided into 22 regions and 94 departments, the Mediterranean island of Corsica (*Corse*) comprising a further two departments. Corsica is 160km (99mi) from France and 80km (50mi) from Italy, covering 8,721km² (3,367mi²) with a coastline of 1,000km (620mi). There are also five overseas departments (*département d'outre-mer/*DOM)

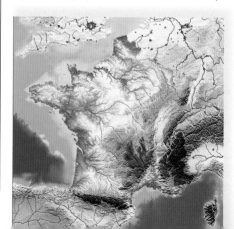

– French Guyana (*Guyane*), Guadeloupe, Martinique, Mayotte and Réunion. – and four overseas territories (*territoires d'outre-mer/TOM*) – French Polynesia (*Polynésie-française*), New Caledonia (*Nouvelle Calédonie*), Saint-Pierre-et-Miquelon and the Wallis and Futuna islands. (Although situated within France, Monaco is an independent principality and isn't governed by France.)

> While other countries suffer deforestation, France has enjoyed a doubling of its forested area in the past two centuries and an increase of 35 per cent (to 16 million hectares/40 million acres) since 1945 – a growth of 30,000ha (75,000 acres) per year – so that forest now covers almost a third of the country.

The north and west of France is mostly low-lying. The basin in the middle of the country, with Paris at its centre, occupies a third of France's land area and is one of Europe's most fertile agricultural regions. The Massif Central to the south is noted for its extinct volcanoes, hot springs and rivers; it has many peaks rising above 1,500m (5,000ft). Mont Blanc – at 4,810m (15,781ft) western Europe's highest mountain – is in the French Alps. In general, the south and southeast of France are mountainous, although despite its many mountain ranges (Alps, Auvergne, Jura, Massif Central, Pyrenees and Vosges), France is largely a lowland country, with most of its area less than 200m (650ft) above sea level.

Almost 90 per cent of France's land is productive, with around one-third cultivated, one-quarter pasture and almost a third forest.

France has a comprehensive network of rivers and canals comprising some 40 per cent of European waterways, including the Garonne, Loire, Rhine, Rhône and Seine. The Loire is France's longest river at 1,020km (634mi). In recent decades, however, France has lost half its wetlands (*zones humides*), which now account for a mere 2.5 per cent of the country's area.

GOVERNMENT

France has a republican form of government since 1792, three years after the Revolution, although it has been much modified and refined over the years and there have been five Republics (new constitutions) lasting from 3 to 70 years: the First from 1792 to 1795; the Second, after a revival of the monarchy, from 1848 to 1851; the Third from 1870 to 1940; the Fourth from 1946 to 1958; and the Fifth from 1958 to the present.

Since 1870 the government has been headed by a president, with a prime minister and two houses of parliament. France's rulers are bound by a written constitution detailing the duties and powers of the president, government and parliament, and the conditions of election. Central government is divided into three branches: executive, legislature and judiciary. The executive is headed by the president, who's the head of state. The legislative branch is represented by parliament, comprising the national assembly and the senate. The constitution is protected by a nine-member constitutional council.

French government has traditionally been highly centralised, edicts regularly issuing from Paris and filtering down to local administrators. However, in accordance with a Decentralisation Law passed in August 2004, a number of responsibilities have been delegated to regional and departmental administrations. *Routes nationales* and minor airports, for example, are now under the control of departments, as are social housing, professional training, and certain other educational, cultural and healthcare functions.

The President

The French president – currently François Hollande who was elected in May 2012 – wields more power than his US counterpart and can assume dictatorial powers in a national emergency. He 'leads and determines the policy of France' and appoints the prime minister and government. He can dissolve the house (once a year) should it pass a vote of no confidence against his prime minister and he has considerable powers in the fields of foreign affairs and defence. The French president lives, appropriately, like a king in the Elysée Palace in Paris.

Elysee Palace

The president is directly elected by the people every five years and must have an absolute majority. Should a candidate not achieve an absolute majority on the first ballot, which is unusual, a second ballot is held two weeks later between the two candidates with the highest number of votes after the first ballot. Just two weeks' campaigning is allowed for the first ballot and one week for the second and there's also a strict limit on election expenses (Americans please note!).

After parliamentary elections (see below) – held every five years, or sooner if the president calls them – the president appoints a Prime Minister (PM). The appointment requires the approval of parliament, therefore the PM is almost always a member of the party that controls the chamber. The Prime Minister serves as head of government and is in charge of domestic policy and day-to-day government. He also recommends for presidential approval the other members of his cabinet.

Although the president can dissolve parliament and call new elections, he can't block legislation passed by parliament but can appeal directly to the people by calling a referendum. This is rarely done (there have been only nine referenda since 1789), the last two in October 2000, when the presidential mandate was reduced from seven to five years, in line with that of the National Assembly (see below), and in May 2005, when the people rejected the EU constitution.

Parliament

Parliament plays a secondary role in France compared with many other democracies, meeting in two sessions for a total of just 120 days a year. It's comprised of two houses, the National Assembly (*Assemblée Nationale*) and the Senate (*Sénat*). The National Assembly is the 'lower' house, to which its 577 deputies (*députés*) are directly elected by the people every five years. Although well paid, many deputies have other jobs as well. The Senate ('upper' house) is appointed indirectly by a college of some 130,000 local councillors. It consists of 348 senators (mostly local politicians), one third of whom are elected every three years. The Senate has limited powers to amend or reject legislation passed by the National Assembly; when an impasse is reached the National Assembly has the final decision.

The French use a modified 'first-past-the-post' voting system for deputies. As with presidential elections, unless a candidate receives over 50 per cent of the votes on the first ballot, there's a second ballot a week later. Only candidates who received at least 12.5 per cent in the first round are eligible, although usually only the top two candidates contest the second round, while first round losers encourage their supporters to back their preferred candidate. Politics is a popular subject for discussion, but when it comes to voting abstentionists are the largest electoral group.

Political Parties

The main political parties in France are: the right-wing *Union pour la Majorité Populaire* (*UMP*), which subsumed the *Rassemblement pour la République* (*RPR*); the conservative Gaullist party founded by de Gaulle; the *Démocratie Libérale* party and the *Parti Radical*; the centre-right-wing *Mouvement Démocratique (MODEM)* formerly the *Union pour la Démocratie Française* (*UDF*), incorporating the *Parti Républicain*, founded by former president Giscard d'Estaing; the left-wing *Parti Socialiste*, and *Parti Communiste Français*; the *Europe écologie – les Verts* (*EELV*) created in 2010, bringing together various political shades of Green; and the extreme right-wing party *Front National*, now led by Marine Le Pen, who succeeded her father the notorious racist Jean-Marie Le Pen.

The concept of 'left' and 'right' in politics originated in France where, after the 1789 Revolution, monarchists sat to the right and republicans to the left of the president of the Assemblée Constituante.

Local Government

For political and administrative purposes France is divided into 22 regions (*région*), 96 departments (*département*), 3,509 cantons (*canton*) and 36,851 communes (*commune*

or *municipalité*). The regions were created in 1972, each consisting of a number of *départements*. Many correspond (more or less) to the old provinces of France such as Burgundy, Normandy and Provence. Each region has an elected council (*conseil régional*) and executive (*conseillers*), its seat being the region's designated 'capital' town (*chef-lieu*). Each *commune* or *municipalité* (see below) contributes a number of *conseillers* according to its size (from a minimum of nine for a commune with under 100 inhabitants, to a maximum of 69 for a town of over 300,000).

Regional elections take place in March and the term of office is six years. Regions are responsible for adult education and certain aspects of culture, tourism and industrial development. The state retains control of general education, justice and health services. Expatriates are entitled to vote in municipal elections and should register on the electoral roll at their *mairie*.

Departments

Each *département* has an elected council (*conseil général*), under the direction of the council's *président*, who vote on the development and budget for the department services for which they're responsible. The *conseil général* is distinct from the prefecture (*préfecture*) run by a prefect (*préfet*), which represents the state in the department. *Départements* are responsible for welfare and social services, while law enforcement through the national police force (*police nationale*), as opposed to the local (municipal) police, is the prefect's responsibility.

Departments are numbered roughly in alphabetical order with a two-digit number, from Ain (01) to Val d'Oise (95). There are also five overseas departments (*départements d'outre-mer/*DOM) – Guadaloupe (951), Martinique (972), Mayotte (976), French Guyana (973) and Réunion (974). The *département* number is used as the first two digits of post codes and the last two digits of vehicle registration numbers. Departmental elections are held every six years.

Communes

Communes vary in size from large cities to tiny villages with a handful of inhabitants and are governed by a municipal council headed by a mayor (*maire*), who's the most important person in the commune and definitely not someone you want to fall out with! Communes control their own town planning, including granting building permits, buildings and environment. The town hall (*hôtel de ville* in towns, *mairie* in villages) also functions as a registry of births, marriages and deaths, passport office, citizens' advice bureau, land registry, council headquarters and general information office.

Mayors

Mayors (*maires*) are both the elected head of the municipal council and representatives of the state and have wide powers, including acting as chief of the local police, issuing

building permits and performing marriages, as well as presiding over local social services, schools, and cultural and sports facilities.

Municipal elections are held to elect the local mayor, whose term of office is six years. Mayors are frequently re-elected and often serve a number of terms of office. The mayor works in conjunction with the municipal council (*conseil municipal*). Almost all prime ministers and presidents of France have been mayors of their home towns, as are most central government ministers: 80 per cent of deputies and 90 per cent of senators.

A controversial aspect of the French political system is the *cumul des mandats*, whereby individuals are allowed to hold more than one post, e.g. at local and national level. The law does, however, prevent you, for example, from being both an MP (*deputé*) and *sénateur* – you can't be in two places at the same time – and from holding two posts where one could favour the interests of the other.

France has three times as many mayors as any other EU country and corruption is even more widespread in local municipal politics than at national level (which is saying something!); in recent decades there has been an increasing number of scandals involving mayors, a number of whom have absconded with public funds. In addition, many towns and cities have been forced to increase taxes to pay for grandiose schemes embarked upon by megalomaniac mayors, costing local taxpayers millions of euros. Unlike members of parliament, however, mayors don't enjoy *immunité parlementaire*, therefore can be prosecuted!

Paris is unique in that it has 20 mayors, one for each *arrondissement*. Since 1977, Paris has also had an 'overall' mayor, chosen by the 163 councillors of the municipal council. Paris is both a *département* and a commune, and therefore its council sits as both a departmental council and a municipal authority. *Arrondissements* are shown on post codes (e.g. 75001 signifies the 1st *arrondissement*) and are also written as *1e, 2e, 3e* (1st, 2nd, 3rd) or *Xe, XVe* and *XXe* (10th, 15th, 20th).

Voting & Elections

Only French citizens aged 18 or older are permitted to vote in French elections, sensibly held on a Sunday. (In fact, they aren't eligible to vote until March of the year after they turn 18.) To register to vote you must have been resident for at least six months in a community. Foreign EU citizens resident in France are eligible to vote in elections to the European Parliament and local municipal elections, provided they're registered at the town hall (first time registrations must be made between 1st September and 31st December), and they may also stand as candidates for councillors in municipal elections. To retain your right to vote in your native country, you may need to register as an 'overseas elector'.

LEGAL SYSTEM

The French legal system is based entirely on written civil law. The system of administrative law was laid down by Napoleon and is appropriately called the *code Napoléon* (Napoleonic code). The code governs all branches of French law and includes the *code civil*, the *code fiscal* and the *code pénal*. It's regularly updated, for example in 1994 a new criminal code was introduced, including clauses on sexual harassment, ecological terrorism, crimes against humanity and maximum jail sentences, which are 30 years.

Judicial System

Franc has two judicial systems: administrative and judiciary. The administrative system deals with disputes between the government and individuals, while the judiciary handles civil

and criminal cases. France doesn't have a jury system (abolished in 1941) but instead has a mixed tribunal made up of six lay judges and three professional judges, with convictions decided by a two-thirds majority. However, in the *cour d'assises* (see below), nine ordinary citizens make up a *jury populaire*.

Under the French criminal law system, cases are heard by a variety of courts, depending on the severity of the alleged offence. Civil courts include a *tribunal d'instance* (for small claims up to around €5,000), a *tribunal de commerce* (for commercial disputes), a *tribunal de sécurité sociale* (for disputes over social security payments), a *tribunal de grande instance* (for cases relating to divorce and adoption, etc., as well as some criminal cases) and a *conseil de prud'hommes* (an arbitration service for labour disputes).

Criminal courts include a *tribunal de police* (for minor misdemeanours such as illegal parking), a *tribunal correctionnel* (for more serious offences), a *cour d'assises* (for major cases) and a *cours d'appel* (for appeals; the supreme appeal court is the *Cour de Cassation*).

Under France's inquisitorial system of justice, suspects are questioned by an independent examining magistrate (*juge d'instruction*). Other types of judge include *juges du siège* (arbitration judges) and *juges d'instance* (presiding judges).

Legal Counsel

Never assume that the law in France is the same as in any other country, as this often isn't the case. Anyone charged with a crime is presumed innocent until proven guilty, and the accused has the right to silence. All suspects are entitled to see a lawyer immediately after their arrest, a person under judicial investigation must be notified in writing, and an examining magistrate may not remand suspects in custody in a case he's investigating.

It's unnecessary to employ a lawyer or barrister (*avocat* – also the word for avocado pear) in a civil case heard in a *tribunal d'instance*, where you can conduct your own case (if your French is up to the task). If you use a lawyer, not surprisingly, you must pay his fee. In a *tribunal de grande instance* you **must** employ a lawyer. An *avocat* can act for you in almost any court of law. A legal and fiscal adviser (*conseil juridique et fiscal*) is similar to a British solicitor and can provide legal advice and assistance on commercial, civil and criminal matters, as well as on tax, social security, labour law and similar matters. He can also represent you before certain administrative agencies and in some courts.

A bailiff (*huissier*) deals with summonses, statements, writs and lawsuits, in addition to the lawful seizure of property ordered by a court. He's also employed to officially notarise documents and produce certified reports (*constats*) for possible subsequent use in legal proceedings, e.g. statements from motorists after a road accident.

If you need an English-speaking lawyer you can usually obtain a list of names from your country's embassy or a local consulate in France. Certain legal advice and services may also be provided by embassies and consulates in France, including an official witness of signatures (Commissioner for Oaths). French residents have the right to a free consultation with a lawyer; ask at your local Tribunal de Grande Instance for information. Legal aid (*aide juridictionnelle*) is available to EU citizens and regular visitors to France on low incomes.

Public Notary

A public notary (*notaire*, addressed as *Maître*) is a public official authorised by the Ministry of Justice and controlled by the Chambre des Notaires. Like a *conseil juridique*, he's also similar to a British solicitor, although he doesn't deal with criminal cases or offer advice concerning criminal law.

A *notaire* informs and advises about questions relating to administrative, business, company, credit, family, fiscal and private law. In respect to private law, a *notaire* is responsible for administering and preparing documents relating to leases, property sales and purchases, divorce, inheritance, wills, loans, setting up companies, and buying and selling businesses. He guarantees the validity and safety of contracts and deeds, and is responsible for holding deposits on behalf of clients, collecting taxes and paying them to the relevant authorities. *Notaires*' fees are fixed by the government and therefore don't vary from one *notaire* to another.

Notaires have a monopoly in the areas of transferring property, testamentary and matrimonial acts, which by law must be in the form of an authentic document (*acte authentique*), verified and stamped by a *notaire*.

MARRIAGE & DIVORCE

The legal age of consent in France is 18, but boys and girls aged between 15 and 18 can be married with the consent of their parents. Non-French citizens are entitled to be married in France, but divorcees and widows must wait 300 days after their divorce or the death of their spouse before being allowed to remarry (in case of pregnancy).

Only some 50 marriages are performed annually for each 10,000 citizens – the lowest per capita number in Europe. As in many other developed countries, the average age for marriage is increasing and is around 30 for men and 28 for women, who on average give birth for the first time at just under 30.

The number of unmarried couples in France has quadrupled to around 2 million in the last decade (among Europeans, only the Swedes

> Almost 7.5 million French citizens live without a partner, around 1 million of whom are divorcees, and the number is growing each year.

are less keen on marriage). It's estimated that 40 to 50 per cent of couples who get married have already cohabited for up to two years. Many couples don't bother to get married and simply live together, but French law distinguishes between partners living together 'unofficially' (*en union libre*) and 'officially' (*en concubinage*). Those living together *en concubinage* have some of the same privileges in law as married couples, including social security. To qualify for these, you may need to obtain a (free) certificate from your town hall testifying that you're living together as man and wife (take identification, proof of address and two witnesses), although town halls aren't obliged to issue them, in which case you can both sign a sworn declaration (*attestation sur l'honneur*) that you live together.

The major disadvantage of *concubinage* is that it isn't recognised under French inheritance laws, so partners can inherit only the portion allowed to non-relatives (see **Wills** on page 204) and they receive no state pension when their partner dies. Cohabiting partners (even those of the same sex) may sign a *pacte civile de solidarité* (PACS), which protects the individual rights of each party and entitles partners to share property rights and enjoy income tax benefits. To make a PACS, you must visit your local *tribunal d'instance* and submit a written statement that you wish to draw up a PACS under law no. 99-944 of 15th November 1999, including details of the division of possessions between you. There's no standard form for this. You must also provide identification, birth certificates, a certificate from the relevant *tribunal d'instance* confirming your place of birth, and sworn statements (*attestation sur l'honneur*) that you live in the area and that there are no legal impediments to your making a PACS, e.g. one of you being married. Inheritance rights are the same as for married couples, but a surviving partner can't claim a 'widow's' or 'widower's' pension (*pension de réversion*).

It's reckoned that over 40 per cent of French children are born out of wedlock and a fifth are raised by a single parent (85 per cent women). Illegitimacy no longer carries the stigma it once did, and all children have the same rights; an unmarried mother (*mère célibataire*) is even paid a generous allowance by the state.

Procedure

To arrange a marriage in France, either partner must apply at least a month in advance to the town hall where they normally live – and must have lived there for at least 40 days. The bride and groom must each provide at least one witness and may provide two, whose names need to be given to the town hall when the wedding is arranged.

Both partners must also provide passports, residence permits (if applicable), birth certificates (stamped by their country's local consulate not more than six months previously), proof of residence in France, and a medical certificate issued within the previous two months. A divorced or widowed person must provide a divorce or death certificate. You may also be required to produce a *certificat de célibat* (proving that you aren't already married) no more than three months old, provided by your embassy and a notarised 'affidavit of law' (*certificat de coutume*), drawn up by a lawyer in your home country, to confirm that you're free to marry. All documents must be 'legalised' (via a signature, seal or stamp from a public official to confirm that it's genuine) in your home country and translated into French by an approved translator.

A civil ceremony, presided over by the mayor or one of his deputies, must be performed in France to legalise a wedding. Although around 50 per cent of couples choose to undergo a church 'blessing' ceremony, it has no legal significance and must take place after the civil ceremony. There's no fee for a marriage in France, although most town halls make a collection in aid of local charities.

Married couples are given a 'family book' (*livret de famille*), in which all major family events such as the birth of children, divorce or death are recorded.

Matrimonial Regimes

Marriages are performed under a matrimonial regime (*régime matrimonial*) that defines how a couple's property is owned during marriage or after divorce or death. If you're married in France, the regime applies to all your land or land rights in France, irrespective of where you're domiciled, and your total assets if you're domiciled in France.

There are four regimes: two communal regimes (*régime communautaire*) and two 'separatist' regimes (*régime séparatiste*). Under a *communauté universelle*, all assets and all debts are jointly owned; under a *communauté réduite aux acquêts*, each spouse retains ownership of their assets acquired before marriage (and assets acquired after marriage in the form of inheritances and gifts), while all assets acquired jointly after marriage are jointly owned. Under a *séparation de biens*, nothing is jointly owned; and under a *participation aux acquêts*, nothing is jointly owned but if the marriage is dissolved, assets acquired during the marriage are divided equally.

A marriage contract isn't obligatory but is strongly recommended. A *notaire* will charge at least €400 to draw one up. If you're married in France and you don't specify otherwise, you're usually subject to a communal regime. If you choose a separatist regime, it's usual to detail

in a notarised contract how your assets are to be disposed of.

If you were married abroad and are buying a house in France your *notaire* will ask you which matrimonial regime you were married under and whether there was a marriage contract. If there was no contract, you'll usually be deemed to be married under a communal regime. You can change your marital regime, but not within two years of drawing up a marriage contract. However, changing your marital regime is expensive (up to €4,000), and can take up to nine months, therefore it's advisable to set up the regime you want when you get married. If you're unsure about the implications of French marital regimes you should seek advice from a *notaire*.

MILITARY SERVICE

France is one of the leading military powers (*force de frappe*) in western Europe and a member of NATO. Defence spending in 2017 will account for around 1.8 per cent of GDP when military pensions are included.

Compulsory military service was suspended in 2001 and hasn't been reintroduced. Instead of military service, males born after 1979 and females born after 1983 must attend a one-day training course, *Journée d' Appel de Préparation à la Défense* (*JAPD*). The course consists of lectures on the army and the country's defence systems, and literacy and numeracy tests. If proof of attending the course can't be provided, you face a variety of sanctions ranging from being excluded from public examinations at school or university to being unable to obtain a driving licence or (far more seriously) a fishing or hunting licence.

If you're aged 18 to 26, you can become a part-time soldier (*volontaire militaire*) for a year, and 18 to 28-year-olds can become 'civil volunteers' (*volontaire civil*) and undertake

various 'missions', e.g. protecting the environment, for between 6 and 24 months.

PETS

The French are generally unsentimental about animals and often keep them as much for practical purposes (e.g. to guard premises or catch vermin) or as fashion accessories as for companionship. However, pets (*animal domestique* or *animal de compagnie*) are more widely tolerated than in many other countries. French hotels usually quote a rate for pets (e.g. €10 per night) and most restaurants allow dogs and many provide food and water (some even allow owners to seat their pets at the table!). There are even exclusive dog restaurants in France.

> Although food shops make an effort to bar pets, it isn't unusual to see a supermarket trolley containing a dog or two (the French don't take much notice of 'no dogs' signs).

There's usually no discrimination against dogs when renting accommodation, although they may be prohibited in furnished apartments. Paris has a pet cemetery (*cimetière des chiens*) at Asnières and there are others in Nice, Toulouse and Villepinte.

Exporting & Importing Pets

If you plan to take a pet to France, it's important to check the latest regulations. Make sure that you've the correct papers, not only for France but for all the countries you'll pass through to reach France. Particular consideration must be given before exporting a pet from a country with strict quarantine regulations in case you wish to re-import it later. For example, if you're exporting a cat or a dog or certain other animals from the UK, you should obtain a 'passport' for them confirming that they've been ISO micro-chipped and that their vaccinations are up to date. You must then continue to have them vaccinated regularly while in France. If you fail to do this and want to bring your pets back to the UK at any time, they'll need to be quarantined for six months.

The cost of a pet passport – available from any vet – and the tests and vaccinations required to obtain one, is around £150-200 in the UK, plus follow-up vaccinations and a fee for a border check on re-entry to the UK. Note that you may have to make arrangements well in advance; for example, a pet must be blood tested at least six months before it can be taken to France. Details of the scheme, known as PETS, can be obtained from the Gov.uk website (www.gov.uk/take-pet-abroad).

You can take up to three animals into France at any time, one of which may be a puppy (three to six months old), although no dogs or cats under three months may be imported. Two psittacidae (parrot-like birds) can be imported into France and up to ten smaller species; all require health certificates issued within five days of departure. Other animals require import permits from the French Ministry of Agriculture.

If you're transporting a pet to France by ship or ferry you should notify the ferry company. Some companies insist that pets are left in vehicles (if applicable), while others allow pets to be kept in cabins. If your pet is of a nervous disposition or unused to travelling it's best to tranquillise it on a long sea crossing. Pets can also be transported by air and certain pets can be carried with you (in an approved container), for which there's a charge. There are a number of companies in the UK that will accommodate your pets while you move, take care of all export requirements and ship them to you when you've settled in, e.g. Pinehawk Kennels & Livestock Shippers (01223-290249, www.pinehawkkennels.org.uk) and Pet Air UK (01725-551124, www.petairuk.com).

Vaccinations

France has almost eradicated rabies by vaccinating foxes, although there have been a number of reported cases in dogs. Although there's generally no quarantine period for animals imported into France, there are strict vaccination requirements for dogs in certain departments, where they must be vaccinated against rabies and have a *certificat contre la rage* or a health certificate (*certificat de bonne santé*), signed by an approved veterinary surgeon and issued no more than five days before their arrival.

Vaccinations (*vaccin*) are initially in two stages, a 'booster' (*rappel*) being administered three or four weeks after the initial injection (*piqure*); a single annual renewal is required. Each injection costs between €35 and €60, depending on the vet. Serums must be administered separately.

Cats aren't required to have regular rabies vaccinations, although if you let your cat roam free outside your home it's advisable to have it vaccinated annually; a rabies vaccination is compulsory for cats entering Corsica or being taken to campsites or holiday parks. All cats must, however, be vaccinated against feline gastroenteritis and typhus.

All vaccinations must be registered with your veterinary surgeon (*vétérinaire*) and be listed on your pet's vaccination card or (preferably) in a *livret international de santé* or an EU pet passport. If you plan to take your pets abroad, the documentation must certify that the animal has been confined to countries that have been rabies-free for at least three years.

Dogs

There are around 17 dogs to every 100 people in France, one of the highest ratios in the world. The French spend some €3 billion on them annually and there's at least one 'poodle-parlour' (*salon de toilettage*) in every town; there's even a canine *pâtisserie* in Paris, called unimaginatively 'Mon Bon Chien', where pampered pooches can be kitted out with *haute couture* clothing and treated to *haute cuisine* 'cakes'!

Dogs don't wear identification discs in France and there's no system of licensing. However, all dogs born after 6th January 1999 must have an official identifying number, either tattooed inside an ear or contained in a microchip inserted under the skin. Some vets favour tattooing (*tatouage*) as the number is visible, whereas reading a microchip (*puce*) requires a machine. Others recommend micro-chipping because a tattoo can be removed or wear off. Identity numbers are kept in a central

computer controlled by the French Society for the Protection of Animals (Société Protectrice des Animaux/SPA, www.la-spa.fr), which is organised on a departmental basis. Contact your nearest SPA office if you lose your pet.

Dogs must be kept on leads in most public parks and gardens and there are large fines for dog owners who don't comply. Note that dogs are forbidden in some parks (even when on leads) and on most beaches in summer. On public transport pets weighing less than 6kg (13lb) must usually be carried in a basket or cage; larger dogs and certain breeds (e.g. pit-bull terriers) must wear a muzzle and be kept on a lead in public places.

The unpleasant aspect of France's vast dog population is abundantly evident on the pavements of towns and cities, where dogs routinely leave their 'calling cards' (officially known as *déjections canines*). You must watch where you walk: many pavements aren't *trottoirs* but '*crottoirs*'.

In Paris and some other cities, there are dog toilet areas. However, most dog owners take their pets to a local park or car park or simply let them loose in the streets to do their business, although allowing your pooch to poop on the pavement is illegal and you can be fined if you don't 'scoop' up after it. At the very least, owners are required to take their pets to the kerb to relieve themselves; you're reminded by dog silhouettes on the footpath in Paris and other cities, where signs encourage owners to teach their dogs to use gutters ('*Apprenez-lui le caniveau*'), which are regularly cleaned and disinfected.

Health & Insurance

Veterinary surgeons (*vétérinaire*) are well trained in France, where it's a popular and well paid profession. Emergency veterinary care is available in major cities, where there are also animal hospitals (*hôpital pour animaux*) and vets on 24-hour call for emergencies. A visit to a vet usually costs €30 to €40. Some vets make house calls, for which there's a minimum fee of around €70 to €85. Taxi and ambulance services are also provided for pets.

Health insurance for pets is available from a number of insurance companies, but usually provides only partial cover. There are essentially two types of pet insurance: insurance against accidents and insurance against illness and accidents. The former costs around €100 per year and covers only medical and surgical costs resulting from accidental injury, e.g. a broken bone, poisoning or a bite by another dog. The latter, which costs at least twice as much, also covers the treatment of certain illnesses and diseases. As with all health insurance, you should check exactly what is and isn't covered, and what conditions apply.

Pet insurance doesn't cover you for third party liability, e.g. if your pet bites someone or causes an accident, which should be included in your household insurance (see page 182); check with your insurer.

POLICE

There are three main police forces in France: the *police nationale*, the *gendarmerie nationale* and the *Compagnie Républicaine de la Sécurité* (CRS). All French police are addressed formally as *monsieur/madame l'agent* and colloquially called *flics* (cops), although there are many less polite names.

The *police nationale* are under the control of the Interior Ministry and are called *agents de police*. They deal with all crime within the jurisdiction of their police station (*commissariat de police*) and are most commonly seen in towns, distinguished by the silver buttons on their uniforms. At night and in rain and fog they often wear white caps and capes.

The *gendarmerie nationale/gardes mobiles* is part of the army, trained by the Ministry of Defence, although it's at the service of and under the operational control of the Interior Ministry. *Gendarmes* wear blue uniforms and traditional *képis*, and are distinguished by the gold buttons on their uniforms. They deal with serious crime on a national scale and general law and order in rural areas, and are responsible for motorway patrols, air safety, mountain rescue, and air and coastal patrols. *Gendarmes* include police motorcyclists (*motards*).

The CRS is often referred to as the riot police as it's responsible for crowd control and dealing with public disturbances, although it also has other duties including life-saving on beaches in summer. Over the years the CRS has acquired a notorious reputation for its violent response to demonstrations (*manifestations*) and public disturbances, although often under extreme provocation. The mere appearance of the CRS at a demonstration is enough to raise the temperature, although it has improved its public image in recent years.

In addition to the three kinds of national police mentioned above, most cities and medium size towns have municipal police (*police municipale/corps urbain*), who deal mainly with petty crime, traffic offences and road accidents. Municipal police traditionally wore a *képi* (like *gendarmes*), although this has been replaced by a flat, peaked cap. While officers of the *gendarmerie nationale*, the *police nationale* and the *CRS* are armed, *police municipale* aren't, unless the local *préfet* and *maire* decide that they should be.

⚠ Caution

The police can stop you and demand identification at any time (*contrôle de papiers*), therefore it's advisable to carry your passport, residence permit (*carte de séjour*) or ID with proof of residence. If you don't have any identification you can be arrested.

If you're arrested, you're only required to state your name, age and permanent address. Never make or sign a statement without legal advice and the presence of a lawyer. Unless your French is fluent, you should make it clear that you don't understand French and, in any case, ask permission to call your lawyer or embassy, which should be able to provide a list of English-speaking lawyers. The police can hold someone in custody for 24 hours, although you're entitled to see a lawyer immediately after arrest, after which the authority of a magistrate is required.

If you lose anything or are the victim of a theft, you must report it in person at a police station and complete a report (*déclaration de vol/plainte*), of which you'll receive a copy. This must usually be done within 24 hours if you plan to make a claim on an insurance policy. If you need to contact the police in an emergency, dialling 17 will put you in touch with your local *gendarmerie* or *commissariat de police*, listed at the front of your local telephone directory.

POPULATION

The population of France was around 65 million in early 2017. The average population density of mainland France is around 120 people per km² (approx. 300 per mi²), one of the lowest in Europe, although it varies enormously from region to region. Paris is one of the most densely populated cities in the world, with over 20,000 inhabitants per km² (over 52,000 per mi²), while in many rural areas there are just a handful. When Paris is excluded, the average population density drops to around 50 people per km² (130 per mi²).

Some 80 per cent of the population lives in urban areas, over 70 per cent in the urban areas of the north, east and the Rhône valley, although the population of industrial cities such as Le Havre, Saint-Etienne and Toulon is in decline. France's urban population doubled between 1936 and 1999, since when the decline in rural population has been reversed. On the other hand, there's a worrying trend of population movement from the north to the south, which puts pressure on water and other resources. This is particularly apparent in the southeast which, as a popular region for retirement, also faces a disproportionate imbalance in age demographics.

France has few large cities compared with other European countries with comparable populations, and Paris (2.24 million) is the only city with over a million inhabitants, excluding its suburban areas. If these are included, Paris has a population of 12.3 million, Lyon 2.2m, Marseille1.7m, Toulouse 1.3m, Lille 1.2m, Bordeaux 1.2m and Nice 1m – the only cities with over 1 million inhabitants – in stark contrast to over 32,500 villages with fewer than 2,000 inhabitants.

The average age of the population is around 41 years, with some 20 per cent aged over 65. France is becoming increasingly popular with retirees, particularly those from the UK, Germany, the Netherlands and Scandinavian countries, which is putting additional strain on its state healthcare and pension systems.

France has around 6 million immigrants (i.e. people not born in France), around 10 per cent of the population – a net increase of over half a million since 1999. Some 2 million have become naturalised, mostly from EU countries. From the early 19th century until the late '50s/early '60s Algeria was a French colony and Morocco and Tunisia protectorates, and there are around 1.5 million North African immigrants in France, around 400,000 people from sub-Saharan Africa, and 700,000 from other parts of Africa and the Caribbean.

France also has a long tradition of welcoming political refugees, who number over 200,000 (most from Eastern Europe, Indo-China, the Middle East and Latin America). It's estimated that there are a further 400,000 illegal immigrants, mostly from Africa and the Middle East (all of whom are subject to forcible repatriation). The majority of immigrants (around 60 per cent) settle in Ile-de-France, Provence-Alpes-Côte d'Azur and Rhône-Alpes.

Immigration is a controversial and emotive subject in France, where there's a degree of racial tension in some areas and overt racism is common – almost 25 per cent of the population regularly vote for the far right *Front National* in presidential elections, which is anti mass immigration. Most French people tolerate EU immigrants, although the same can't be said of Africans and Arabs. The majority of North Africans, for example, exist in ghettos in run-down suburbs, particularly north of Paris, with large families existing on incomes well below the official poverty line in a vicious circle of deprivation and lack of opportunity.

RELIGION

France has officially been a secular state since the Revolution and therefore has a long tradition of religious tolerance; residents have freedom of religion without hindrance from the state or community, and the majority of the world's religious and philosophical movements have religious centres or meeting places in Paris and other major cities.

The majority of the population is Christian, by far the largest number belonging to the Catholic faith (around 62 per cent of the population) and a mere 2 per cent Protestants. The second-largest religious group is Muslims (6 per cent), mostly immigrants from North Africa, and France is also home to some 700,000 Jews.

Details of mosques in France can be found on http://mosquee.free.fr and a list of synagogues at www.pagesjaunes.fr (enter *Synagogues* in the first box and then the name of the city or town where you're looking for a synagogue).

Religious observance continues to decline and attendance at mass has dropped to below 15 per cent (attendance is lowest in Paris, particularly among those aged 18 to 35). With well under 50 per cent of marriages consecrated in church and only 45 per cent of babies baptised, parish priests have lost much of their traditional influence and there's a serious shortage of recruits for the priesthood.

However, few French are atheists, although many are agnostics.

Church and state were officially divorced in 1905, since when all churches have been state owned and the church is responsible only for 'running' them. On the other hand, the Catholic church is prominent in education, where it maintains many private schools separate from the state education system, although largely funded by the state (see **Private Schools** on page 113). An attempt to abolish state funding for religious schools by the Socialists in the '80s generated fierce opposition and was quickly abandoned.

For information about local places of worship and service times contact your local town hall or tourist information office. Churches and religious centres can be found online and are listed in the Yellow Pages under *Églises* and *Cultes* (e.g. *Culte israélite* for synagogues), and include American and English churches in Paris and other major cities.

There are over 50 Anglican churches in France; details of English-language services throughout France (and indeed the world) are contained in the *Directory of English-Speaking Churches Abroad*, published by the Intercontinental Church Society (www.ics-uk. org).

SOCIAL CUSTOMS

All countries have strange social customs and France is no exception. As a foreigner you'll probably be excused if you accidentally insult your hosts, but it's better to be aware of accepted taboos and courtesies, especially as the French are much more formal than most foreigners (especially Americans and Britons) imagine.

Greeting

When you're introduced to a French person, you should sa\y 'good day, Sir/Madam' (*bonjour

madame/monsieur) and shake hands (a single pump is enough – neither limp nor knuckle-crushing). *Salut* (hi or hello) is used only among close friends and the young. When saying goodbye it's customary to shake hands again. In an office everyone shakes hands with everyone else on arrival at work and when they depart (so that the amount of work done is in inverse proportion to the number of staff).

It's also customary to say good day or good evening (*bonsoir*) on entering a small shop and goodbye (*au revoir madame/monsieur*) on leaving. *Bonjour* becomes *bonsoir* around 6pm or after dark, although if you choose *bonsoir* (or *bonjour*), don't be surprised if the response isn't the same. *Bonne nuit* (good night) is used when going to bed or leaving a house in the evening. On leaving a shop you may be wished *bonne journée* (have a nice day) or variations such as *bon après-midi, bonne fin d'après-midi, bon dimanche* or *bon week-end*, to which you should reply *merci*, adding *vous aussi, vous de même* or *et vous*. The standard and automatic reply to *merci* is *je vous en prie* (you're welcome).

Titles should generally be used when addressing or writing to people, particularly when the holder is elderly. The president of a company or institution should be addressed as *monsieur* (*madame*) *le président* (*la *présidente*), a courtesy title usually retained in retirement. The mayor must be addressed as *Monsieur/Madame le Maire* (even female mayors are *le Maire!*).

Kissing

To kiss or not to kiss, that is the question. When negotiating this social minefield, it's best to take your cue from the French. You shouldn't kiss (*faire la bise*) when first introduced to an adult, although young children will expect to be kissed. If a woman expects you to kiss her, she'll offer her cheek. Note that men kiss women and women kiss women but men don't kiss men unless they're relatives or very close friends. The 'kiss' isn't usually a proper kiss, more a delicate brushing of the cheeks accompanied by kissing noises, although some extraverts will plant a great wet smacker on each side of your face.

The next question is which cheek to kiss first. Again, take your cue from the natives, as the custom varies from region to region (and even the natives aren't always sure where to start). Finally, you must decide how many kisses to give. Two is the standard number, although many people kiss three or four or even six times. It depends partly on where you are in France.

The British travel agent Thomas Cook has published a *French Kissing Guide*, according to which four kisses are the norm in northern France, three in the mid-west and southern central areas and two in the west, east and extreme south, a single kiss being acceptable only in the department of Charente-Maritime! Much also depends on how well you know the person concerned: acquaintances may kiss twice, friends four times and old friends six! Kissing usually takes place when you take your leave, as well as when you greet someone. It's also customary to kiss everyone in sight – including the men if you're a man – at midnight on New Year's Eve!

Vous & Tu

When talking to a stranger, use the formal form of address (*vous*). Don't use the familiar form (*tu/toi*) or call someone by his Christian name until you're invited to do so. Generally the older, senior (in a business context) or simply local person will invite the other to use the familiar *tu* form of address (called *tutoiement*) and first names; when it happens, the switch is often sudden and you should pick up on it immediately or you'll forever be stuck on formal terms.

The familiar form is used with children, animals and God, but almost never with your

elders or work superiors. However, the French are becoming less formal and the under 50s often use *tu* and first names with work colleagues (unless they're of the opposite sex, when *tu* may imply a special intimacy!) and will quickly switch from *vous* to *tu* with new social acquaintances, although older people may be reluctant to make the change.

Some people always remain *vous*, however often you meet them, such as figures of authority (the local mayor) or those with whom you've a business relationship, e.g. your bank manager, tax officials and policemen.

Gifts

If you're invited to dinner by a French person (which is a sign that you've been accepted into the community), take along a small present of flowers, a plant or chocolates. Gifts of foreign food or drink aren't generally well received unless they're highly prized in France such as Scotch whisky; foreign wine, however good the quality, isn't recommended!

Some people say you must never take wine, as this implies that your hosts don't know what wine to buy, but this isn't necessarily the case. If you do take wine, however, don't expect it to be served with the meal. It will almost certainly be put aside for a future occasion; your hosts will already have planned the wine for the meal and know that a wine needs to settle before it can be drunk. Flowers can be tricky, as to some people carnations signify bad luck, chrysanthemums are for cemeteries (they're placed on graves on All Saints' Day), red roses signify love and are associated with the Socialists, and yellow roses have something to do with adultery – and marigolds (*soucis*) simply aren't *de rigueur*. If in doubt, ask a florist for advice – or take a nice bunch of wildflowers!

Eating & Drinking

You shouldn't serve any drinks (or expect to be served one) before all the guests have arrived – even if some are an hour or more late! If you're offered a drink, wait until your host has toasted everyone's health (*santé*) before taking a drink. **Never** pour your own drinks (except water) when invited to dinner. If you aren't offered a(nother) drink, it's probably time to go home.

> ## ☑ SURVIVAL TIP
>
> Always go easy on the wine and other alcohol; if you drink to excess you're unlikely to be invited back!

The French say *bon appétit* before a meal and you shouldn't start eating until your hosts do. It's polite to eat everything that's put on your plate. Cheese is served before dessert.

Conversation

The French love detailed and often heated discussions, but there are certain topics of conversation that need handling with care or avoiding altogether. These include money, which is generally mentioned only when complaining about how expensive things are or boasting of how large a motoring fine has been incurred; it's a major *faux pas* to ask a new acquaintance what he does for a living, as his job title will often give an indication of his salary.

Far safer to stick to discussions about food and drink, without, however, comparing French food and drink with that of your home country – unless you are praising French gastronomy! When conversing, even in the midst of a heated debate avoid raising your voice, which is considered vulgar (although you may interrupt, which is considered normal). Note also that the French often stand close when engaging in conversation, which you may find uncomfortable or even threatening at first.

Greeting Cards

The sending of cards, other than birthday cards, isn't as common in France as in some other countries. It isn't, for example, usual to send someone a card following a bereavement or after passing a driving test. Instead of Christmas cards, the French send New Year cards, but only to people they don't usually see during the year.

The design of most French greetings cards is on a par with the worst in other countries. More acceptable cards may be found in some bookshops, although the range rarely goes much beyond reproductions of works of art.

Dress

Although the French are often formal in their relationships, their dress habits, even in the office, are often extremely casual. Note, however, that the French tend to judge people by their dress, the style and quality being as important as the correctness for the occasion (the French often wear 'designer' jeans to dinner). You aren't usually expected to dress for dinner, depending of course on the sort of circles you move in. On invitations, formal dress (black tie) is *smoking exigé/tenue de soirée* and informal dress is *tenue de ville*.

Phone Calls

Always introduce yourself before asking to speak to someone on the telephone.

Surprisingly, it's common to telephone at meal times, e.g. noon to 2pm and around 8pm, when you can usually be assured of finding someone at home. If you must call at these times, you should apologise for disturbing the household.

Noise

It's common for there to be noise restrictions in French towns and villages, particularly with regard to the use of lawnmowers and other mechanical tools. Restrictions are imposed locally and therefore vary, but in general, noisy activities are prohibited before around 8 or 9am each day, after 7pm on weekdays and Saturdays and after noon on Sundays, and additionally at lunchtime on Saturdays.

TIME DIFFERENCE

Like most of the continent of Europe, France is on Central European Time (CET), which is Greenwich Mean Time (GMT) plus one hour, from October to March and GMT+2 the rest of the year. The change to 'summer time' (*l'heure d'été*) takes place on the last Sunday in March and to winter time (*l'heure d'hiver*) on the last Sunday in October. Time changes are announced in local newspapers and on radio and TV, and officially take place at 2am. (In 1997, the French tried to abolish the change of time but were overruled by Brussels!)

Times in France, for example in timetables, are usually written using the 24-hour clock, when 10am is written as 10h or 10.00 and 10pm as 22h or 22.00. Midday (*midi*) is 12.00 and midnight (*minuit*) is 24.00 or 00.00; 7.30am is written as 7h30 or 07.30. (Note: in this book we have used am/pm.) However, the French

Paris at Noon					
London	Jo'burg	Sydney	Auckland	Los Angeles	New York
1100	1300	2200	2400	0500	0800

use the 12-and 24-hour clocks interchangeably in conversation and it's wise to make sure you've understood. In some French towns, clocks strike twice, with a minute's pause in between, just in case you missed it the first time!

The time (in summer) in selected major foreign cities when it's midday in Paris is shown in the table below. You can find the local time in any country or major city via the internet, e.g. www.timeanddate.com/worldclock.

TIPPING

Tips (*pourboire*, literally 'in order to drink') aren't as freely offered as in the US or even the UK, and have become less common since the introduction of the euro. In some places you may even come across signs forbidding tipping (*pourboire interdit*)! Whether or not you should tip may depend on whether a service charge has already been included in the price. If service is included it should be indicated by the words *service compris* (SC), *service et taxe compris* (STC) or *prix nets/toutes taxes comprises* (TTC), which means that prices are inclusive of service and value added tax (TVA). If service is extra, *service non compris* (SNC) or *service en sus* may be indicated.

Service is now automatically included in all restaurant bills, although you may still leave a tip if you've had exceptional service. In hotels, a 15 per cent service charge is usually included in the bill. In bars and cafés, prices usually include service when you sit at a table but not when you stand at the bar (it should be shown on the menu or bill or the *tarif des consommations*). It's usual to leave your small change on the bar or in the dish provided.

Those who are usually tipped include porters (€1 to €2 per bag, which may be a fixed fee), group tour guides (€1 to €2 for a morning or afternoon), taxi drivers (10 to 15 per cent) and hairdressers (10 per cent). In top-class hotels

it's normal to tip a bellboy, porter, chambermaid or other staff members if you ask them to perform extra services. In public toilets where there's an attendant there's usually a fixed charge and you aren't required to tip, although when no charge is displayed it's usual to leave around €0.50.

Christmas is generally a time of giving tips to all and sundry, including the postman (*facteur*), garbage collectors (*éboueurs*) and firemen (*sapeurs-pompiers*), who will often call in early December or November 'offering' you a calendar, for which you're nevertheless expected to pay – unless you don't want your post delivered, your rubbish collected or any house-fires extinguished for the following 12 months!

The size of such tips depends on how often someone has served you, the quality and friendliness of the service, your financial status and, of course, your generosity. Generally €5 to €15 is acceptable, although you may wish to give more to the *gardienne* of your apartment block (it pays to be nice to her!). Large tips are, however, considered ostentatious and in bad taste (except by the recipient, who will be your friend for life).

If you're unsure who or how much to tip, ask your neighbours, friends or colleagues for advice (who will all tell you something different!).

Sanisette

TOILETS

French public toilets vary considerably in their modernity (or antiquity!) and in addition to some of the world's worst, France – always a country of stark contradictions – also has some of the best. The French use a variety of names to refer to a toilet including *toilettes*, WC (bizarrely pronounced 'VC' – an abbreviation for *double-VC)*, *waters*, *lavabos*, *cabinets* (all in the plural, even if there's only one – as there often is) and colloquially *petit coin* (the little corner) and other less polite terms. Public toilets are labelled *messieurs/hommes* and *dames/femmes*.

Urinals (properly termed *Vespasiens*, after the Emperor Vespasian, who introduced them to ancient Rome, but more commonly referred to as *pissoirs* or *pissotières*) are thankfully no more, and have been replaced by unisex, 24-hour *sanisettes* or 'superloos': cylindrical metal booths topped with a *'Toilettes'* sign. In some towns and cities their use costs up to around €1, although all *sanisettes* in Paris are free. You're

forbidden to allow small children (e.g. under ten) to use them on their own as they may be unable to open the door (a small child was once swept into a sewer by the cleaning process and drowned!), and relieving yourself in public can earn you a fine.

In cities and towns, public toilets are also found at railway and bus stations, in parking garages and in the street. In towns, there are often public toilets with attendants (commonly known as *'Dame Pipi'*), where there's a fixed charge of around €1. If no charge is displayed, it's normal to leave around €0.50. Toilet paper is often dispensed (reluctantly) sheet by sheet by the attendant. In some rural areas you're given a key or even a detachable door handle to an outside toilet.

In many restaurants and bars, men and women share a common WC and there may be a urinal next to the wash basin. In cheap bars and restaurants there may be no toilet paper. Some toilets have no light switch and the light is operated automatically when you lock the door (to prevent people leaving the light on when they leave). In private residences, Americans should ask for the toilet and not the bathroom (*salle de bains*), as the toilet is often separate from the bathroom.

Most French bathrooms have a *bidet* in addition to a toilet bowl; these are for 'intimate ablutions' and aren't footbaths, drinking fountains or toilets! They're also common in hotels, where rooms may have a washbasin and a *bidet* but no toilet bowl, although they're going out of fashion. French toilets employ a variety of flushing devices including a knob on top of the cistern which is pulled upwards, a push button on the cistern behind the bowl (often with two 'settings': short and long flush), a chain, or even a foot-operated button on the floor (in public toilets).

If a building has a septic tank (*fosse septique*), certain items mustn't be flushed down the toilet, including sanitary towels, paper other than French toilet paper (which is designed to disintegrate), disposable nappies (diapers), condoms or anything made of plastic. You should also not use standard bleaches, disinfectants and chemical cleaners in systems with septic tanks (special products are available), as they can have a disastrous effect on their operation and create nasty smells!

In Paris, it's common to see young children (assisted by their parents) relieving themselves in the gutter (*caniveau*), which is where dogs are also supposed to do their business (the gutters are swept and washed daily). In rural areas, the lack of public toilets is no obstacle to many Frenchmen, who are happy to relieve themselves by the side of the road (and even in your garden!) whenever the urge strikes them; they may make little attempt to conceal themselves behind a tree or other object, often not even bothering to turn their backs to passing women or children. Those of a delicate disposition, beware!

19.
THE FRENCH

*W*ho are the French? What are they like? Let's take a candid and totally prejudiced look at them, tongue firmly in cheek, and hope they forgive my flippancy – or that they don't read this bit, which is why it's at the back of the book. (French readers and Francophiles, please note: this chapter isn't supposed to be taken too seriously!)

The typical French person is artificial, elitist, hedonistic, enigmatic, idle, civilised, insular, a hypochondriac, bloody-minded, spineless, a suicidal driver, misunderstood, inflexible, pseudo-intellectual, modern, lazy, disagreeable, seductive, complaining, a philosopher, authoritarian, cultured, gallant, provincial, educated, sophisticated, aggressive, flirtatious, unsporting, egocentric, unbearable, paternalistic, insecure, racist, an individual, ill-disciplined, formal, cynical, unfriendly, creative, emotional, irritating, narrow-minded, charming, unhygienic, obstinate, vain, laid-back, a socialist and a rightwing conservative, serious, long-winded, indecisive, convivial, unloved, callous, bad-tempered, garrulous, inscrutable, ambivalent, infuriating, anti-American, adventurous, incomprehensible, superior, ignorant, impetuous, a gourmet, blinkered, decadent, truculent, romantic, extravagant, reckless, sensuous, pragmatic, aloof, chauvinistic, capitalistic, courteous, chic, patriotic, xenophobic, proud, passionate, fashionable, nationalistic, bureaucratic, conceited, arrogant, dishonest, surly, rude, impatient, articulate, chivalrous, brave, selfish, imaginative, amiable, debauched, boastful, argumentative, elegant, a lousy lover, egotistical, cold, a good cook, sexy, private, promiscuous, contradictory, political, intolerant,

inhospitable, brusque, handsome, an Astérix fan, and above all – insufferably French!

You may have noticed that the above list contains 'a few' contradictions (as does life in France), which is hardly surprising as there's no such thing as a typical French person. Apart from the numerous differences in character between the inhabitants of different regions of France, the population encompasses a potpourri of foreigners from all corners of the globe. However, while it's true that not all French people are stereotypes (some are almost indistinguishable from 'normal' humans), I refuse to allow a few eccentrics spoil my arguments...

Living among the French can be a traumatic experience, and foreigners are often shocked by French attitudes. One of the first things a newcomer needs to do is discover where he fits in, particularly regarding class and status. In many ways the French are even more class and status conscious than the British (it was the Normans who introduced class into the UK), with classes ranging from the aristocracy (*les grandes familles*, otherwise known as the guillotined or shortened classes) and upper bourgeoisie, through the middle and lower bourgeoisie to the workers and peasantry. The French class system is based on birthright rather than wealth, and money doesn't determine or buy status (so *ploucs nouveaux riches* needn't apply).

> As in most developed countries, there's a huge and widening gap between the rich and the poor, e.g. business tycoons and the lowest-paid workers, particularly those living in rural areas.

The French are renowned for their insularity (worse than the Japanese!) and can't stand foreigners. However, if it's any consolation, the French reserve their greatest enmity for their fellow countrymen (everybody hates Parisians – even other Parisians). The French are Alsatians, Basques, Burgundians, Bretons, Corsicans, Normans, Parisians, Provençals, etc., first and French second. Parisians believe that anybody who doesn't live in Paris is a peasant (*plouc*) and beneath contempt. Paradoxically, most Parisians have a yearning to live in the country (*la France profonde*) and escape to it at every opportunity.

Every setback is seen as part of an international conspiracy (naturally concocted by *les Anglo-Saxons*) to rob France of its jobs, culture, language and very identity. The

French bemoan the American influences seeping into their lives, such as *le fast food* (known as *le néfaste food* – 'unhealthy food'), American English, and worst of all, US 'culture', symbolised by Disneyland Paris (which patriotic French people are praying will go broke – again) and McDonald's 'restaurants' (known as *'macdos'*), which have become a target for self-styled cultural 'guardian angels', battling to prevent the Americanisation of France. However, French youth devours everything American including its clothes, films, music, food, drinks, toys, technology and culture, and French people of all ages pepper their speech with Anglicisms – often feigning ignorance that the words have been pinched from English.

Which brings us to a subject dear to every French person's heart – food. As everyone knows, food was a French invention (along with sex, the guillotine and VAT) and eating is the national pastime. The French are voracious carnivores and eat anything that walks, runs, crawls, swims or flies. They're particularly fond of all the nasty bits that civilised people reject including hoofs, ears, tails, brains, entrails and reproductive organs (the French are anything but squeamish). They also eat repulsive things such as snails and frogs' legs. A nation of animal lovers, the French are particularly fond of the tastier species such as horses and songbirds, which are usually eaten raw with garlic (it's essential to develop a tolerance to garlic if you're to live in France). The French have an ambivalent attitude towards 'pets', and those they don't pamper are often treated abominably.

Not surprisingly, the French are obsessed with their livers (when not eating those of force-fed geese) and bowel movements, both of which have an intimate relationship with food and drink. The customary treatment for a liver crisis (*crise de foie*) and most other ailments is the suppository, used to treat everything from

times. France always seems to be teetering on the edge of anarchy and revolution, and mass demonstrations have a special place in French political culture. The *CRS* (riot police) are the only people capable of communicating with rioting people, which they do by whacking them on the head with a large baton. Not surprisingly, the French are the world's leading consumers of tranquillisers, not to mention aspirins to counter the effects of being frequently bashed on the head.

The French complain loud and long about their leaders and the merest mention of politics is a cue for a vociferous argument. They're contemptuous of their politicians, which isn't surprising considering they're an incompetent, licentious and corrupt bunch of buffoons who couldn't organise a *soûlerie* in a vineyard. Politicians rate lower than prostitutes in the social order and the quality of the service they provide (prostitutes have morals and principles and do a sterling job – ask any politician!).

The French (through Jean Monnet) invented the European Union (EU), a fact which should be patently obvious to anyone, considering it's one of the most bureaucratic, corrupt and dictatorial organisations in the world. They believe that the EU was a splendid institution while it pursued French ambitions and was led by France, but are ambivalent about it since all the Eastern European rabble were admitted and are positively hostile to Turkey's proposed accession. General de Gaulle was adamant that the intractable British should never be allowed to join and the French have since been doing their utmost to keep them at arm's length (but surprisingly don't seem so happy now that they're leaving the EU!).

France is the most bureaucratic country in the world, with almost twice as many civil servants as Germany and three times as many as Japan. In order to accomplish anything remotely official in France, 98 forms must

the common cold to a heart attack (the French are a nation of hypochondriacs and, when not eating, they're popping pills). They're never happier than when they're complaining about something, and protests (*manifestations*) are commonplace and an excuse for a good riot.

Civil disobedience is the national sport and the French take to the barricades at the drop of a beret. France has numerous self-help groups (called anarchists in other countries) and many French people, e.g. fishermen, hunters, farmers and truck drivers, are a law unto themselves. Obeying senseless edicts such as motoring laws, prohibitive signs (e.g. no parking, no smoking, no dogs, no riots, etc.) and other trivial rules is a matter of personal choice in France – and most French choose not to. Although France is ostensibly a country of written rules, regulations and laws, they exist solely to be waived, bent or adapted (*système débrouillard* or *système D*) to your own advantage.

The French, who are difficult to govern at the best of times, are impossible to rule in bad be completed in quintuplicate, each of which must be signed by 47 officials in 31 different government departments. Only then do you get your bus pass! It's the fault of all those French cheeses; as de Gaulle so succinctly put it: "It's difficult to rule a nation with 265 cheeses" (or possibly 365, 400 or even 750). It's even harder to govern a country that has no idea how many cheeses it has!

The French aren't exactly noted for their humility and variously describe France (*la Grande Nation*) as the most cultured of countries, the light of the world, and a nation destined by God (who's naturally French) to dominate the continent. Naturally, Paris is the capital of civilisation and the city of light. France lives on its past glories (*la gloire*) and clings tenaciously to its colonies long after others had seen the light. French history is littered with delusions of grandeur (*la grandeur française*), which spawned such

> The French language has divine status in France and is the language of love, food and the Gods. The French cling to it as their last vestige of individuality and its propagation by the foreign service is sacrosanct (mock it at your peril!).

infamous megalomaniacs as Charlemagne, Napoleon, de Gaulle, and the most famous Frenchman of all, Astérix.

France yearns for foreign adulation, the predominance of the French language and culture, and to be hailed as the undisputed leader of Europe. The French person's favourite word is appropriately *supérieur* (nobody **ever** accused the French of being modest).

The French love their language and habitually use it as a blunt instrument to intimidate uneducated foreigners, i.e. anyone who doesn't speak it (only in France are tourists treated with contempt for not speaking the language). To fully understand the French you need an intimate knowledge of their beautiful and romantic language, which is the key to their spirit and character. In practice this consists of learning just two words, *merde!* and *NON!*, which can be used effectively to deal with every situation, as was aptly demonstrated by General de Gaulle.

When not eating, the French are allegedly making love. They're obsessed with sex and have a long tradition of debauchery. French men think they're God's gift to women and are in a permanent state of arousal. Every attractive woman is a potential conquest, especially foreign ones, some of whom have a reputation for being 'easy' (if you want to know how good your wife is in bed, the saying goes, ask your French friends!).

The French use sex to sell everything from cars to mineral water (what others find sexist, the French find sexy) and lack modesty in all things, discarding their clothes at every opportunity. French women enjoy being objects of desire and most care little for women's liberation and indulge their 'macho' (i.e. selfish) men, most of whom couldn't change a nappy if their lives depended on it.

The French are renowned for their sexual peccadilloes and are credited with inventing sadism (the Marquis de Sade), brothels (*bordellos*), French letters (Condom is a French town), masturbation and adultery. In France, *c'est normal* for a woman to seek lovers and for a man to have mistresses. If a married man is a philanderer it's a source of pride, a mark of respect and nothing to be ashamed of (a real vote-catcher for politicians!). A mistress is a status symbol, the absence of which casts grave doubts on a man's virility and sexual predilections.

Despite not washing, living on garlic and wearing their socks for weeks on end, Frenchmen have amazingly established a reputation for suave, seductive charm (surely women aren't still attracted to Alain Delon and Gérard Depardieu?). However, despite his formidable reputation, the Frenchman's performance in bed is similar to his performance in the battlefield: lots of pomp and ceremony, but when the pantaloons are down he empties his cannon out of range and rolls over. Fittingly, the national symbol is the resplendent cockerel, which seduces and impregnates the submissive hens and then crows (*cocorico*!) triumphantly, even when it has nothing to boast about (after which it's cooked in wine and eaten). However, despite the fact that the rooster services many hens, the evidence is that he doesn't satisfy them (around half of French women declare their sex lives to be unsatisfactory).

The French are formidable sportsmen and have produced a long line of sporting heroes (although their names are difficult to recall). Among the most popular French sports are sex; beating the system (e.g. fare evasion, cheating the tax man, claiming unlawful social security and defrauding the EU); stock-car racing on public roads; corruption, fraud and sleaze; falling off skis; running (away from the Germans); falling off bicycles while following Americans, Belgians, Spaniards and assorted other foreigners around France; losing at football (1998 was a temporary aberration); *boules* (a form of marbles played by southerners plastered on *pastis*); rioting; horse riding (to escape faster from rampaging Germans); shooting themselves in the feet; tennis and sex. It's widely acknowledged that the French are cheats, poor losers and have absolutely no notion of *le fair-play*. After all, how can a nation which doesn't play cricket or baseball possibly be trusted to play by the rules?

Enough frivolity – let's get down to serious business! Like most capitalist countries, France is a sorely divided nation. While the elite and privileged bourgeoisie luxuriate in the sun, the inhabitants of the poor suburbs and immigrant

ghettos remain permanently in the shadows, plagued by poor transport, soaring crime levels, extremist politics, and an acute sense of dereliction and hopelessness. There's a festering racial problem, with suppressed and disadvantaged Africans and Arabs (enticed to France as cheap labour) locked in a vicious circle of poverty and deprivation.

The increasingly destitute farming communities and thousands of rural villages are also firmly anchored in second-class France. The human fallout from *la bonne vie* and high unemployment occupy the streets and *métro* tunnels of French cities. France also suffers from increasing drug abuse, alcoholism, racism and violence. However, by far the biggest challenge facing France's leaders is how to reform the economy – e.g. debt-ridden public companies, a yawning social security deficit and endless benefits and workers addicted to ever shorter working hours, time off and holidays – without provoking a(nother) revolution.

The French do, however, have a few good points. They've managed (largely) to preserve the splendour of their countryside and the charm and beauty of their villages, towns and cities. They enjoy the best (although least adventurous)

> The French (unlike many other nations) haven't turned their backs on their roots and strong family and community ties, and loyalties are a prominent feature of French life.

cuisine in the world and many of the world's great wines. They have good public services, fine schools, exceptional social security benefits (although the country can't afford them), superb hospitals, excellent working conditions and employee benefits, and a first class transport system with magnificent *autoroutes* and among the world's fastest trains. The country enjoys a generally high standard of living, low inflation and a relatively healthy economy (despite the gloom).

France is one of the most cultured countries in the world and the French are renowned for their insatiable appetite for gastronomy, art, literature, philosophy and music. Paris is home to some of the world's greatest museums, monuments and architectural treasures, and is one of the world's most attractive and romantic cities and its cleanest major capital (London and New York please note) – apart from the canine deposits on pavements.

France is highly competitive on the world stage, notably in foreign affairs, business, technology, sport and culture, and is one of the few developed countries with the vision and boldness to conceive and execute grandiose schemes (*les grands projets*). The French are justifiably proud of their achievements and France is no longer an island unto itself, its traditional insularity having been replaced by a highly developed sense of international responsibility. It remains one of the most influential nations in the world and a positive power for good, particularly in the field of medicine, where *Médecins sans Frontières* and *Médecins du Monde* do exemplary work.

While French bureaucracy is enough to discourage anybody, ordinary French people usually couldn't be more welcoming (apart from Parisians). If you're willing to meet them halfway and learn their language you'll invariably be warmly received by the French, who will go out of their way to help you – and 'educate' you in the finer points of civilised living. Contrary to popular belief, they aren't baby-eating ogres and, provided you make an effort to be friendly and speak French, they're likely to overwhelm you with kindness. Although it's difficult to get to know the French, when you do you invariably make friends for life.

Anyone planning to make their permanent home in France should bear in mind that assimilation is all-important. If you don't want to live **with** the French and share their way of life, language, culture and traditions, you're probably better off staying at home.

The mark of a great nation is that it never breeds indifference in foreigners – admiration, envy, hostility or even blind hatred, but never indifference! Love it or hate it, France is a unique, vital, civilised, bold, sophisticated and vibrant country.

In the final analysis, the French enjoy one of the world's best lifestyles and what many believe is the finest overall quality of life. Few other countries offer such a wealth of intoxicating experiences for the mind, body and spirit – and not all out of a bottle! – or provide a more stimulating environment in which to live and work. (But don't tell the French – they insufferable enough as it is!)

Vive la République! Vive la France! Vive les Français!

20.
MOVING HOUSE OR LEAVING FRANCE

W hen moving house or leaving France, there are numerous things to be considered and a 'million' people to inform. The checklists contained in this chapter will make the task easier and may even help prevent an ulcer or nervous breakdown – provided you don't leave everything to the last minute.

MOVING HOUSE

When moving house within France, bear in mind the following:

♦ If you're renting accommodation, you must usually give your landlord at least three months' notice (refer to your contract). Your resignation letter must be sent by registered post (*lettre recommandée avec accusé de réception*).

♦ Inform the following, as applicable:

- your employer;
- your present town hall and the town hall in your new community within a month of taking up residence. They'll change the address on your *carte de séjour*, if applicable.
- your local social security (Caisse Primaire d'Assurance Maladie/CPAM) and family allowance (Caisse d'Allocations Familiales) offices;
- your local income tax office (Centre des Impôts) and *trésorerie*;
- your local electricity/gas and water companies (at least two days in advance);
- France Télécom (and other phone companies) if you've a telephone. You can have your new number announced to callers for six months.

- your regional TV licence centre (Centre Régional de la Redevance Audiovisuelle) if you've a TV and other TV companies (cable, satellite);
- your insurance companies, e.g. health, car, house contents and public liability; hire purchase companies; lawyer; accountant; and local businesses where you've accounts. Obtain new insurance, if applicable.
- your banks and other financial institutions, such as stockbrokers and credit card companies. Make arrangements for the transfer of funds and the cancellation or alteration of standing orders.
- your family doctor, dentist and other health practitioners. Health records should be transferred to your new practitioners.
- your children's schools. If applicable, arrange for schooling in your new community (see **Chapter 9**). Try to give a term's notice and obtain copies of any relevant school reports and records from current schools as well as a *certificat de radiation*.
- all regular correspondents, publications to which you subscribe (including professional and trade journals), social and sports clubs, and friends and relatives. Arrange to have your post redirected by the post office by completing

a permanent change of address card (*ordre de réexpédition définitif*), available from post offices, at least four days in advance.

– your local consulate or embassy if you're registered with them.

♦ If you've a French driving licence or a French-registered car and are remaining in the same department, you must return your licence and car registration document (*carte grise*) and have the address changed (see page 138). If you're moving to a new department, you must inform both your current and new *préfectures*.

♦ Return any library books or anything borrowed.

♦ Arrange removal of your furniture and belongings (or hire a vehicle if you're doing your own removal).

♦ If you live in rented accommodation, obtain a refund of your deposit from your landlord.

♦ Ask yourself (again): 'Is it really worth all this trouble?'

LEAVING FRANCE

Before leaving France for an indefinite period, you should do the following in addition to the things listed above under Moving House:

♦ Check that your own and your family's passports are valid.

♦ Give notice to your employer, if applicable.

☑ **SURVIVAL TIP**

Check the entry requirements of your country of destination, e.g. visas, permits or vaccinations, by contacting the local embassy or consulate in France. An exit permit or visa isn't required to leave France.

♦ Check whether you qualify for a rebate on income tax and social security payments

(see **Chapter 13**). Tax rebates are normally paid automatically. If you've contributed to a supplementary pension scheme, a percentage of your contributions will be repaid, although your pension company will require proof that you're leaving France permanently.

♦ Obtain a copy of your health and dental records and a statement from your health insurance company stating your present level of cover. You may wish to arrange health and dental check-ups before leaving France.

♦ Make arrangements to sell or let your house or apartment and other property in France.

♦ Arrange to sell anything you aren't taking with you (car, furniture, etc.) and to ship your belongings. Find out the procedure for shipping your belongings to your country of destination. Check with the local embassy in France of the country to which you're moving. Forms may need to be completed before arrival. If you've been living in France for less than a year, you're required to re-export all imported personal effects, including furniture and vehicles (if you sell them, you may have to pay tax or duty).

♦ If you've a French-registered car that you plan to take with you, you can drive abroad on your French registration plates for a maximum of three months.

♦ Pets may require vaccinations or may need to go into quarantine for a period (see page 273), depending on your destination.

♦ Contact France Télécom (see **Chapter 7**) and anyone else well in advance if you need to recover a deposit.

♦ Arrange health, travel and other insurance (see **Chapter 13**). Terminate any French loans and lease or hire purchase contracts, and pay all outstanding bills (allow plenty of time, as some companies are slow to respond). Check whether you're entitled to a rebate on your car and other insurance. Obtain a letter from your French motor insurance company stating your no claims bonus.

♦ Check whether you need an international driving licence or a translation of your

French or foreign driving licence for your country of destination.

♦ Give friends and business associates in France a temporary address, telephone number and email address where you can be contacted abroad.

♦ If you'll be travelling or living abroad for an extended period, you may wish to give someone 'power of attorney' over your financial affairs in France so that they can act on your behalf in your absence. This can be for a fixed period or open-ended and can be limited to a specific purpose only. You should, however, obtain expert legal advice before doing this.

Bon voyage!

Château de Chambord, Loire

APPENDICES

APPENDIX A: USEFUL WEBSITES

*T*he following list of websites (by subject) will be of interest to newcomers planning to live or work in France.

General Information

About France (http://about-france.com).
Alliance Française (www.alliancefr.org). The famous French language school.
Alliance Française in Paris (www.paris.alliancefr.fr).
Anglo Info (www.angloinfo.com). Information and forums specific for various regions including Aquitaine, Brittany, Dordogne, French Riviera, Limousin, Normandy, Paris/Isle-de-France and Poitou-Charentes.
Bonjour (www.bonjour.com). French tuition.
British in France (www.britishinfrance.com). Comprehensive information for the British community in France.
British Embassy in Paris (www.gov.uk/government/world/organisations/british-embassy-paris and www.british-consulate.org/british-embassy-in-france.html).
Cityvox (www.cityvox.com). Information about eating out, accommodation, foreign food shops, etc. in selected towns in France.
Electricité de France (www.edf.fr).
L'Etudiant (www.letudiant.fr). Information for students in French.
Europa Pages (www.europa-pages.com). Directory of European language courses.
Expatica (www.expatica.com/fr). One of the best sources of information for anyone living in France.
France Guide (www.franceguide.fr). Tourist information in English.
French-at-a-Touch (http://french-at-a-touch.com). General information on France and links to many other sites.
French Embassy in London (www.ambafrance-uk.org).
French Entrée (www.frenchentree.com). Information on every aspect of living in France and a useful forum.
INSEE (www.insee.fr). Office of national statistics: population, unemployment, salaries, etc. (in English and French).

Invest in France Agency (www.invest-in-france.org). Useful information on living and working in France.

Legifrance (www.legifrance.gouv.fr). Official legal information.

Météo France (www.meteofrance.com). Weather and climate in France.

Moving to France Made Easy (www.moving-to-france-made-easy.com). Plenty of information about life in France.

Online Newspapers (www.onlinenewspapers.com/france.htm). Links to dozens of French newspaper publishers' sites.

Pages Jaunes (www.pagesjaunes.fr). The French Yellow Pages.

Paris Info (www.parisinfo.com). The website of the Paris Convention & Visitors' Bureau.

Paris Notes (www.parisnotes.com). A subscription newsletter about Paris, published ten times a year.

Pavillon Bleu (www.pavillonbleu.org). A list of 'blue flag' beaches in France (awarded by the Foundation for European Education and Environment).

Le Point (www.lepoint.fr). Articles and surveys on all aspects of French life from the consumer magazine *Le Point*.

Pratique (www.pratique.fr). Practical information about life in France (in French).

Le Progrès (www.leprogres.fr). General information in French.

Que Choisir (www.quechoisir.org). Reports and articles from the consumer magazine *Que Choisir*.

This French Life (www.thisfrenchlife.com). Articles about setting up a variety of necessary services, from bank accounts to internet connection, as well as some of the more enjoyable things about life.

US Embassy in Paris (www.amb-usa.fr).

Webvivant (www.webvivant.com). Online community for English speakers in France and Francophiles everywhere.

English-language News, Newspapers & Magazines

Agence France Press (www.afp.com). One of the world's largest news agencies.

Connexion (www.connexionfrance.com). Newspaper offering news, information and classified ads for English-speaking expats in France.

Expatriates Magazine (http://paris.expatriatesmagazine.com). Essential reading for foreigners living in Paris.

France Diplomatie (www.diplomatie.gouv.fr/en). Site from the Ministry of Foreign Affairs offering diplomatic news.

France magazine (www.completefrance.com/our-magazines/france-magazine). French lifestyle magazine.

France 24 (www.france24.com/en). French global news TV channel in English.

French Property News (www.completefrance.com/our-magazines/french-property-news). The ultimate househunters' guide to the French property market.

Languedoc Living (www.languedocliving.com). English-language website providing French local and national news, events and life stories for expats living in the Languedoc region.

Living France magazine (www.completefrance.com/our-magazines/living-france). Lifestyle magazine for visitors and residents.

The Local (www.thelocal.fr). French news headlines, plus features, advice and discussion about living in and moving to France.

Lost in France (www.lost-in-france.com). Guide to living in France, French property and holidays.

Metropole Paris (www.metropoleparis.com). Weekly Parisian news, including features, photos, events and cartoons.

News in Normandy (http://newsinnormandy.com). Daily news from and about the Normandy region.

Paris Voice (http://parisvoice.com). Magazine for English-speaking Parisians including restaurants, books, music, exhibitions and trends.

Radio France (www.radiofrance.fr).

Radio France International (http://en.rfi.fr). English-language service featuring international news and regular reviews of French newspapers in English.

Riviera Insider (www.riviera-press.fr/insider). Daily news from the French-Italian Riviera and the Principality of Monaco since 2002.

Riviera Magazine (www.riviera-magazine.com). Dedicated to the culture, events, and economy of the French Riviera. Includes a hotel directory and tourism details.

Government Ministries

Ministry of Culture & Communications (www.culture.fr).

Ministries of the Economy and Finance and of Budgets and Accounting (www.finances.gouv.fr). Economic and tax information.

Ministry of Education (www.education.gouv.fr).

Ministry of Foreign & European Affairs (www.diplomatie.gouv.fr/en). Information (in English) about French foreign policy.

Prime Minister (www.premier-ministre.gouv.fr). Information (in English) about the French Prime Minister's role and function.

Service Public (www.service-public.fr). Official French government portal, with links to all ministry and other sites.

Employment

Agence pour la Création d'Entreprises (www.apce.com). Help for company founders in French.

Cadre Emploi/Cadres Online (www.cadremploi.fr and www.cadresonline.com). For executive or managerial positions

Pôle Emploi (www.pole-emploi.fr). French national employment agency.

Keljob (www.keljob.com). Job search portal.

Property & Accommodation

Coast & Country (http://coast-country.com). English-speaking estate agents on the Côte d'Azur.

De Particulier à Particulier (www.pap.fr). Advertisements in the French property magazine *De Particulier à Particulier* (English-language version available).

Entre Particuliers (www.entreparticuliers.com). Property advertisements.

Faire Construire sa Maison (www.construiresamaison.com). Site of the magazine *Faire Construire sa Maison*.

FNAIM (www.fnaim.com). French federation of estate agents.

Foncia (www.foncia.fr). Rental accommodation specialists.

France Property Shop (www.francepropertyshop.com). Huge range of properties for sale.

French Entree (www.frenchentree.com). A wealth of information for anyone planning to buy property or live in France.

Gîtes de France (www.gites-de-france.com). Principal national organisation regulating self-catering accommodation.

Green-Acres Services (www.green-acres.com). Property agents.

Immonot (www.immonot.com). Property listed with *notaires* and information on buying.

Immoprix (www.immoprix.com). Average property and building land sale prices by type, size, town, area, department and region.

ImmoStreet (www.immostreet.com). Properties for sale and rent; also has automatic calculator showing repayment amounts for mortgage purchases.

Journal des Particuliers (www.journaldesparticuliers.com). Advertisements in the French property magazine *Le Journal des Particuliers*.

Logic-Immo (www.logic-immo.com). French estate agents' property advertisements.

Notaires de France (www.notaires.fr). Property listed with *notaires* and information on buying.

Salut France (http://salut-france.com). French property search agents.

Se Loger (www.seloger.com). Properties for sale and rent plus quotations for insurance, removals and building work.

Terrains (www.terrain.fr). Building land for sale and information on buying land.

Communications

Air

Aéroports Français (www.aeroport.fr). Details of and links to all French airports.

Air France (www.airfrance.com).

BMI (www.flybmi.com).

British Airways (www.britishairways.co.uk).

EasyJet (www.easyjet.com).

Flybe (www.flybe.com).

Ryanair (www.ryanair.com).

Sea

Brittany Ferries (www.brittanyferries.com).
Condor Ferries (www.condorferries.co.uk).
Norfolkline (www.norfolkline.com).
P&O Ferries (www.poferries.com).
Sea France (www.seafrance.com).
Transmanche (www.transmancheferries.com).

Other Public Transport

Eurolines (www.eurolines.com). International coach services.
Eurostar (www.eurostar.com). International rail services.
Eurotunnel/Le Shuttle (www.eurotunnel.com). Car transport through the Channel Tunnel.
Motorail (www.frenchmotorail.com). Travelling by rail with your car in France.
National Express (www.nationalexpress.com). International coach services.
Rail Europe (www.raileurope.com). Eurostar/*TGV* link.
RATP (www.ratp.fr). Parisian regional transport authority.
SNCF (www.sncf.fr). French national railways.
Trans'bus (www.transbus.org). Information about urban public transport in France.

Motoring

ASFA (www.autoroutes.fr). Information about French motorways and tolls.
Automobile Association/AA (www.theaa.co.uk).
Bison Futé (www.bison-fute.equipement.gouv.fr). French road traffic reports.
Mappy www.iti.fr). Road route planning through France.
Royal Automobile Club/RAC (www.rac.co.uk).

APPENDIX B: MAPS

*T*he map opposite shows the 22 regions and 96 departments of France (excluding overseas territories), which are listed below. The departments are (mostly) numbered alphabetically from 01 to 89. Departments 91 to 95 come under the Ile-de-France region, which also includes Ville de Paris (75), Seine-et-Marne (77) and Yvelines (78), shown in detail opposite. The island of Corsica consists of two departments, 2A and 2B.

01 Ain	32 Gers	64 Pyrénées-Atlantiques
02 Aisne	33 Gironde	65 Hautes-Pyrénées
2A Corse-du-Sud	34 Hérault	66 Pyrénées-Orientales
2B Haute Corse	35 Ille-et-Vilaine	67 Bas-Rhin
03 Allier	36 Indre	68 Haut-Rhin
04 Alpes-de-Hte-Provence	37 Indre-et-Loire	69 Rhône
05 Hautes-Alpes	38 Isère	70 Haute-Saône
06 Alpes-Maritimes	39 Jura	71 Saône-et-Loire
07 Ardèche	40 Landes	72 Sarthe
08 Ardennes	41 Loir-et-Cher	73 Savoie
09 Ariège	42 Loire	74 Haute-Savoie
10 Aube	43 Haute-Loire	75 Paris
11 Aude	44 Loire-Atlantique	76 Seine-Maritime
12 Aveyron	45 Loiret	77 Seine-et-Marne
13 Bouches-du-Rhône	46 Lot	78 Yvelines
14 Calvados	47 Lot-et-Garonne	79 Deux-Sèvres
15 Cantal	48 Lozère	80 Somme
16 Charente	49 Maine-et-Loire	81 Tarn
17 Charente-Maritime	50 Manche	82 Tarn-et-Garonne
18 Cher	51 Marne	83 Var
19 Corrèze	52 Haute-Marne	84 Vaucluse
21 Côte-d'Or	53 Mayenne	85 Vendée
22 Côte-d'Armor	54 Meurthe-et-Moselle	86 Vienne
23 Creuse	55 Meuse	87 Haute-Vienne
24 Dordogne	56 Morbihan	88 Vosges
25 Doubs	57 Moselle	89 Yonne
26 Drôme	58 Nièvre	90 Territoire de Belfort
27 Eure	59 Nord	91 Essonne
28 Eure-et-Loir	60 Oise	92 Hauts-de-Seine
29 Finistère	61 Orne	93 Seine-Saint-Denis
30 Gard	62 Pas-de-Calais	94 Val-de-Marne
31 Haute-Garonne	63 Puy-de-Dôme	95 Val-d'Oise

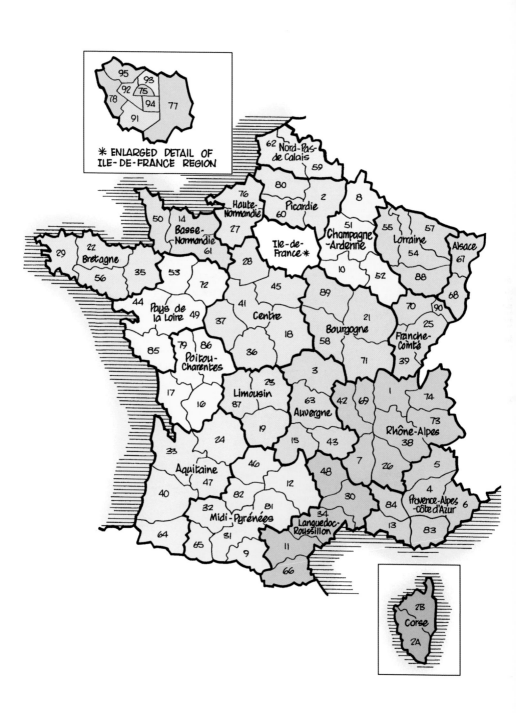

CITIES & AIRPORTS

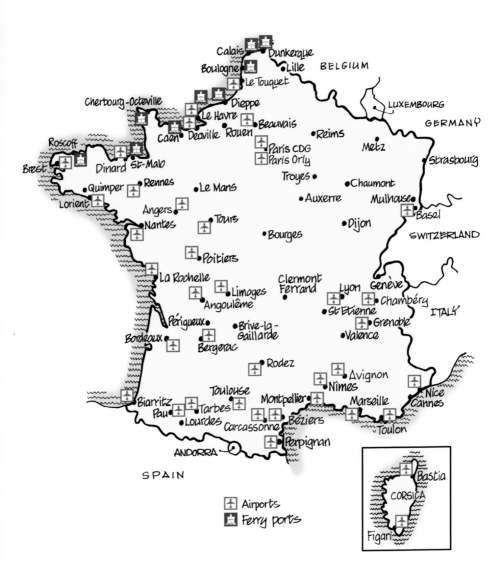

TGV RAIL LINES

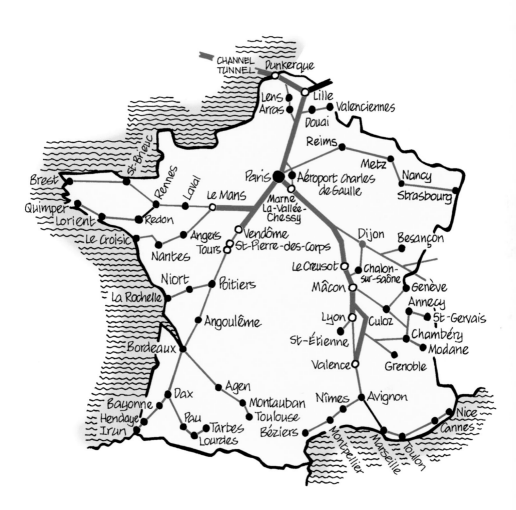

MOTORWAYS

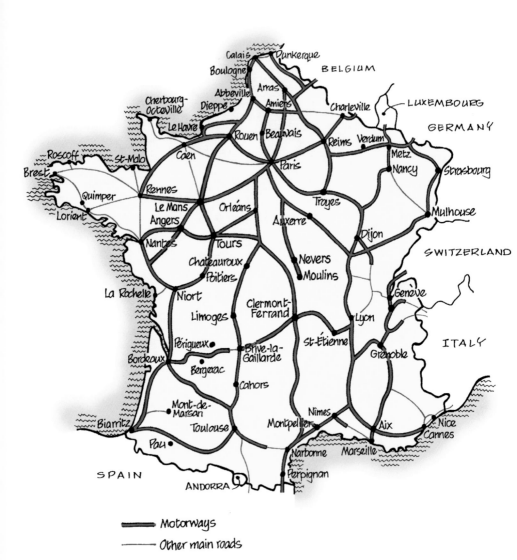

———— Motorways

——— Other main roads

INDEX

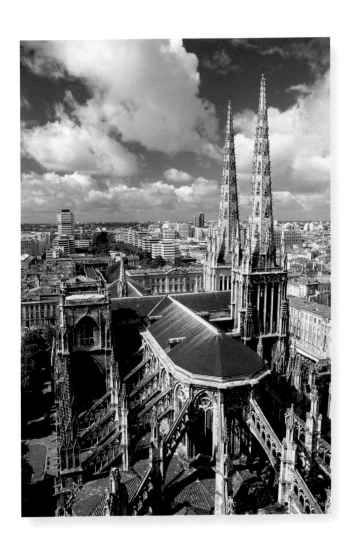

SKETCHBOOK SERIES

£10.95

ISBN: 978-1-907339-37-0
Jim Watson

A celebration of one of the world's great cities, London Sketchbook is packed with over 200 evocative watercolour illustrations of the author's favourite landmarks and sights. The illustrations are accompanied by historical footnotes, maps, walks, quirky facts and a gazetteer.

Also in this series:

Cornwall Sketchbook (ISBN: 9781909282780, £10.95)
Cotswold Sketchbook (ISBN: 9781907339108, £9.95)
Devon Sketchbook (ISBN: 9781909282704, £10.95)
Lake District Sketchbook (ISBN: 9781909282605, £10.95)
Yorkshire Sketchbook (ISBN: 9781909282773, £10.95)

London's Secrets: Peaceful Places

ISBN: 978-1-907339-45-5, 256 pages, hardback, £11.95

David Hampshire

London is one of the world's most exciting cities, but it's also one of the noisiest; a bustling, chaotic, frenetic, over-crowded, manic metropolis of over 8 million people, where it can be difficult to find somewhere to grab a little peace and quiet. Nevertheless, if you know where to look London has a wealth of peaceful places: places to relax, chill out, contemplate, meditate, sit, reflect, browse, read, chat, nap, walk, think, study or even work (if you must) – where the city's volume is muted or even switched off completely.

London for Foodies, Gourmets & Gluttons

ISBN: 978-1-909282-76-6, 288 pages, hardback, £11.95

David Hampshire & Graeme Chesters

Much more than simply a directory of cafés, markets, restaurants and food shops, *London for Foodies, Gourmets & Gluttons* features many of the city's best artisan producers and purveyors, plus a wealth of classes where you can learn how to prepare and cook food like the experts, appreciate fine wines and brew coffee like a barista. And when you're too tired to cook or just want to treat yourself, we'll show you great places where you can enjoy everything from tea and cake to a tasty street snack; a pie and a pint to a glass of wine and tapas; and a quick working lunch to a full-blown gastronomic extravaganza.

London's Cafés, Coffee Shops & Tearooms

ISBN: 978-1-909282-80-3, 192 pages, £9.95

David Hampshire

This book is a celebration of London's flourishing independent cafés, coffee shops and tearooms – plus places serving afternoon tea and breakfast/brunch – all of which have enjoyed a renaissance in the last decade and done much to strengthen the city's position as one of the world's leading foodie destinations. With a copy of *London's Cafés, Coffee Shops & Tearooms* you'll never be lost for somewhere to enjoy a great cup of coffee or tea and some delicious food.

London's Best Shops & Markets

ISBN: 978-1-909282-81-0, 256 pages, hardback, £12.95

David Hampshire

The UK is a nation of diehard shoppers. Retail therapy is the country's favourite leisure activity – an all-consuming passion – and London is its beating heart. It's one of the world's most exciting shopping cities, packed with grand department stores, trend-setting boutiques, timeless traditional traders, edgy concept stores, absorbing antiques centres, eccentric novelty shops, exclusive purveyors of luxury goods, mouth-watering food emporiums, bustling markets and much more.

see www.londons-secrets.com

London's Best-Kept Secrets

ISBN: 978-1-909282-74-2, 320 pages, £10.95
David Hampshire

London Best-Kept Secrets brings together our favourite places – the 'greatest hits' – from our London's Secrets series of books. We take you off the beaten tourist path to seek out the more unusual ('hidden') places that often fail to register on the radar of both visitors and residents alike. Nimbly sidestepping the chaos and queues of London's tourist-clogged attractions, we visit its quirkier, lesser-known, but no less fascinating, side. *London Best-Kept Secrets* takes in some of the city's loveliest hidden gardens and parks, absorbing and poignant museums, great art and architecture, beautiful ancient buildings, magnificent Victorian cemeteries, historic pubs, fascinating markets and much more.

London's Hidden Corners, Lanes & Squares

ISBN: 978-1-909282-69-8, 192 pages, £9.95
Graeme Chesters

The inspiration for this book was the advice of writer and lexicographer Dr Samuel Johnson (1709-1784), who was something of an expert on London, to his friend and biographer James Boswell on the occasion of his trip to London in the 18th century, to 'survey its innumerable little lane and courts'. In the 21st century these are less numerous than in Dr Johnson's time, so we've expanded his brief to include alleys, squares and yards, along with a number of mews, roads, streets and gardens.

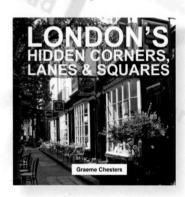

A Year in London: Two Things to Do Every Day of the Year

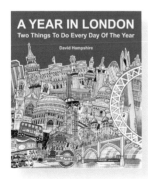

ISBN: 978-1-909282-68-1, 256 pages, £11.95
David Hampshire

London offers a wealth of things to do, from exuberant festivals and exciting sports events to a plethora of fascinating museums and stunning galleries, from luxury and oddball shops to first-class restaurants and historic pubs, beautiful parks and gardens to pulsating nightlife and clubs. Whatever your interests and tastes, you'll find an abundance of things to enjoy – with a copy of this book you'll never be at a loss for something to do in one of the world's greatest cities.

see www.londons-secrets.com

LONDON'S HIDDEN SECRETS

ISBN: 978-1-907339-40-0
£10.95, 320 pages
Graeme Chesters

A guide to London's hidden and lesser-known sights that aren't found in standard guidebooks. Step beyond the chaos, clichés and queues of London's tourist-clogged attractions to its quirkier side.

Discover its loveliest ancient buildings, secret gardens, strangest museums, most atmospheric pubs, cutting-edge art and design, and much more: some 140 destinations in all corners of the city.

LONDON'S HIDDEN SECRET'S VOL 2

ISBN: 978-1-907339-79-0
£10.95, 320 pages
Graeme Chesters & David Hampshire

Hot on the heels of London's Hidden Secrets comes another volume of the city's largely undiscovered sights, many of which we were unable to include in the original book. In fact, the more research we did the more treasures we found, until eventually a second volume was inevitable.

Written by two experienced London writers, LHS 2 is for both those who already know the metropolis and newcomers wishing to learn more about its hidden and unusual charms.

LONDON'S SECRET PLACES

ISBN: 978-1-907339-92-9
£10.95, 320 pages
Graeme Chesters & David Hampshire

London is one of the world's leading tourist destinations with a wealth of world-class attractions. These are covered in numerous excellent tourist guides and online, and need no introduction here. Not so well known are London's numerous smaller attractions, most of which are neglected by the throngs who descend upon the tourist-clogged major sights. What London's Secret Places does is seek out the city's lesser-known, but no less worthy, 'hidden' attractions.

LONDON'S SECRET WALKS

ISBN: 978-1-907339-51-6
£11.95, 320 pages
Graeme Chesters

London is a great city for walking – whether for pleasure, exercise or simply to get from A to B. Despite the city's extensive public transport system, walking is often the quickest and most enjoyable way to get around – at least in the centre – and it's also free and healthy!

Many attractions are off the beaten track, away from the major thoroughfares and public transport hubs. This favours walking as the best way to explore them, as does the fact that London is a visually interesting city with a wealth of stimulating sights in every 'nook and cranny'.

see www.londons-secrets.com